ACUA
Underwater Archaeology
Proceedings
2013

edited by
Colin Breen and Wes Forsythe

An Advisory Council on Underwater Archaeology Publication

© 2013 Advisory Council on Underwater Archaeology

Library of Congress Control Number: 2013951491

Made possible in part through the support of
the Society for Historical Archaeology.

Cover Image: *Divers deployed on a sunken schooner in the village of Strangford, Ireland.* ca. 1885.
National Museums Northern Ireland 2013, Ulster Museum MS382.

Contents

Foreword vi

Below Sea-Level: Combining Palaeolithic and Underwater
Archaeology in the Eastern Mediterranean Sea 11
    Christina Papoulia

The 1725 *Nuestra Señora de Begoña*: Ongoing Investigations
of a Spanish Merchant *Fragata* in La Caleta de Caucedo,
Dominican Republic 19
    Matthew J. Maus and Charles D. Beeker

Talegas and Hoards: The Archaeological Signature of
Contraband on a 1725 Spanish Merchant Vessel 31
    John W. Foster, Matthew J. Maus and
    Anna Rogers

Sultan: Cleveland's Grindstone Wreck 39
    David VanZandt, James Paskert and Kevin Magee

Site Formation Processes of the Wreck of the U.S. Steamer
Convoy in Pensacola Bay, Florida 49
    Christopher T. Dewey

Roman Lead Ingots From Shipwrecks: A Key to
Understanding Immigration From Campania, Southern
Latium, and Picenum in the Mining District of Carthago
Nova in the Late Republican and Early Imperial Eras 57
    Michele Stefanile

Ceramics from 18th century Dutch and English Shipwrecks:
A Survey of Southern Baltic Sea, Poland 65
    Joanna A. Dąbal

Bajo Hornos Reef: A Trap for Ships and Cultural Materials 75
    Ricardo Borrero and Roberto Junco

The Formation of a West African Maritime Seascape:
Atlantic Trade, Shipwrecks, and Formation Processes on the
Coast of Ghana 83
    Rachel L. Horlings

The Maddalena Archipelago Maritime Target Survey: A Collaborative Effort toward the Enhancement of Maritime Cultural Heritage 93
    Secci Massimiliano, Claudia Giarrusso, Giulia Nieddu, Alessandro Porqueddu and Pier Giorgio I. Spanu

Ports and Settlements in the Gulf of Oristano: A Coastal and Underwater Archaeological Approach..105
    Orrù Paolo, Emanuela Solinas, Pier Giorgio I. Spanu and Raimondo Zucca

Edward Rhodes – His Booke: Examining Trade Routes, Functions, and Vessel Performance in the 17th Century Through Primary Source Documents 113
    Scott A. Tucker

Digitally Reconstructing the Newport Medieval Ship: 3D Designs and Dynamic Visualisations for Recreating the Original Hull Form, Loading Factors, Displacement, and Sailing Characteristics 123
    Toby Jones, Nigel Nayling and Pat Tanner

Ship Reconstruction and Digital Modeling: the Example of the Aber Wrac'h 1 Wreck (France)..131
    Alexandra Grille

3D Laser Scanning for the Digital Reconstruction and Analysis of a 16th-Century Clinker Built Sailing Vessel............................137
    Pat Tanner

Digital Documentation for Many Purposes: The Barcode 6 Boat as a Case Study...151
    Tori Falck, Inger Marie Egenberg and Hilde Vangstad

Managing Submerged Prehistoric Landscapes: New Approaches in the Southern North Sea..159
    Edward Salter

Developing Foresight, Threat Analysis And Risk Assessment to Further the Management of the Marine Historic Environment Of England...167
    Ian Oxley

Researching, Protecting and Managing England's Marine Historic Environment 173
    Alison James

Petrolheads: Managing England's Early Submarines 179
    Mark Dunkley and Hanna Steyne

Managing Change on UK Wreck Sites Through
Community-Based Recording: The London Recording Project 185
    Graham Scott

Underwater Archaeological Parks in Greece: The Cases of
Methoni Bay – Sapienza Island and Northern Sporades, from
a Culture of Prohibition to a Culture of Engagement 191
    Panagiotis Georgopoulos and Tatiana
    Fragkopoulou

Foreword

Maritime Archaeology at Leicester 2013

The 46th Annual conference on Historical and Underwater Archaeology took place in Leicester, England from the 9th to the 12th January 2013. The conference theme was 'Globalization, immigration, transformation', three processes that are embedded within the subject area of maritime archaeology. The organisers were especially interested in examining the emergence of capitalist society and the expansion of colonial activity across the globe. Particular emphasis was placed on the emergence of early modern society within the broader context of the Atlantic social world. Further examination was encouraged of the movement of peoples across these geographical regions and the processes that drove migration whether forced or willing. Significant change was introduced across the globe as a consequence of these processes and the attendance of academics from over 60 countries reflected an interest in change that continues to resonate in contemporary society. The choice of the host city of Leicester was a further reflection of the nature of these changes. It is the UKs most diverse and multicultural city and has been a focus of immigration by people of south Asian, African and Caribbean descent.

The range and diversity of the papers at Leicester provided a broad cross section of the subject and illustrated its expanding sphere of geographical interest. 123 papers and posters were submitted directly to underwater or maritime sessions and a large number of further papers had a strong maritime component. It is interesting that the term 'underwater' still seems to set maritime papers apart in separate sessions and creates an artificial division between archaeological remains on land and those underwater. At the conference the archaeology of a number of small islands were presented solely as terrestrial concerns, however their content would fall firmly within the maritime sphere. Geographically the papers were primarily concerned with North West Europe and North America but both South America and the Mediterranean region were strongly represented. Interestingly, many of the Mediterranean papers adopted a broader chronological range than traditionally would be presented at SHA conferences and represent the wider temporal limits of historical archaeology in this region. A number of papers were also presented concerning south east Asia and from parts of the Indian Ocean. While participants from these regions were very welcome they unfortunately remain a very small minority. Most speakers came from the Global North and it must surely become a stronger ambition of the SHA to encourage more attendees from the Global South. Practitioners from Africa and other areas where the discipline is poorly developed must be supported in their efforts to protect and promote the maritime archaeology of their regions.

In terms of content the maritime/ underwater papers followed a relatively traditional route. There remains a strong focus on the management and protection of the underwater cultural resource, the investigation of individual shipwreck sites and the adaption of new technologies to the study of underwater material. Increasingly deep-water archaeology is featuring more on the conference programmes as the awareness of this resource develops. Fewer papers took a more landscape/ seascape orientated approach and where this did happen it tended to be European based. Public engagement was a strong theme across the broader conference. While the SHA has consistently featured papers encouraging avocational divers to participate in archaeological projects a number of papers at Leicester were concerned with broader public engagement outside the diving community. This more inclusive approach is to be welcomed. We look forward to the day when maritime archaeology has as much public recognition and appreciation as marine biology, for example.

This has been an interesting volume to bring together and we feel it reflects the subject as it presented itself at Leicester. Each of the contributors are to be thanked for their submissions and the timely way they dealt with deadlines. We would like to thank the members of the organizing committee who worked tirelessly to run a highly successful conference: Prof. Sarah Tarlow, Prof. Audrey Horning, Dr Alasdair Brooks and Emma Dwyer. We would like to particularly thank Knic Pfost of the PAST Foundation who brought this volume together with great humour and professionalism.

Dedication

Tragically, as this publication was being brought together one of the contributors, Rachel Horlings, had a fatal accident while leading an underwater project in Ghana. Rachel was a graduate of Florida State University and completed her doctorate at Syracuse University's Maxwell School in 2011. She had worked on a number of underwater projects across the globe but had a special interest in west Africa. Her death is a huge loss to the discipline, she had contributed much - and had much to give.

We dedicate this volume to her memory

Colin Breen
Wes Forsythe

Centre for Maritime Archaeology
School of Environmental Sciences
University of Ulster
Northern Ireland
BT52 1SA

ACUA
Underwater Archaeology
Proceedings
2013

Below Sea-Level: Combining Palaeolithic and Underwater Archaeology in the Eastern Mediterranean Sea

Christina Papoulia

The area of the eastern Mediterranean is a focal point for the study of the earliest acts of globalization. Palaeolithic archaeology provides the tools for the analysis and interpretation of the material record of the early hominins who passed through and occupied this part of the world. However, since the early pleistocene, the constant environmental fluctuations between glacials and interglacials have caused major alterations in the ice sheets resulting in sea-level changes. Consequently, large land masses which could have been occupied by our early ancestors are now hidden deep below sea-level.

This paper deals with the current evidence for early migrations in the eastern Mediterranean and explores the potential of encountering Palaeolithic artifacts below the sea-level of the Aegean and Ionian Sea. Finally, the prospects for combined Palaeolithic and Underwater investigations and the need for an interdisciplinary collaboration is stressed.

Introduction

In accordance with the general theme of this year's conference, this paper focuses on the earliest acts of "globalization" in the eastern Mediterranean, particularly in the area of the Aegean and Ionian Sea, and pushes the time-scale back to early Prehistory. To do so, it draws upon the current archaeological evidence for early hominin occupation in the region, it takes into account the paleo-environmental reconstructions and explores the potential of encountering palaeolithic artifacts under the sea-level of the Aegean and Ionian Sea.

Underwater investigations in the eastern Mediterranean have traditionally shed light on a number of shipwrecks from the historical and prehistoric periods, after all, the area has always been a major crossroad and a melting point for a number of cultures. In the majority of cases in the past, any kind of research conducted under the sea-level had been rather defined as strictly "Maritime" instead of "Underwater" in the broader sense. The oldest sites which have been systematically studied in the Aegean region have yielded Neolithic and Bronze Age finds. As Gusick and Faught (2011: 29) have pointed out,

> *The underwater archaeology of submerged prehistoric sites is following a path somewhat similar to that of shipwreck archaeology; however, interest in developing specific methods for the underwater archaeology of prehistoric sites has begun to grow within the last few decades.*

One of the most well-known submerged prehistoric settlements in the Aegean is Pavlopetri, situated off the southeastern coast of Peloponesse, while interesting finds have been recovered from the Agios Petros site of the Sporades islands in the northern Aegean. Both of these sites are currently at the centre of a debate regarding their future exploitation as underwater cultural parks (Georgopoulos and Fragkopoulou, this volume; and references therein). At the same time, the only specimens coming from underwater sites and dating back to the Palaeolithic come from the Ionian Sea, off the coast of Kerkyra, and were collected almost 30 years ago (Flemming 1985; 1998). No systematically organized investigations with up-to-date methods have yet focused on the exploration of the eastern Mediterranean in terms of early hominin occupation on the continental shelf.

Palaeolithic Archaeology in the Eastern Mediterranean

Palaeolithic Archaeology in Greece has, for decades, focused on certain caves & rock-shelters of mainland Greece, primarily Epirus and the Peloponnese, while the plentiful islands have been overlooked for various reasons, one of which was the premise that early humans were incapable of successfully crossing the open sea. Although the first archaeological implications for pre-sapiens presence on islands were published more than 30 years ago, these were laregly ignored, partially because some of them were interpreted by non-lithic specialists or by amateur archaeologists.

In the Greek peninsula, Early Palaeolithic stone tools have been found in just a few open-air sites; they are surface finds, and in most cases lack stratigraphic context (Tourloukis 2010). Interestingly, after half a century of Palaeolithic research in Greece, half of the sites which have been attributed to the early Palaeolithic in terms of stone tool technology and associated context have been found on islands, both of the Aegean and Ionian Sea. The oldest fossil hominins found belong to the species of *Homo heidelbergensis* and come from the Petralona cave site in Northern Greece (Galanidou 2004; Grün 1996; Harvati et al. 2009; Hennig et al. 1982). The most common palaeolithic sites, however, are open-air, usually red-soil, Middle Palaeolithic ones, with Mousterian stone-tools that have traditionally been attributed to Neanderthal groups. The few Neanderthal fossils found in Greece are mainly teeth specimens that come from caves and rock-shelters of the southern Peloponnese (Harvati et al. 2009; Harvati et al. 2013). A young individual (most probably a Neanderthal) has been thought to have left his or her footprints at Theopetra cave in Thessaly (Manolis et al. 2000). The majority of the Middle Palaeolithic sites in Greece are low altitude, coastal or near-coastal, with a notable concentration in western Greece, west of the Pindus mountains. Recently, though, the exploitation of inland locations situated on high altitudes of the Pindus mountains have also been recorded in Macedonia, Northern Greece (Efstratiou et al. 2006; 2011). Epirus is a resource-rich area which had been extensively occupied by Neanderthals and perhaps *Homo heidelbergensis* as well. The rich in archaeological finds and raw material sources sites of northwestern Greece do not stop at the present-day Epirotic coast but continue in the Ionian islands such as Kerkyra, Lefkada, Kefalonia and Zakynthos (Cubuk 1976; Kavvadias 1984; Kourtessi-Philipakis 1999; Papagianni 2000; Foss 2002). Although not all of the above present-day islands were indeed islands during the Pleistocene, a couple of them (i.e. Kefalonia and Zakynthos) seem to have been separated from mainland Greece during the period under study (Ferentinos et al. 2012). The fact that Mousterian and possibly older lithic assemblages (Cubuk 1976; Kourtessi-Philipakis 1999; Foss 2002; Tourloukis 2010)—however no palaeoanthropological remains—have been found on these two islands implies a certain degree of sea-crossing abilities.

It has long been accepted that early hominins did not and were not capable of exploiting marine resources. Similarly any capacity for navigation skills in pre-Modern Human species was, until recently, out of the question. However, it has now been proved that marine resources were consumed and utilized by Neanderthals in Spain since at least 150 ka (Cortés-Sánchez et al. 2011); certain kinds of marine mollusk shells were also retouched and used as tools, as is the case at Mousterian sites in Greece and Italy (Darlas and De Lumley 2004; Douka and Spinapolice 2012), or transformed into personal ornaments embodying symbolic expression, as is the case with several sites in the Iberian peninsula (Zilhão et al. 2010). The critical role of early hominin adaptations to coastal environments (Bicho and Haws 2008) has lately been further elaborated by implications for sea-faring activities by early hominin species which occupied the eastern part of the Mediterranean before the arrival of Homo sapiens. New challenging archaeological and geological data published during the last decade argue for Pleistocene sea-faring activities taking place in the southern Ionian and southern Aegean Sea (Mortensen 2008; Kopaka and Matzanas 2009; Strasser et al. 2010; 2011; Ferentinos et al. 2012). The region has now become a central field in the study of early hominin migrations, since it could have been either an obstacle or a crossing point during a vast period of our early prehistory.

Geomorphological Reconstructions

The present morphology of the Eastern Mediterranean, in particular the Aegean Sea with the plentiful islands and the large coastal-zone—the largest in the whole Mediterranean region—is a result of tectonic, volcanic activities and global sea-level changes. The constant environmental fluctuations between glacials and interglacials have caused major alterations in the ice sheets resulting in sea-level changes. The majority of what are now seen as islands were, during most of the Palaeolithic, attached either to mainland Greece (e.g. Kerkyra, Lefkada) or Turkey (e.g. Lemnos, Lesvos, Kos etc.). As Athanassas, et al., (2012: 237) have rightly pointed out,

> *During climatically cool periods in the geological record the currently submerged continental shelf emerged in the form of extensive plains. This newly exposed land became available for hunter-gatherers to temporarily settle, wander, or hunt for game. That situation was occasionally interrupted by events of sea level rise, diminishing the available land, and compelling human adaptation, to a new allocation of resources.*

In order to reconstruct the palaeo-geographic map, the global eustatic curve in addition to the bathymetric and tectonic data need to be taken into account. Unfortunately, though, most of the sea-level reconstructions in the Eastern Mediterranean have focused on the Last Glacial Maximum or later, Holocene stages, due to better resolutions. According to a broad paleogeographic reconstruction proposed by Lykousis (2009: 2041) and based on seismic reflection profiles, "during the isotopic stages 8, 10, 11 and 12, almost the 50-60% of the present Aegean Sea was land with extensive drainage systems, delta plains and large lakes in the central and North Aegean". Consequently, large land masses which could have been occupied by our early ancestors are now hidden deep below the sea-level.

Evidence for Early Hominin Migrations—the "Sea-faring" Hypothesis

It has been proposed that "during periods of low sea level early hominins and anatomically modern humans could probably cross from Morocco to Spain, from Tunisia to Sicily, and from Eritrea to Yemen, as well as by the land route through Sinai" (Flemming et al. 2003: 61). In the Eastern Mediterranean, islands such as Crete or Gavdos have been isolated from the mainland since the Miocene. Due to the fact that lithic artifacts have been collected from sites on these islands, certain questions regarding early navigation skills have lately been addressed (Mortensen 2008; Kopaka and Matzanas 2009; Strasser et al. 2010; 2011). Milos, an island of the Cyclades, has also provided evidence of morphologically early Palaeolithic chopping tools, made of coarse-grained volcanic material. However, since these were surface finds, no stratigraphic information could be provided (Chelidonio 2001). Strasser and team (2010: 187) have implied for the finds from Crete that "an African or Near Eastern origin is as likely as an Anatolian or mainland Greek one". However, a sea-faring hypothesis directly from Africa to Gavdos or Crete seems too far-fetched, since the bathymetric data exhibit great depths in the Libyan Sea (Mitsopoulou 2008); thus the distance for a non-stop trip is very large and the sea currents can be very unpredictable and dangerous, but most importantly, Crete is not visible from the coast of Libya, even with the best climatic conditions. On the other hand, sea-crossings would have been necessary in order to move even from Antikythera to Crete and from Crete to Gavdos or from Milos to other islands of the Cyclades and from there back to the mainland; thus the sea-faring scenario should be further tested by examining any potential sea-routes (Papoulia 2014). According to palaeontological data, several endemic species have been found in western Crete, one of which (*Mamuthus Creticus*) is thought to have arrived in the Lower or Middle Pleistocene probably through the Kythera – Antikythera way, at times when the sea-level was low (Poulakakis et al. 2006). A similar route should be tested for the early hominins who reached Crete. In addition, further multidisciplinary research, on the islands east and west of Crete as well as the Cyclades, is needed in order to provide better answers to the question of early sea-faring (Papoulia 2014).

In the case of the Ionian islands of Kefalonia and Zakynthos it is easier to imagine early hominins attempting to cross the water of the inner Ionian Sea, which would have looked more like a lake rather than the open sea (Ferentinos et al. 2012). In such cases one is dealing with less dangerous, yet not trouble-free, sea-crossings. On-going research at the inner Ionian Archipelago, northeast of Kefalonia, conducted by the University of Crete in collaboration with the 26th Ephorate for Prehistoric and Classical Antiquities, under the direction of Dr. Nena Galanidou, is bound to provide new insights on the issue.

Future Prospects for Underwater Palaeolithic Research

Although for too many years the scientific community was extremely pessimistic in terms of the potential for underwater investigations of the early human prehistory, it has now become clear that Early Palaeolithic research in the Eastern Mediterranean will remain incomplete without targeted underwater archaeological investigations, in the Aegean and Ionian Sea. According to the paleo-geographic reconstructions, the Aegean would have been a terrestrial wetland, ideal not only as a crossing route, but also as a refuge for early hominins (Lykousis 2009; Tourloukis 2010; Tourloukis and Karkanas 2012).

A couple of decades ago three Acheulean handaxes were found in depths of 7–8m, off the coast of Table Bay in South Africa. "The handaxes were embedded in oxidised soil resting on bedrock, and covered by a metre or more of marine sand" (Flemming 2004: 1226). On the north coast of France the submerged site near Fermanville has yielded a large number of Mousterian tools and debitage, thus indicating Middle Palaeolithic occupation (Scuvée and Verague 1988). A few years ago Flemming (2010, 276) was insisting that "it is reasonable, at least at the intellectual level, to consider the potential [of encountering palaeontological and archaeological remains] for the whole continental shelf, and for the last million years." In the last few years, multidisciplinary research conducted by international teams in different parts of Europe have discovered large numbers of stone-tools and mammal fossils of early and middle Pleistocene dates and even organic materials of later dates, all exceptionally preserved (Benjamin et al. 2011; Bailey and Sakellariou 2012).

The fact that archaeological and palaeontological material of the Pleistocene have survived marine transgression under circumstances (Flemming 2004) renders with optimism potential Underwater Palaeolithic projects, even in the very tectonically active region of the Aegean. Such discoveries should be able to provide new and important insights in the study of early hominin migration routes and subsistence strategies. Tourloukis and Karkanas (2012: 9) have rightly pointed out the limited potential of encountering Lower Palaeolithic implements in the region since, as they note, "half of what would have been the 'Greek Lower Palaeolithic record' is currently underwater, forever virtually lost". While it is true that "the importance of the submarine data should not be exaggerated" (Flemming 2003: 62), if archaeologists keep ignoring the potentials of targeted underwater palaeolithic projects in the eastern Mediterranean, they will also have to keep dealing with "misleading or even false explanations for what really happened in prehistory" (Flemming 2003: 62). In the Ionian Sea, Levallois-Mousterian lithic specimens have been found by diving roughly 200 m off the coast of the island of Kerkyra at a depth of about 5 m (Flemming 1985; 1998). According to Flemming (2003: 69), palaeolithic sites in the Mediterranean "could exist to a depth of – 140 m, and should exist near potential crossing points". However, in Greece all systematic underwater surveys have thus far focused on the exploration of later phases of human prehistory, such as the Neolithic or the Bronze Age. Underwater Neolithic finds were also discovered in the northern Aegean Sea, at the Sporades island complex. On-shore surveys on one of the Sporades islands, Alonissos, have also proved the significant Neanderthal occupation in the area (Panagopoulou et al. 2001). As for the southern Aegean, it has been argued that "The Cyclades Plateau cannot be considered as an area of high archaeological potential with respect to the Middle and Upper Palaeolithic, because preservation of material is not favored due to erosion, and access is impossible due to deep burial." (Tourloukis 2010: 170). However, it should in no respect be overlooked, since geographically it would have played an important role in the history of early hominin migrations. Perhaps it should not be the starting point for Palaeolithic Underwater investigations but rather be part of on-shore palaeolithic surveys first, as Tourloukis (2010) has rightly suggested, since the evidence at hand are not yet strong enough to suggest intensive palaeolithic occupation.

On the other hand, western Greece and especially the Ionian islands seem to be the place to focus at first. The fact that it is a well studied area in terms of Palaeolithic remains and geological formations, the proximity of the islands to the western part of mainland Greece and the numerous coastal caves and rock-shelters which might possibly continue underwater, are some of the elements which could facilitate future Underwater Palaeolithic projects. Other areas expected to reveal underwater early Palaeolithic finds are possibly the Sporades island complex, as well as the eastern Aegean islands, which would in their majority be connected to Turkey, thus in the Early and Middle Pleistocene would have been the western coastal border for any hominin groups migrating from Asia to Europe. Even if they did not cross over to the Cyclades, Rhodes or Crete, they would have certainly taken advantage of the numerous benefits of the Aegean coast. As far as the sea-faring hypothesis is concerned, we can only now make rational assumption as to whether or not Neanderthals, for instance, were capable sea-farers. What we know for sure is that they were very skilled knappers who made use of specialized knapping techniques; they were the first to manufacture and efficiently use composite tools by hafting a lithic point on a wooden shaft, and they had been also very sophisticated and cooperative hunters. They buried their dead, and transformed surfaces, such as marine shells for personal ornamentation, as well as their own bodies with ochre tattoos, demonstrating their capacity for abstract and innovative thinking (Papoulia 2014 and references therein).

Potential underwater palaeolithic finds will be able to further contribute to the study of early migrations in the Mediterranean Sea and in some cases maybe also confirm or not the assumptions for early sea-crossings, especially now that new techniques are "providing the momentum for a rapidly expanding field of investigation", as Bailey and Flemming (2008, 2153) have rightly pointed out.

Conclusions

To conclude, the initial aim of this paper was to bring to light the need for, and the prospects of, combined Underwater Palaeolithic projects in the eastern Mediterranean. Such projects should aim to understand the potential Pleistocene crossing points and the significance of archaeological prehistoric sites on the continental shelf of the Aegean and Ionian Sea. Important prerequisites for such research, apart from the issue of funding, which will in any case be—at least—challenging, such projects will need to take into account certain components such as accurate bathymetric data; a refined analysis of sea-level changes and tectonics; the palaeo-landscape morphology; the vegetational, faunal, and palaeo-climatic data available; as well as a detailed determination of morphological characteristics such as deep basins, river channels and bedrock depressions (Benjamin 2010; Gusick and Faught 2011). A collaboration between palaeolithic archaeologists, palaeoanthropologists, geologists, geo-archaeologists, palaeontologists, and of course specialized underwater archaeologists is crucial. Finally, as Tourloukis (2010: 170) has already noted, at this point, perhaps the most promising and realistic scenario for Greece would be the development of underwater research projects "as parts of broader land-based investigations", or "as the seaward extensions" of terrestrial palaeolithic surveys.

Acknowledgments

My supervisor Dr. Nena Galanidou is acknowledged for her guidance throughout my on-going PhD research and for entrusting me with the lithic material from the Inner Ionian Sea Archipelago Project. Dr. Giorgos Iliopoulos and Dr. Constantin Athanassas have provided me help and references regarding palaeontological and geoarchaeological issues. I would also particularly like to thank Massimiliano Secci for inviting me to participate in the session entitled "Maritime Archaeology: a Mediterranean Perspective" and both my Italian and Greek colleagues for the post-conference pints, for transferring Mediterranean vibes to Leicester and thus making my fleeting visit to the city really worth it.

References

ATHANASSAS, CONSTANTIN, YANNIS BASSIAKOS, GÜNTHER A. WAGNER, AND MICHAEL E. TIMPSON
    2012   Exploring Paleogeographic Conditions at Two Paleolithic Sites in Navarino, Southwest Greece, Dated by Optically Stimulated Luminescence. Geoarchaeology 27 (3): 237-258.

BAILEY, G, AND N FLEMMING
    2008   Archaeology of the Continental Shelf: Marine Resources, Submerged Landscapes and Underwater Archaeology. Quaternary Science Reviews 27 (23-24): 2153–2165.

BAILEY, GEOFF N., DIMITRIS SAKELLARIOU AND MEMBERS OF THE SPLASHCOS NETWORK
    2012   SPLASHCOS: Submerged Prehistoric Archaeology and Landscapes of the Continental Shelf. Antiquity 86 (334). http://antiquity.ac.uk/projgall/sakellariou334/

BENJAMIN, JONATHAN
    2010   Submerged Prehistoric Landscapes and Underwater Site Discovery: Reevaluating the 'Danish Model' for International Practice. The Journal of Island and Coastal Archaeology 5 (2): 253–270.

BENJAMIN, JONATHAN, CLIVE BONSALL, CATRIONA PICKARD, AND ANDERS FISCHER (EDITORS)
    2011   Submerged Prehistory. Vol. 1. Oxbow, London.

BICHO, N, AND J HAWS
    2008   At the Land's End: Marine Resources and the Importance of Fluctuations in the Coastline in the Prehistoric Hunter–gatherer Economy of Portugal. Quaternary Science Reviews 27 (23-24): 2166–2175.

CHELIDONIO, GIORGIO
    2001   Manufatti Litici Su Ciottolo Da Milos (Isole Cicladi). Pegaso, Rivista Annuale Di Cultura Mediterranea, 1:117–148. Il Prato, Padova.

CORTÉS-SÁNCHEZ, MIGUEL, ARTURO MORALES-MUÑIZ, MARÍA D SIMÓN-VALLEJO, MARÍA C LOZANO-FRANCISCO, JOSÉ L VERA-PELÁEZ, CLIVE FINLAYSON, JOAQUÍN RODRÍGUEZ-VIDAL, ET AL.
    2011   Earliest Known Use of Marine Resources by Neanderthals. PLoS ONE 6 (9): e24026.

CUBUK, G.A.
    1976   Altpaläolitische Funde Von Den Mittelmeerterrassen Bei Nea Skala Auf Kephallinia. Archäologisches Korrespondenzblatt 6: 175–181.

DARLAS, ANDREAS, AND HENRY DE LUMLEY
    2004   La Grotte De Kalamakia (Areolopis, Grèce). Sa Contribution à La Connaissance Du Paleolithique Moyen De Grèce. In Le Paleolithique Moyen. Sessions Generales Et Posters. Actes Du XIVème Congrès UISPP, Université De Liège. Belgique, 2–8 Septembre 2001., pp. 255–234. British Archaeological Reports. International Series 1239, Oxford.

DOUKA, KATERINA, AND ENZA ELENA SPINAPOLICE
    2012   Neanderthal Shell Tool Production: Evidence from Middle Palaeolithic Italy and Greece. Journal of World Prehistory 25 (2): 45–79.

Efstratiou, Nikos, Paolo Biagi, Diego E Angelucci, and Renato Nisbet
    2011   Middle Palaeolithic Chert Exploitation in the Pindus Mountains of Western Macedonia, Greece. Antiquity 85 (328). http://www.antiquity.ac.uk/projgall/biagi328/

Efstratiou, Nikos, Paolo Biagi, Paraskevi Elefanti, Panagiotis Karkanas, and Maria Ntinou
    2006   Prehistoric Exploitation of Grevena Highland Zones: Hunters and Herders Along the Pindus Chain of Western Macedonia (Greece)." World Archaeology 38 (3): 415–435.

Ferentinos, George, Maria Gkioni, Maria Geraga, and George Papatheodorou
    2012   Early Seafaring Activity in the Southern Ionian Islands, Mediterranean Sea. Journal of Archaeological Science 39 (7): 2167–2176.

Flemming, Nicholas C.
    1985   Ice Ages and Human Occupation of the Continental Shelf. Oceanus 28: 18–26.

    1998   Archaeological Evidence for Vertical Tectonic Movement on the Continental Shelf During the Palaeolithic, Neolithic and Bronze Age Periods. In Coastal Tectonics. Geological Society Special Publication, I.S. Stewart and Claudio Vita-Finzi, editors, pp. 129–146. Geological Society, London.

    2004   Submarine Prehistoric Archaeology of the Indian Continental Shelf : A Potential Resource. Current Science 86 (9): 1225–1230.

    2010   Comment on Jonathan Benjamin's 'Submerged Prehistoric Landscapes and Underwater Site Discovery: Reevaluating the "Danish Model" for International Practice'. The Journal of Island and Coastal Archaeology 5 (2): 274–276.

Flemming, Nicholas C, Geoff N Bailey, V Courtillot, Geoffrey C P King, Kurt Lambeck, F Ryerson, and Claudio Vita-Finzi
    2003   Coastal and Marine Palaeo-Envi – Ronments and Human Dispersal Points Across the Africa-Eurasia Boundary. In The Maritime and Underwater Heritage, C.A. Brebbia and T Gambin, editors, pp. 61–74. Wessex Institute of Technology Press, Southampton.

Foss, P.
    2002   The Lithics. In Kephallenia: Archaeology and History: The Ancient Greek Cities, K. Randsborg, editor, pp. 77-148. Acta Archaeologica 73, Blackwell Munksgaard, Copenhagen.

Galanidou, Nena
    2004   Early Hominids in the Balkans. In Balkan Biodiversity: Pattern and Process in the European Hotspot, H. I. Griffiths, B. Kryštufek, and J. M. Reed, editors, pp. 147–164. Kluwer Academic Publishers.

Gusick, Amy E, and Michael K Faught
    2011   Prehistoric Archaeology Underwater: A Nascent Subdiscipline Critical to Understanding Early Coastal Occupations and Migration Routes. In Trekking the Shore: Changing Coastlines and the Antiquity of Coastal Settlement, Nuno F. Bicho, Jonathan A. Haws, and Loren G. Davis, editors, pp. 27–51. Springer, New York NY.

Grün, R.
    1996   A Re-analysis of Electron Spin Resonance Dating Results Associated with the Petralona Hominid. Journal of Human Evolution 30: 227–241.

Hennig, G. J., W. Herr, E. Weber and N. I. Xirotiris
    1982   Petralona Cave Dating Controversy Nature 299: 281–282.

Harvati, Katerina, Eleni Panagopoulou, and Curtis Runnels
    2009   The Paleoanthropology of Greece. Evolutionary Anthropology 18 (4): 131–143.

Harvati, Katerina, Andreas Darlas, Shara E. Bailey, Thomas R. Rein, Sireen El Zaatari, Luca Fiorenza, Ottmar Kullmer and Eleni Psathi
    [2013]   New Neanderthal remains from Mani peninsula, Southern Greece: The Kalamakia Middle Paleolithic cave site. Journal of human evolution, 2013. Available at: http://www.ncbi.nlm.nih.gov/pubmed/23490263 [Accessed March 24, 2013].

Kavvadias, G
    1984   Palaeolithic Kefalonia: The Fiskardo Culture. Fitrakis, Athens (in Greek).

Kopaka, Katerina, and Christos Matzanas
    2009   Palaeolithic Industries from the Island of Gavdos, Near Neighbour to Crete in Greece. Antiquity 83 (321). http://antiquity.ac.uk/antiquityNew/projgall/kopaka321/

Kourtessi-Philipakis, Georgia
    1999   The Lower and Middle Palaeolithic in the Ionian Islands. In The Palaeolithic Archaeology of Greece and Adjacent Areas, Geoff N. Bailey, Eugenia Adam, Eleni Panagopoulou, Catherine Perles and Kostas Zachos, editors, pp. 282–287. British School at Athens, London.

Lykousis, V.
    2009   Sea-level Changes and Shelf Break Prograding Sequences During the Last 400ka in the Aegean Margins: Subsidence Rates and Palaeogeographic Implications. Continental Shelf Research 29 (16): 2037–2044.

Manolis, Sotiris, Leslie Aiello, R Henessy, and Nina Kyparissi-Apostolika
    2000   Middle Palaeolithic Hominid Footprints from Theopetra Cave (Thessaly, Greece). In Theopetra Cave: Twelve Years of Excavation and Research 1987-1998. Proceedings of the International Conference, Trikala (6-7 November 1998), Nina Kyparissi-Apostolika, editor, pp. 81–93. Greek Ministry of Culture and Institute for Aegean Prehistory, Athens (in Greek).

Mitsopoulou, Vassiliki
    [2008]   The Impact of Tectonic and Eustatic Changes on Large Mammal Migrations in the Southern Aegean During the Middle and Upper Pleistocene. Undergraduate Dissertation, Department of Geology, University of Patras (in Greek).

Mortensen, Peder
    2008   Lower to Middle Palaeolithic Artifacts from Loutro on the South Coast of Crete. Antiquity 82 (317). http://www.antiquity.ac.uk/ProjGall/mortensen/index.html

Panagopoulou, Eleni, Eleni Kotjabopoulou, and Panagiotis Karkanas
    2001   Geoarchaeological Research in Alonnisos: New Evidence on the Palaeolithic and Mesolithic in the Aegean Region. In The Archaeological Research in Northern Sporades, Adamantios Sampson, editor, pp. 121–151. Municipality of Alonnisos, Alonnisos (in Greek).

Papagianni, Dimitra
    2000   Middle Palaeolithic Occupation and Technology in Northwestern Greece: The Evidence from Open-air Sites. British Archaeological Reports 882. Archaeopress, Oxford.

Papoulia, Christina
    [2014]   Seeing Is Believing or Believing Is Seeing? The Lithic Evidence for Early Sea-Crossing in the Eastern Mediterranean Sea. In HOBET Conference Proceedings. The Interdisciplinary Forum on Human Origins: Behaviour, Environment and Technology. Liverpool 26-28 January 2012.

Poulakakis, Nikos, Aris Parmakelis, Petros Lymberakis, Moysis Mylonas, Eleftherios Zouros, David S Reese, Scott Glaberman, and Adalgisa Caccone
    2006   Ancient DNA Forces Reconsideration of Evolutionary History of Mediterranean Pygmy Elephantids." Biology Letters 2 (3): 451–4.

Runnels, Curtis, and Tjeerd H Van Andel
    1993   A Handaxe from Kokkinopilos, Epirus, and Its Implications for the Paleolithic of Greece." Journal of Field Archaeology 20 (2): 191.

Runnels, Curtis N, and Tjeerd H. van Andel
    2003   The Early Stone Age of the Nomos of Preveza: Landscape and Settlement. Hesperia Supplement: Landscape Archaeology in Southern Epirus, Greece Volume 1, 32: 47–134.

Scuvée, Frédéric, and Jean Verague
    1988   Le Gisement Sous-marin Du Paléolithique Moyen De L'anse De La Mondrée à Fermanville, Manche. C.E.H.P-Littus, Cherbourg.

Strasser, Thomas F., Eleni Panagopoulou, Curtis N Runnels, Priscilla M. Murray, Nickolas Thompson, Panagiotis Karkanas, Floyd W. McCoy, and Karl W. Wegmann
    2010   Stone Age Seafaring in the Mediterranean: Evidence from the Plakias Region for Lower Palaeolithic and Mesolithic Habitation of Crete. Hesperia 79: 145–190.

Strasser, Thomas F., Curtis Runnels, Karl Wegmann, Eleni Panagopoulou, Floyd Mccoy, Chad DiGregorio, Panagiotis Karkanas, and Nick Thompson
    2011   Dating Palaeolithic Sites in Southwestern Crete, Greece. Journal of Quaternary Science 26 (5): 553–560.

Tourloukis, Vaggelis
    2010   The Lower and Middle Pleistocene Archaeological Record of Greece. Leiden University Press, Leiden.

Tourloukis, Vangelis, and Panagiotis Karkanas
    2012   The Middle Pleistocene Archaeological Record of Greece and the Role of the Aegean in Hominin Dispersals: New Data and Interpretations. Quaternary Science Reviews 43: 1–15.

Zilhão, João, Diego E Angelucci, Ernestina Badal-García, Francesco d'Errico, Floréal Daniel, Laure Dayet, Katerina Douka, et al.
    2010   Symbolic Use of Marine Shells and Mineral Pigments by Iberian Neandertals. Proceedings of the National Academy of Sciences of the United States of America 107 (3): 1023–8.

• • • • • • • • • • • • • • • •

Christina Papoulia
PhD candidate in Prehistoric Archaeology
Department of History & Archaeology
University of Crete
University Campus Gallos
74100 Rethymnon
Crete, Greece
+30 6977418334 / +30 2130417839
christina_papoulia@hotmail.com

The 1725 *Nuestra Señora de Begoña*: Ongoing Investigations of a Spanish Merchant *Fragata* in La Caleta de Caucedo, Dominican Republic

Matthew J. Maus
Charles D. Beeker

This paper provides an introduction to the Spanish merchant fragata, Nuestra Señora de Begoña, and a summary of Indiana University's (IU) ongoing archaeological investigations at the site of its 1725 sinking at La Caleta de Caucedo in the Dominican Republic. Archival research and key archaeological findings in the beach area at La Caleta are presented. Early finds suggest that the historical and archaeological records are consistent, and that the cove is a spillage area with the Begoña shipwreck buried nearby off shore. The cultural resources represented by the Begoña are demonstrated to be in peril. While IU is documenting and recovering the most threatened cultural resources within the cove, this paper also proposes the establishment of a Living Museum in the Sea Marine Protected Area to protect the Begoña and associated biology in the public interest.

Historical Record

The *Nuestra Señora de Begoña San Francisco Xavier y las Animas*, alias *Las Tres Hermanas* (The Three Sisters), was an early 18th-century Spanish merchant vessel plying *la Carrera de Indias*, or the Route of the Indies, between the Canary Islands and the Spanish America. Historical records describe the vessel as a three-masted *fragata de 90 toneladas* or 90-ton frigate (Archivo General de Indias [AGI] 1725). While the *Begoña* was smaller than average, *fragatas* were typically about 125 feet long and 25 feet wide. Frigates were the most common vessels in the Spanish treasure fleets, or *flotas*, sailing the Route of the Indies in the 18th century, as their trim design allowed them to move heavy loads much faster than lumbering galleons. However, on its final voyage the *Begoña* did not sail in either of the New Spain or *Tierra Firme flotas* which departed every two or three years in the early 1700s (Walton 1994:165). Instead the ship plied the Atlantic Ocean as a *suelto*, or a trading vessel permitted to sail outside of the *flotas*. *Sueltos* carried 87 percent of all shipping between Spain and the Americas from 1684 to 1745 (Deagan 2002:26-30).

According to the manifest, the primary cargo of the *Begoña* was cacao (*Theobroma cacao*) shipped as whole beans, in paste, or in bricks mixed with honey (*turrones*), along with a smaller component of the dyewood *Palo de Campeche*, or Campeachy Wood (*Haematoxylum campechianum*) (Table 1). Venezuelan plantations in the 18th century provided the bulk of cacao to Spain, principally from the port of *La Guaira*. From 1670, cacao plantations increasingly relied upon African slave labor as indigenous populations disappeared. Ships of many nations engaged in the now infamous "Three-way Trade", exchanging European manufactured goods for African slaves, who were sold for plantation products, such as Venezuelan cacao, for importation to Europe on the return voyage (Cambridge World History of Food 2000; Coe & Coe 2007:187-191) The *Begoña* was also transporting mail and packages along with an official cargo of 8761 silver pesos bound for church and military officials in the Canary Islands (AGI 1725).

The *Begoña* left port for the last time on 30 April 1725 from *La Guaira de Caracas*, Venezuela. The crew was bound for *La Aguada de Puerto Rico* to resupply before the Atlantic crossing towards their homeport of Tenerife in the Canary Islands. En route to Puerto Rico, the ship encountered severe weather in the Caribbean Sea. Forced westward by the storm, the crew attempted to dock at Santo Domingo, but rough waves and a leaking hull prevented the *Begoña* from crossing the sandbar at the mouth of the *Rio Ozama*. Two passengers disembarked in the ship's launch to bring a pilot to guide the frigate into port, but the weather prevented their return. After four days, wind and current broke the ship's anchor cable, forcing the *Begoña* towards the iron shore east of Santo Domingo. Fearing the impending impact, captain, master, and owner of the *Begoña*, Don Theodoro Garces de Salazar, chose to run the vessel aground at the only visible opening in the approaching rock line: a tiny sandy beach called *La Caleta de Caucedo*. On 21 May 1725 the crew beached the vessel there in two fathoms and abandoned ship. While everybody made it to shore alive, the *Begoña* and its cargo were a total loss (AGI 1725).

Cargo	Quantity
Cocoa beans (cacao en grano)	2652 bushels (1768 fanegas)
Bricks of cocoa and honey (turrones)	102 (1 fanega each)
Cocoa paste (cacao en pasta)	550 pounds (22 arrobas)
Campeachy wood (palo de campeche)	3500 pounds (35 quintales)
Silver Pesos (pesos de plata doble)	8761

TABLE 1. 1725 NUESTRA SEÑORA DE BEGOÑA REGISTERED CARGO (CARACAS MANIFEST).

Of the 35 people on the *Begoña*, 27 are recorded in the manifest as crew (Table 2). The division of labor listed on the manifest is consistent with social hierarchy on Spanish ships since at least the 16th century. Pages, apprentices, and sailors served under specialists and officers while everybody answered to the ship's master (Pérez-Mallaína 1998:75-92). The remaining seven people were passengers, of which only one is mentioned in the manifest. The Franciscan Fray Diego Francisco y Banes registered 1950 pesos bound for church officials in Spain when he boarded the *Begoña* in *La Guaira*. The names of the other six are only known from testimonies after the wrecking event (AGI 1725).

The intentional grounding of the *Begoña* resulted in no loss of life. However, with the ship's longboat documented as being in Santo Domingo, it is unclear how the crew and passengers saved themselves and some belongings. It is assumed they used a lifeline to be transported to shore. In his testimony Don Theodoro described use of an *andarivel*, or lifeline, to rescue the official cargo of six *talegas*, or sacks, of 1000 silver pesos each from the cot in his cabin. Furthermore, it is clear that the ship's occupants did manage to save some of their most valued possessions. Shipwreck survivors were intercepted on the road to Santo Domingo by a military detachment responding to the shipwreck. Suspicious of precious metals in the survivors' possession, the detachment confiscated all gold and silver. It took fifteen horses to carry the valuables back to Santo Domingo, which precipitated an investigation of the shipwreck by a colonial commission. The resulting documents from the investigation are kept in Seville, Spain at the *Archivo General de Indias* and provide a detailed historical record of the *Begoña* (AGI 1725).

The investigation found the crew to be in possession of coins and articles valued at over 21,000 pesos while only 8,761 were officially registered. Declaring that the captain must have been aware of the discrepancy, the authorities sentenced Don Theodoro Garces de Salazar to 3 years in prison with another 10 years prohibition of sailing the Route of the Indies. Scholarship suggests that contraband was the norm in the colonial Spanish empire. While many officials tolerated or profited from this illicit trade, the contraband made obvious by the *Begoña's* wrecking so near to Santo Domingo proved impossible for the colonial government to ignore (Boxer 1972; Lyon & Purdy 1982).

Simultaneous with the court proceedings, the commission hired 15 divers and a sloop to salvage the *Begoña*. Divers were hampered by sand, which filled their excavations faster than they could dig with hoes and shovels. Nevertheless, the sloop returned to Santo Domingo on 9 June 1725 with objects apparently recovered from the top deck including three masts and topmasts with some rigging, seven planks, one *esmeril*, part of the bilge pump, two anchors, and 382.5 silver pesos. This was the last recorded salvage attempt (AGI 1725).

La Caleta de Caucedo

La Caleta de Caucedo is on the south coast of the Dominican Republic approximately 21 kilometers east of the historic *Zona Colonial* in the national capital, Santo Domingo. The most notable characteristic of the site is a 34.5-meter long sandy beach, oriented northwest to southeast. The beach is situated at the interior extreme of a small cove, which penetrates 50 meters into the shoreline, and is bound by inaccessible iron shore cliffs that extend unbroken for over 14 kilometers in either direction. Today, the beach is surrounded by urban development along the east-west highway, *Autopista Las Americas*, and is therefore a popular and often crowded local bathing destination.

The site is located within the *Parque Nacional Submarino La Caleta*, which the Dominican Ministries of Environment and Culture established in 1984 to protect the extensive coral reef habitat and known cultural resources within its boundaries. Since then, the government has sunk multiple modern vessels in park waters to create artificial reefs and promote dive tourism.

Officers and Specialists		
Name	*Duty*	
Don Theodoro Garces de Salazar	captain, master, administrator	(capitán, maestro, administrador)
Lic. Don Francisco Pérez	chaplain	(capellán)
Don Pedro Rodríguez Muñoz	secretary	(escribano)
Cristóbal de Vera	pilot	(piloto)
Gregorio de Silva	assistant pilot	(ayudante de piloto)
Manuel Bravo	boatswain	(contramaestre)
Domingo Martín	assistant boatswain	(guardián)
Juan Baptista Carrillo	master gunner	(condestable)
Domingo de Ortega	steward	(despensero)
Juan García	surgeon and barber	(cirujano y barber)
Skilled Sailors (marineros)		
Miguel Francisco	Joseph Theodoro	Juan de León
Salvador Barriento	Pedro Toledo	
Apprentice Sailors (mozos)		
Joseph Fernández	Juan Amaro	Joseph Felles Fadaje
Cristóbal Alventos	Miguel Antonio	Juan Lorente
Manuel Yanes	Pedro Raymundo	
Pages (pajes)		
Sebastián Tadeo	Nicolás Francisco	
Cooks (cocineros)		
Thomas de los Santos	Luis Fernández	
Passengers		
Fray Diego Francisco y Banes	Domingo Hernández Perima	Alférez Phelipe de Páez
Don Nicolás Bartolomé Lordelo	Thomas González	Joseph Rodríguez
Baltazar de Acosta	Joseph Albanes de San Pedro	

Table 2. 1725 Nuestra Señora de Begoña: Crew and Passengers.

While the park is mostly underwater it also includes grounds near the beach, which contain evidence of a pre-historic Taíno settlement. Previous investigation by Dominican archaeologists found Chicoid subseries ceramics at *La Caleta*, identifying the site as belonging to the Boca Chica cultural horizon from ca. AD 1000 – 1500 (Rouse 1992:32,110-112; Veloz Maggiolo 1972:127-150,159). In recent years, a museum was constructed in the park, but today the structure is roofless with open pits containing exposed pre-historic human remains.

Near-shore submerged cultural resources are also in peril. Locally, it is common knowledge that there is a shipwreck near the beach. In the 1980s residents removed a cannon after its exposure from storm scour. More recently, Indiana University (IU) has documented local men hunting for coins in the sand between waves. These threats became more pressing in early 2010, when an American treasure hunting company applied for permits to salvage the *Begoña*.

Summary of Field Work (2010 – 2012)

In order to document and protect the imperiled cultural resources at *La Caleta*, IU offered to provide technical training to the Dominican government and begin archaeological investigations there. By invitation of the Ministry of Culture, IU commenced work at *La Caleta* in March 2010 by providing a Technical Workshop on Underwater Cultural Heritage and Introductory Scientific Diving to divers and snorkelers from the Dominican Navy and Ministries of Culture and Environment. This workshop was coupled with the first exploratory remote sensing and archaeological excavation at *La Caleta*, funded by a National Geographic Society Waitt Grant. In addition to diver-deployed remote sensing in the beach area, Panamerican Consultants Inc. (2010) conducted a remote sensing survey outside of the cove with a boat-towed proton magnetometer. The 2010 excavation exposed a single concentration of artifacts, including cannonballs, unidentified metal concretions, and a large concretion of silver coins near the beach, together designated Feature 1 (Figure 1) (Beeker 2010; Foster et al, this volume). After the 2010 fieldwork, IU paused operations at *La Caleta* to conduct archival research at the *Archivo General de Indias* in *Seville*, Spain and acquire funding for more excavation at the site.

In March 2012, IU resumed excavations at *La Caleta* with funding from the Eli Lilly and Company Foundation and in collaboration with The Children's Museum of Indianapolis. In March and May 2012 IU exposed two artifact concentrations in the beach area, designated Features 2 and 3 (Maus 2012a; Maus, Keller, Bleichner 2012). Feature 2 is centered on a cannon and includes a scatter of artifacts found within a 3-meter radius, including a smallsword hilt and a large concretion of silver dinnerware. Feature 3 is a 2.8 by 2.1 meter Pleistocene limestone rock suspended in the sand column. Mixed prehistoric, historic, and modern cultural material was found in the compact sand beneath the rock, apparently concentrated together by wave action. Also, two concretions of silver coins cemented in the shape of their bags, or *talegas* (Foster et al, this volume), were found adjacent to the eastern edge of the bedrock lens.

Three additional features were identified in December 2012 (Maus 2012b). In Feature 4, the most seaward excavation to date, divers found a small crushed pot in the sand column and a small timber segment under two meters of sand. Prior to fully excavating this feature, IU reoriented excavation shoreward to

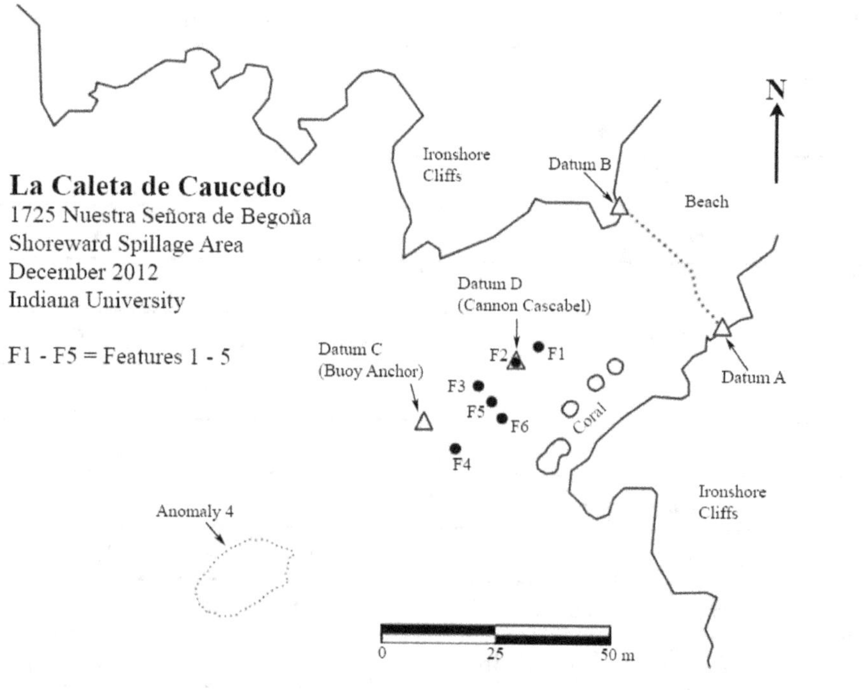

FIGURE 1. LA CALETA SITE PLAN AFTER DECEMBER 2012 EXCAVATIONS (INDIANA UNIVERSITY, 2013).

focus on more threatened resources. Future excavation will be necessary to determine if the timber represents a ship component, such as a spar, or is unrelated to the *Begoña*. Feature 5 includes a large concretion, possibly the contents of a sea chest, and the surrounding scattered assemblage. Feature 6 is another catchment area similar to Feature 3 and yielded the densest concentration of artifacts yet found at *La Caleta*.

Underwater topography gently inclines towards the beach. The sand surface is only 3 meters deep at the mouth of the cove, the current seaward limit of excavations. The substrate is mostly loose sand with sheltered pockets of friable compact sand. The sand column narrows towards shore. In Feature 4 the Pleistocene limestone bedrock lays beneath two meters of sand, but just 0.5 meters in Feature 1.

While the water is usually calm, the effects of powerful wave forces are apparent. In December 2012, the beach was scoured to bedrock after Hurricane Sandy. In every excavation, prehistoric, historic, and modern cultural materials were consistently found mixed together at all depths and therefore clearly not in primary context. In addition, most objects were not found on the bedrock, but in the sand column apparently subject to occasional wave displacement. Furthermore, many small objects were found crushed, demonstrating an additional environmental threat to near shore cultural materials.

Methods

Divers excavated anomalies with a venturi jet connected by fire hose to a 23 horsepower water pump deployed either on shore or in an inflatable boat. Divers conducted remote sensing of the excavation area using handheld JW Fischers 8X Metal Detectors and a JW Fischers PT-1 Pipe Tracker proton magnetometer to locate magnetic anomalies within the cove, guide active excavation, and check dredge tailings for small objects.

Distance and bearings from onshore Datum Points A and B to large objects and artifact concentrations were measured using spotting scopes and plotted by trilateration. Underwater, divers measured and plotted *in situ* objects, concentrated assemblages, and other points of interest with reel tape measures and compass bearings from established underwater Datum Points C (concrete spar buoy anchor) and D (cannon cascabel). However, due to ongoing wave transport, most objects were exposed in the sand column, out of primary context. As a result of the frequent turbulence churning up the local sand environment, these objects often slid down the cascading sand slopes during active excavation, thus precluding *in situ* documentation, and were instead recorded in association with the nearest Feature.

Panamerican Consultants (2010) conducted the remote sensing survey outside of the cove and a Trimble DSM12/212 Differential GPS system with a Marine Magnetics SeaSPY overhauser magnetometer towed by a 28-foot Boston Whaler loaned to IU by the *Oficina Nacional de Patrimonio Cultural Subacuático* for survey purposes. Transects were spaced at 50-foot intervals and the entire survey area covered approximately 400 meters by 250 meters, oriented northwest by southeast.

Armaments

In March 2012, excavation exposed one muzzle-loaded smooth bore cast-iron cannon under 0.5 meters of sand in a tumbled position with the touchhole down and the muzzle facing 305° northwest. This cannon is the central object in Feature 2 and its cascabel is designated Datum D. It is 1.68 meters long with the first reinforcement ring at 30 cm and the second at 66 cm from the cascabel. The 10 cm diameter trunnions are low, centered on the bottom of the bore, and situated 81 cm from the cascabel. The bore, partially concreted, is approximately 10 cm in diameter suggesting it fired a 6-pound ball.

Local residents removed one cannon from the beach after exposure from storm scour in the 1980s. This cannon is now lost, but government photographs show a cast-iron muzzle-loaded cannon of similar dimensions to the one described above, but differs with very low trunnions centered on the barrel bottom. Together, these two cannons intimate an eclectic design and relatively small caliber that one might expect on an 18th century merchant vessel. The *Begoña* armaments registry lists 10 cannons and 2 *pedreros* of which two cannons and one *pedrero*, likely referred to as an *esmeril* by the contemporaneous salvors, are now accounted for (AGI 1725).

A concreted flintlock firearm was recovered from Feature 6 in December 2012. While concretion currently prevents detailed description of the action, the barrel measures 53 cm long with a .51 caliber bore. Thirty *escopetas*, or light muskets, were registered on the *Begoña* (AGI 1725). *Escopeta* usually designates a smooth bore, flintlock sporting or militia firearm with a patilla type miquelet lock and was present in the Americas from ca. 1680 to 1825. While examples vary, most have a barrel length of 87.6 – 99 cm and were standardized at .69 caliber in 1728. (Brown 1980:172-174; Deagan

2002[2]:276-279; Lavin 1965:168; Neal 1956:10). However, one example, fabricated for mounted use circa 1750, has a smaller than average barrel of 72 cm and a .54 caliber bore (Brinkerhoff & Chamberlain 1972:27). If the weapon recovered in Feature 6 is in fact one of the 30 *escopetas*, it is very diminutive for the style, but may be a smaller sporting variant or an intentionally shortened *escopeta* for ship service.

Twelve lead projectiles were recovered in Features 1 and 3. Seven are identified as cast musket balls that exhibit mold sprues and lines. These range in diameter from .65 to .72 caliber with an average mass of 34.1 grams. The other five pieces exhibit a freeform, irregular shape and lack any casting marks. The freeform projectiles are smaller, ranging from .52 to .61 caliber with an average mass of 17.5 grams. These are likely scatter shot, which was commonly used in the colonial period to improve the effectiveness of musket fire (Brown 1980:114). Taken together, these lead balls and shot could have been fired by most *escopetas*, but are all too large for use with the Feature 6 firearm.

The bronze hilt of a smallsword was found in Feature 2 1.85 meters west (270°) from Datum D. The ferrous blade is broken and missing, but the bronze hilt, 18.5 cm from button to guard, exhibits the characteristic features diagnostic of a European smallsword including a lobate quillon below two finger-guard branches terminating in double oval shell guards (Brinkerhoff & Chamberlain 1972:97-99, Mcnab 2010:142-145). While 12 *chafarotes*, or cutlasses, are listed on the *Begoña* manifest, this weapon is likely not one of them. Smallswords are indicators of high social status as officers and other elite males typically carried these functional dress weapons (Brinkerhoff & Chamberlain 1972:97-99) and are unlikely to have been grouped with more common swords in the ship's armory.

Sea Chests

In May 2012, divers exposed a 32.13 kilogram concretion of silver dinnerware resting on top of an eroded wooden board in Feature 2, 1 meter west (270°) of Datum D. The assemblage was found beneath 0.5 meters of sand and rock. For description of the silver dinnerware concretion see Foster, et al. (this volume).

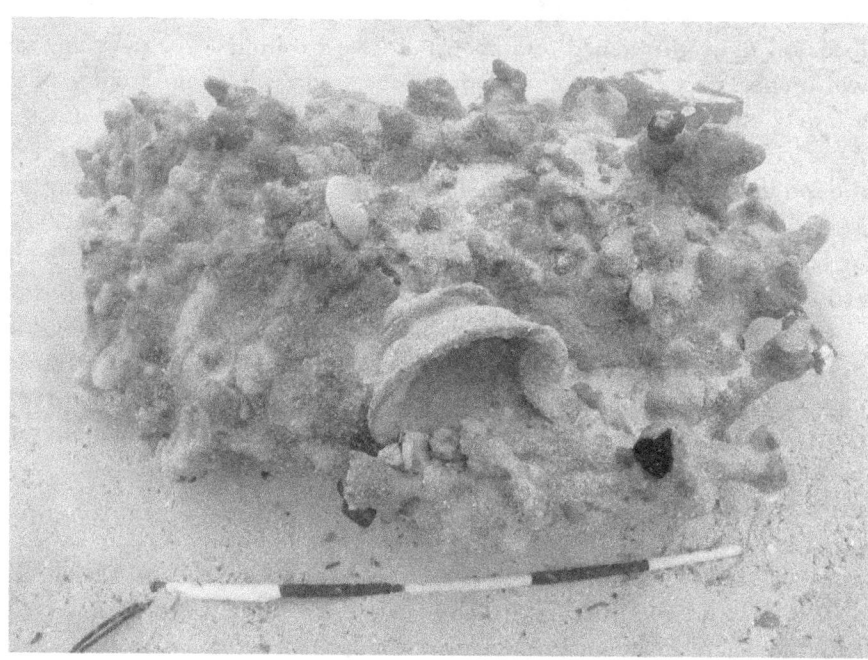

FIGURE 2. CONCRETION OF UNIDENTIFIED METAL OBJECTS WITH CHALICE IN SITU IN FEATURE 5 (INDIANA UNIVERSITY, 2012).

The wooden board measures 81 cm long, 26 cm at its widest, and 2 cm thick. These dimensions correspond to the size of the dinnerware concretion found on top of the wood. In addition, an impression of one of the silver plates on the bottom of the concretion is visible on the wood surface. These observations support the interpretation of this assemblage as a chest bottom below its contents.

After the shipwreck, when questioned by the Spanish colonial authorities as to the location of the ship's manifest, Captain Don Theodoro Garces de Salazar responded

> *...that he was carrying the manifest from Caracas in a big cedar trunk which also had his color dress clothes with other things of consequence and the ship's log and other parts of the manifest; of which the bottom fell out and it was pulled out empty from the shore at La Caleta with nine other passengers' boxes that also came out bottomless without gaining anything from them... [Author's translation] (AGI 1725)*

The degraded cellular structure of the wooden chest bottom has so far prevented identification of the tree species. Prior to microscope observation, wood samples were macerated and added to a wet mount. Preliminary

FIGURE 3. DETAIL OF ONE OF FOUR IDENTICAL BUTTONS FROM LA CALETA, FEATURING A SHELL DISK CARVED WITH A FLOWER MOTIF SET INTO A BRASS BACKING WITH WIRE SHANK (ILLUSTRATION BY LOREN CLARK, 2012).

results thus obtained indicate the presence of tapered tracheid-like cells suggesting that the wood is from an unidentified gymnosperm, and therefore possibly cedar. While this early information is tantalizing, there is no accounting for the possibility that every chest on the *Begoña* was made of cedar.

Another large concretion was recovered from Feature 5 in December 2012. The concretion is 76 cm by 36 cm by 24 cm tall and consists of a compact jumble of heavily concreted elongated metal objects with a small chalice visible on top (Figure 2). These dimensions, the compact nature of the jumbled metal objects, and Don Theodoro's description of multiple boxes lost on the way to shore suggest that the Feature 5 concretion may represent the contents of another sea chest. Additional conservation and analysis is necessary to determine the composition of this concretion prior to conclusive interpretation.

High Status Personal Effects

In May 2012, a covered tankard was found in Feature 3. X-Ray Fluorescence (XRF) spectra recorded with a Bruker Tracer III-SD Handheld XRF Analyzer, identifies the tankard material as an alloy of silver and copper covered in a gilding of gold and mercury. While the cup lid and base are badly deteriorated, the three-part lid hinge is still articulated and features an ornamental female head, or caryatid, protruding 2.25 cm from the scrolled handle. The cup is crushed and still partially cemented, but ongoing conservation continues to expose intricate scrolling and embossment.

A crushed silver basin was found in Feature 6. The intact but deformed vessel prevents most measurements, but the mouth diameter is 11.23 cm across. The base consists of a 10.32 cm diameter round foot with decorative fluting on the underside. Conservation has revealed intricate etching on the body along with evidence of gilding. An 8 cm long handle is mounted on the side with a caryatid similar to that found on the tankard. No makers' marks are visible on this or any other pieces, though they could be obscured by the remaining concretion.

Two cast silver candlestick stems were recovered in December 2012. One was found cemented to the chamber pot and the other was found near a silver candlestick base in Feature 5. The stems are 10.0 cm and 8.7 cm long with one and two knops respectively and are morphologically similar to the three pairs of stems and bases on the silver dinnerware concretion. The former stem has a threaded screw inserted into the base and was concreted to a crushed silver wax pan. The silver candlestick base is 14.5 cm square and 0.65 cm thick and lacks ornamentation or other marks. The base is crushed with a 2 cm thick wood fragment trapped within the folded halves. Together, these objects may represent an attempt to conceal illicit transport of precious metals to Europe as personal effects that were lost during attempted transport to shore.

Brass

A total of four identical compound buttons were found in Features 1, 5, and 6. The exterior circular face of the buttons range in diameter from 1.54 to 1.82 cm. Three of the buttons are intact with a brass backing, but only one retains its wire shank. Inset onto the backing is a shell disk with a 6-petal flower with alternating leaves carved into the exterior surface (Figure 3). The carving is identical on each button. Button use in all social strata of the Spanish empire increased throughout the 18th century, as French fashion influenced Spain and its colonies after the accession of Bourbon King Felipe

FIGURE 4. A BRASS WINE CASK SPIGOT. THE STOPCOCK IS OPEN (INDIANA UNIVERSITY, 2012).

V in 1700. As buttons became more popular, they also became more complex with two and three-piece buttons made from a wide variety of materials, including shell (Deagan 2002:157-173).

A brass spigot was recovered in Feature 3 and measures 20.7 cm long and 9.4 cm from the valve bottom to the top of the stopcock, which is in the open position (Figure 4). The stem tapers to a 1.3 cm diameter orifice and the faucet mouth is 1.5 cm square. This spigot likely was used to tap wine barrels, source of the crew's most appreciated ration (Pérez-Mallaína 1998:140-145). While the interaction of wave forces and moving sand may have forced the stopcock into a more compact open position, drinking the ship's wine stores before an impending wreck is a documented coping mechanism (Gibbs 2006:11-12).

Ceramics

Excavation has uncovered both historic and prehistoric ceramics in mixed contexts throughout the beach area. Spanish and pre-historic Taíno ceramics were recovered throughout the excavation area in mixed context. Feature 6 accounts for majority of ceramics so far recovered, with 96 historic and 60 pre-historic sherds found in a mixed context. The historic ceramics at *La Caleta* are almost exclusively Middle Style Unglazed Coarse Earthenware Spanish Olive Jars with visible interior wheel lines. Middle Style Olive Jars date from ca. AD 1560 to 1800, and represent the most frequently found Spanish ceramics in the Americas. Olive Jars were ubiquitous in Spanish colonial life, probably due to their prevalence in shipping, and were used to store goods, especially liquids (Deagan 1987:30-34). The pre-historic ceramics, identified as of the Chicoid subseries, are easily differentiated from the olive jars by the absence of interior wheel lines and the presence of exterior decorative incisions. The Chicoid subseries is associated with the classic Taíno of Hispaniola from ca. AD 1000 – 1500 and was in use until the European contact period (Rouse 1992:32,110-112; Veloz Maggiolo 1972:127-150). The ceramics appear utilitarian, or for body ornamentation, and not representative of religious uses (Beeker, Conrad, and Foster 2002).

Discussion

Armaments and high status objects, especially those made of silver, represent artifact categories disproportionately predominant relative to the dearth of non-elite personal effects and absence of the ship's structural components in the beach area. While the resistance of noble metals to corrosion, such as the brass, silver, and gold documented here, may exaggerate their representation in the archaeological record, the absence of a comparable quantity of ferrous artifacts is conspicuous. It is clear from the court archives that the crew prioritized salvage of precious metals immediately after the shipwreck. These observations suggest that the cultural resources in the beach area represent valuables, and the arms to guard them, lost during attempted transport to shore by the ship's crew.

The current hypothesis is that the hull component of the *Begoña*, including a ballast pile, remnant structure, artillery, and a more concentrated assemblage of cargo and personal effects, is further seaward from the beach area. Supporting evidence for this position includes:

- The lack of the ship's structural components, such as drift pins, fasteners, hardware, timbers, or rigging.

- No ballast pile. While some scattered ballast stones are present in the beach area, they are insufficient to account for the ship's entire ballast and are small enough to have been transported shoreward by wave action.

- A lone cannon in a tumbled position with most *Begoña* artillery unaccounted for.

- Historical description of the shipwreck in 2 *brazos*, or 4 meters, of water whereas the cove is 3 meters at its deepest.

- Captain's testimony of the loss of sea chests during attempted transport to shore and the identification of one or two chests in the archaeological record suggests the ship lies seaward.

The magnetic survey of the waters around *La Caleta* identified a total of 6 magnetic anomalies (Panamerican Consultants 2010). Of these, Anomaly 4 appears most likely to represent the hull of the *Begoña*. The anomaly is elliptical in shape with the long axis pointing towards the beach. This orientation is consistent with the intentional grounding of the vessel. Furthermore, the sand surface at Anomaly 4 is four meters deep, consistent with the historical recorded depth of the shipwreck's final resting place under 2 *brazos,* or fathoms, of water (AGI 1725). Divers investigating the anomaly observed only a featureless sandy bottom, suggesting it is likely buried under deep sand. While excavation of the anomaly will be necessary in order to verify if it is in fact the *Begoña*, the anomaly's location seaward of the cove and deep overburden means that it is not under immediate threat.

Findings from the beach zone at *La Caleta de Caucedo* continue to support the hypothesis that the archaeological assemblage in the cove does not represent the shipwreck itself, but instead the attempted transport to shore from the shipwreck by the crew and contemporary salvage efforts by the colonial government. Furthermore, wave action has mixed cultural resources in all excavations and is likely to have moved smaller artifacts from the shipwreck towards shore.

Conclusions

The *Begoña* represents a unique opportunity for the archaeological study of an early 18th century Spanish shipwreck beside detailed corresponding historical sources. Ongoing excavations at *La Caleta* will continue to focus on documentation and, when necessary, recovery of the threatened cultural resources in the beach zone. In the future, IU is considering test excavations of Anomaly 4 to verify if it represents the shipwreck of the *Begoña*, but this resource is not under imminent peril.

IU is working with local, national, and international actors to expand the DR National System of *los Museos Vivos del Mar*, or Living Museums in the Sea, to preserve the unique and significant cultural resources at *La Caleta* for future generations. Living Museums of the Sea are Marine Protected Areas that preserve significant submerged cultural resources and the associated biology by promoting sustainable tourism such as underwater parks (Hanselmann and Beeker 2008). With the support of the DR *Oficina Nacional de Patrimonio Cultural Subacuático* and the US Agency for International Development, IU has already established three Living Museums in the Sea in the DR, including the Captain Kidd *Museo Vivo del Mar* at the 1699 shipwreck of the *Quedagh Merchant*. These underwater preserves are popular local tourist destinations and, as a result, associate local economic incentive with the protection of submerged cultural resources and the associated biology.

Considering the presence of a pre-historic Taíno settlement and its proximity to Santo Domingo, established in 1496 by Bartolomé Colón, *La Caleta* offers a compelling interpretation opportunity to tell the story of the indigenous peoples of Hispaniola, the European conquest of their world, and the subsequent colonial system, of which ships such as the *Begoña* were integral. Enhancement and interpretation of these unique resources, both on land and underwater, will benefit the local community by promoting sustainable tourism and protecting their unique cultural patrimony. Only by associating the preservation of these resources with the wellbeing of *La Caleta* can we hope for the *Begoña* to last another 288 years.

Acknowledgements

We would like to express our special thanks to the Eli Lilly & Company Foundation and The Children's Museum of Indianapolis for their generous support of this project, to the National Geographic Society Waitt Grants Program for funding the initial exploratory remote sensing survey, and the USAID for initial sponsorship of the Dominican Republic National System of Living Museums in the Sea. In addition, we would like to thank the following DR government institutions for their support of this research: *la Oficina Nacional de Patrimonio Cultural Subacuático, el Ministerio de Cultura,* and *el Ministerio de Medioambiente*. We are grateful to

Dr. D. Bish, Indiana University, for x-ray diffraction analyses of the button shell insets. Also, we recognize the many valued contributions of the following individuals: Francis Soto, Pedro Borrell, John Foster, Geoffrey Conrad, Isabel Brito, Bruce Kaiser, Anna Rogers, Loren Clark, Jessica Keller, Mylana Haydu, Barry Bleichner, Lydia Barbash-Riley, Rodrigo Parra-Ferro, Olivia Thomas, Samuel Erotas, Benjamin Ivers, Emily Palmer, and Abigail Yates. Finally, special thanks to the 2012 Our World Underwater Scholarship Society scholars, Megan Cook, Yoland Bosiger, and Oscar Svensson, and Ocean Technology Services for their on-site assistance.

References

ARCHIVO GENERAL DE INDIAS [AGI]
    1725   En la Ciudad de Santo Domingo (In the City of Santo Domingo). Commission proceedings, Escribania 9c, Legajo 2, Pieza 9, Archivo General de Indias, Seville, Spain.

BEEKER, CHARLES
    2010   Report on the Technical Workshop in Underwater Cultural Heritage and Introductory Scientific Diving (March 2010). Report to the Dominican Republic Ministries of Culture and Environment from Indiana University – Bloomington.

BEEKER, CHARLES D., GOEFFREY W. CONRAD, AND JOHN W. FOSTER
    2002   Taíno Use of Flooded Caverns in the East National Park Region, Dominican Republic. *Journal of Caribbean Archaeology*, 3:1-26.

BOXER, C.R.
    1972   A Question of Contraband: the Old Colonial Trade. *History Today* 22(3):204-213. London.

BRINCKERHOFF, SYDNEY, AND PIERCE CHAMBERLAIN
    1972   *Spanish military weapons in colonial America, 1700-1821*. Stackpole Books, Harrison, Pa.

BROWN, M.L.
    1980   *Firearms in colonial America : the impact on history and technology, 1492-1792*. Smithsonian Institution Press, Washington.

CAMBRIDGE WORLD HISTORY OF FOOD
    2000   A History of American Cacaos. Cambridge University Press, Cambridge, United Kingdom. <https://oberon.ius.edu/login?url=http://www.credoreference.com/entry/cupfood/a_history_of_american_cacaos>. Accessed 11 February 2013.

COE, SOPHIE D. AND MICHAEL D. COE
    2007   *The true history of chocolate*. New York Thames and Hudson.

DEAGAN, KATHLEEN
    1987   *Artifacts of the Spanish colonies of Florida and the Caribbean, 1500-1800, Vol. 1: Ceramics, Glassware, and Beads*. Smithsonian Institution Press, Washington DC.

    2002   *Artifacts of the Spanish Colonies in Florida and the Caribbean, 1500-1800, Vol. 2: Portable Personal Possessions*. Smithsonian Institution Press, Washington DC.

GIBBS, MARTIN
    2006   Cultural Site Formation Processes in Maritime Archaeology: Disaster Response, Salvage and Muckelroy 30 Years on. *The International Journal of Nautical Archaeology*, 35(1):4-19.

HANSELMANN FREDERICK H. AND CHARLES D. BEEKER
    2008   Establishing Marine Protected Areas in the Dominican Republic: A Model for Sustainable Preservation. En Langley, S. y Mastone, V. (Eds.) ACUA Underwater Archaeology Proceedings 2008. Columbus: PAST Foundation

LAVIN, JAMES
    1965   *A history of Spanish firearms*. New York: Arco.

LYON, EUGENE AND BARBARA A. PURDY
    1982   Contraband in Spanish Colonial Ships. *Itinerario*, 6(2):91-108.

MAUS, MATTHEW J.
    2012a   Preliminary Field Report of Archaeological Investigations at La Caleta de Caucedo: A Proposed Living Museum of the Sea, May 2012. Report to the Dominican Republic Ministries of Culture and Environment from Indiana University – Bloomington.

    2012b   Preliminary Field Report of Archaeological Investigations at La Caleta de Caucedo: A Proposed Living Museum of the Sea, December 2012. Report to the Dominican Republic Ministries of Culture and Environment from Indiana University – Bloomington.

MAUS, MATTHEW J., JESSICA A. KELLER, BARRY J. BLEICHNER
    2012   Preliminary Field Report of Archaeological Investigations at La Caleta de Caucedo: A Proposed Living Museum of the Sea, March 2012. Report to the Dominican Republic Ministries of Culture and Environment from Indiana University – Bloomington.

McNAB, CHRIS (EDITOR)
    2010   *Swords: A Visual History*. Dorling Kindersley Limited, London.

NEAL, W. KIETH
    1955   *Spanish guns and pistols*. London: G. Bell and Sons.

PANAMERICAN CONSULTANTS, INC.
2010   Submerged Cultural Resources Survey of the Begoña Shipwreck Site Offshore La Caleta, Near Santo Domingo, Dominican Republic. Report to the Dominican Republic Ministry of Culture.

PÉREZ-MALLAÍNA, PABLO E.
1998   *Spain's Men of the Sea: Daily Life on the Indies Fleets in the Sixteenth Century.* The Johns Hopkins University Press, translator Carla Rahn Phillips, Baltimore.

ROUSE, IRVING
1992   *The Tainos: Rise and Decline of the People Who Greeted Columbus.* Yale University Press, New Haven.

VELOZ MAGGIOLO, MARCIO
1972   *Arqueologia Prehistorica de Santo Domingo.* McGraw-Hill Far Eastern Publishers Ltd, Singapore.

WALTON, TIMOTHY R.
1994   *The Spanish Treasure Fleets.* Pineapple Press Inc., Sarasota, FL.Matthew J. Maus

. . . .

Matthew J. Maus
Office of Underwater Science
Indiana University, SPH 058
Bloomington, IN 47405
mmaus@indiana.edu

Charles D. Beeker
Office of Underwater Science
Indiana University, SPH 058
Bloomington, IN 47405
cbeeker@indiana.edu

Talegas and Hoards: The Archaeological Signature of Contraband on a 1725 Spanish Merchant Vessel

John W. Foster
Matthew J. Maus
Anna Rogers

Nuestra Señora de Begoña, a Spanish merchant vessel bound from Caracas to Tenerife, was wrecked at la Caleta de Caucedo in the Dominican Republic in 1725. An investigation of the incident resulted in charges being brought against Captain Don Theodoro Garces de Salazar and his conviction of silver smuggling. Contemporary salvage of the Begoña cargo was only partially successful, but some 21,000 pesos in silver were recovered including "six talegas found under the captain's bed." Only 8,761 pesos were registered as formal cargo.

Archaeological testing at the site has begun to record further evidence of contraband. Two additional talegas (moneybags) have been recovered and a hoard of coins in the shape of a canvas bag or satchel. Silver dinnerware and the remnants of a wooden chest have also been recovered. This paper describes the talegas and hoard and presents numismatic details recorded to date. The Begoña's archaeological signature of a contraband cargo is beginning to emerge.

Introduction

The storm was unrelenting. The *Nuestra Señora de Begoña San Francisco Xavier y las Animas,* alias *Las Tres Hermanas* wallowed heavily in the huge seas, her pumps working constantly to keep her afloat. Captain Don Theodoro Garces de Salazar gathered the passengers and crew to discuss options. Attempts to reach harbor in Puerto Rico were impossible due to contrary winds, and the bar of the Ozama River thwarted refuge in Santo Domingo. Riding so low in the water, the obstruction could not be cleared. For four days the ship searched for a harbor, but none could be found. Finally, as agreed by all on board, the captain sailed directly into the only opening on an ironshore coast, a small cove known as *la Caleta de Caucedo* – wrecking the ship. The date was May 21, 1725.

The seamanship of Captain Garces de Salazar resulted in the safe landing of 35 crew and passengers from the merchant frigate. As they gathered their tattered belongings on the beach, the ship was pounded by heavy swells and broke apart against rocks protecting the cove. The cargo of cacao was swept away and attempts to rescue personal belongings were only partially successful. The 90-ton frigate set to carry them from La Guaira in the province of Caracas to Tenerife in the Canary Islands was no more.

The *Begoña*'s loss may have been unremarkable except for the trial and conviction of Captain Garces de Salazar for silver smuggling. Spanish authorities in Santo Domingo compared the registered value of salvaged items with those listed on the ship's manifest. Although the original document was lost in the wrecking, along with the captain's personal effects, a copy from Caracas was produced and the Captain held responsible for the discrepancy. Trial records indicate some 21,000 pesos in silver were recovered by contemporary salvage and confiscated from the *Begoña*'s passengers while only 8,761 pesos were officially registered.

After beaching the ship, the crew salvaged six *talegas,* or bags of 1,000 pesos each, from beneath the captain's bunk. This accounts for 6,000 of the 8,761 pesos registered onboard. Most of the remaining registered cargo was lost by Diego Francisco y Barnes of the Order of St. Francis. He signed up as a passenger to Tenerife and placed 1,950 pesos onto the register of the ship. He lost it all in the *Begoña*'s wrecking and whether it was recovered in the salvage is not known. The remainder, save 811 pesos, must be contraband (*Archivo General de Indias* 1725).

The problem of unregistered contraband was widespread throughout the Iberian shipping empires (Lyon and Purdy 1982: 92; Boxer 1972). Even on royal fleets organized to carry gold and silver back to Spain, smuggling was common. The *avería*, a regular assessment of shipped goods, funded much of the protection efforts carried out by the Spanish crown. Added to that were regulations establishing custom duties (*almojarifazgo*) and Royal taxes on the founding and minting of precious metals (*quinto*). The result was a well-organized and systemic effort to avoid payment (Lyon and Purdy 1982:92). As an example, the 11 Spanish ships of the 1715 treasure convoy carried a registered 6,486,066 pesos in gold and silver bullion and coin. All were lost

FIGURE 1. THE FOSTER CLUMP IS A LARGE COIN CONCRETION WITH A CIRCULAR SHAPE. IT MAY HAVE BEEN CONTRABAND CONCEALED IN THE FALSE BOTTOM OF A BARREL. THE CONTENTS ARE 4- AND 8 REALES COINS FROM THE MEXICO CITY MINT. THE CONCRETION IS BEING PRESERVED INTACT AS AN INTERPRETIVE ARTIFACT FROM THE 1725 SPANISH MERCHANT FRIGATE.

in a devastating hurricane that scattered wrecks along a 50-mile stretch of Florida coast. Spanish salvage efforts began immediately and lasted until 1719. Over 8,500,000 pesos were saved (Marx 1980:116). Modern salvage efforts have added considerably to that total so we can now estimate that the contraband cargo was probably equal to that officially registered (Smith 1988:96).

Indiana University excavations in partnership with the government of the Dominican Republic have begun to yield coins and silver that were apparently carried on board the *Nuestra Señora de Begoña*. This paper presents information about these archaeological artifacts. Keeping in mind that our focus to date has been the cove itself and not the deeper offshore area thought to contain the *Begoña's* hull (Maus and Beeker, this volume), the coin and silver sample may increase considerably over time, altering initial interpretations. Nonetheless, some interesting observations and patterns can be seen emerging from the documentary evidence and archaeological analyses. Documents produced for the trial of Captain Garces de Salazar help us separate registered coinage from contraband and thus characterize the nature of contraband coins and cargo from a 1725 Spanish merchant frigate.

La Caleta de Caucedo is located on the south coast of the Dominican Republic 21 kilometers east of historic Santo Domingo. *La Caleta*, or the small cove, refers to a 34.5 meter long sandy beach recessed 50 meters into low ironshore cliffs that shroud the beach on both sides. Indiana University (IU) began underwater archaeological investigation of the beach area in March 2010 and has since conducted excavations in March, May, and December 2012. To date, IU has designated Features 1 to 6, each representing concentrated archaeological assemblages, within the beach zone which is interpreted to represent the shoreward spillage area. A magnetic anomaly located approximately 50 meters seaward of the excavation limits may represent the buried hull remains of the *Begoña* shipwreck (Maus, Beeker, this volume: Figure 1).

Excavations at *La Caleta* are ongoing under the authority of *la Oficina Nacional de Patrimonio Cultural Subacuático*. The goals are: 1) to recover artifacts from the shallow beach zone that are subject to periodic exposure and collection; 2) to identify the source of submerged artifacts and their relationship to the 1725 merchant frigate *Nuestra Señora de Begoña;* and 3) to train Dominican officials in practical methods of underwater cultural resource management within the national park.

Description and Numismatic Profile of *Nuestra Señora de Begoña* Coins

A sequence of buried magnetic features has been identified offshore in the shallow, high-energy zone of La Caleta. They have proven to contain a mixture of 18th century shipwreck artifacts, coins, Taíno pottery and modern debris. Three coin concretions have been recovered – not cemented to bedrock substrate, but "floating" in a sand matrix that averages 1.4m in thickness. This unusual stratigraphic context after 288 years may be due to periodic storm waves that sweep the cove and churn many centuries of accumulated deposits. Some individual coins have also been recovered.

The first coin concretion (some call it the "Foster Clump") was discovered in the cascading sidewall while excavating a cannonball assemblage designated Feature 1 (Maus, Beeker, this volume: Figure 1). It weighs 6150.7g or 13.6 lbs. (Figure 1). The concretion remains intact although exposed coin surfaces have been cleaned to permit identification. Thus far, five 4-*reales* and twenty-two 8-*reales* have been noted in the circular concretion. All are shielded coins from the Mexico City mint as indicated by visible marks or Florenzada cross on the reverse (Menzel 2004:81). All visible coins in this clump display the Bourbon shield of Philip V on the obverse side. The "Foster Clump" retains the form of a container long since lost to time. It may have been a coin hoard in a circular satchel or perhaps the false bottom of a barrel.

Two "*talegas*" or concretions of former moneybags have also been recovered (Figure 2). They were found together at a depth of about 1 meter in the sand substrate of Feature 3. No other artifacts were found in direct association. Both *talegas* are currently undergoing conservation so their full numismatic details remain to be documented as treatment proceeds. Nonetheless, the following is known:

The smaller *talega* weighs 2795g or 6.16 lbs. It is composed of small coin denominations of 1, 2, and very few 8-*reales* concreted together in their moneybag. To date, 55 coins have exfoliated from the *talega* with the following mints observed: 4/55 Lima mint, 5/55 Potosí mint, 32/55 Mexico City mint, and 14/55 indeterminate. The average date of small *talega* coins is 1688. The earliest visible date is 1682 and the latest 1712. Theoretical dates based on the shield era of cob coins (1572-1734), including the Habsburg shield (1572-1700) and Bourbon shield (1700-1747), can be placed in the range of 1572-1734 when the cob style coin was replaced by milled coins (Menzel 2004:80).

The larger *talega* is currently undergoing analysis. It is intact and measures 13.6 by 9.5 by 6.3 cm. Its weight is 3.520 g or 7.76 lbs. It appears to be similarly composed of small denominations. Both coin concretions retain the shape of the original moneybag frozen in time although cloth remnants did not preserve.

Most excavation units have resulted in the recovery of loose coins – individual examples and small coin concretions. These are being analyzed and added to the coin inventory as conservation reveals their details. Several unique coins have been identified, including:

1. A rare, counterstamped, pillars and waves,

FIGURE 2. TWO TALEGAS RECOVERED FROM THE LA CALETA SITE AWAIT CONSERVATION. THESE ARE COIN CONCRETIONS FROZEN IN TIME. THE LEATHER OR CLOTH HAS NOT PRESERVED, BUT THE CONTENTS ARE MAINLY 1-REAL AND 2-REALES COINS. THEY WERE PROBABLY UNREGISTERED INDIVIDUAL HOARDS CARRIED ON BOARD THE BEGOÑA.

8-*reales* coin from the Santa Fé de Bogotá mint in Colombia (Figure 3a). Identifiable features on the obverse include crowned shield with quadrants of castles and lions, partial name of Charles II (1665-1700) (Menzel 2004), Roman numeral VIII (8-*reales*). Obverse features include partial legend "Rex" (King), a counterstamp over pillars, and the motto "Plus Ultra."

2. A possible Potosí minted coin weighing 4.4 g with a crown counterstamped over a Greek cross on the reverse, and the obverse indeterminate (Figure 3b). Similar coins in the Florida State collection are thought, perhaps, to indicate incorporation into the Danish West Indies economy (Craig 2000:36).

3. A 1-*real* demonstration piece as identified by an intentionally punched hole with a clear entry and exit (Figure 3c). Weighing 2.1 g, identifiable features on obverse include date of (1)701, mint mark "L" for Lima mint, "1" for denomination, motto "PL VS VL" for Plus Ultra, and assayer mark "H" for Francisco Hurtado (Menzel 2004:199). The Jerusalem cross appears on the reverse. This is probably not an official piece, but rather a family heirloom that

was modified at home, worn, and subsequently re-entered circulation.

4. Double struck coin—a 1-*real* double-struck coin also referred to as "doubling" (Menzel 2004:8) features the misalignment of design (Figure 3d). Weighing 1.8 grams, identifiable features on the reverse include pillars and waves, date of (16)82, mint mark "P" for Potosí, "1" for denomination, motto "PL VS VL TRA" Plus Ultra, assayer mark "V" representing Pedro de Villar (Menzel 2004:317).

5. Several snipped coins have been recovered. One example, weighing 3 grams was minted in Mexico City. Since the majority of minted coins were in denominations of 4 and 8-*reales*, snipping was sometimes necessary to produce smaller denominations for change for a particular transaction. This coin appears to be a quarter of 4-*reales* that would have weighed 13.73 grams when minted.

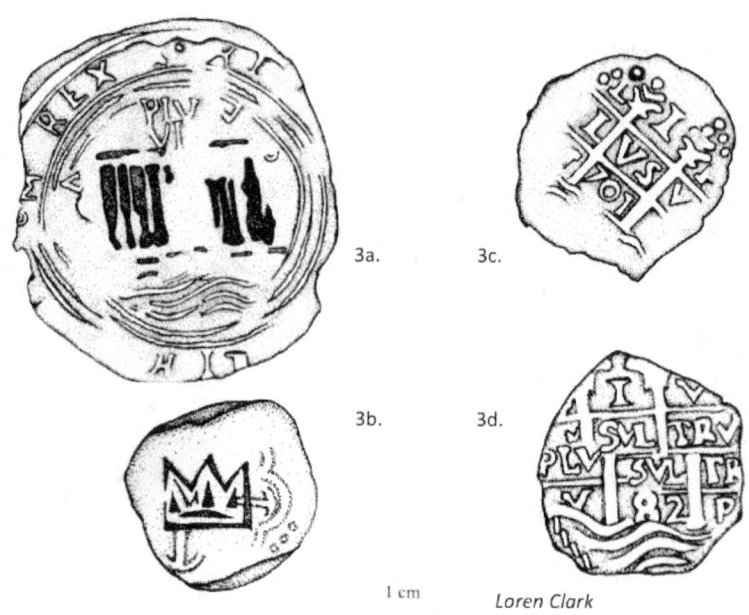

FIGURE 3. DIAGNOSTIC COINS FROM THE LA CALETA SITE. 3A. A RARE COUNTERSTAMPED, PILLARS AND WAVES, 8-REALES COIN FROM THE SANTA FÉ DE BOGOTÁ MINT IN COLOMBIA; 3B. A CROWN COUNTERSTAMPED OVER A GREEK CROSS ON A VERY WORN COB COIN; 3C. A 1-REAL DEMONSTRATION PIECE THAT MAY HAVE BEEN A FAMILY HEIRLOOM; 3D. A 1-REAL DOUBLE-STRUCK COIN FROM (16)82.

A database for all coins is being created. Four mints are represented: Mexico City, Potosí, Lima and Santa Fé de Bogotá. The sample of individual coins conserved and analyzed is small at present (n = 88), but is expected to grow as more excavation and conservation of coin concretions are done. Some 76% of all coins can identified by mint: Mexico City (70.1%), Lima (14.9%), Potosí (13.4%), and Santa Fé de Bogotá (1.4%). For coins with a visible date stamp, the average mint year is 1694.2 with a range of 1682 to 1712.

The smaller *talega* has been replicated in collaboration with The Children's Museum of Indianapolis. This allows presentation of the contraband story with a museum-quality replica, while allowing the original coin concretion to be dissolved and its contents studied. Coins that have been cleaned in order to record identifiable features have undergone electrolytic reduction.

One interesting exercise of this analysis is estimating the number of coins in each concretion. This was done by measuring the weight of each exfoliated coin, and comparing it to the whole. The average weight of 1-*real* is 2.0556g and of 2-*reales* is 3.0769g in our sample. Critical is the estimate of denomination ratio for each concretion. The concretion weight was then divided by the average exfoliated coin weight within 1 standard deviation – giving an estimate of the number of coins in each concretion. The results predict the smaller *talega* should contain 1,113 coins; the larger one should reveal 1,307. We will know in time if this estimating process provides a reasonable projection for the number of coins or their value within each concretion.

Metallurgy

Some initial results from XRF have been received. A total of six coins have been examined. As expected, the Mexico City examples differ slightly from the Potosí and Lima ones. It is hoped that once a metallurgical profile is established with a larger sample, it will be possible to identify the mint from very worn coins on the basis of metallurgy.

A second result is more interesting. The crown counterstamp from the Potosí mint (Figure 3b) is apparently not the result of the 1652 mint debasement scandal.

Silver content of the coin measures 92-95% – – normal for Spanish cobs, and thus it seems likely this coin was not devalued at Potosí, but stamped and accessioned into a regional economy sometime during its circulation.

Contraband Silver from a Chest

Salvage records indicate most of the personal belongings on board the Begoña were stored in wooden chests. At least 10 were damaged and their contents lost in the wrecking (Maus and Beeker, this volume). From expansion of an excavation unit that exposed a cannon, Feature 2, the catchment beneath a table rock slab was revealed. Inside was what we believe to be the remains of a chest containing silver dinnerware (Figure 4).

Two plate stacks were recovered. By matching the embossment on the bottom, it is possible to reassemble them and outline the shape of the storage chest lost in the wrecking. A portion of the wood bottom was also recovered showing platter marks. Conservation work on this material has just begun, but an initial inventory of the silver has identified: 26 silver platters, 4 different sizes (D= 24.5 – 46.5cm); 6 forks (four 4-tine, two 5-tine); 2 spoons; 3 matching pairs of candlesticks and bases, one crushed wax pan; and a single candlewick scissors. These objects were carefully packed in the bottom of a wooden chest.

The total silver component weight is 32.13 kg (70.83 lbs). When cleaning and conservation are complete, we shall know whether any hallmarks and tax stamps are present on the platters or forks. So far they seem to be absent, implying this silver was packed as unregistered contraband.

Mexico City Cob Silver compared to Silver Platter

Initial XRF studies provide an interesting elemental profile for the silver platter. It most closely resembles that of the Mexico City silver cobs on the Foster clump. While silver, copper, and gold proportions are different between these two objects, the elemental profiles visually appear to be very similar whereas coins from Potosí and Lima produce more different profiles. This implies the trace elemental profile of silver coins could be consistent from the same mint / source, enabling the association of silver objects with their place of origin despite the lack of mintmarks. The preliminary data suggests the silver plate may have been produced in Mexico City. To verify this conclusion, we will need much more XRF sampling, but the initial results show promise.

Comparison with Coins from other Spanish shipwrecks

Sedwick and Sedwick (2007) show 55 known shipwrecks have produced Spanish cob coins worldwide. This listing is undoubtedly missing many other wrecks that have been salvaged without much notice, but in spite of the widespread discovery of Spanish coins from shipwrecks, archaeological analyses of these materials has been rare. Three published examples provide comparisons for the coins being associated with *Nuestra Señora de Begoña*, but keep in mind that all were carrying royal cargoes as opposed to the humble merchant frigate. Still, these show the preferred means of transporting Spanish coinage.

Silver and gold specie were stored in individual bags packed inside chests or shipping crates on Spanish vessels

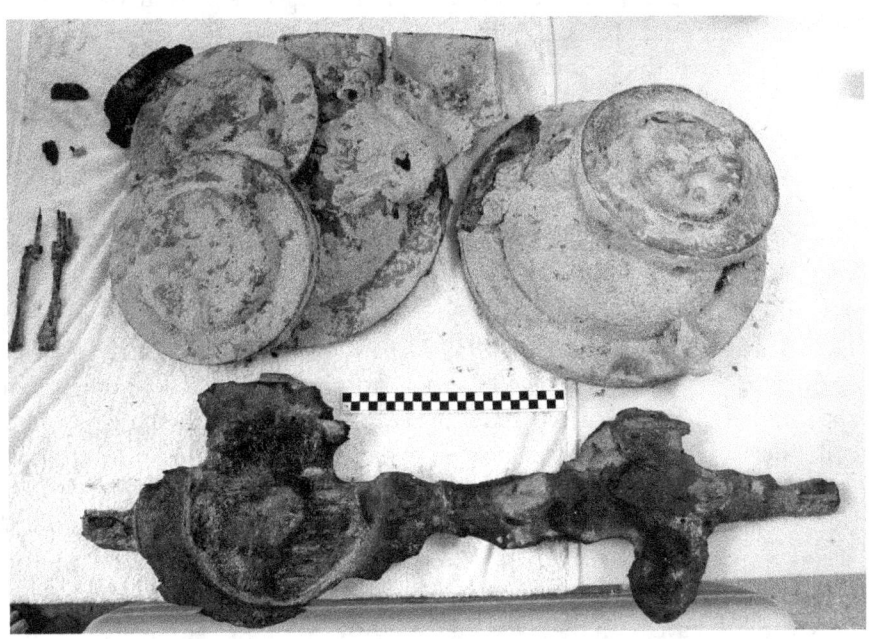

FIGURE 4. SILVER OBJECTS AND THE REMAINS OF A CHEST WERE RECOVERED FROM THE SITE. SOME 26 SILVER PLATTERS, ALONG WITH FORKS, SPOONS, CANDLESTICKS AND BASES, ONE CRUSHED WAX PAN, AND A SINGLE CANDLEWICK SCISSORS WERE PACKED IN A WOODEN CHEST. THE SILVER WEIGHS 32.13KG AND IS THOUGHT TO BE PART OF THE CONTRABAND CARGO. A PORTION OF THE WOODEN BASE HAS PRESERVED IMPRESSION MARKS FROM THE SILVER PLATTERS.

carrying cargo back from the New World. The chests seem to vary somewhat over time. According to the published studies of the *Nuestra Señora de Atocha* (1622), the standard chest was a simple shipping crate of two sides, two ends and undifferentiated tops and bottoms. Made from rosewood planks (*Dalbergia sp.*), the dimensions are given as: 1) tops/bottoms 57.2 cm L by 22.3 cm W; 2) sides 57.1 cm L by 16.9 cm W; 3) ends 18.7 cm L by 16.8 cm W (Malcolm 2001).

These *Atocha* crates had no hinges or latching hardware; they were simply nailed shut. Chest #A85-2313 may have been typical. It weighed 59.1 kg (130 lbs 7oz.) and contained 2,225 coins packed in bags (Malcolm 2001). Sorted by denomination, there were twelve 2-*reales* (.005%); 661 4-*reales* (29.7%), and 1,454 8-*reales* (65.3%). This demonstrates the clear preference for shipping higher denomination coins to Spain.

Nuestra Señora de la Concepción was a Spanish vice-flagship lost in 1641 on reefs off the north coast of Hispaniola. Spanish authorities failed in repeated attempts to salvage the cargo, and four more unsuccessful attempts were made throughout the 17th century. In 1687 the English captain William Phips relocated the wreck and retrieved one quarter of a million pounds. Several twentieth-century expeditions failed to find the wreck until the historian Peter Earle found the logbook of Phips' ship and working with treasure hunter Burt Webber, located the Spanish galleon once more. Gold, silver, ceramics, glass, and an astrolabe were found, among the wreckage of the *Concepción*. Excavations deep within an encompassing coral reef revealed a sealed wooden chest containing porcelain cups and silver table wares as packed by their wealthy owner. The chest had a false bottom concealing 1,440 contraband silver coins. An estimated 60,000 total coins were recovered (Smith 1988:5; Fine 2006:62; Borrell 1983:97).

Analysis of one of the 1,300 cedar storage chests aboard the *Capitana* of the *Flota* of 1715 revealed a container 3-feet wide, 2-feet long and one foot deep (J. Brandon, personal comm.). In each were "three bags of gunnysack-type material, with 1,000 pesos of 4 and 8-*real* coins in each bag" (Burgess and Clausen 1976:116). The total coin concretion weighed 250 lbs. This seems to have been the standard for registered cargo in 1715.

The fact that Spanish vessels would go to elaborate measures to secure silver and to conceal contraband should not be too surprising. According to Steven Stern, the Spanish conquest was driven by three desires: 1) the quest for utopia, 2) the lust for gold and riches, and 3) the desire to bring the Christian faith to Amerindians (1992:7-8). In discussing motivation, Stern notes:

> *The lust for gold and riches is well known. Diaz del Castillo acknowledged it in a matter-of-fact way in his conquest chronicle. The Aztec informants of Bernardino de Sahagún offered a more striking portrait: a fetish for gold so powerful that the sight and feel of it threw conquistadors into a trance-like state of joy and fingering, an uncontainable exuberance. The Andean oral tradition reproduced by Felipe Guaman Poma de Ayala summed up the obsession with riches in the story of an encounter between an Indian and a Spaniard in Cuzco, the old Inca capital. The Indian asked what it is that Spaniards ate. The answer: gold and silver (1992:7-8).*

Summary and Conclusions – Characteristics of Spanish Maritime Contraband from an 18th Century Merchant Frigate

In surveying the archaeological literature on coins, there seem surprisingly few analyses of shipwreck coins as artifacts. In fact, the *Oxford Handbook of Maritime Archaeology* – "a comprehensive survey of the field through the eyes of nearly fifty scholars," has no listing for coins in its index (Catsambis et al. 2011). Moreover, while there is a widespread assertion that extensive contraband was carried on 17th and 18th century Spanish vessels, little archaeological evidence is normally presented. Other than determining the *terminus post quem* (time after which) for the shipwreck, coins seem to have been bypassed in comparison with other artifact classes.

Analyses of coins and silver from *Nuestra Senora de Begoña* are beginning to cast light on activities of its passengers and crew. The two *talegas* recovered archaeologically are not the larger 1,000 peso moneybags used for registered cargo on the *Begoña*. It is clear from trial records that Capt. Garces de Salazar had six – 1,000 peso containers in his possession. They were registered cargo. The *talegas* thus far recovered seem likely to be individual contraband. The Foster clump is also likely an individual unregistered hoard.

Based on patterns observed to date, the following are characteristics of contraband from an outbound 18th century Spanish merchant vessel:

1. Coins of highly diverse origin reflecting individual hoards.

2. Containers of different size and dimension (as opposed to standard containers/packaging) with a tendency toward small hoard packaging.

3. A tendency for small coin denomination – indicating individual ownership.

4. A "piggy-bank" effect – coins of extended circulation and considerable wear including heirloom coins. One may expect a large range of dates and clipped coins. Individual examples tend to be lighter in weight from use than official standards.

5. Other contraband evidence including unregistered and unstamped silver plate and silverware, candlesticks and other silver objects, or concretions shaped by a former container that provides evidence of a false bottom for concealing coins or silver.

Smaller denominations were favored for New World commerce. As Craig notes, "Small denomination coins needed to facilitate daily marketplace transactions, were in short supply and tended to stay in the viceroyalties where they originated. Conversely, official convoys carrying the royal treasury back to Spain were normally composed mainly of 4 and 8-*reales* coinage" (2000:74.)

This is clearly demonstrated in the coins recovered from the *Atocha* (1622). Of 113,863 coins recovered from salvage efforts in 1985, 0.005% (110) were 1-*real* pieces; 15.0% (17,088) 2-*reales*; 21.8% (24,853) 4-*reales*; and 63.1% (71,808) 8-*reales*. (Malcolm 2001).

There is also historical precedence for use of cacao to conceal contraband silver and gold. Lyon and Purdy note: "in 1744, the taking of a Franco-Spanish prize led to the discovery that in each of 800 pannier-baskets of cacao, a gold bar had been cached to evade taxation. Gold was found in the ship's knees and even in the hollowed out shoe-soles of the prisoners" (1982:101). It may be that cacao shipments were favored for contraband transport.

Contraband aboard Spanish vessels was widespread and efforts to combat it were ineffective. In the words of a Spanish captain from 1685: "The King's Treasury is like an owl, from which every little bird plucks a feather" (Boxer 1972:207). *Nuestra Señora de Begoña*, a merchant frigate lost at *la Caleta de Caucedo* in 1725, may have been only a metaphorical owlet, but it is producing important information regarding silver contraband and the activities of its passengers and crew. Future studies will seek to expand and refine this information while preserving its historical maritime legacy as a Living Museum of the Sea in the Dominican Republic.

Acknowledgements

The authors recognize the generous support provided this project by the Eli Lilly & Company Foundation and The Children's Museum of Indianapolis. The USAID has provided critical assistance in furthering establishment of Living Museums of the Sea in the Dominican Republic. The Peace Corps program of the Dominican Republic has provided valuable assistance in our efforts. The following Dominican government institutions are singled out for their support of this research: *la Oficina Nacional de Patrimonio Cultural Subacuático, el Ministerio de Cultura*, and *el Ministerio de Medioambiente*. The coin illustrations in Figure 3 were skillfully done by Loren Clark. We likewise recognize the valued contributions of the following individuals: Charles Beeker, Francis Soto, Pedro Borrell, Geoffrey Conrad, Roger Smith, Isabel Brito, Courtney Michalik, Jessica Keller, Mylana Haydu, John Brandon, Lydia Barbash-Riley, Colleen Ferris, Rodrigo Parra-Ferro, Benjamin Ivers, Glenn Farris, Olivia Thomas, and Emily Palmer.

References

ARCHIVO GENERAL DE INDIAS (AGI)
1725   En la Ciudad de Santo Domingo (In the City of Santo Domingo). Commission proceedings, Escribania 9c, Legajo 2, Pieza 9, Archivo General de Indias, Seville, Spain.

BORRELL, PEDRO J.
1983   *Historia y Rescate del Galeon Nuestra Señora de la Concepción*. Museo de Casas Reales, Comisión de Rescate Arqueológico Submarino de la República Dominicana. Santo Domingo.

BOXER, C.R.
1972   A Question of Contraband: the Old Colonial Trade. *History Today* 22(3):204-213. London.

BURGESS, ROBERT F. AND CARL J. CLAUSEN
1976   *Gold, Galleons and Archaeology: A History of the 1715 Spanish Plate Fleet and the True Story of the Great Florida Treasure Find*. The Bobbs-Merrill Company, Indianapolis/ New York.

CATSAMBIS, ALEXIS; BEN FORD AND DONNY L. HAMILTON (EDS.)
  2011 *The Oxford Handbook of Maritime Archaeology.* Oxford University Press, New York.

FINE, JOHN CHRISTOPHER
  2006 *Treasures of the Spanish Main: Shipwrecked Galleons in the New World.* The Lyons Press, Guilford, Conn.

LYON, EUGENE AND BARBARA A. PURDY
  1982 Contraband in Spanish Colonial Ships. *Itinerario* 6(2):91-108.

MALCOLM, CORY
  2001 The Cargo of Coins Aboard *Nuestra Señora de Atocha*, or "The Treasure Chest Defined." *The Navigator* 16 (5).

MARX, ROBERT F.
  1980 The 1715 Treasure Fleet. IN: *Archaeology Under Water*, Keith Muckelroy, ed. pp. 116-117. McGraw-Hill, New York.

MENZEL, SEWALL
  2004 *Cobs, Pieces of Eight and Treasure Coins: The Early Spanish-American Mints and their Coinages 1536-1773.* The American Numismatic Society, New York.

SEDWICK, DANIEL AND FRANK SEDWICK
  2007 *The Practical Book of Cobs.* Fourth edition. Self Published, Winter Park, Florida.

SMITH, ROGER C.
  1988 Treasure Ships of the Spanish Main: The Iberian-American Maritime Empires. IN: *Ships and Shipwrecks of the Americas*, George F. Bass, ed. pp. 87-106. Thames & Hudson, London.

STERN, STEVE J.
  1992 Paradigms of Conquest: History, Historiography and Politics. *Journal of Latin American Studies* 24:1-34. Cambridge   University Press.

. . . .

John W. Foster
Indiana University
8654 Amber Oaks Court
Fair Oaks, CA 95628
916-673-7343 w
916-967-6607 h
parkarky@yahoo.com

Matthew J. Maus
Office of Underwater Science
Indiana University, SPH 058
Bloomington, IN 47405
717-856-2360 w
812-340-0501 h
mmaus@indiana.edu

Anna Rogers
Office of Underwater Science
Indiana University, SPH 058
Bloomington, IN 47405
812-322-2075
annaroge@umail.iu.edu

Sultan: Cleveland's Grindstone Wreck

David VanZandt
James Paskert
Kevin Magee

Due to a novice captain's error in judgment, the brig Sultan foundered in Lake Erie off Cleveland, Ohio, during a storm in 1864. As the vessel came to rest in shallow water only a few miles from shore with its masts exposed, six of the eight crew climbed the rigging in an effort to survive. One by one, however, they succumbed to the fury of the storm leaving a sole survivor to be rescued and share the harrowing tale. The wreck was discovered in 2011 by the Cleveland Underwater Explorers (CLUE) with the assistance of associate Rob Ruetschle. A reconnaissance survey was conducted, and the wreck was determined to be the Sultan based on a number of unique features including its deck cargo of large grindstones.

Introduction

The brig *Sultan* was built by James Averill at Chicago, Illinois, in 1848 and officially enrolled by the District of Chicago on 27 July 1848 (District of Chicago 1848). Constructed of oak and measuring 127 feet in length, 24 feet in breadth, 9 feet 4-5/8 inches in depth, and 267-00/95 tons, the *Sultan* had one deck, two masts, no galley, and a billet head (District of Chicago 1848). It should be noted that the word "brig," as historically used in the Great Lakes region, refers to a vessel with two masts, the foremast being square-rigged and the mainmast being fore-and-aft rigged. Outside the Great Lakes region, "brigantine" is used to describe this style of rigging, and the word "brig" is alternatively used to describe a vessel with two square-rigged masts. The historical/regional use and meaning of the word "brig" will be used throughout this work.

The *Sultan* was owned and operated out of Chicago from the time of its construction in 1848 until May of 1854 when it was sold to H. C Walker & Co. of Buffalo, New York, who had the brig completely refitted (Maritime History of the Great Lakes 2013a). These repairs were necessitated by the last of several unfortunate accidents which occurred during the 1853 shipping season. On 6 June 1853 the *Sultan* capsized and sank five miles from Chambers Island, Green Bay, Lake Michigan. The wreck was successfully raised in early July 1853 (Maritime History of the Great Lakes 2013b), repaired at Chicago during August and September, and returned to service (Maritime History of the Great Lakes 2013c). Just two months later, on 11 November 1853, the *Sultan*, loaded with a cargo of railroad iron intended for the Galena Railroad, went ashore and was heavily damaged at Forty Mile Point, Lake Huron. Salvors were successful in salvaging the cargo of railroad iron, which was then sent to Chicago, but due to the lateness of the season, the *Sultan* was left to endure the winter of 1853-1854 in the shallow waters near Forty Mile Point. Efforts to salvage the *Sultan* were renewed the following spring, and it was pumped out and released from the shore (Maritime History of the Great Lakes 2013a).

An additional incident occurred on 4 November 1856 when the *Sultan*, loaded with a cargo of wheat, went ashore on the east side of Lake Huron about fifty miles above Goderich, Ontario, near old Port Bruce, Ontario, Canada. The cargo of wheat was lightered off, and the brig was released and subsequently taken to Detroit, Michigan, where it was repaired later that same month (Maritime History of the Great Lakes 2013d). The *Sultan* was purchased by Robert Mills of Buffalo in April of 1858 (District of Buffalo 1858) and continued in the lumber and grain trade until April of 1859 when Mills sold the brig to the mercantile firm of Dibble & Co. of New York, New York (District of Buffalo 1859). On 2 June 1859 the *Sultan* sailed from Buffalo to the city of New York via the Welland Canal and St. Lawrence River. On 5 November 1859 the *Sultan* was registered at the Port of New York (District of Buffalo 1859) and commenced an interesting two-year saltwater career trading between New York and various ports in North and South Carolina.

The *Sultan* made regular trips between New York, New York, and Georgetown, South Carolina (*The New York Times* 1860a:8, 1860b:8, 1860c:8, 1861a:8). The nature of the cargos loaded in New York and freighted to Georgetown is not known. Entry records for freight loaded in Georgetown and landed in New York consistently describe these cargos as "naval stores" (*The New York Times* 1860b:8, 1861a:8). The definition of "naval stores" has yet to be determined. Upon the commencement of the Civil War in 1861, Dibble apparently used his various long-established connections with many high ranking U.S. military officers to conduct trade between New York and several southern coastal ports still under the control of the U.S. military (Dibble 1864:14-16).

In late August 1861 the *Sultan* sailed in ballast from Havana, Cuba, to New York City under the command of Captain Sutton (*The New York Times* 1861b:8). Captain Sutton had been the master of the *Sultan* during its entire saltwater career. Exactly why the *Sultan* was in Havana and departed with no cargo is still unknown. On 9 September Mrs. Sutton, the brig's cook and the wife of Captain Sutton, died and was buried at sea. The *Sultan* arrived in New York City on 11 September and was "anchored in the Lower Quarantine" as reported in the 'Marine Intelligence' column in *The New York Times* (*The New York Times* 1861b). Just over three weeks later, on 4 October 1861, the *Sultan*, under the command of Captain Sutton, cleared New York for Chicago, Illinois (*The New York Times* 1861c:8) thus ending its saltwater career.

Dibble & Co. ultimately sold the *Sultan* in June of 1862 to Thatcher, Burt & Co., merchants located in Cleveland, Ohio (District of Cuyahoga 1862) who had the brig completely rebuilt in December by Cleveland shipbuilder Foote & Keating (The Cleveland Morning Leader 1864:4). Thatcher, Burt & Co. owned and operated the *Sultan* until the time of its final loss.

It is important to note that the last enrollment issued to the *Sultan*, No. 62, dated 28 June 1862 (District of Cuyahoga 1862), states the breadth of the vessel to be 28 feet, which conflicts with the breadth of 24 feet indicated on all of the *Sultan's* previous enrollments. This same document certifies the tonnage as 267-00/95, which is unchanged from all of the previous enrollments. The tonnage could not remain the same if the breadth of the vessel was altered. The breadth on the last enrollment appears to be incorrect and is undoubtedly a transcription error which occurred when the information was copied from the previous enrollment.

The Sinking

The seas were running high when the tug *Ajax* towed the *Sultan* out of Cleveland at 1:00 P.M. on Saturday, 24 September 1864 (*The Cleveland Leader* 1864:4). The crew of eight consisted of newly appointed Captain Nelson Webster of Fairport, Ohio; First Mate Eleazor Spear of Kirtland, Ohio; Second Mate and brother of the Captain Douglas Webster of Fairport, Ohio; Steward Christopher Roe of Euclid, Ohio; Seaman James Greer of Dunnville, C.W. [Ontario, Canada]; Seaman Stephen Johnson of Fairport, Ohio; Seaman Monroe Ellsworth of Fairport, Ohio; and Seaman Barney Carroll of Dunnville, C.W. [Ontario, Canada] (*The Cleveland Leader* 1864:4). The brig was bound for Buffalo, New York, with a cargo of 200 tons of grindstones shipped by J. McDermott & Co., Wilson, Crittenden & Co. and B. Clough along with some hickory lumber and a small quantity of staves (*The Cleveland Herald* 1864:3). The grindstones came from the Amherst and Berea, Ohio, areas, which were famous for the quality of their stone, and many of the larger grindstones were stacked on the deck rather than in the cargo hold.

Prior to departing, Captain Webster was advised by more than a few people including George W. Gardner, one of the principals in the firm of Thatcher, Burt & Co., owner of the *Sultan*, that he should stay in port as the seas were too high to risk making the trip at that time. Some years later Mr. Gardner would recall:

> *We had just appointed a young fellow to captain and I called him aside and told him that the trip was not a matter of life and death and he had better wait until the storm abated. He was ambitious, however, to make a record and insisted upon going out, saying that he could land the cargo in Buffalo easily on Monday morning (Marine Reviews 1901:17).*

The crew had the pleasure of having four ladies aboard the *Sultan* on the upbound trip from Buffalo, and the wives of Captain Webster and Steward Christopher Roe were aboard while the *Sultan* was docked in Cleveland. The wives left by train for their homes prior to the *Sultan's* departure (*The Cleveland Leader* 1864:4).

As the *Sultan* passed out of the Cuyahoga River and into the open waters Lake Erie, the heavy seas began to lift and drop the brig more and more. As predicted by those who had warned Captain Webster to stay in port, the *Sultan* struck bottom on the bar near the mouth of the river and "pounded it very heavily five or six times" (*The Cleveland Leader* 1864:4). When the brig was well out into the lake, the towline was cast off, the sails were set, and the crew manned the pumps to determine if any damage had been sustained. No more water than usual was found in the bilge, and it appeared that no damage had been done (*The Cleveland Leader* 1864:4).

Not long afterward, the *Sultan* began "laboring heavily, the waves dashing over her" (*The Cleveland Leader* 1864:4). Working its way down the lake and well heeled over in the high wind and seas, the *Sultan* made little progress. The order was soon given to start throwing a portion of the deck load of grindstones overboard "for the purpose of easing her" (*The Plain Dealer* 1864:3). At the same time, one of the crew entered the forecastle and discovered that the brig was leaking badly. The pumps were manned, but it soon became obvious that the brig was settling so Captain Webster ordered the *Sultan* put about in an attempt to run the brig onto the beach (*The Plain Dealer* 1864:3).

After sailing and drifting down the lake about two miles, the *Sultan* lurched and rolled on its side. The waves knocked off the cabin, and the deck load of grindstones shifted to the starboard side as staves, hickory timber, and cabin contents—including the trunks of the crew—were pitched into the lake. The *Sultan* was surrounded by wave-tossed debris that was "beating about the waves as if a "school" of whales had been there pounding and "thrashing" the sea for a meal" (*The Cleveland Leader* 1864:4).

The *Sultan* was now off Euclid, Ohio, eight miles below Cleveland and about three miles from shore. Recognizing that the shifted deck load made it impossible for the *Sultan* to right itself, the crew realized the brig would soon be on the bottom. The small boat was cut loose but quickly filled with water. After ten minutes of futile bailing First Mate Eleazor Speer abandoned any hope of using the small boat for rescue (*The Cleveland Leader* 1864:4). He then jumped onto the bulwarks and joined the rest of the crew as they began climbing the rigging with the *Sultan* settling fast below them. Seamen Monroe Elsworth and Barney Carroll, however, jumped into the nearly-filled small boat and drifted away in the high seas (*The Cleveland Leader* 1864:4). The last time anyone saw Ellsworth and Carroll they were standing up in the small boat about half way between the wreck and shore (*The Plain Dealer* 1864:3).

When the *Sultan* struck bottom, First Mate Speer, Captain Webster, Second Mate Webster, and Seaman Johnson were clinging to the main top gallant mast while Seaman Greer and Steward Roe were similarly perched on the fore top gallant mast (*The Plain Dealer* 1864:3). With the *Sultan* resting on the bottom on its beam ends and swaying back and forth with the surge of every passing wave, the positions of the crew were very precarious. As the masts swayed back and forth, the jerking motion made clinging to the rigging "next to impossible" (*The Cleveland Leader* 1864:4). It was now 3:30 p.m.

Seaman Johnson decided to abandon his position on the main top gallant mast and join Steward Roe and Seaman Greer on the fore top gallant mast where they planned to cut the yard loose and use it to float to shore (*The Cleveland Leader* 1864:4). Johnson made the difficult swim to the foremast and stopped there to rest for a moment. Suddenly the mast broke, and Johnson, Roe, and Greer were all cast into the surging lake (*The Cleveland Leader* 1864:4). The exhausted Johnson sank immediately, but Roe and Greer were able to swim to the main-mast and take refuge there. Just over an hour later, with darkness setting in, a large wave wrenched the main-mast from its step throwing Roe and Greer into the lake never to be seen again (*The Cleveland Leader* 1864:4). The remaining three crew members, Captain Nelson Webster; his brother, Second Mate Douglas Webster; and First Mate Eleazor Spear, now found their situation even more difficult. Un-stepped, the mast swayed and jerked much worse than before with each passing wave. Spear was on top of the top gallant with Captain Webster located just below him and Second Mate Webster just below the Captain. Separated by only a few feet, they had to shout to hear one another over the crashing waves and howling wind (*The Cleveland Leader* 1864:4).

At approximately 9:00 p.m. Captain Webster realized his brother, Second Mate Douglas Spear, had fallen from or was washed off the main-mast and into the lake (*The Cleveland Leader* 1864:4). In the darkness the Captain called to his brother but received no reply. He shouted to Spear, "Doug' is gone; Doug' is gone. Do you see him? Can you see him?" (*The Cleveland Leader* 1864:4). Soon the rain stopped, and the sky cleared. The Captain and Mate talked about rescue with the Captain commenting about what his wife might think if she knew of his predicament, and that he was glad she did not know (*The Cleveland Herald* 1864:3). Some hours later Spear heard a splash and called out to the Captain but received no reply. The Captain was gone, and Spear believed that he either fell asleep and fell from the mast or was so exhausted that he could no longer hold on (*The Cleveland Herald* 1864:3). Either way, First Mate Eleazor Spear was alone and the last of the eight man crew aboard what was now the wreck of the brig *Sultan*.

Spear slid down the mast to the place that had been occupied by Captain Webster since the swaying of the mast was less dramatic there. Fearing that he would succumb to the same fate as his fellow crew members, Spear used a piece of 'hamberline' that he had in his pocket to make two loops for his feet. He then secured it to the rigging making it easier to stand and hold onto the swaying mast (*The Cleveland Leader* 1864:4). During the coming hours he would shift his weight periodically

 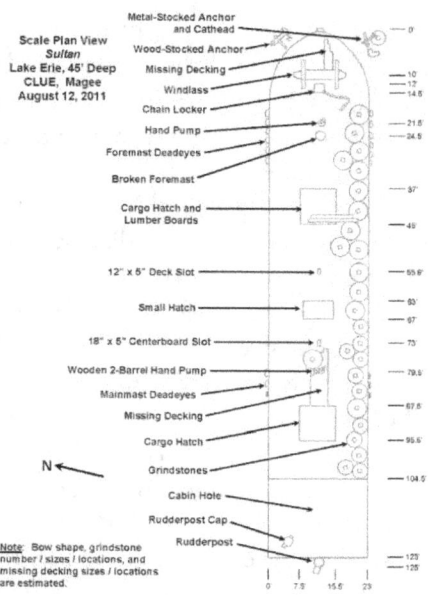

FIGURE 1. SULTAN SIDE SCAN SONAR IMAGE AND RECONNAISSANCE SURVEY SKETCH (SIDES CAN IMAGE BY DAVID VANZANDT, SKETCH BY KEVIN MAGEE).

from one foot to the other in an attempt to avoid fatigue. It seemed like dawn would never come as Spear continued to hang on and hope (*The Cleveland Herald* 1864:3). When dawn did come, Spear could see shore clearly, and he waved his hat to let people on shore know that there was someone still aboard the wrecked brig (*The Cleveland Leader* 1864:4).

Rescued

George Gardner of Thatcher, Burt & Co., owner of the *Sultan*, received news late Saturday afternoon that a vessel was "in distress" (*Marine Reviews* 1901:17) off Euclid and the crew was in the rigging. He immediately knew that it had to be the *Sultan* as only hours before he had advised Captain Webster not to make the trip to Buffalo until the weather improved. Mr. Gardner later recollected:

> *I received word that a vessel was in distress off Euclid Creek and that the crew were lashed to the cross-trees. The vessel was rolling frightfully and the crew were being submerged half of the time. I made up my mind that that was our brig, the Sultan, and I went down to the river to see if I could get some one to go out to help her. The only steamer in was the Northwest. I asked the captain if he would go out but he was afraid he would get stuck on the bar and declined. There was one tug near the government pier and I asked the captain of her if he wouldn't go out. He said that his insurance wasn't high enough. I asked him how much more he wanted and when he said $4000 I volunteered to get it and pay the premium on it and to go out with him. He then said that the sea was too high and he wouldn't risk it. I had to wait then until 4 o'clock in the morning when the Detroit & Cleveland steamer came in. She stopped at the government pier, as was her custom then, to discharge freight. In a moment or two Capt. McKay came down on the dock. I related the circumstances to him. He didn't wait for me to ask him to go out but said very quietly, "I'll be ready to back out in three minutes." He then asked me if I had a sharp knife. I told him I would have one by the time the steamer reached the wreck. When we got to the wreck there was only one man lashed to the rigging left. The rest had drowned. The captain said "I am going to run her nose across her quarters, so you lean over and cut that man loose from the rigging. You'll have to work quick for I shall have to back out at once to save myself from being crushed." Well, he sent her bow over the boat and we cut the man loose. He was unconscious but we had some brandy on board and soon revived him (Marine Review 1901:17).*

The above description of the rescue differs significantly from the newspaper accounts which were undoubtedly based on interviews with sole survivor Eleazor Spear. The *Cleveland Leader* stated the following:

> *The North Star made a pass for him but missed. Then the City of Cleveland came up, her rail passing about three feet below the yard to which he was lashed. He sprang aboard nimbly, having perfect use of his limbs, not being at all benumbed by the exposure to waves and chilly air (The Cleveland Leader 1864:4).*

Perhaps the brandy influenced Spear's recollection of the rescue during his interviews with the press just after the *City of Cleveland* docked in Cleveland. Perhaps an ambitious and newly appointed reporter, not unlike an ambitious and newly appointed Lake Captain, decided to stretch things a bit to make a name for himself by embellishing his story. Regardless, Spear was rescued at about 8:00 A.M. on Sunday morning thanks to the skill and courage of Captain George McKay, Master of the Steamer *City of Cleveland*. Just weeks later, in October of 1864, in recognition of and appreciation for this gallant act and others that preceded it, the citizens of Cleveland presented Captain McKay with a gold watch and chain "suitably inscribed" (*Marine Reviews* 1901:17). During the weeks that followed the sinking of the *Sultan*, most of the bodies of the lost crew members came ashore or were found floating in the lake. Thereafter, the brig *Sultan* quickly became a forgotten shipwreck like the hundreds of others on the bottom of Lake Erie.

Discovery

The Cleveland Underwater Explorers (CLUE) began searching for the *Sultan* in 2007. CLUE is a non-profit corporation founded in 2001 whose membership includes avocational divers, historians, and archaeologists dedicated to researching, locating, and documenting the shipwrecks and submerged cultural heritage in the Great Lakes with an emphasis on Lake Erie. CLUE is based in Cleveland, Ohio, on the southern shore of Lake Erie. In 2007 CLUE covered a two square mile area based upon historical research. In 2008 an additional square mile was searched. The wreck was not located and the project was shelved in deference to other projects. However, during 2011, in discussions with fellow shipwreck searcher and CLUE associate Rob Ruetschle (who had previously located the shipwreck), he strongly suggested that CLUE should revisit its original search area. Upon examining the 2007 side scan data, it was discovered that the tow fish, on the second transect of the original search area, passed parallel to the wreck. Furthermore, the wreck lay almost exactly along the bottom return making the wreck barely detectable in the data. On 12 August 2011, CLUE returned to the site to precisely locate the shipwreck and complete the first dives.

Figure 1 contains a high resolution side scan sonar image and the preliminary plan view developed after the first reconnaissance survey dives on 12 August 2011. Photographic and video images were gathered at the site, and several of these images are shown in Figure 2. The *Sultan* sits upright on a sandy bottom in 42 feet of water. It has settled into the sand to a firmer sub-bottom underneath the hull, and it remains mostly intact in a partially buried state. Silt has filled the interior spaces of the ship, and the slight west-to-east current helps keep the upper structure of the wreck free of silt. Due to its depth the wreck is not subject to shallow water ice damage, wind-driven surface currents, or wave action. Zebra or quagga mussels cover vertical surfaces of the wreck to a moderate degree.

The ship's bow has no bowsprit, is pointed east, and stands five feet high off the sandy mud bottom. The hull sides are intact, and the majority of the decking is present. Two anchors are present and visible lying on the bottom off either side of the bow. A wood-stocked anchor is partially buried on the port side. A metal-stocked anchor is mostly buried on the starboard side with a grind stone on top of it and a 90 degree-shaped wooden cathead still attached to it. The bow of the ship features a prominent cutwater with a notch for the missing bowsprit, which is located on the bottom further to the east. A windlass is on the forward deck just aft of the bowsprit notch. Behind it is a small square access opening in the deck for the chain locker. Chain runs out of this opening and along the starboard deck. Anchor chain is wrapped around the spool of the windlass as well. Aft of the chain

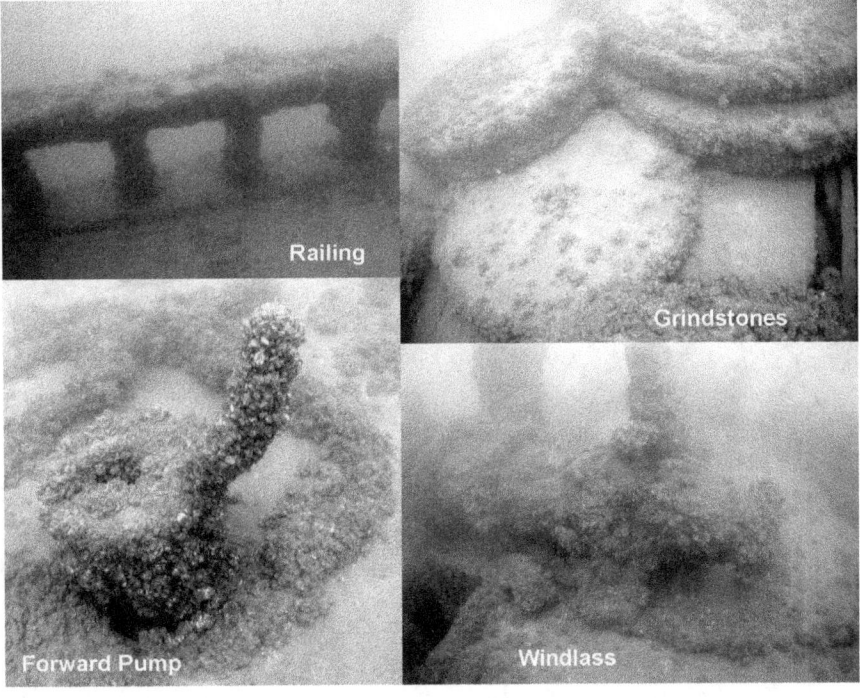

FIGURE 2. SULTAN RECONNAISSANCE SURVEY PHOTOS (PHOTOS BY DAVID VANZANDT)

Category	Historic Value	Measured Value
Dimensions	127 ft. x 24 ft. x 9 ft. 4 in.	125 ft. +0 ft./-6 ft. x 23 ft. +0 ft./-1 ft.
Type of Vessel	2-masted brig	2-masted brig
Head Style	Billet	Billet
Cargo	Lumber, staves, and grindstones	Lumber and grindstones
Depth	36 feet (11 m)	42 feet (13 m)
Orientation	Partially on side with NW wind, downbound	Bow east, Starboard list
Location	Near Euclid, Ohio	Near Euclid, Ohio

TABLE 1: SULTAN FEATURES COMPARISON

locker is a single-barrel hand pump. The remains of the foremast, which is broken off at deck level, are located behind this pump. Along the railings adjacent to the foremast are the remains of six large deadeyes on each side. The deadeyes are no longer attached to the railings, and their chainplates are bent down parallel to the hull suggesting the mast was violently wrested from the standing rigging. The large number of deadeyes indicates that the foremast was square-rigged.

The ship has an obvious list of about 30 degrees to starboard, and the railings on both sides are mostly intact. Starting near the foremast are stacks of round grindstones piled up on the deck against the starboard railing. The stacks of grindstones, some two or three high with several rows, continue all the way to the stern along the starboard railing. The larger stones, about 5.5 feet in diameter, are located forward, and the smaller stones, about 3.5 feet in diameter, are located towards the stern. Behind the foremast stub is a cargo hatch. Two long boards protrude out from the after side of the hatch toward the starboard side and are likely remnants of the secondary cargo of lumber. Amidships is a small slot in the deck followed by a small hatch and another small slot. This is the location of a centerboard, although no centerboard box is visible inside the silt-filled hold as viewed through the center hatch, and no centerboard winch is present at the aft slot. A single, large, 5-foot diameter grindstone rests wedged on the centerline against a two-barreled wooden pump immediately behind the aft slot. The mainmast is missing but it stood in this area as evidenced by the chainplates designed to accommodate three deadeyes each and located on both rails adjacent to this location. The deadeyes are missing on the starboard side railing and two of the three deadeyes remain on the port side railing. A strip of missing centerline decking continues all the way to another cargo hatch aft of the pump.

Beyond the aft cargo hatch is a raised wooden combing that spans the entire beam and once formed the front of the now missing cabin. Grindstones are wedged against this combing and the starboard railing but do not spill into the cabin space. Floor joists are present where the cabin floor was once located. The transom is missing. The rudderpost stands high off the bottom and is turned slightly to port. The rudder cap, which would have been mounted on top of the rudderpost and turned with a wheel, can be seen lying inside the cabin on the port side. A line of grindstones that spilled from the boat as it drifted and sank is visible in the distance on the bottom of the

FIGURE 3. ANTHONY SHAW MAKER'S MARK ON PLATE (PHOTOS BY DAVID VANZANDT)

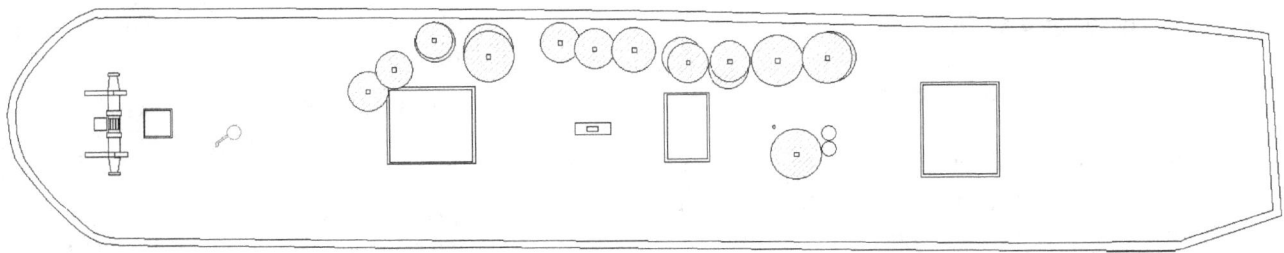

FIGURE 4. SULTAN PRELIMINARY SITE PLAN (IMAGE BY DAVID VANZANDT)

lake beyond the stern. The wreck's dimensions were measured at 125 feet long by 23 feet in beam, which compares closely to the 127 feet by 24 feet indicated on the *Sultan*'s various enrollments.

Furthermore, several ceramics, including a cup and several plates, were found on the wreck with maker's marks indentifying the manufacturer as Anthony Shaw of Great Britain. These marks date to the period of ca. 1860-1882. This tableware appears to be one of the designs manufactured by Shaw and distributed exclusively in the United States. It was likely stocked on the brig as part of its standard galley dishware, probably during the *Sultan*'s time in New York City from 1859-1861. A photo of a plate with the maker's mark is shown in Figure 3.

Identification

The identification of the shipwreck as the brig *Sultan* was accomplished using the VanZandt Historic Shipwreck Identification Method (VHSIM) developed by David VanZandt, one of the authors (VanZandt 2009). The historical data available for the *Sultan* was categorically evaluated against the acquired archaeological data from the wreck site. The results of the evaluation confirm that the shipwreck discovered is the *Sultan*. Table 1 describes some of the features used to identify the wreck and how they compare to the known historic values.

Mooring and Archaeological Survey

Since this wreck is located in a highly trafficked location near shore and could be easily located with information publicly available, the decision was made to work with the Maritime Archaeological Survey Team (MAST) to place a mooring on the wreck to prevent anchor damage from recreational and commercial boats. In addition, a full archaeological survey to document the shipwreck was proposed. MAST is a group of avocational divers involved in the archaeological survey and mooring of shipwrecks in Ohio waters. CLUE assisted MAST with the project's fund raising efforts through presentations at local dive shops and scuba shows throughout the winter of 2011-2012. Sufficient funds were raised to both properly install a mooring at the shipwreck site and perform the detailed archaeological survey. The mooring was approved in late 2011 and installed in the late spring of 2012. The wreck was opened to the general diving public with a special charter to the wreck on 26 May 2012. The archaeological survey was performed by MAST divers over the summer of 2012 under the direction of CLUE's Director and Chief Archaeologist, David VanZandt. The survey results are now in the process of being documented and will be published by MAST at a later date. Figure 4 contains the preliminary site plan of the survey data plotted to date.

Site Management

MAST has added the *Sultan* to their ongoing Lake Erie mooring project. The mooring provides both use and protection functions. By placing a permanent anchor block, jump line to the wreck, and a seasonal mooring buoy, the wreck will have greater diver access, thus promoting cultural tourism, while protecting the shipwreck by eliminating the need to drag or grapple the wreck with boat anchors. The mooring and jump lines also provide a more direct and safer path to the wreck than an errantly snagged anchor line.

Acknowledgements

The authors would like to thank the entire Cleveland Underwater Explorers organization for their support and assistance with the *Sultan* project. They would also like to thank the Great Lakes Historical Society for their unwavering support over the years. Additionally, the authors would like to thank 3H Consulting Ltd. for providing their Site Recorder 4 survey software, which is currently being used to develop the site plan for the wreck site from the MAST survey data.

References

THE CLEVELAND HERALD
    1864   Terrible Disaster. *The Cleveland Herald* September 26:3. Cleveland, Ohio

THE CLEVELAND LEADER
    1864   Terrible Disaster on the Lake. *The Cleveland Leader* September 26:4. Cleveland, Ohio

DIBBLE, C. B.
    1864   *Orders, Correspondence, &c., &c., Relating to the Expulsion of C. B. Dibble from the Department of North Carolina.* Press of Wynkoop, Hallenbeck & Thomas, New York.

DISTRICT OF BUFFALO
    1858   Enrollment No. 26, 26 April 1858, Records of the Bureau of Marine Inspection and Navigation, Record Group 41, National Archives, Washington, DC.

    1859   Enrollment No. 17, 19 December 1859, Records of the Bureau of Marine Inspection and Navigation, Record Group 41, National Archives, Washington, DC.

DISTRICT OF CHICAGO
    1848   Enrollment No. 40, 27 July 1848, Records of the Bureau of Marine Inspection and Navigation, Record Group 41, National Archives, Washington, DC.

DISTRICT OF CUYAHOGA
    1862   Enrollment No. 62, 25 June 1862, Records of the Bureau of Marine Inspection and Navigation, Record Group 41, National Archives, Washington, DC.

MARITIME HISTORY OF THE GREAT LAKES
    2013a   *Sultan* (Brig), aground, 11 Nov 1853. http://images.maritimehistoryofthegreatlakes.ca/40078/data?n=3. Accessed 4 February 2013.

    2013b   *Sultan* (Brig), 1 Sep 1853. http://images.maritimehistoryofthegreatlakes.ca/30704/data?n=1. Accessed 4 February 2013.

    2013c   *Sultan* (Brig), capsized, 10 Jun 1853. http://images.maritimehistoryofthegreatlakes.ca/39860/data?n=2. Accessed 4 February 2013.

    2013d   *Sultan* (Brig), aground, 4 Nov 1856. http://images.maritimehistoryofthegreatlakes.ca/40555/data?n=4. Accessed 4 February 2013.

MARINE REVIEW
    1901   Pleasing incident aboard the Erie, 6 June 1910:17, Penton Press, Cleveland.

THE NEW YORK TIMES
    1860a   Marine Intelligence, *The New York Times*, 27 August 1860:8, New York.

    1860b   Marine Intelligence, *The New York Times*, 20 September 1860:8, New York.

    1860c   Marine Intelligence, *The New York Times*, 6 November 1860:8, New York.

    1861a   Marine Intelligence, *The New York Times*, 17 June 1861:8, New York.

    1861b   Marine Intelligence, *The New York Times*, 12 September 1861:8, New York.

    1861c   Marine Intelligence, *The New York Times*, 7 October 1861:8, New York.

THE PLAIN DEALER
    1864   Terrible Lake Disaster. *The Plain Dealer* September 26:3. Cleveland, Ohio

VANZANDT, DAVID M.
    2009   'A Systematic Method for the Identification of Historic Era Shipwrecks', Master's thesis, Department of Archaeology, Flinders University, Adelaide, South Australia.

David Michael VanZandt, MMA, RPA
Director/Chief Archaeologist
Cleveland Underwater Explorers, Inc.
1226 Lakeland Avenue
Lakewood, OH 44107
440-625-2308
clue@clueshipwrecks.org
dvanzandt@sbcglobal.net

James Edward Paskert
Director of Historic Research
Cleveland Underwater Explorers, Inc.
2619 Remsen Road
Medina, OH 44256
440-625-2356
paskertj@zin-tech.com

Kevin Scott Magee
Co-Director
Cleveland Underwater Explorers, Inc.
4363 West 182nd Street
Cleveland, Ohio 44135
440-625-2281
kevin.magee@zin-tech.com

Site Formation Processes of the Wreck of the U.S. Steamer *Convoy* in Pensacola Bay, Florida

Christopher T. Dewey

This paper examines the site formation processes of the U. S. steamer Convoy that burned and sank in the Pensacola Pass in March 1866. The vessel's Civil War history and the deliberate and opportunistic salvage operations conducted during the nineteenth and twentieth centuries are discussed. The paper compares a recent survey of the wreck site, completed by archaeologists from the University of West Florida, with a U. S. Navy survey from 1987. The result of this research is a comprehensive examination of the cultural and natural forces that created the contemporary wreck site.

Introduction

Beneath the strong currents and churning eddies of the Pensacola Pass rests the remains of the nineteenth-century steamer *Convoy*. Although the wreck site enjoyed nearly a century of undisturbed rest, the emergence of scuba equipment and the advance of the channel scarp have caused the wreck much distress in recent decades. Through a study of the cultural and physical processes that affect the shipwreck, the evolution of the wreck site from the sinking to the present day can be determined; many of the processes are still at work.

Archaeologists and graduate students at the University of West Florida (UWF) examined *Convoy's* historical record and compared their findings to the archaeological evidence they encountered in the Pensacola Pass during the 2012 field season. The researchers' goal was to determine the wreck's site formation processes in order to identify how the wreck has changed over time and possibly how the site may evolve in the future.

The U. S. Steamer *Convoy*

New York shipwright Thomas Stack completed the side-wheel steamer *Convoy* in his Williamsborough shipyard in 1862, and he launched the steamer in January 1863. *Lloyds American Registry* listed the Leary Brothers as *Convoy's* owners at the time of the vessel's construction (Lloyd's of London 1870:610). *Convoy* was a nondescript cargo vessel, a long-haul truck of the time. The steamer was 54.9 m (180 ft.) in length and just over 7.9 m (26 ft.) in the beam; the 2.7 m (9 ft.) depth of the hold allowed the ship to carry 344.7 mt (380 tons) of cargo. One single-cylinder, walking-beam, steam engine with a 1.0 m (40 in.) diameter piston and a 3.0 m (10 ft) stroke powered the two 7.6 m (25 ft.) diameter paddle wheels. A single tubular boiler was located in the hold (*New York Times* 1863:6). *Convoy* had a single enclosed deck designed for river navigation (Lloyd's of London 1870:610).

Artist Herbert Valentine (1863) painted *Convoy* in 1863 for the War Department; Figure 1 is a digital representation of that painting. The vessel in Valentine's painting matches the description in Lloyds, and the vessel's name is emblazoned on the paddle-wheel housing. The walking beam steam engine is clearly visible aft of *Convoy's* stack. Valentine titled his work "Steamer *Convoy* carried mail from Hilton Head to St. Helena, S. Carolina." The title accurately represented the nature of the ship's work during the Civil War, as reflected in the historical record.

Operating out of Fort Monroe in Virginia, the steamer carried cargo and personnel along the Atlantic coast in support of the Union Army. After the war, the Army transferred *Convoy* to the Gulf Coast where the steamer served as the dispatch boat for the Army in Texas (*Daily National Intelligencer* 1865:5). On the evening of 21 March 1866, *Convoy's* honorable career ended on the waters of Pensacola Bay (Wise 1866:2). An oil lamp overturned in the engine room igniting a fire that destroyed the ship and forced the crew took into the lifeboats (*New York Times* 1866:5). The initial report indicated that one crewmember lost his life; however, subsequent reports revealed that the entire crew escaped the blaze (Wise 1866:2).

Convoy sank in 3.4 m (11 ft.) of water south of Fort Barrancas in the Pensacola Bay; part of the superstructure was visible above the water. In 1876, the *New York Herald* (1876:8) reported that *Convoy's* boiler drum and connecting rod protruded from the water and looked much like a navigation buoy. The U. S. Army Corps of Engineers (USACE) decided in 1877 that the wreck was a hazard to navigation and contracted to remove *Convoy's* remains. In November 1878, a salvage crew used blasting powder to break up the wreck and then cut away

FIGURE 1. "STEAMER CONVOY CARRIED MAIL FROM HILTON HEAD TO ST. HELENA, S. CAROLINA" BY HERBERT VALENTINE (COURTESY OF THE NATIONAL ARCHIVES).

the portions of the ship that extended above the water (Damrell 1879:801). What remained of Convoy lay at the bottom of Pensacola Bay for over one hundred years.

Archaeological Research

Convoy's initial archaeological investigation began with a 1987 survey of the wreck by Tidewater Atlantic Research (TAR) under contract to the U.S. Navy. The TAR dive team used closed circuit television and still photography to develop a detailed site plan. They reported a large debris field consisting of hull structure and sheathing, ship's machinery, ceramics, and fasteners scattered over an area measuring approximately 43 m (140 ft.) by 15 m (50 ft.). The engineering machinery included boiler fragments and pieces of the ship's steam cylinder (U. S. Navy 1987). The high quality photographs and detailed site diagram were particularly useful during the 2012 survey. The wreck's charted depth, from the hydrographic survey of Pensacola Bay conducted by the National Oceanic and Atmospheric Administration (NOAA) in 1989, was approximately 4.6 m (15 ft.) (NOAA 2006).

The 2012 field effort started with magnetometer and side-scan sonar surveys of the site, which the research team compared to the written descriptions and the site plan from the 1987 survey. Surprisingly, the charted depth of the wreck from the 2009 NOAA hydrographic survey was 3.9 m (13 ft.), but the surrounding water was in excess of 7.6 m (25 ft.) (NOAA 2011). The chart showed that the wreck should have exhibited approximately 3.0 m (10 ft.) of relief, but side-scan sonar images indicated much lower relief. An orientation dive in May 2012 verified the wreck's location and confirmed that the debris field was no higher that a few feet off the bottom.

The UWF dives continued in late June, and the dive teams set out to map the extent of the debris field and identify features from the 1987 survey. Figure 2 shows the extents of the debris field. The dive team's first impression of the wreck was that it resembled the site documented in the 1987 survey with a few notable exceptions. First, the depth of the site was different. The charted depth in 1987 was approximately 4.6 m (15 ft.) (NOAA 2006), yet the wreck was significantly deeper in 2012; the depth at north end of the site was 7.6 m (25 ft.), while the south end was nearly 10.7 m (35 ft.). A difference of between 3.0 m (10 ft.) and 4.6 m (15 ft.) seemed extreme even considering the intervening two decades. Second, the wreck was spread over a much larger area. The north-south measurement was similar to

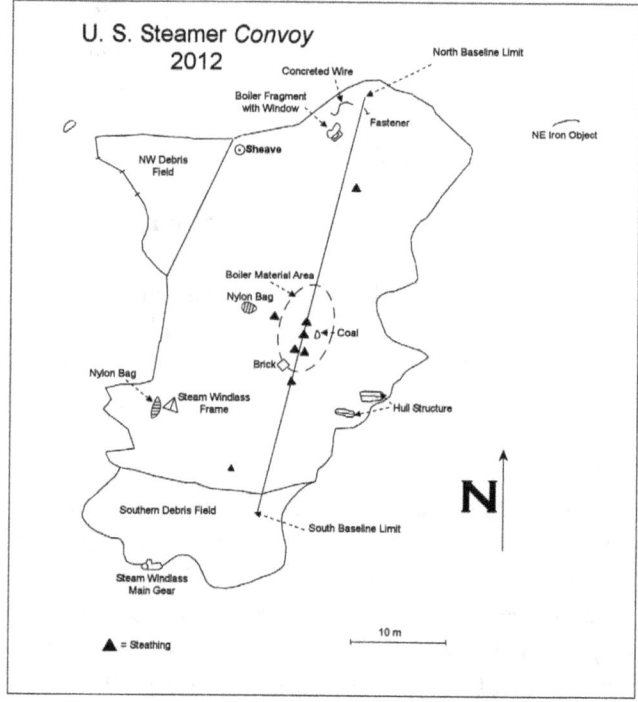

FIGURE 2. CONVOY SITE DIAGRAM (DIAGRAM BY AUTHOR, 2012).

the 1987 U. S. Navy survey, but the east-west extents were nearly twice as great. The drawing and photos from the 1987 survey gave the impression of isolated outcroppings of features and artifacts interspersed among large areas of loose sand; this was not the case in 2012. The present wreck was more akin to a continuous debris field of concreted features and artifacts with little loose sand between. Third, the debris field extended much farther to the northwest (Figure 2). At first, the team thought they had found a separate artifact scatter that might have indicated a second wreck, but they determined that the scatter was part of a single, continuous field of concreted metal objects.

Late in the dive season the crew discovered another large area of debris to the south of the main wreck site that included a 2.0 m (6.6 ft.) long object that was clearly the main gear of the steam windlass (Figure 3). A reexamination of the wreck revealed that the capricious currents had scoured the new southern debris field down to the hardpan sediment beneath. Approximately one half meter (1.5 ft.) of sand had previously covered the area. Additionally, fresh sand deposits covered large sections of the east side of the wreck.

The team spent the last two days of the dive season locating and photomapping other diagnostic features. The object identified as the steam windlass on the 1987 survey was most likely part of the frame for the device; it was located 20 m (65.6 ft.) north of the actual windlass main gear, although its orientation had changed approximately 90 degrees. The dive team also discovered evidence of opportunistic salvage by sport divers including numerous modern lines and ropes around the wreck and nylon fabric covering some features; the sport divers may have used the material as a type of homemade lift bag system.

Geophysical Findings

The most significant discrepancy between the 1987 U. S. Navy survey and the wreck's current condition was the depth. Approximately 3.0 m (10 ft.) to 4.6 m (15 ft.) of sand disappeared from beneath the wreck between NOAA hydrographic surveys in 1989 and 2009 (NOAA

FIGURE 3. STEAM WINDLASS WITH WILDCAT (PHOTO BY AUTHOR, 2012).

2006, 2011). The northward and westward retreat of the channel scarp during the 20 years between hydrographic surveys removed the sand as part of the natural process of sediment redistribution. Figure 4 shows the progressive retreat of the northern channel scarp from 1859 to 2009. The 2011 navigation chart, which used sounding data from the 2009 NOAA hydrographic survey, clearly showed the location of the wreck with a depth of 4 m (13 ft.) and the nearby soundings in excess of 6.1 m (20 ft.). The wreck retained some sediment beneath it and the ebb and flow of the tidal current scoured the area around the wreck. During the ensuing three years between the 2009 hydrographic survey and the 2012 diver investigations, the current likely eroded the remaining sediment beneath the wreck until it came to rest on the hardpan sediment beneath (NOAA 2011).

The strong currents of the Pensacola Pass are the likely cause of the frequent changes in the wreck's appearance. The 3.0 m (10 ft.) difference in depth between the north and south ends of the wreck indicates that the erosion process beneath the debris may not be complete. The wreckage settles a little closer to the hard packed substrate with each tide cycle. Different portions of the wreck are uncovered as the current brings new sand deposits to some areas and removes sand from other areas exposing the few remaining wooden hull fragments to the deleterious effects of exposure to salt water. The large amount of Muntz metal sheathing and tacks without their accompanying wood structure found among the

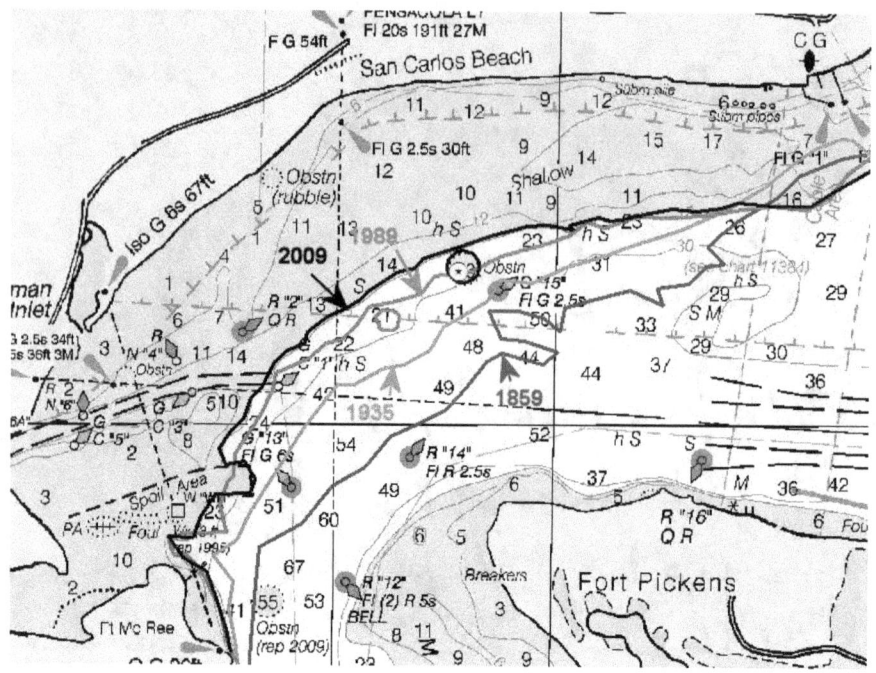

FIGURE 4. CHANNEL SCARP RETREAT 1859-2009. SOUNDINGS IN FEET. (FIGURE BY AUTHOR 2012, MODIFIED FROM NOAA'S HISTORICAL MAP AND CHART COLLECTION).

concreted iron features indicates that most of the hull structure has already succumbed to the elements.

Maritime Site Formation Process Theory

Keith Muckelroy (1978) grouped both cultural and non-cultural transformations into extracting filters and scrambling devices. Extracting filters work to remove parts of the ship from the wreck site, while scrambling devices rearrange artifacts and features at the site (Muckelroy 1978:159-184). By removing portions of the ship, extracting filters play an important role in the evolution of the wreck site. The extracting forces of the process of wrecking often carry away or consume sections of the ship that never become part of the wreck site. Other extracting filters remove portions of the wreck site after the initial process of sinking, including artifact and feature deterioration by physical, chemical, and biological forces. Muckelroy listed salvage operations and archaeological excavations as extraction filters because they removed artifacts and features from wreck sites (Muckelroy 1978:165-169).

Muckelroy divided scrambling devices into two broad categories, the process of wrecking and seabed movement. During the wrecking process, the ship system suffers a catastrophic failure that causes the rearrangement of artifacts and features on the bottom. The process continues for many years as the wreck site breaks up and settles. Once the wreck becomes part of the seascape, the process of seabed movement causes the site to develop into the present day site (Muckelroy 1978:169-182). Interestingly, Muckelroy did not list salvage efforts as scrambling devices despite the tendency of such operations to move or reorient objects on the seafloor.

Martin Gibbs (2006) expanded Muckelroy's process models for cultural maritime site formation processes. Gibbs based his research on models used in disaster studies in which "(human activities) can be viewed and investigated within a process-oriented framework of consistent stage that embraces both the physical progress of the event and the behaviors that take place in each phase" (Gibbs 2006:7). The five major stages of a disaster fit well into a systems approach to studying shipwrecks; they include pre-impact, impact, recoil, rescue, and post-trauma stages (Leach 1994:8). Gibbs's disaster phased process is a framework that researchers may use to define the cultural site formation processes of a shipwreck (Gibbs 2006:7-8). These processes are equally applicable to non-cultural processes.

Convoy's Site Formation Processes

UWF archaeologists applied Martin Gibbs's crisis/disaster process model (2006:7-8) to the historical, archaeological, and geophysical findings from *Convoy's* wreck to identify Muckelroy's (1978) extraction filters and scrambling devices. The result is a comprehensive accounting of the cultural and physical forces that have contributed to the evolution of the shipwreck in a high-energy environment.

Pre-Impact, Impact, and Recoil Phases

Some of the factors that contributed to *Convoy's* demise are found in the historical record and others can only be inferred. Colonel George Wise, of the U. S. Army Quartermaster Department, described the steamer's loss as a direct result of the use of coal oil in the engineering space. *Convoy's* mishap was not a unique occurrence; "I cannot too strongly condemn the practice of using this inflammable material for illuminating purposes on shipboard, it being the frequent cause of loss to life and property" (Wise 1866:122).

Other processes are not as clearly attributable to the ship's loss. The training of the crew to control an oil spill and combat a small fire can be brought into question. An oil spill and the resultant fire should not have caused the destruction of the entire vessel. Yet, the ship's design may have contributed to its loss as a poorly designed ship might have prevented the crew from reaching the fire before it grew out of control.

The crew may have had time to jettison some of the more explosive and combustible items in an effort to save their ship; such actions would have been extracting filters. Firefighting equipment such as buckets of sand or water and fire axes were likely displaced as the crew battled the blaze in the engine room. All these actions changed the wreck site; jettisoning acted as an extraction filter, and the movement of the firefighting equipment worked as a scrambling device.

The crew departed the burning ship quickly. The *New York Times* (1866:5) reported "the captain and crew were obliged to escape in boats in their night clothes." The newspaper article provides two important clues that influenced the wreck. First, the rapid departure of the crew indicates that they had little time for crisis or survivor salvage. Some crewmembers awakened by the alarm might have had time to retrieve personal items before abandoning ship, but most had little time to do so. Most of the crew probably left their few personal possessions aboard the steamer as the vessel burned and sank. An example of personal gear found on the wreck site is the two kaolin pipes that were possibly left behind as the sailors abandoned ship.

The second clue from the 1866 *New York Times* article that might affect the wreck was that the crew escaped in boats. These boats were probably *Convoy*'s lifeboats, carried for just such an occasion. The crew likely rowed to the nearest shore in Pensacola Bay, which was approximately 800 m (880 yds.) from the wreck site. Because the crew removed the lifeboats from the ship, no lifeboat debris should have been found on the wreck site. Accordingly, no such features or artifacts were recovered.

Post-Disaster Phases

The systematic salvage operation by the U.S. Army Corps of Engineers (USACE) in 1879 had a dramatic effect on the current wreck site. The official report of the salvage effort described the removal of the engine and machinery and the use of blasting powder to break apart the wreck (Damrell 1879:801). The 2012 dive team discovered a large debris field northwest of the main area of wreckage. The northwest debris area is outside the most plausible location of *Convoy*'s hull indicating that it is likely a separate scatter associated with another event. In order to access *Convoy*'s engine and boiler, the 1879 salvage crew probably had to remove the frame structure around the engine seen in Figure 1. The framework resembles much of the debris found in the northwest scatter area (Figure 2). It is likely that the salvage team cut or pulled the frame assembly from around the engine and boiler and deposited the wreckage northwest of the steamer's hull, resulting in the debris scatter documented by the 2012 UWF dive crew. The dive team also identified a sheave of a block, also known as a wheel of a pulley, near the northwest debris area. While *Convoy* carried many such blocks for handling cargo, the location of this sheave may indicate that the salvage crew might have used it to hoist the frame assembly away from the main wreck.

Further evidence of the 1879 salvage operations is indicated by the location of the steam anchor windlass main gear more than 20 m (66 ft.) south of the windlass frame (Figure 2). The main gear assembly rests well outside the likely extents of *Convoy*'s hull, and the salvage crew may have separated the main gear from the windlass frame as they removed portions of the steamer's hull. A steam tug or steam powered winch might have been employed to detach the windlass sections.

The nineteenth-century salvage work acted as both an extraction filter and as a scrambling device. Clearly, the extraction of much of the ship's engine and half of its hull influenced the wreck site visible on the bottom today. Beyond the possible removal and deposition of the engine framework and the anchor windlass main gear, the salvage crew likely moved other sections of the ship in order to access other areas or reduce the wreck's profile above the bottom.

The wreck site remained relatively undisturbed by humans from the completion of the salvage operations in 1879 until widespread use of scuba by recreational divers in the early 1960s. Storms and spring tide currents acted as extracting filters by uncovering sections of the wreck and exposing the soft portions (wood, cloth, leather, hemp etc.) to deterioration by biological and chemical processes. Scrambling devices were also at work as pieces of the wreck, weakened by chemical and biological actions, were likely redistributed around the site or carried away by strong currents and storm surge from hurricanes.

Scuba divers knew the location of *Convoy*'s wreck site by the early 1960s; it became, and remains today, a popular dive site for spearfishing and relic hunting. Many divers took artifacts from the site; reportedly, they removed bottles, flatware, ceramic sherds, and other items (Madden 2012, Sharar 2012). The sport divers' actions represent extracting filters as they removed artifacts from the site, and they also acted as scrambling devices when various portions of the wreck were moved around the bottom possibly to access areas the divers hoped would contain valuable artifacts (Madden 2012).

Scuba divers continue to remove artifacts from the wreck, and the physical, biological, and chemical processes have reduced the wreckage visible above the bottom. However, starting about 1989, an additional physical force began to influence the site and acted as an additional scrambling device. Significant scour of the sediments around the wreck began as the migrating channel scarp approached the site (Figure 4). The 1989 hydrographic survey showed *Convoy*'s wreck site at a depth of 4.6 m (15 ft.) on the edge of the channel scarp, where the shallow flats meet the deeper water of the natural channel. The strong tidal currents likely accelerated the extracting filter effects of the physical processes on the remaining wreck site. By the time of the 2009 hydrographic survey, the navigational chart indicated that the current had eroded the sand around the wreck to a depth in excess of 6.1 m (20 ft.), but the wreck remained at a depth of 4 m (13ft.). The wreck retained some sediment beneath it as the surrounding sand was scoured around the wreck. By the time UWF divers accessed the wreck site in 2012, the currents had eroded the sediment beneath the wreck so that the shallowest portion of the site was 7.6 m (25 ft.) deep, while deepest portion was nearly 10.7 m (35 ft.) below the surface.

The scouring effects of the tidal current were likely amplified by the unintended consequences of dredging operations in the Pensacola Ship Channel and the Intra-Coastal Waterway (ICW) channel. The effect of the dredging, known as "bank slump" that happens when the sides of a dredged channel fall into the channel, likely accelerated the migration of the channel scarp (Browder and Dean 1999:20).

The increased sediment erosion acted as a scrambling device by rearranging artifacts and features as the wreckage settled to the hardpan sediment at the bottom of the natural channel. A clear example of this rearranging effect is the orientation of the steam windlass frame whose apex pointed west in 1987 (U. S. Navy 1987:16), but was recorded pointing north in 2012. The object is much too heavy to have been moved by divers and its orientation likely shifted ninety degrees as it settled to the bottom of the channel.

Summary

The history of *Convoy*'s wreck site formation is evident from the historical, archaeological, and hydrographic records; the ship was subject to cultural and physical processes that removed artifacts and features and other actions that scrambled the vessel's remains on the bottom of the Pensacola Pass. Cultural factors generally caused change to occur rapidly, such as the deliberate and opportunistic salvage efforts that removed or rearranged sections of the wreck immediately. However, one might make the case that the use of coal oil lamps in *Convoy*'s engine room was one cultural process that took a long time to influence the wreck, assuming that the lamps were in use from the ship's commissioning to its demise.

Physical processes worked more slowly. The two most significant physical factors, the erosion of sediments beneath the wreck and the deterioration of the wooden components, required many years to achieve their full effect. By contrast, the wreck's appearance changed with each tide cycle as the shifting sand covered and uncovered different portions of the site. The cultural and physical site formation processes continue to change the wreck, but with this study, we have a more complete understanding of the forces that influence the site.

Acknowledgements

The author wishes to acknowledge the support of the University of West Florida (UWF) Archaeological Institute that funded the research, the Florida Bureau of Archaeological Research, the U. S. General Services Administration (GSA), the Florida Public Archaeology Network (FPAN), the Naval Facilities and Engineering Command (NAVFAC) Southern Region, Tidewater Atlantic Research (TAR), West Florida Historic Preservation Inc. (WFHPI), and National Oceanographic and Atmospheric Administration (NOAA) Office of Coast Survey. The author owes special thanks to Drs. Elizabeth Benchley, John Bratten, Greg Cook, Amy Mitchell-Cook, Hilde Snoeckx, Gordon Watts, and Della Scott-Ireton, and 2012 UWF Maritime Field School divers.

References Cited:

BROUSSARD, LARRY W.
    1988   The *Judah*: Sunken Civil War Schooner Harbored in Shifting Sands for 125 Years. *Skin Diver*, July, 164-167.

BROWDER, ALBERT E. AND ROBERT G. DEAN
    1999   *Pensacola Pass, FL Inlet Management Study*. University of Florida, Gainesville, FL.

DAILY NATIONAL INTELLIGENCER
    1865   From Fortress Monroe. *Daily National Intelligencer* 25 August, Washington, District of Columbia.

DAMRELL, A. N.
    1879   Report of the Chief Engineer. *Annual Report of the Chief of Engineers 1879*, Washington, DC.

GIBBS, MARTIN
    2006   Cultural Site Formation Processes in Maritime Archaeology: Disaster Response, Salvage and Muckelroy 30 Years on. *The International Journal of Nautical Archaeology* 35(1):4-19.

LLOYD'S OF LONDON
    1870   *Lloyd's American Registry of Ships 1860-1870*. Lloyd's of London, London, United Kingdom.

MADDEN, JOE
    2012   Interview by Christopher T. Dewey, 9 June. Manuscript and audio file, The Steamer *Convoy* Project, University of West Florida Oral History Department, Pensacola, Florida.

MUCKELROY, KEITH
    1978   *Maritime Archaeology*. Cambridge University Press, Cambridge, United Kingdom.

NATIONAL OCEANIC AND ATMOSPHERIC ADMINISTRATION (NOAA)
    2006   Hydrographic Chart 11383, Pensacola Bay.

    2011   Hydrographic Chart 11383, Pensacola Bay.

NEW YORK HERALD
    1876   Notice to Mariners. *New York Herald* 26 February, New York, New York.

NEW YORK TIMES
    1863   Steamers Building or Recently Completed for the Merchant Service. *New York Times* 26 January. New York, New York.

    1866   ALABAMA. Total Destruction of a United States Steamer – One Person Killed Several Injured. *New York Times* April 6, New York, New York.

SHARAR, FRITZ
    2012   Interview by Christopher T. Dewey, 12 June. Manuscript and audio file, The Steamer *Convoy* Project, University of West Florida Oral History Department, Pensacola, Florida.

U. S. NAVY
    1987   Underwater Archaeological Investigations Gulf of Mexico and Pensacola Bay, Florida. *Gulf Coast Strategic Homeporting*. Naval Facilities Engineering Command, Southern Division. Charleston, South Carolina.

VALENTINE, HERBERT E.
    1863   Painting, "Steamer *Convoy* carried mail from Hilton Head to St. Helena, S. Carolina.", National Archives and Record Administration, College Park, Maryland. ARC Identifier 533209 1863. <http://arcweb.archives.gov>. Accessed 20 March 2012.

WISE, GEORGE D.
    1866   Third Division – Ocean and Lake Transportation. *Report of the Secretary of War*, p. 2. Washington, District of Columbia.

. . . .

Christopher T. Dewey
Freelance Maritime Archaeologist
Portland, Oregon
Christopher.T.Dewey@gmail.com

Roman Lead Ingots From Shipwrecks: A Key to Understanding Immigration From Campania, Southern Latium, and Picenum in the Mining District of Carthago Nova in the Late Republican and Early Imperial Eras

Michele Stefanile

Roman lead ingots from the mines of Carthago Nova (modern Cartagena in south-east Spain), found in several shipwrecks in Western Mediterranean, constitute an extraordinary source for understanding the immigration of people from Campania, Southern Latium and Picenum in the newly conquered provinces of Hispaniae – an interesting historical phenomenon described by contemporary authors, and which formed the basis for the Romanization of the Iberian Peninsula.

The analysis of the gentilitia inscribed on the ingots, cross-referenced with Latin epigraphic data from Roman Spain and the Italian Peninsula, permits in most cases the identification of the nuclei of origin of several families, and allows us to retrace their routes to Carthago Nova, their stories, and their destinies in their new home. It also allows us to understand more fully the cultural connections between Carthago Nova and the homeland of the immigrants.

Introduction

Ancient lead from the sea is a very interesting key to understanding immigration in the Roman world. This study aims to reconsider a particular type of ancient artifact from an underwater context, namely the marked lead Roman ingots from the Iberian mines, in order to reconstruct the massive displacement of people from Campania, Southern Latium and Picenum to the provinces of *Hispaniae* during the Late Republican and Early Imperial Ages. This subject is part of a wider study, undertaken in 2007 at the University of Alicante, and resulted in a doctoral project (University of Naples "L'Orientale"). The project focused on the study of Romanization in the Eastern part of the Iberian Pensinsula, on the basis of the entire epigraphic documentation available. Some preliminary results of this work have been published to date (Stefanile 2009, 2011, 2013), others are forthcoming.

Iberia at the Dawn of Romanization

It is sufficiently well known that soon after the end of the Second Punic War and the Carthaginian's last defeats in *Astapa* (206 BC) and *Gadir*, the Romans took the place of the Barcids in the control of the Southern and Eastern coastal strips of the Iberian Peninsula. Within a short time houses, roads, harbours, public buildings, wall paintings, mosaics, floors and pottery began to show the imprint of Rome. In this complex historical process a key-role was played by the Senate of Rome, through the action of people such as *Tiberius Sempronius Gracchus* and other governors. It is essential, however, to note the actions of those who moved to the newly conquered provinces, within the two great parallel flows of people very well described by M.A. Marin Diaz (1988). On the military side, a huge amount of soldiers were stationed in *Hispaniae* owing to the continuous state of war, together with a great number of people that gravitated around the legions. On the civilian side, a very high number of people poured into the newly conquered territories of Iberia for two centuries after the end of the Second Punic War. They came to exploit the rich resources available, partly inherited by the Barcids, partly obtained with diplomacy or taken away by force from the Iberian people. In this 'land of promises', as Richardson (1997: 67) defined *Hispaniae*, there was an abundance of agricultural land, attractive to an Italic population under the strain of an increasing land crisis, as well as forests, pastures and fishing. In particular, there was an incredible abundance of metal mines, in the district of *Carthago Nova*, in the area of *Castulo*, and in many other areas of the Peninsula.

The Mining District of Carthago Nova

The mining district of *Carthago Nova*, on the hills around the city founded by Hasdrubal a few years before the arrival of the Romans, was probably one of the first major poles of attraction for the Italics that reached Iberia after the end of the Second Punic War. Its incredible richness was one of the reasons for the rapid recovery of Carthago's economic situation after the end of the first war against the Romans and the heavy conditions imposed by the treaty of *Lutatius* in 241 BC. When, in 209 BC, Hasdrubal's *Qart Hadashat* in Iberia was conquered, Rome took possession of an extraordinary wealth reported by *Livius* in a famous chapter of his work (XXVI, 47).

In a very short time, the Romans started to exploit the mines, and export the metals, especially silver and lead, through the excellent triple-basin natural port of the city. *Polybius* wrote, reported by *Strabo* (III, 2, 10), the mines had a diameter of four hundred *stadia*, with a daily profit of twenty five thousand *drachmae* and more than forty thousand people involved in the work. Another ancient source, the historian *Dyodorus* (V, 36), adds an important detail to our knowledge of this matter, that is the arrival of people from Italy to exploit those mines: "after the Romans had made themselves masters of Iberia, a multitude of people from Italy have swarmed to the mines and taken great wealth away with them, such was their greed".

Lead Ingots from the Sea

Due to the evidence provided by ancient shipwrecks sunk in the Mediterranean, we have a large number of ingots from the mines of *Carthago Nova* and, for later periods, from other Iberian mines. Parker, in his famous inventory (1992), recorded 46 shipwrecks with lead ingots in their cargoes; more recent discoveries, for example in Sicily, have increased this number (Thisseyre 2008).

When the Romans began to manage the export of metals from *Hispaniae*, these ingots (Figure 1), tended to be standardized by type, shape and weight, and by the presence of seals impressed on the surface bearing the names of individuals or societies (Domergue 1990).

Sometimes other inscriptions testify to further steps in the export of the ingots (Figure 2). There are examples of wrecks sunk before the arrival of the Romans and before the birth of *Carthago Nova*. The ingots from these vessels include very rough examples from the shipwreck at Mazarron, or in the shape of a *Pinna nobilis* shell from the Cabrera II wreck, but do not include inscriptions. They cannot tell us anything about the people involved in managing, producing, exporting and transporting the metal, in contrast to Late Republican ingots (Domergue, 1990; Alonso Campoy, 2009). Much has been written regarding these cargoes, and some very exhaustive works on mining and ingots have been produced. In particular, the work of Domergue (1965, 1966, 1990, 1994, 2004, 2009a, 2009b) has provided the most complete and detailed study currently available.

The origin of the *massae plumbeae* from *Carthago Nova*, has been verified not only on the basis of the typological or epigraphic information available, but also through isotope analyses (Trincherini et al., 2010). Cores recovered from Greenland and compared with the isotopic records have shown that the greatest part of lead dust circulating in Earth's atmosphere in the 1st century BC came from the mines of *Carthago Nova* (Trincherini et al., 2010).

Apart from work by Domergue on individual families of great interest, for example the *Planii*, from *Cales*, there is no real prosopographical study on the topic. Domergue's indications on the possible origins of the *gentes*, in most of the cases are just simple suggestions based on a first reading of the names, or on some details such as the mention of the *tribus*, were frequently taken in the later literature in an uncritical and passive way.

Figure 1. A lead ingot from Carthago Nova marked by Cn. Atelllius Cn. f. Miserinus, found in Ischia, in the Gulf of Naples (Photo by author, 2009).

FIGURE 2. MINOR INSCRIPTIONS ON ONE OF THE SMALL SIDES OF THE INGOTS MARKED BY CN. ATELLIUS CN. F. MISERINUS (PHOTO BY AUTHOR, 2009).

The Origin of the Gentes Involved in the Exploitation of the Mines

By crossing the information present on the ingots with the Latin epigraphic data from the Iberian and Italian Peninsulas, this research is trying to provide a more precise and better documented answer to the question of the origin of these *gentes*. It is obtaining data that confirms the widely accepted idea of a strong presence of people from Campania, allowing the determination of more *nuclei* of origin in that region. It is a meaningful datum that offers new ideas for discussion and acquires added significance when compared with archaeological evidence from the *Carthago Nova* area with strong imprints from Campania and with interesting parallels in the same areas of origin of the *gentes*. Below, we present some cases where a few remarks can be made:

The Atellii

For the *Atellii*, for example, it is possible to go beyond the general mention of *Campani* given by Domergue (1990, 321) and retaken by Abascal (1997) on the basis of the simple indication of the tribe *Menenia*, given to some towns in *Campania* after the *bellum sociale* and for that reason also constituting a *terminus post quem*. Their marked ingots are found in numerous wrecks: Mahdia in Tunisia (*CIL* 1(2) 2396); Mal di Ventre in Sardinia (Salvi, 1992); in the middle of an impressive cargo of more than one thousand ingots of several families, in Capo Testa, Sardinia (Gandolfi 1983, *EDR* 81552); Portopalo di Capo Passero in Sicily (Thisseyre *et al.* 2008); and in Ischia near Naples – an underwater find not associated with shipwreck (Stefanile, 2009, *EDR* 116575).

The family, whose members usually bear the *praenomen Cnaeus*, is very well documented in *Carthago Nova* (Abascal and Ramallo 1997, n. 74, 119, 120 and *CIL* 2 3449, 3450, 3451). The *Atellii* quickly gained wealth, prestige and power, reaching and maintaining the city rank of magistrates, as shown by the production of coins with the *legenda P. Atellius* (probably the first mint in the history of the city, *RPC* 146); *Cn. Atellius Ponti(lienus)* (*RPC* 169) and *Cn. Atellius Flaccus* (the last production, *RPC* 185-186).

In the 1st century AD, which coincides with the decline and extinction of lead production in *Carthago Nova*, a funerary inscription for a *libertus* with an Iberian name (*CIL* 2 3450), in a plate decorated with an agricultural scene suggests perhaps the transition of the *Atellii* towards a more traditional type of wealth (Abascal and Ramallo 1997, n. 74, *CIL* 2 3450, Koch 1978, Pena Gimeno 1999). Their possession of land put to agricultural use and the exploitation of indigenous workers may also have occurred together with mining at an earlier date. A very small group of *Atellii* in the rest of

Hispaniae indicates a clear concentration of the family in the area (*CIL* 2 3603, 3405, 3003 and *AE* 1983 609).

The ingots suggest a century-long involvement with mining activity – the latest of them (the one found in Ischia in the seventies and then forgotten) can be dated back to the years around the beginning of the first millennium (Stefanile 2009, 564). Minor inscriptions, visible on the ingot can retrace the different steps from producer to consumer.

On the geographical origin of the family has thus far been confined to the general area of *Campani*. However the location can be narrowed further, as for other families, due to the reduced dispersion of the *nomen* in Italy during the Republican Age. For the *Atellii*, the evidence is mostly concentrated in the Gulf of Naples, and particularly in the city of *Herculaneum*, where there were at least four people, although with different *praenomina*, and whose inhabitants were registered in the *tribus Menenia* like those of *Pompeii, Surrentum, Nuceria, Stabia* (*AE* 1993 462 – *EDR* 103437 and *CIL* 10 1403). A relationship between the *Atellii* and the city of *Atella* (between *Neapolis* and *Capua*), whose inhabitants were registered in the *Falerna* tribe, is not demonstrable despite the name.

The Messii

Another interesting case is that of the *Messii*. One ingot, marked by a *C. Messius L. f.* (Domergue 1966, n. 13, *CIL* 11 6722-13), appears among the ingots of the *Planii, Calvii, Aquinii* and *Utii*, in the Bajo de Dentro 1st century BC wreck, in front of the *Cabo de Palos*, at the exit of Cartagena's harbour. The *Messii* are not so well evidenced in *Carthago Nova* as the *Atellii*; however, in one funerary inscription of the Augustan period (Koch 1978, 256-258, n. 3 and Abascal 1997, 369-371, n. 153) mentions a *libertus* of the family, *M. Messius M. l. Samalo, faber lapidaries*. In the rest of *Hispaniae* during the first century AD the *Messii* scattered in various directions. In this case too, Domergue (1990, 321) indicated a possible Campanian origin. Indeed, various nuclei of the family are concentrated in Campania, both in the cities around the Gulf of Naples and in the north of the territory. But while the Phlaegrean and Puteolan references are quite late, and therefore less significant, and those from *Pompeii* clearly cannot be after 79 AD (among them there is also a very ancient Oscan inscription of an *aedilis*), are all characterized by different *praenomina*, the focus in Northern Campania, between Capua, Cales, Teanum and Southern Latium, provides us with a significant documentation for the 3rd century BC, with a good spread of the *praenomen Caius*. It's also important to point out that the presence in *Delos* of the *Messii* (like many other families involved in trade from *Hispaniae*) indicates a marked propensity towards the maritime trade by this *gens* in the 2nd century BC.

Particularly significant, because of the dating, onomastics, personal history, and for being in the core of an area closely related to *Carthago Nova*, as is shown by the histories of other families and by the massive import of Calenian pottery, is a *C. Messius, tribunus plebis* and supporter of *Pompeus* in 57 BC, *aedilis curulis* in 55 BC, *legatus* of Caesar in Gallia in 54 BC and in Africa in 46 BC, *censor* of *Teanum Sidicinum*, mentioned by Cicero (*Ad Atticum* 8,11,2). Some later proofs from the same *Teanum* and from its close surroundings confirm the presence of this *gens* with important roles in the administration at least until the Flavian Age (when we can count on a *Messius Scaeva, IIvir* of *Forum Popilii* – *EDR* 079493).

The Fiduii

The case of the *Fiduii* is relatively simple due to the extreme rarity of the *nomen* – *C. Fiduius C. f.* who exports lead in a company together with *Sp. Lucretius Sp. f.* (probably belonging to another Campanian family) is mentioned on some ingots from the Escombreras wreck, off Cartagena (Domergue 1990, n. 1015; Alonso Campoy 2005) and from a shipwreck found at the end of the 1990s in Ventotene, in the Pontine islands (Arata, 1999).

Until recently just one text with the name of a *Fiduius* (one *Fiduia mulieris liberta*) was known. Mentioned together with an *Augustalis* in *Cales* (*CIL* 10 8379), in the middle of Northern Campania, they were from the same city as very active families in *Carthago Nova*. During recent research a second *Fiduia* was discovered in a new, unpublished, late-republican inscription, again from *Cales*, so strengthening the identification of the origin of the *gens*.

The Calvii

Members of another family probably from Campania, the *Calvii* (*Marcus* and *Sextus*), are present on five ingots (Domergue 1966 and 1990) from the previously mentioned Bajo de Dentro wreck. Domergue relates them with the *Calvii* in *Cori*, in Southern Latium, but we could lean towards a different hypothesis: etymologically connected with the Oscan name *Kalovios*. *Calvius* is a *nomen* that, in addition to the concentration in *Cori*, can be found in Northern Campania, once again in *Cales*. As well as a *quattuorvir* (*CIL* 10 4644) and a *sevir Augustalis* (*CIL* 10 4645), appears one *Calvia* around the middle of the 1st century BC (*EDR* 108426). Less significant are the testimonies from *Puteoli* (*CIL* 10 2220, 2222 and *CIL* 10 2221 / *EDR* 077683)) and *Misenum* (*EE* 8-1 434), all dating from the 2nd century AD.

The Aurunculeii

The *Aurunculeii*, that appear on ingots (Domergue 1990 n. 1007 and 1008) found in Cartagena and in Campofrio. They are known through the names *L. Aurunculeius L. [-] At[—-]* and *L. Aurunculeius L. l. C[ot]ta*. The latter may be related to the *legatus* of Caesar in Gallia, Lucius Aurunculeius Cotta, who was killed by the Eburonii in 54 BC (Caesar, *Bellum Gallicum*, 2,11,3; 4,22,5; 4,38,3), and through the name of *Aurunculeia* in a funerary inscription from *Carthago Nova* (Abascal and Ramallo 1997, n.121 / *AE* 1987 657). They recall once again Northern Campania: Auruncan are the lands between the Garigliano River, the Roccamonfina volcano and the Volturno River, and *Suessa Aurunca* in the heart of that territory, is considered the birthplace of the *gens* by Castrèn (1975). Nevertheless, even if there are many literary references showing that the *Aurunculeii* played high-position roles in Rome by the Republican Age – e.g. the first *praetor* of Sardinia in 209 BC (Livius, 27,6,12 and 27,41,9), the *praetor urbanus* of 190 BC (Livius, 36,45,9 and 37,2,55) and the ambassador sent to Prusa in Bythinia in 155 BC (Polybius 33,1-2) – there are no members of this family in the Auruncan territory. *Aurunculeii* can be found all around this centre (*CIL* 14 3731 – *Tibur*; *CIL* 9 4048 – *Carseoli*; *AE* 1975, 302 – *Marruvium*; *CIL* 9 2388 – *Allifae*; *AE* 1909 45 – *Pompeii*; *CIL* 10 5688 and *AE* 2006 277 – Isola Liri), but none inside it. The oldest, however, are also the closest to the centre. It seems possible, therefore, to tend towards an Auruncan – northern Campanian origin.

The Pontilieni

An especially interesting case is the *Pontilieni*, who appear as *Societas M. C. Pontilienorum* in 709 of about 1000 lead ingots found in the cargo of the ship sunk off Mal di Ventre in Sardinia (Salvi, 1992, 2012). Their *nomen*, attested only in ingot epigraphy, has been linked to a Sabellian root, as a variant of the Oscan-Umbran linguistic group. That fact, combined with the presence of the suffix *–ien*, typical of the Middle-Hadriatic area, and with mention of the tribe *Fabia*, has allowed us to connect this family to the territory of the *Picenum*. In this same area, moreover, are found several names

Gens	Origin
Appii	Unknown
Appuleii	Gulf of Naples
Aquinii	Other
Atellii	Gulf of Naples
Aurunculeii	Northern Campania
Calvii	Northern Campania
Carulii	Northern Campania
Cornelii Poliiones	Northern Campania
Dirii	Gulf of Naples
Fiduii	Northern Campania
Furii	Northern Campania
Gargilii	Unknown
Iunii	Unknown
Laetilii	Unknown
Lucretii	Gulf of Naples
Messii	Northern Campania
Nonae Nucerini	Gulf of Naples
Nonii Asprenates	Other
Planii	Northern Campania
Pontilieni	Other
Raii	Other
Roscii	Northern Campania
Seii	Gulf of Naples
Turullii	Other
Varii Hiberi	Unknown
Utii	Gulf of Naples

TABLE 1. THE GENTES ATTESTED ON THE LEAD INGOTS FROM CARTHAGO NOVA AND THEIR POSSIBLE ORIGIN

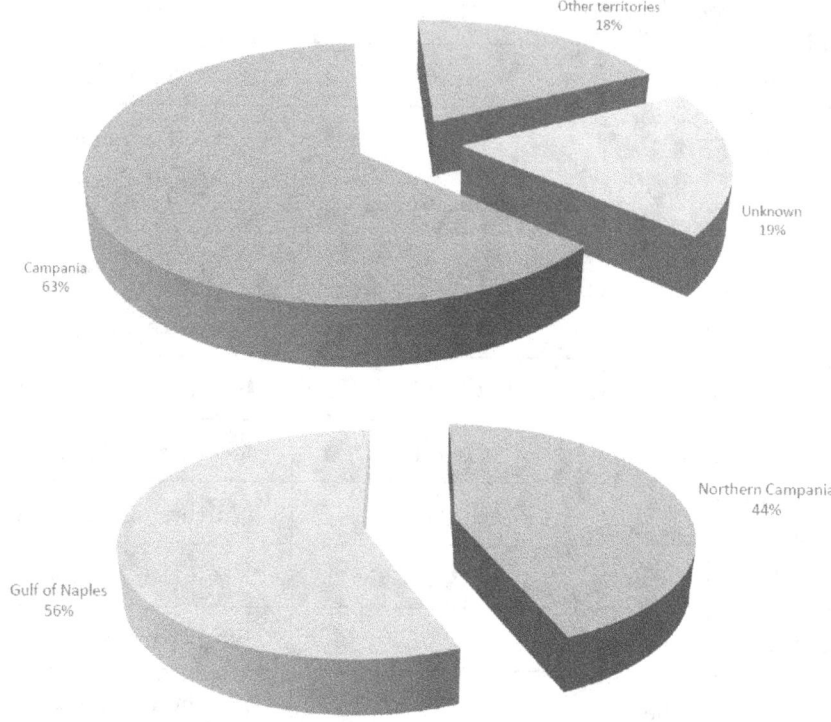

FIGURE 3 (TOP). ORIGIN OF THE GENTES ATTESTED ON LEAD INGOTS FROM CARTHAGO NOVA.

FIGURE 4 (BOTTOM). ORIGIN OF THE CAMPANIAN GENTES ATTESTED ON THE LEAD INGOTS FROM CARTHAGO NOVA.

63% of the family groups involved in the lead export.

With the exception of cases as the *Pontilieni*, or the *Raii* from the Lower Adriatic regions, or the *Turullii*, perhaps from the territory of the *Marsi*; the majority of the families arrived in *Hispaniae* from two areas of Campania: on one hand, the Gulf of Naples and the cities surrounding it, on which there is an excess of documentation provided by the Vesuvian sites; on the other, the territory between Capua and Southern Latium, and especially its centre, *Cales – Teanum*. Among the Campanian people, 56% came from the northern part of the region, and 44% from the Gulf of Naples.

We may imagine that for the cities of the Gulf of Naples the port of departure was *Puteoli*, and for those in the north it may have been *Minturnae*. This city, at the mouth of the Garigliano River and on the border between *Latium* and *Campania* is the ideal starting point for whole Auruncan territory, for the area of *Cales – Teanum*, and for the towns of Southern Latium, along the river Liri. The rich epigraphic evidence of Late Republican *Minturnae* in some cases can confirm this hypothesis: if we enlarge the focus, not only on lead producers but on all Campanian people in *Carthago Nova* and surroundings, there are many cases in which we find clear evidence of a relationship with this city.

originating from the same linguistic root – these are almost acceptable as variants of the *nomen Pontilienius*. The form *Pontulenus* also appears in Ostia, in an inscription dedicated to a *navicularius* of the Hadriatic Sea.

The origin of the *Pontilieni* in the *Picenum* is an important point, because it shows the existence of a regional group alternative and contemporary to the Campanian one, involved in the export of the Iberian lead. This is demonstrated by some other names too (*Nonii Asprenates, Turullii*). The relationship between eastern part of *Hispaniae* and *Picenum* has been shown very convincingly by Maria José Pena Gimeno, in a recent paper on the presence of the tribe *Velina* in Mallorca and on the settlements of *Palma* and *Pollentia* in the same island (Pena Gimeno 2004).

Conclusion

In Table 1 and in the graphs attached (Figures 3 and 4), it is very easy to observe a predominance of Campanian people among the Italics involved in exploiting *Carthago Nova* mines. People from Campania constituted the

The presence of contemporary families with economic interests in *Carthago Nova* and *Delos*, often indicated in *Minturnae* and *Brundisium*, may indicate the existence of a complex network based on long distance maritime trade, towards east and west, thanks to two harbours well connected through the Via Appia.

The histories of people and families that only epigraphy is able to render give depth and colour to the archaeological data and lists of parallels and comparisons. *Opus signinum* floors, so similar to those of contemporary Campania, suddenly appearing around the mines of *Carthago Nova*, funerary monuments recalling those of Capua, Formia or Quarto Flegreo, manmade stelai and Calenian pottery acquire a deeper and fascinating meaning when connected to these families.

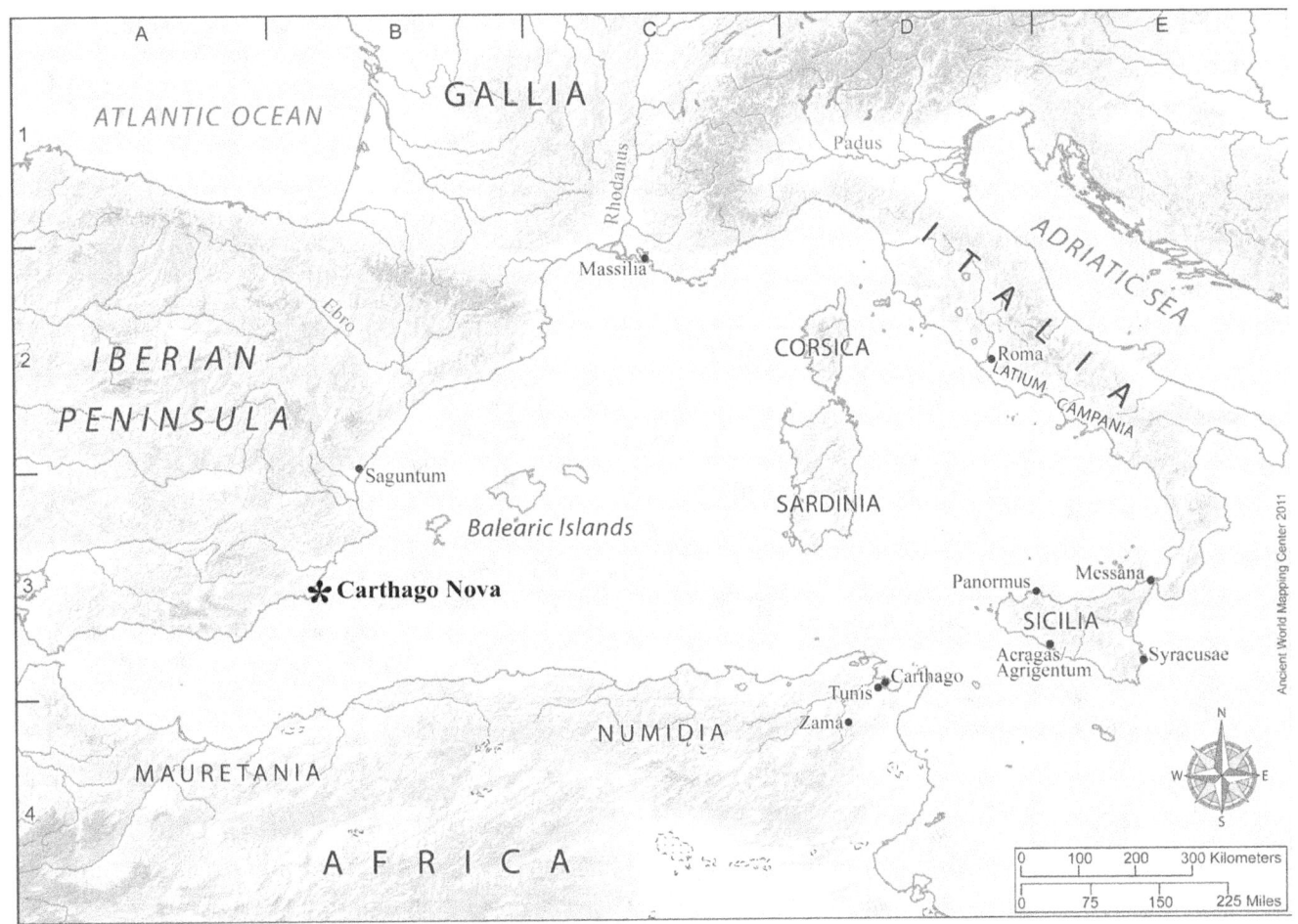

FIGURE 5. THE WESTERN MEDITERRANEAN SEA AND THE POSITION OF CARTHAGO NOVA.

References

ABASCAL PALAZÓN, JUAN MANUEL & RAMALLO ASENSIO, SEBASTIANO
1997　*La ciudad de Carthago Nova: la documentación epigráfica*, Murcia: Universidad de Murcia.

ALONSO CAMPOY, DANIEL
2005　Scombraria : la historia ocvlta bajo el mar : arqueología submarina en Escombreras, Cartagena : 1 junio-4 septiembre, MMV 2005, MARQ, Museo Arqueológico de Alicante, Murcia: Fundación Cajamurcia.

2009　Minería y tráfico marítimo. Pecios y enclaves costeros para el estudio de la actividad minera en Carthago Nova. *Argentum*, 1: 11–55.

ARATA, FRANCESCO PAOLO
1999　Il museo di Ventotene. *L'Archeologo Subacqueo*, 14.

CASTRÉN, PAAVO
1975　*Ordo populusque Pompeianus: polity and society in Roman Pompeii. Acta Instituti Romani Finlandiae, vol. 8*, Roma: Bardi.

DOMERGUE, CLAUDE
1965　Les Planii et leur activité industrielle en Espagne sous la République. *Mélanges de la Casa de Velázquez*, 1(1): 9–27.

1966　Les lingots de plomb romains du Musée Archéologique de Carthagène et du Musée Naval de Madrid. *Archivo Español de Arqueología*, 39: 41–72.

1990　*Les Mines de la péninsule Ibérique dans l'Antiquité romaine. Collection de l'école française de Rome, 127*, Roma.

1994　Production et commerce des métaux dans le monde romain : l'exemple des métaux hispaniques d'après l'épigraphie. In *Epigrafia della produzione e della distribuzione, Actes de la VIIe Rencontre franco-italienne sur l'épigraphie du monde romain (Rome, 5-6 juin 1992)*: 61–91.

2004　Un parcours a travers les lingots de plomb romains d'Espagne (1965-2003). *Pallas*, 66:105–117.

2009a　Les lingots de plomb romains des mines de Sierra Morena. L'identification par les isotopes du plomb. Questions de méthode. In *Actes de la table Ronde ACI Métal, Université de Toulouse-le Mirail*.

2009b L'exportation des métaux de l'Occident méditerranéen à l'époque romaine. L'exemple de la Gaule et de l'Hispanie. In *Porti antichi e retroterra produttivi, Atti Congresso Livorno 2009*.

GANDOLFI, DANIELA
1983 Il relitto di Capo Testa (S. Teresa di Gallura, SS). Prima campagna 1978. *Forma Maris Antiqui*, XI-XII(1975-1981): 40–68.

KOCH, MICHAEL
1988 Las grandes familias en la epigrafia de Carthago Nova. In *I Congreso Peninsular de Historia Antigua (Santiago de Compostela, 1986)*: 403–407

MARÍN DÍAZ, MARIA AMALIA
1988 Emigracion, colonizacion y municipalizacion en la Hispania republicana, Granada: Universidad de Granada.

PARKER, ANTHONY J.
1992 Ancient shipwrecks of the Mediterranean & the Roman provinces, Oxford: Archaeopress.

PENA GIMENO, MARIA JOSÉ
1999 La epigrafia funeraria de Carthago Nova. In *Atti dell'XI Congresso Internazionale di Epigrafia Greca e Latina (Atti Convegno Roma 1997)*. Roma.

2004 La tribu Velina en Mallorca y los nombres de Palma y Pollentia. *Faventia: Revista de filologia clàsica*, 26(2): 69–90

RICHARDSON, JOHN
1997 Una terra di promessa. In J. Arce, S. Ensoli, & E. La Rocca, eds. *Hispania Romana. Da terra di conquista a provincia dell'Impero*. Milano: Electa, 67–72.

SALVI, DONATELLA
1992 La massae plumbeae di Mal di Ventre. In A. Mastino, ed. *L'Africa Romana. Atti del IX Convegno di Studio (Nuoro, 13-15 dicembre 1991)*. Sassari: Gallizzi: 661–672.

2012 Mercanti e imperatori: bolli, marchi e monete provenienti da scavi subacquei. In *Ricerca e confronti 2010 ATTI Giornate di studio di archeologia e storia dell'arte a 20 anni dall'istituzione del Dipartimento di Scienze Archeologiche e Storico-artistiche dell'Università degli Studi di Cagliari (Cagliari, 1-5 marzo 2010) ArcheoArte. ArcheoArte. Rivista elettronica di Archeologia e Arte*: 241–260

STEFANILE, MICHELE
2009 Il lingotto di piombo di Cn. Atellius Cn. f. Miserinus e gli Atellii di Carthago Nova. Ostraka, XVIII(2): 559–565.

2011 Sailing towards the west. Trade and traders between the Peninsula Iberica and the Campania between the II century B.C. and the I century A.D. In *SOMA 2011, Proceedings of the GAMA Symposium on Mediterranean Archaeology-Catania 2011*. Oxford: Archaeopress.

2013 On the routes of the Iberian lead. New data and new remarks on the presence of gentes from Campania in Hispania between the II century B.C. and the I century A.D. on the basis of marked lead ingots. In *SOMA 2012, Proceedings of the GAMA Symposium on Mediterranean Archaeology-Florence 2012*. Archaeopress.

TISSEYRE, PHILIPPE ET AL.
2008 The lead ingots of Capo Passero: Roman global Mediterranean Trade. *Oxford Journal of Archaeology*, 27(3): 315–323

TRINCHERINI, PIER RENATO. ET AL.
2010 The identification of lead ingots from the Roman mines of Cartagena (Murcia, Spain): the role of lead isotope analysis. *Journal of Roman Archaeology*, 22(1): 123–145

. . . .

Michele Stefanile
Dipartimento Asia, Africa, Mediterraneo
Università degli Studi di Napoli "L'Orientale"
Via D. Fontana 81
80128
Napoli
Italia
archeologia_subacquea@yahoo.it

Ceramics from 18th century Dutch and English Shipwrecks: A Survey of Southern Baltic Sea, Poland

Joanna A. Dąbal

The geographic scope of this paper is the Southern Baltic Sea, Poland, Gdansk area. Underwater survey was conducted by archaeologists from the Maritime Museum in Gdansk. Two 18th-century shipwrecks were explored: an English ship; the General Carleton of Whitby, lost in 1785; and a Frisian vessel, De Jonge Seerp, sunk in 1791. In this paper two ceramic assemblages from these 18th-century merchant shipwrecks are compared. Ceramic analysis is presented to shed light on sailors' meals and their onboard habits. The material culture and ceramics in particular have helped define the "economic origins of the ship". This paper summarizes information about the types of ceramics used on 18th-century vessels.

Introduction

Underwater investigations of shipwrecks provide a wealth of information for archaeological studies. These findings can shed light on the living habits of the ship's crew. Raw material indicates commonly used goods by sailors aboard merchant ships at a specific time period. From studied wrecks we can attempt to interpret some aspects of everyday life for the sailors aboard two ships in the 18th century, based on underwater excavations (shipwrecks W-32 and W-27 were excavated by underwater archaeologists from Maritime Museum of Gdansk: Przemysław Smolarek, Waldemar Ossowski, Tomasz Bednarz and Iwona Pomian).

The two shipwrecks have different origins—English and Dutch—but both sank at a similar time, at the end of the 18th century in the southern area of the Baltic Sea (presently the territorial waters of Poland). There have been many studies identifying the two shipwrecks and their structures (Smolarek 1987; Ossowski 2003; 2007; 2008; Bednarz 2007; Bednarz Kaczor 2011). Preliminary results of the ceramics found on W-32 were also previously published; this article will confirm some of the information already published and will draw further conclusions (Dąbal 2008).

Wreck W-32, *General Carleton of Whitby*

The wreck *W-32* was discovered about 463 meters from the shoreline near Dębki, north of the intersection where the Piaśnica River flows into the Baltic Sea. Remains of the vessel's hull lie at a depth ranging from 4.7 to 7.4 meters (Ossowski 2003:320).

During the excavation in 1995-1999, remains of a hull with even keel, keelson, and forestern were discovered. Whole constructs, 29 meters by 8 meters and 1.5 meter high, were found well preserved (Ossowski 2003:321). From the inside of the vessel, iron rods and sheets were recovered from the main cargo (Ossowski 2003:321). The discovery of the ship's bell was a crucial find in the identification of the vessel. The ship's bell was inscribed with the words: GENERAL CARLETON OF WHITBY 1777 (Ossowski 2003:324; Wróblewska 2008:154). Lastly, remains of this wooden merchant ship suggest that it was a two or three-mast sailing ship with a cargo capacity of about 200 tons (Ossowski 2008:62).

The ship's bell and further findings alluded to an English origin of the wreck. Deeper research into English archives revealed information about the ship's owner, the crew, and voyages it took since birth to the sinking event (Baines 2008). Nathaniel Campion, born in Whitby, was the owner of the ship (Baines 2008:65). The vessel was named after Guy Carleton (1724-1808), a Canadian governor (1768-1778) and commander of the British troops in the American War for Independence (Baines 2008:69). Thomas Pyman was the first captain of the ship. *General Carleton of Whitby's* first voyage was from London to Hull (Baines 2008:71-72). After that, the vessel was sailing regularly between London to Ryga and Hull to other Baltic ports (Baines 2008:77-79). William Hustler became the captain of the ship in 1782. That year, during the American War, all available English fleets, including *General Carleton of Whitby*, came to America to help in the evacuation of Savannah (Baines 2008:84-85). The vessel came back from Port Royal, Jamaica to Portsmouth in February 1783 (Baines 2008:85). That same year, Nathaniel Campion died and the vessel became the property of his wife, Margaret. The new owner continued to utilize the vessel for transportation of goods. The vessel was mainly used to carry wood from Norway and other Baltic ports to England (Baines 2008:88-89). Records from the archive registries showed that there were 18 men aboard *General Carleton of Whitby* in the year of 1785: the captain,

Vessels' Type	No. of Forms from the Shipwreck
chamber pots	12
pot	2
bottles	5
jars	4
bowls	7
tea or coffeecups	4
mugs	1
mustard pots	2
lids	1
plates	5
total number of vessels	**43**

TABLE 1. LIST OF VESSELS FROM W-32 SHIPWRECK.

William Hustler; the first mate, John Swan; the second mate, Robert Clark; the carpenter, John Pearson; the cook, James Woolf; the ship's boy, John Frazer; sailors, John Johnson, Richard Trueman, James Hart, John Thompson, Richard Neal, John Noble, Nicolas Theaker, George Taylor, John Purvis, Andrew Gibson, Andrew Noble and Thomas Eades (Baines 2008:88-89). The ship's last voyage was planned to be from London to Stockholm. In Stockholm port, the ship was loaded with 230 heavy lasts of iron and remained in port until 30 August (Baines 2008:90). On 26 September 1785, *General Carleton of Whitby* encountered a big storm on the Baltic Sea while on route to England. A report by Helsingor in the Lloyd's registry under the date of 4 October states that *General Carleton of Whitby* was seen a week ago (27 September) on the Baltic Sea having been damaged and possibly changing route towards Gdansk (Baines 2008:90). However, the vessel never got to the port of Gdansk; instead, had probably stopped at a small harbor near Debki attempting to repair damages. It is possible that another change of weather sank the ship at that location. Another report from Lloyd's dated 21 September states that *General Carleton of Whitby* on route from Stockholm to London lost in the Baltic Sea and all crew missing, except three people (Baines 2008:92).

Information given in this report was not precise enough to estimate the accurate number of survivors. At the site of the wreckage explored by present day archaeologists, there were no remains of any crew found. It is almost certain that Capitan William Hustler died during the storm. Confirmation of his death could be alluded from a document stating that his son was adopted on 8 March 1786 by his grandmothers, Jane Hustler and Ann Brown (Baines 2008:94). It is almost certain that first mate, John Swan was a survivor of the shipwreck (Baines 2008:94).

Ceramics from W-32 wreck

During the underwater survey, 169 pottery sherds were excavated from the wreck. From those loads, there was a total of 44 vessels which were all found on the stern. After analyzing the different characteristics of the pottery, it could be distinguished into four groups: redware (33% of total collection), creamware and pearlware (39%), stoneware (21%) and porcelain (7%). The items found varied from plates, mustard pots, mugs, tea and coffee cups, bowls, and bottles (Table 1).

Analyzing the technology used in manufacturing those items exemplifies English creamware, probably from Staffordshire workshops and European porcelain made in Liverpool, Londyn-Chelsa, Leeds or Worcester manufactures (Wills 1964:40-41; Miller, Stone 1970:42, 91; Konietzka 1981:142-143; Savage 1981:124-129, 207-218; Barker 1990:166). A smaller group of storage containers represent jars, bottles, and pitchers. Brown stoneware jars were made in England, probably in London or Bristol (Savage 1981:48-53; Draper 1984:33-35, Hume 2001:168-180). Stoneware bottles and pitchers were made in Stadt Lohn-Freden and Frechen workshops (Elling 1994; Gaimster 1997:208-211). Containers for preparing or heating meals are represented only with two redware pots made in local (English) workshops (Hume 2001:81-87; Copland-Griffiths, Draper 2002:147-150). The last distinguished forms are London type redware chamber pots (Hume 2001:81-87; Copland-Griffiths, Draper 2002:147-150). It can be concluded that 91% of the collection were of tableware made in English workshops and factories. The other 9% were made in German workshops.

Though all the ceramics sunk with the ship in 1785, it does not mean they were all made in the same time period. According to the different shape of the ceramic, it is possible to trace its origin to a specific time period. For instance, redware pots and chamber pots might be widely dated throughout the 18th century (Hume 2001:81-87; Copland-Griffiths, Draper 2002:147-150). More recent to the date of sinking are pearlwares and creamwares which might be dated late 70's or early 80's of the 18th century (Baart, Krook, Lagerweij 1986:92-95; Barker 1990:182; Cantwell, diZerega Wall 2001:215). Porcelain is dated no earlier than the 80's of the 18th century (Wills 1964:40-41; Konietzka 1981:142-143; Savage 1981:124-129, 216-218). The list of pottery explored from the shipwreck is incomplete but still large enough to shed light on the role of pottery in the everyday life of sailors.

Wreck W-27, De Jonge Seerp

Wreck *W-27* was found in the Northern Port of Gdansk in 1985 (Smolarek 1987:484). Remains of the vessel were scattered in an area of about 2000 m² at a depth of 26 meters in which parts of the hull, keelson, and stern were found(Bednarz, Kaczor 2011:145).

According to registered data, it was estimated that a vessel found was about 30 m long and 6 meters wide (Bednarz 2007:468). During the excavation a well preserved stern with a clover-leaf-shaped head was found (Bednarz, Kaczor 2011:150, 155). Dendrochronological analysis provided information on the chronology of the wood used and the area it was cut from (Bednarz, Kaczor 2011:156). According to this data, wood was delivered from Lusatia and the southern shore of North Sea, cut no later than 1761 (Bednarz, Kaczor 2011:156).

After thirteen archaeological seasons over 10,000 artifacts from the wreck were explored (Bednarz 2007:468). During the excavation, parts of the merchant ship's armory were found: two swivel guns and a small cannon (Bednarz 2007:468). Coins discovered in the wreck were important to verify the chronology. A total of 77 coins were found, the latest one was one French sole dated 1778-1793 (Bednarz 2007:468). Dates ranging from 1784 to1789 were also on textile lead seals. The wheelbarrow was found with the date 1791 engraved onto the deck (Bednarz 2007:468).

Preserved structure of the ship and its raw materials collected during the excavation were enough to preliminarily identify the type of ship, its origin, and date of sinking. Wreck W-27 was identified as Dutch kuff which sank in the early 90's of the 18th century (Bednarz 2007:468). This information was verified with the research from the archives. According to historical data, the shipwreck actually turned out to be the remains of Frisian kuff *De Jonge Seerp*, skipped by Johannes

Vessels' Type	No of Forms from the Shipwreck
tea or coffeecups	15
saucers	20
plates	23
bowls	26
jugs	7
teapot	1
strainers	2
lids	3
spittoons	2
bottles	11
jars and pots	12
total number of vessels	**122**

TABLE 2. LIST OF VESSELS FROM W-27 SHIPWRECK.

Leenders (Bednarz, Kaczor 2011:158-159). Maritime accident reports from 1791 include information about the collision between Frisian kuff carrying unknown cargo and an English ship, *The Recovery* (Bednarz, Kaczor 2011:158-159). The collision had taken place in the Northern Port during its departure (Bednarz, Kaczor 2011, s. 159). Current studies are inconclusive; however, it is almost certain that the wreckage found is remains of *De Jonge Seerp*, which sunk in 1791.

Ceramics from W-27 wreck

From the shipwreck, there was 4071 pottery sherds found. The exact location of 88 pieces was uncertain; therefore, these pieces were excluded from analysis. The assemblage of 3983 shards was restored into 122 dishes. The largest number of vessels was located in the front and the middle part of the wreck. After analyzing the vessels, it can be brought down into several categories: redware (35%), whiteware (2%), greyware (1%), blackware (2%), stoneware (14%), faience (39%), and porcelain (7%). The most numerous in this group are

FIGURE 1. STORAGE VESSELS FROM SHIPWRECKS: W-32 AND W-27.

tableware: teapot, coffee pots, teacups, saucers, plates, bowls, and jugs (Table 2).

Technologically this group consists of faience including cream and pearlware, redware, blackware, and porcelain. Faience plates and bowls were made probably in Harlingeen workshops (Bartels 1999:215). Redware bowls and painted plates were also Frisian origins (Klijn 1995:96, 98; den Braven, Fermin, Groothedde 2008:47; Bartels 1999:139, 684; Havers, Klinkenberg, van Oostveen, Vermeulen 2006:30). One greyware jug was probably made in Danish workshops, but identification of it is still not certain. Creamware, pearlware, and blackware were produced in Staffordshire factories (Barker 1990; Thijssen 1993). Porcelain saucers and teacups are of good, quality Chinese origin (Baart, Krook, Lagerweij 1986:95-102, Carswell 2000:184-185; Schönborg 2002:218-219).

Storage vessels were represented by bottles, jars, tripots, and pots. Technologically they are characterized as redware, whiteware, and stoneware. Most workshops were precisely identified. Stoneware bottles were made in Frechen and Stadt LohnVreden workshops (Gaimster 1997:279; Adler 2005:26-66). Redware jars and whiteware pots are of Frisian production. Whiteware workshops in that region were located in Leeuwarden and Lammer (Bartels 1999:163). Jars were most probably made in one of the big production centers, like Leeuwarden (Klijn 1995:96, 98; den Braven, Fermin, Groothedde 2008:47). Tripot storage vessels are most probably from Oosterhout or Bergen op Zoom (van Gangelen, Lenting 1993:185).

Typical kitchen-ware was not found from the wreck, although, it is possible that some redware vessels were possibly used for preparing meals and eating. The last group of vessels was categorized as hygienic vessels and was represented with two spittoons. Two examples found on the wreckage were made in Northern Netherlands and Staffordshire regions (Kilarska 2003:138).

Analysis of the assemblage from the wreck is clear and dated as a whole archaeological complex at 1791. It was found that there were also some differences in the chronology of the vessels. Chinese porcelain (Qianlong) might be considered as an antique. Danish pitchers and Dutch faiences were made in the 60's of the 18th century (Bartels 1999:870; Carswell 2000:186; Schönborg 2002:218). Redware Frisian vessels are widely dated at the 2nd half of the 18th and beginning of the 19th century (before 1815) (Bartels 1999:139, 684; Havers, Klinkenberg, van Oostveen, Vermeulen 2006:30). Frisian faiences and English ware are dated approximately at late 80 and 90's of 18th century (Baart, Krook, Lagerweij 1986:92-95; Barker 1990, s. 182; Bartels 1999:163, 185; Cantwell, diZerega Wall 2001:215). Stoneware vessels were made at the end of the 18th century (Gaimster 1997:208-211; Heege 2009:22-23).

In the *W-27* case, it can be assumed that most of the pottery from the vessel was found. The ship probably sunk immediately after the collision which is why it was not robbed and the cargo, equipment and other items were preserved as a whole, unlike the *W-32* wreck. Although, the entire assemblage is still not complete.

Ceramics on 18th century merchant ships

It is a great scientific endeavor to compare two well dated pottery assemblages from shipwrecks. Both vessels sunk in similar time 1785 and 1791. Different origin of ships, English and Frisian, might be used to observe differences between those vessels.

Three general groups of ceramic forms were distinguished on both ships: tableware, storage vessels, and hygienic vessels.

Storage vessels are divided into three general forms: bottles, jars, and pots (Figure 1). At *General Carleton of Whitby*, those types of equipment comprised of 18% of all pottery. At *De Jonge Seerp*, storage vessels represented 19% of the total group. It is an obvious conclusion that except for pottery containers, food and drinks were stored in wooden, glass, and pewter vessels. However, food and drinks stored in pottery containers had a better taste than the ones stored in wooden and pewter ones. Bottles and pitchers were used for wine and beer storage (Gaimster 1997:209; Smith 2008:12-13). The presence of wine on board is also confirmed by wineglasses. On the *W-32*, bottles had the holding capacity of 1.5 liters to 5 liters. On the *W-27*, there were more bottles found, but their holding capacity ranged between 1.5 liters and 2.5 liters. Historical data of the ships' bills from the 18th century confirmed that beer and wine were a part of the basic menu for sailors (Łączyńska 2012:294). In general, it is very characteristic for 18th century ships to have wine and beer bottles which were made in Stad Lohn-Vreden or Frechen workshops.

Another group of containers are jars. Those found on the *W-32* were English made and those excavated from the *W-27* were Frisian made. The origin of pottery used on specific ships was not a coincidence but rather a rule because the pottery was bought at the place of origin. It is not clear what could have been held in the English jars but the Frisian pots were specifically made to hold butter and eggs (Malaguzzi 2009:198). These products appear in sailors' bills from the end of the 18th century (Łączyńska 2012:294-295). Butter was a very basic food addition, but eggs were eaten rather occasionally. The last group of storage vessels was those which could have a variety of uses, all different kinds of pots were present on both wrecks.

Tableware was the largest group of pottery (52% on W-32 and 78% on W-27). These types of forms were probably used both for serving meals, and in some cases, for preparing meals. Three general groups were present on both ships: specific forms, plates and bowls, and drinking vessels. The presence of the first group was able to reveal the food preferences of the ship's crew during the voyages (Figure 2). On the *W-32* wreck, two mustard pots were found. This is an interesting find because mustard, as well as other spices, appear more often in sailors' diet in the second half of the 18th century, but is still not common (Łączyńska 2012:294-295). Another specific form in the *W-27* assemblage is a lobster dish. It is a very unique find from shipwrecks and, according to recent publications, have no analogy in that type of context. From the Frisian wreck, the lid of a sugar pot was also excavated. Sugar was an expensive commodity which was usually bought in small amounts (Łączyńska 2012:294-295). The last type of vessel in this group is Frisian faience strainers. Strainers were used for drying boiled fish (van Dam 2000:185). Those strainers were found on *W-27* confirming that fish was served on board.

There was a big variety in tableware on the ship, mainly different types of plates and bowls (Figure 2). On both ships, English creamware sets were found: royal edge plates, mocha bowls, and tortoiseshell bowls. Redware plates and bowls and faience plates were also registered.

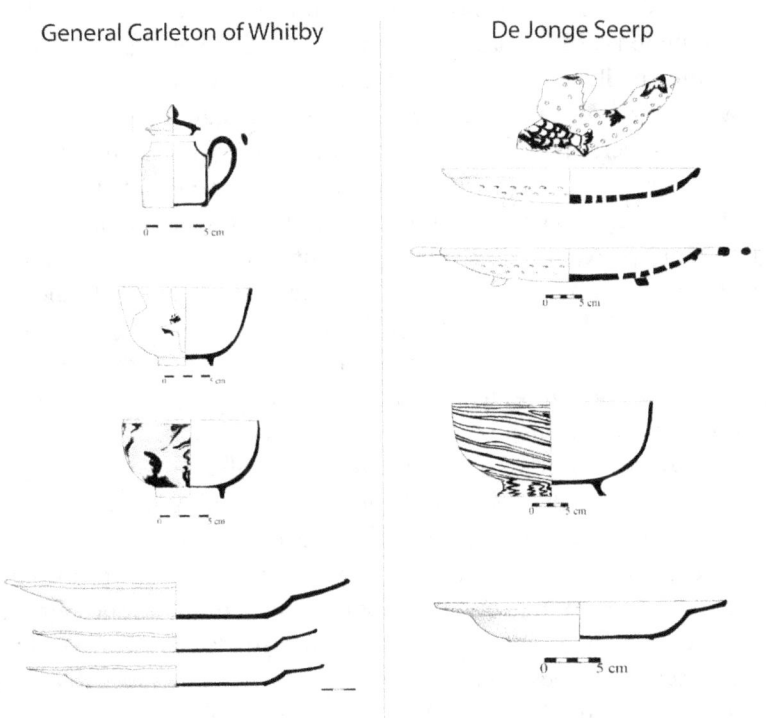

FIGURE 2. TABLEWARE (SPECIFIC FORMS, PLATES AND BOWLS) FROM SHIPWRECKS: *W-32* AND *W-27*.

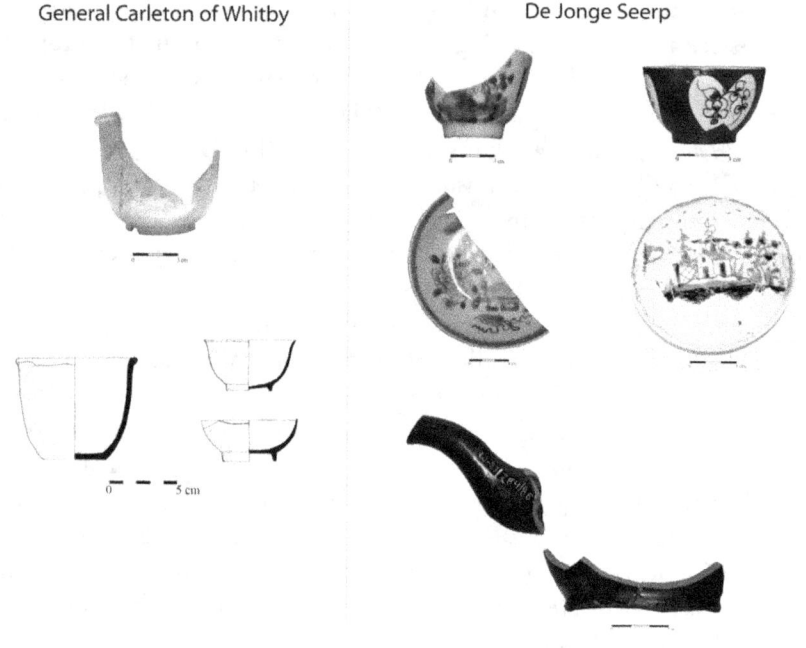

FIGURE 3. TEA AND COFFEE VESSELS FROM SHIPWRECKS: W-32 AND W-27.

Such a great variety of tableware suggests that there was a great selection of meals served on board; however, because there were no remains of food found, this cannot be confirmed. According to historical sources, there were weekly rationed amounts of meat. The most common kinds were salted pork and beef (Coy, Hamilton-Dyer, Oxley 2005:564-573). Analyses of plate sizes show that shallow and smaller-in-size plates were used for serving meat were found on English shipwreck. The bigger and deeper plates were used for serving soups. These types of dishes were found on both shipwrecks. There were also other shapes of bowls found on both wrecks which might be interpreted as vessels for serving different type of fruits and vegetables which were acquired fresh at every port visited (Łączyńska 2012:295-296).

Other tableware forms were drinking vessels (Figure 3). On both ships, tea and coffee sets were present. Those drinks seemed to be important for sailors. Drinking coffee was also confirmed with parts of coffee mills found on the W-32 and the W-27. English sailors drank tea and coffee from creamware and white stoneware cups, and Frisian sailors preferred Chinese porcelain and creamware. The presence of at least three examples of the same type of decorations and shape of cups and saucers suggests that on the W-32 there were at least two sets (for six persons), and on the W-27 at least three sets (for six persons). At De Jonge Seerp, tea was served in blackware teapots. Drinking coffee and tea are also widely historically confirmed (Łączyńska 2012:296).

The last category of pottery might be hygienic vessels (Figure 4). At General Carleton of Whitby, there were assemblages of redware chamber pots found. At De Jonge Seerp, there were two spittoons present. Spittoons were used for spitting tobacco in enclosed places. This find indicates individual habits of sailors. Twelve chamber pots from the W-32 with scratches on the inside were at first interpreted as bowls for common use. However, further research and iconography (for example: "Invasion" by W. Hogarth, 1756) showed that there was another use of this vessel on board. It is possible that chamber pots were used as tar containers. This idea may be partly confirmed by a broken chamber pot with a round hole made in the body from the inside. The size and the way the hole was made fit a metal object used for heating tar found on the wreck. The metal objects and brushes found indicate that they were used to maintain and repair the ship's hull.

According to both assemblages of pottery it is important to identify the number of sailors on board. In case of General Carleton of Whitby, information is very precise. There were eighteen young men on the ship. The number of sailors on the Frisian vessel is not that certain. On this type of ship there were usually eight to ten sailors but it was possible to sail with six people. This information compared with number of vessels suggest that sailors preferably ate the ceramic dishes.

Comparing both collections we could determine the basic diet of sailors from the different forms of vessels present. For certain, both crews had soups, fruits, (probably) bread with butter and had drunk beer, wine, coffee and tea. There are also some possible differences indicated by types of dishes from English shipwreck that the English crew was eating meat which might be served with mustard. The Frisian sailors preferred fish and seafood but that does not exclude meat at all.

According to types and dating of vessels it is also possible to indicate some individual's habits. It is likely we can specify those preferences according to preserved examples. At least one Frisian sailor chewed tobacco and used spittoons. Some antique individual vessels found on the Frisian ship could indicate that they were family souvenirs or brought from foreign voyages. In this context, the Danish pitcher, the Dutch faience jug, or the Chinese porcelain might be considered a foreign or family souvenir.

The amount and quality of analyzed pottery imply that there were probably not many "status" differences between sailors. None of the rare items found represent a higher economic status of the crew. But, on the other hand, the presence of tea and coffee sets or antique vessels might be considered as less common, and thus perhaps more noble.

FIGURE 4. HYGIENIC VESSELS FROM SHIPWRECKS: W-32 AND W-27.

Analyzing products from pottery workshops enables archaeologists to determine the place of origin of the ship. The term might refer to "construction place", "legal place", or "economic place" (Kleij 1997:181). Pottery from wrecks might help pinpoint the economic place of origin—the place where they began and ended their journeys.

It may be assumed that the pottery on board was rarely changed. Eventually, new vessels were added to old sets. In both wrecks considered, according to historical data, economic place of origin is easily pinpointed. For the *General Carleton of Whitby* it was England – Whitby, Hull, and London; and for *De Jonge Seerp* it was Frisia – one of Frisian ports or Amsterdam.

Most of the pottery from the English ship came from local manufactures (91%), and storage vessels were made in Germany (9%). On the Frisian ship, Dutch pottery represents 43%, English ware – 41%, German stoneware – 9% and Chinese porcelain – 7%.

These statistics are becoming a "mirror" phenomena for pottery products present in local markets in England and Netherlands at the end of 18th century. Similar to Frisian wreck groups of pottery that were excavated in Amsterdam (Gawronsky 2011). Also, similar to those from *W-32* pottery assemblages that are known from many ports of England such as London, Liverpool, or Chester (Davey 2008).

Concluding investigative studies of the entire group of finds, and comparing them to the situation in the local market of the region in one specific period, might give the most precise results. In many cases, casual and low-quality vessels workshops (like redware) might indicate the economic origin of the ship. It must also be considered that some pottery workshops and manufacturers specialized in supplying ships with vessels. These types of workshops were, for example, Frechen and Stadt Lohn-Freden.

Conclusions

Ceramic assemblages from wrecks W-32 and W-27 are a valuable resource for studying aspects of everyday life onboard merchant ships. Different origins of both ships, English and Frisian, gave the possibility of searching for dissimilarities in aspects of everyday life. Further comparative studies with other vessels might confirm the interpretations contained here. Published ceramic assemblages from 18th-century wrecks like *HMS Swift*, *Boscawen*, *Machault*, *Texelstroom IV*, and *Älvsnabben* have drawn similar conclusions. However, these examples are still not enough to get a broader understanding of social phenomena. In some cases, the presentation of the material has not allowed for detailed statistical analyses.

Pottery and other items used during the sea and ocean voyages are part of material culture, which is still being researched in an unsatisfactory matter. Comparing different groups of findings from shipwrecks and city excavations with studies and analyses of scientific disciplines, as well as historical and iconographic sources could give a better view of everyday life, peoples' habits, and economy in the past.

This paper is an attempt at such a study which may provide new understandings of past centuries.

References

ADLER, BEATRIX
2005 *Early stoneware steins from the Les Paul Collection: a survey of all German stoneware centers from 1500 to 1850*, Dillingen.

BAINES, STEPHEN
2008 The History of General Carleton, and of some of those connected with her, In: *The General Carleton Shipwreck, 1785*, Gdansk: 65-94.

BAART, JAN M., KROOK, W., LAGERWEIJ, A.C.
1986 Opgravingen aan de Oostenburgermiddenstraat, In: *Van VOC tot Werkspoor. Het Amsterdamse industrierrein Oostenburg*: 81-142.

BARKER, DAVID
1990 *William Greatbatch: A Staffordshire Potter*, London.

BARTELS, MICHIEL
1999 *Steden in Scherven*, Zwolle-Deventer.

BEDNARZ, TOMASZ
2007 Wrak W-27 jako przykład osiemnastowiecznego holenderskiego statku handlowego, In: *XV Sesja Pomorzoznawcza*, Elbląg: 467-476.

BEDNARZ, TOMASZ, KACZOR, DARIUSZ.
2011 Próba identyfikacji XVIII-wiecznego wraka W-27 na podstawie analizy porównawczej źródeł archeologicznych i archiwalnych, *Acta Universitatis Nicolai Copernici, Archeologia XXXI, Archeologia Podwodna 6*:142-163.

DEN BRAVEN, J.A., FERMIN, H.A.C., GROOTHEDDE, MICHAEL
2008 Van achetuin tot achterbuurt. Archeologisch an historisch onderzoek aan de Wanne – Lievenheerseeg te Zutphen. *Zutphense Archeologische Publicaties 35*.

CANTWELL, ANNE-MARIE, DIZEREGA WALL, DIANA
2001 *Unearthing Gotham, The Archaeology of New York City*, Yale University Press.

CARSWELL JOHN
2000 *Blue & White. Chinese porcelain around the Word*, The British Museum Press London.

COPLAND-GRIFFITHS, PATRICIA, DRAPER, JOE
2002 *Dorset Country Pottery. The kilns of the Verwood district*, Wiltshire

COY J., HAMILTON-DYER S., OXLEY I.
2005 Meat and fish: the bone evidence, In: *Before the Mast: Life and Death Aboard the Mary Rose. The Archaeology of the Mary Rose*: 564-586.

DĄBAL, JOANNA.
2008 An attempt to recreate the ceramic vessel selection, In: *The General Carleton Shipwreck, 1785*, Gdansk: 223-234.

VAN DAM, JAN D.
2004 *Delffse Porceleyne. Dutch delftware 1620-1850*, Amsterdam.

DAVEY, PETER, J.
2008 Merseyside: the archaeological evidence for trade, *Journal of the Merseyside Archaeological Society, vol. 12*, Liverpool: 161-171.

DRAPER JOE
1984 Post-Medieval Pottery 1650-1800, Shire.

ELLING WILHEL
1994 *Steinzeug aus Stadtlohn und Vreden*, Vreden.

GAIMSTER, DAVID.
1997 *German stoneware 1200-1900. Archaeology and Cultural History*, London.

VAN GANGELEN, H., LENTING, J.J.
1993 Steengoed, In: *Schans op de grens*: 309 – 333.

GAWRONSKI, JERZY
2012 *Amsterdam Ceramics: A City's History and an Archaeological Ceramics Catalogue (1175-2011)*, Amsterdam.

HAVERS, GEERTJE, KLINKENBERG, VICTOR, VAN OOSTVEEN, JAN, VERMEULEN, BAART
2006 Materiaal uit gesloten vondsten, Catalogus, *Razende mannen onrutige vrouwen. Archeologisch en historisch ondrzoek naar de vroegmiddeleeuwse nederzetting, een adellijke hofstede en St. Elizabethsgasthuis te Deventer*, Deventer: 1-72.

HEEGE, ANDREAS
2009 Steinzeug *in der Schweiz (14.-20.Jh.). Ein Überblick über die Funde im Kanton Bern und den Stand der Forschung zu deutschem, französischem und englischem Steinzeug in der Schweiz*, Bern.

HUME, IAN N.
2001 *If These Pots Could Talk. Collecting 2 000 Years of British Household Pottery*, Hannover-London.

KLEIJ, PIETER.
1997 The identification of a ship's place of departure with the help of artifacts, In: *Artifacts from Wrecks. Dated Assemblages from the Late Middle Ages to the Industrial Revolution. Oxbow Monograph 84*:181-190.

KILARSKA, ELŻBIETA
2003 Fajanse z Delft w dawnym Gdańsku, Gdańsk.

KLIJN E.M.Ch.F.
1995 *Lead-glazed earthenware in the Netherlands*, Arnhem.

KONIETZKA L.P.
1981 *Europees Porselein*, Utrecht/Antwepen.

ŁACZYNSKA, EWA
2012 Na co dzień i od święta – menu gdańskich ludzi morza w XVIII wieku, In: Historia naturalna jedzenia. Między antykiem a XIX wiekiem; Gdańsk: 293-306.

MALAGUZZI S.
2009 Wokół stołu, Warszawa.

MILLER J.J., STONE L. M.,
1970 Eighteenth-Century Ceramics from fort Michilimackinac. *A study in Historical Archaeology*, Smithsonian Institute Press, Washington D.C.

OSSOWSKI, WALDEMAR
2003 Archeologiczne badania wraków statków żaglowych z XVIII wieku prowadzone przez Centralne muzeum Morskie w Gdańsku, In: *XIII Sesja Pomorzoznawcza, tom 2*:313-334.

2007 Badania nowo odkrytych wraków z XVIII-XIX wieku w polskich obszarach morskich w latach 2003-2005, In: *XV Sesja Pomorzoznawcza, materiały z konferencji 30 listopada – 02 grudnia 2005*:477 – 490.

2008 Archaeological underwater excavation of wreck W-32, *The General Carleton Shipwreck, 1785*, Gdansk: 35-64.

SAVAGE, GEORGE
1981 *English Ceramics*, New York, org. ed 1961.

SCHÖNBORG G.N.
2002 Kinesiskt porslin i Stockholm, In: *Upptaget. Arkeologi i Stockholm inför 2000-talet*: 215-224.

SMITH, FREDERICK H.
2008 *The Archaeology of Alcohol and drinking*, University Press of Florida.

SMOLAREK, PRZEMYSŁAW
1987 Badania podwodne w Bałtyku w latach 1979-1986, *Kwartalnik Historii Kultury Materialnej, R. 35*, nr 3:465-495.

THIJSSEN J.R.
1993 Engelse indutriële keramiek, In: *Schans op de Grens*: 281-308.

WILLS, GEOFFREY
1964 *The country life book of English China*, London.

WRÓBLEWSKA, ELŻBIETA
2008 The ship's bell, 1777, *The General Carleton Shipwreck, 1785*, Gdansk: 151-158.

. . . .

Joanna A. Dąbal
Institute of Archaeology and Ethnology
Gdansk Univeristy
Poland
Bielańska 5 st.
80-851 Gdańsk
Poland
tel./fax. +48(58)523 37 10
joannadabal@gazeta.pl

Bajo Hornos Reef: A Trap for Ships and Cultural Materials

Ricardo Borrero
Roberto Junco

Little attention has been given to the underwater cultural resources of Veracruz, one of the most important ports in the Americas from the 16th to the 19th century. An archaeological rescue carried out in August 2010 by the Subdirección de Arqueología Subacuática (SAS) at the Bajo Hornos reef in the southern part of the harbor yielded several archaeological remains that testify to the port's commercial dealings, as well as to its intense nautical activity. For more than three decades, SAS, the branch of Instituto Nacional de Antropologia e Historia (INAH) in charge of underwater archaeology in Mexico, has been active in diverse projects in interior waters such as lakes and caves as well as in the Gulf of Mexico, the Pacific Ocean and the Caribbean Sea (Luna 2011:123). The survey carried out was not extensive to the whole reef, but rather to a small area affected by the construction of a Marina in the vicinity and the canal that was dug for it; regardless, the opportunity to work there opened up a window into the underwater archaeological record of Veracruz. Different ship remains were identified and recorded, presenting interesting clues to shipbuilding traditions used in the Gulf of Mexico in historic times. Among these, a 6 by 6 meter structure was excavated, which appears to correspond to the remains of the hull of Basque ship. The sample of artifacts collected and documented includes ceramics, glass fragments and ammunition that together present an interesting portrait of the products used and consumed by the population of New Spain, later Mexico.

Bajo Hornos Reef, Veracruz

The port of Veracruz was the first Spanish settlement on what is today Mexican territory and by far its most important harbor. Discovered in 1518 by Grijalva and established as a town of the crown by Cortés in 1519, it took eighty years and four attempts at allocation prior to the final decision to set the city in La Gallega reef, where the first stones of the mighty fortress of San Juan de Ulua were laid (Junco 2012: 96). Bajos Hornos is located south of La Gallega. It forms part of the Veracruz reef system, one of the biggest in the Gulf of Mexico. The eleven reefs that compose the system are set in a pattern that follows the bow shaped coastal line. "The seabed is topographically complex due to the presence of shallow banks, reefs and islands forming a series of channels with variable horizontal dimensions and depths" (Salas-Pérez and Granados-Barba 2008: 284). Although navigation would have been unsafe and difficult, the location of the port was taken based on the strategic properties of the island of San Juan de Ulua and the surrounding natural barriers that helped to shelter the fleets coming from Seville against the raging northern winds known as *Nortes*. These winds affect the area between the months of October and February and are the major cause of naval accidents in the area to this day. *Nortes* are a phenomenon resulting from the violent access of polar continental air masses to the Gulf of Mexico, and vary between 40 and 120 km per hour, frequently attaining hurricane status (Montero et al. 1996: 43). As described by routers and documents dating back to the 16th century, these feared winds frequently untied ships fastened by iron chains to the walls of the fortress, or made them crash against each other when the port was crowded, causing the wreckage of a great quantity of anchored ships throughout its history (Haring 1918: 204).

During the one-week rescue fieldwork carried out in 2010, several shipwreck remains were located in the surveyed area of the reef. The efforts were hindered by hurricane Karl, which interrupted the archaeological intervention. Work continued after the event but the excavated trenches and materials located were already covered with sediment and trash carried by the overflow of rivers nearby (Carrillo 2011: 26). Further work on site is programmed for this year, with plans to relocate sites and collect data. One of the very first finds consisted in a couple of wood planks articulated by two 3.3 cm diameter treenails. The biggest one measures 170 x 30 x 20 cm. Excavating the perimeter with a water lift, two smaller planks were found joined with square nails and treenails. Some meters to the northeast, isolated wooden remains were also found, severely affected by the dredging of the channel. After mapping and documenting with photographs, this cluster of materials registered as *Orejas* and *Jiníguaro* sites were reburied; no further research has been carried out.

A less disturbed site, known as *Reina*, was found in the southeast area of the reef, at the end of the canal being dug by the marina during construction. In order

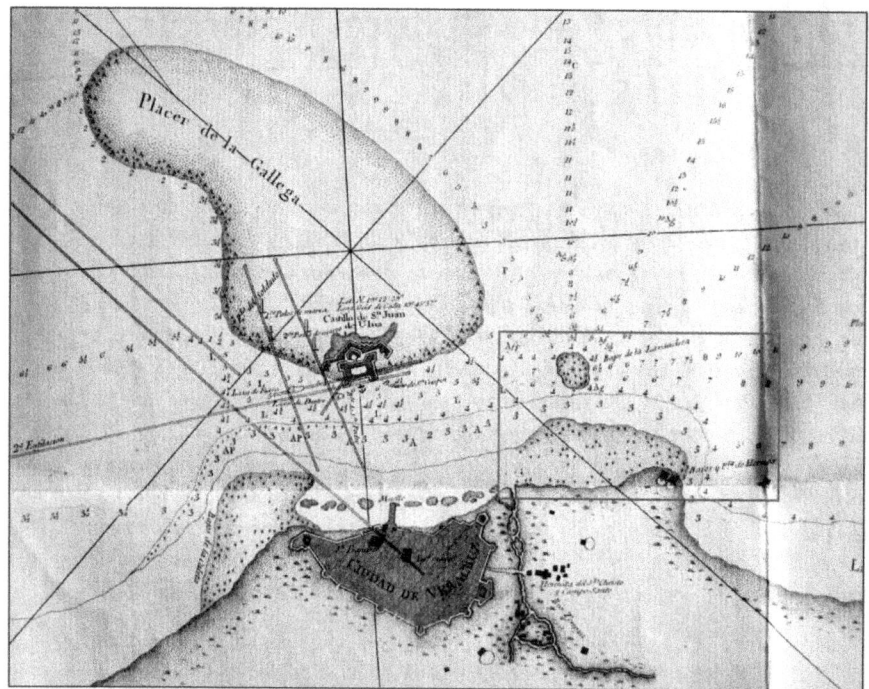

FIGURE 1. ANCIENT MAP OF THE PORT OF VERACRUZ MADE BY DON BERNARDO DE ORTA IN 1798. COPYRIGHT INAH-SAS ARCHIVE.

to protect such archaeological findings, the planned course of the waterway was modified (Carrillo 2011: 21). The two wood structures that make up the site are located at a depth of 2 meters and rest 10 m apart from each other (Figure 2). The smaller one seems to be part of the hull of a minor vessel with the interior facing the surface. It was covered with some river stones, dead coral, and sand in which were found ceramics and glass fragments from different time periods. The structure is made up of eleven planks, the largest 2.3 m by 26 cm and 6 cm thick, jointed with twelve frame timbers. They are held together with 46 square iron nails of 1 cm thickness—of which only the holes in the concretion left in wood remain—and 16 treenails with an average diameter of 3 cm. The presence of diagonal planks, which form a 45-degree angle with the frame timbers—apparently to strengthen the assemblage—plus the absence of curvature, led to the hypothesis that it was part of the stern panel of a ship. Further southwest, the other structure encountered on the site was located and partially excavated. It comprises 11 longitudinal strakes and 16 futtocks, tightly arranged, showing evidence of a solid constructed hull. According to Carrillo, the remains pertained to the port or starboard side of a ship under the waterline. Some of the longitudinal strakes are 5 m long by 30 m wide. The outer hull is facing the surface, and square, concreted iron nails and treenails can be noted throughout. Triangular incisions around the iron nails on the strakes were documented (Figure 3). They measure 2.5 cm on each side with that same depth, and are a trademark of Basque shipbuilding tradition as suggested by Robert Grenier, who led the excavation of the Red Bay wreck, a 16th century Basque whaler, well documented by National Parks Canada. Furthermore, a lead sheet was found associated to the hull. Lead sheeting of the hull is traditional of Spanish and Portuguese ships of the 16th and early 17th Centuries. However, it is not conclusive that this is part of the sheeting of the hull, and could well be a fix to stop leaks in the hull—a technique used until the 18th Century. Other related nautical artifacts are an iron hook, as well as an iron axis sheave with some rope still attached. These artifacts undoubtedly pertained to the rigging of ships, but it is unlikely they belonged to the remains of the ship described above.

Formation Processes in Bajo Hornos

To study the surveyed area of Bajo Hornos, the first step was to understand the formation process of the archaeological deposits within the reef. Thus, archival and bibliographical research was conducted to comprehend historical currents and wind patterns that constrained and affected its nautical dynamics, as well as the relation between the reefs and the port. From this analysis, it was conclusive that before the renovations of the harbor in the 20th Century, Bajo Hornos acted as a trap for ships and cultural materials deposited on the seabed due to the currents running from North to South. Furthermore, the dramatic changes in the port, mainly extensive dredging, new wharfs, and breakwaters, distorted the setting of artifacts already deposited in the seabed in prior periods, moving them south to Bajo Hornos and consolidating the current archaeological record. The context itself, when excavated, showed that there is no readable stratigraphy but rather a mix of materials moving around the reef. This is because the slow growth of coral gives way to a long exposition of the sites, which get contaminated with artifacts from close wrecks and

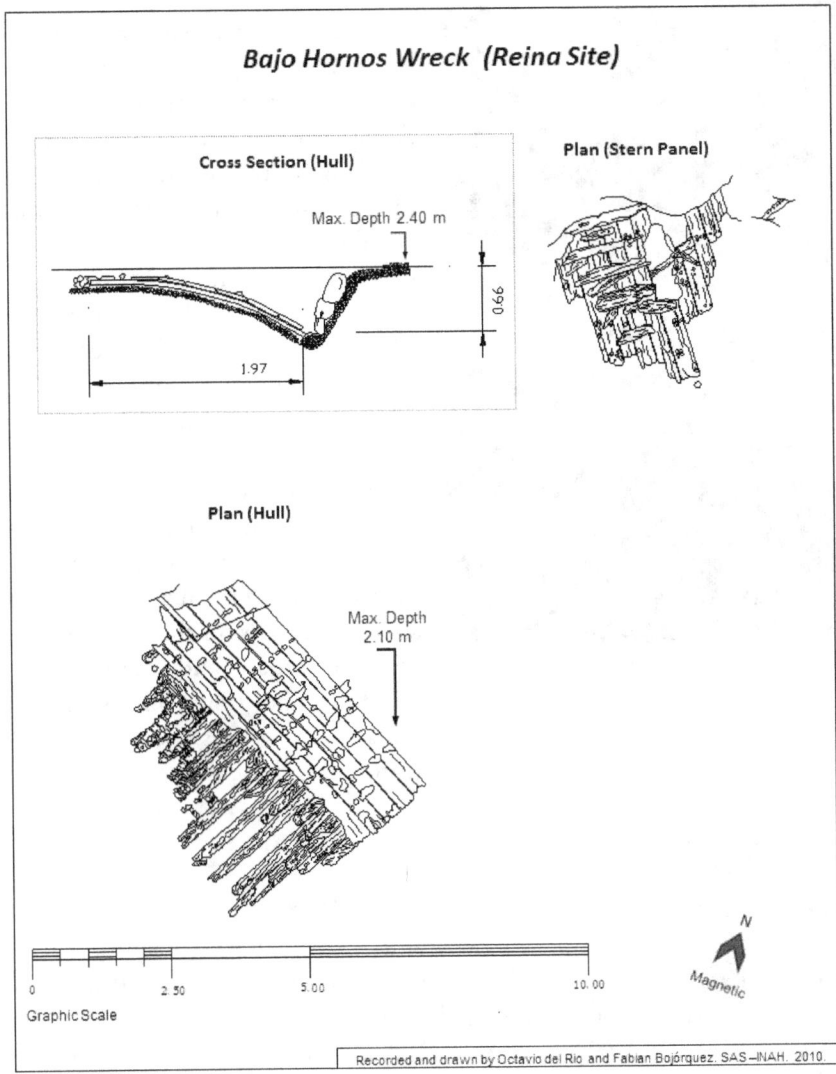

FIGURE 2. BAJO HORNOS WRECK (REINA SITE). MODIFIED PLAN AND CROSS SECTION. ORIGINALLY DROWN BY OCTAVIO DEL RIO AND FABIAN BOJÓRQUEZ. COPYRIGHT INAH-SAS ARCHIVE.

other materials moved around by human and natural disturbances (Muckelroy 1976: 283). These wrecks were carried southeast until they got trapped in the Lavandera and Bajo Hornos reefs (Carrillo 2011: 17). Sediment is constantly being deposited in the reef from city pollution to be then blown away with the *Nortes*.

Basque Shipbuilding Tradition

One of the strongest correlations between the Reina site or Bajo Hornos wreck and 16th Century Biscayan shipwrecks is the use of a combination of oak treenails of about 25 mm and iron nails of between 10 and 12 mm to fasten planks and frames of the hull. According to Loewen, the use of both iron and wooden nails distinguishes Biscayan shipwrecks from northerly wrecks, such as the Mary Rose, which have only treenails; and from more southerly wrecks, especially from the Mediterranean, which contained only iron nails (Loewen 1998: 193). Considering this combination, Red Bay research concluded that the treenails were used to make the assembly stronger, when planks and frames were already joined with ferrous nails. Furthermore, another characteristic of Basque naval construction tradition is the triangular marks or countersinks at the outboard face of the planks around the iron nails which were made with a small adze to keep "...the drill from slipping or from splitting the wood and later, it ensured that the head of the nail did not protrude from the surface of the plank" (Loewen 1998: 194). Countersinks also contributed to hold the resin applied to protect the hull and the nail (Loewen 2007: 118). Another important characteristic of 16th Century Basque ships is the use of oak in frames, the planking of the hull and in various other parts of the structure. Archaeobotanical analysis of a plank sample taken from the large structure at the Reina site by Susana Xelhuantzi and Mariana Tovalín of the Subdirección de Laboratorios (INAH) was identified as *Quercus sp*. Furthermore, the same genus was identified for a sample of a treenail taken at the site. Oak matches with the wood type utilized for the *Red Bay* vessel treenails. Unfortunately the analysis could not determine the geographical origin of the woods.

Minor Basque Wooden Vessels

At the beginning of the 16th Century, hundreds of vessels of under 25 tons sailed in the ports of Biscay and Guipúzcoa. Based on the documentary evidence, Michael Barkham asserts that the biggest ones were the *lanchas*, specifically conceived for the military purpose of protecting the Atlantic coasts of the Peninsula and the English Channel. A bit smaller, *pinazas*, were mainly utilized for tuna, hake and bream fishing, but also for local privateering, towing big ships, coastal transportation,

FIGURE 3. TRIANGULAR COUNTERSINKS OF THE BAJO HORNOS WRECK, WHICH IS CHARACTERISTIC OF BASQUE SHIPBUILDING TECHNIQUES. OCTAVIO DEL RIO. COPYRIGHT INAH-SAS ARCHIVE.

and inshore trade. Between the minor mid types were the *galeones, chalupas* and *pinazas*, used for inshore fishing, whale hunting, coastal transportation, privateering, and towing. Finally, *bateles* and *esquifes* were even smaller than the aforementioned; they were usually towed or carried onboard bigger ships as auxiliary boats (Barkham, 1998: 202). During the first half of the 16th Century, *pinaza* seemed to be a generic term to vaguely refer to both big and small inshore fishing vessels (Gaiztarro 1956). In turn, *galeones* and *chalupas*, frequently encompassed under the generic term, were more technical words to describe small open vessels, propelled by oars and sails and used for whale hunting and sardine, codfish, and conger eel fishing. Although the word *galeones* acquired a new meaning around 1550, when it started to be used as reference to much bigger and armed ships employed in transatlantic trade, presumably there were very few differences between these two types of vessels during the first part of the 16th Century. According to Barkham, *galeones* may have been constructed using the Atlantic lapstrake or clinker built technique, and *chalupas* using the Mediterranean carvel planking or strake to top tradition. Judging by the measurements of the futtocks and frame timbers found between the structures, the wreck of the Reina site is likely to be a minor wooden vessel. Applying the equations derived from the suggested proportions of ships contained in the first Spanish, Portuguese and English naval treatises of Escalante de Mendoza (2 depth: 5 beam: 7 length) or even Tomé Cano and Joao Baptista Lavanha (1 depth: 2 beam: 3 length) to the average lengths of the better preserved futtocks and frame timber remains, the measurements of the Reina site wreck suggest it to be a vessel of less than 15 m. This length coincides with some *mayor pinazas* sizes, which notwithstanding, according to the documentary evidence analyzed by Barkham, should have 0,43 depth: 1 beam: 3,65 length as proportions. So, as its origin, the type to which the Reina ship pertained will remain undisclosed until further field seasons shed some light on the upper works, number of masts and lengths of longitudinal and transversal structural remains, as well as the keelson, the futtocks, and the master frame.

Artifacts

The archaeological materials recovered from Bajo Hornos are made up mainly of ceramics and glass. Analysis of over 300 objects collected in the survey area was carried out. Among the ceramics there is English porcelain from the early 18th to late 19th Centuries, some medical containers, cups, bowls and plates of Creamware; transfer printed ceramics identified as Davenport "Tendrill" from between 1794-1887, Liverpool "Lasso" from between 1840 and 1871, and Staffordshire ware from 1845 – as well as others with diverse motifs, such as Chinese styles and landscapes. This raises a question in regard to the trade of Transfer printed wares with Chinese motifs imported to Mexico. Did Transfer printed wares with Chinese designs substitute the Chinese porcelains of the old trade route of the Manila Galleon (1565 to 1815)? In any case the motifs kept being acquired in Mexico at a cheaper price. Mayolica plates and bowls make up a substantial part of the collection and the types – San Luis, San Agustin, Aucilla and Aranama – were identified. Stoneware, such as gin bottles, 19th Century beer bottles and Bristol ginger bottles are also present. Interestingly, of the 16th to 18th Century olive jars discovered, several contained tar

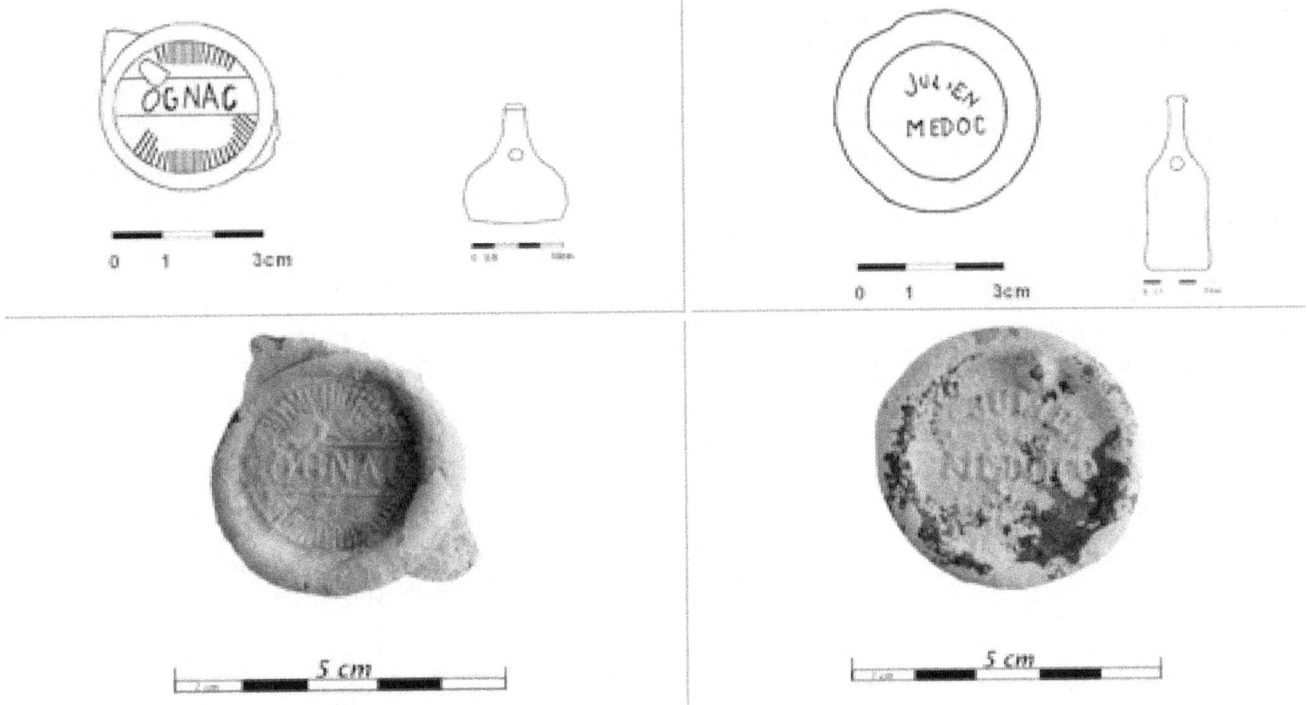

FIGURE 4. MARKS OF XIX CENTURY FRENCH WINE FORM THE REGION OF MEDOC AND COGNAC. COPYRIGHT INAH-SAS ARCHIVE.

remains used for the caulking of ships. Two orange bricks were located, along with many pieces of glass pertaining to ink containers, a candlestick holder, wine bottle caps, and bottles such as 19th Century French wine from the regions of Cognac and Medoc (Figure 4). Finally, two ammunitions of different kinds were recovered, one of them round and the other pointed. Once the collection was catalogued, the interpretation of groups and single objects was integrated into a coherent discourse of Mexican history to be exhibited to the public. For example, the English ceramics that range from the 18th to the 19th Centuries reflect the historical tension between the crowns of Spain and England on trade restrictions – smuggling that gave way to open commerce. Other objects in the collection reiterate the presence of foreign powers on Mexican territory during the 19th Century, such as a bullet from the period of the second French invasion in 1862 with the famous storming of the San Juan de Ulua fortress, among others.

Historical archaeologists usually engage with artifacts in contexts related to their consumption, however, the study of shipwrecks has been an interesting aspect of historical archaeological inquiry that has traditionally looked at aspects of exchange, since they often reveal the sort of items that traveled the trade routes across continents. That is, of course, those items that survive the conditions of submerged sites, such as ceramics; "Studies of ceramics recovered from shipwreck excavations have proven particularly useful in understanding the nature of international trade" (Barker 2006: 220). Maritime archaeology has therefore played an important role in the study of global trade and local uses, since not only does it look at the nature of shipments and the movement of material culture throughout the world, but in terms of the local context, with the ship itself becoming a local moving society. The case for the materials in Bajo Hornos, where the remains have been deposited from port activities and ships wrecked in the area but not on the reef itself, permits us to look in general terms at these artifacts as meaningful evidence of trade and consumption patterns, as supported by Parker three decades ago in his defense of the Mediterranean "ship graveyards" archaeological potential (Parker 1981).

Conclusion

The rescue survey and excavation of 2010 at Bajo Hornos reef by the Subdirección de Arqueología Subacuática INAH, opens up possibilities for the underwater study of one of the most important ports in the Americas until the 19th Century and the virtual door to New Spain and later 19th Century Mexico. The shipwreck remains that were located, as well as the ceramics, glass, and other objects documented, serve as ideal materials with which to examine processes of trade, cultural influence, and consumption. Furthermore, the materials are worthy illustrations for exhibits and other cultural projects in the region. It is conclusive that the reef of Bajo Hornos has, in the past, acted as a trap for materials submerged in the port of Veracruz, due to currents and winds coming form the North and the location of the reef south of the fortress/port of San Juan de Ulua. Furthermore, the extensive dredging and port modifications that disturbed the archaeological record in the early 20th century contributed to the movement of artifacts and wrecks to the reef. Thus, cultural materials from all periods have gathered in this reef. This cluster of artifacts and wrecks is very interesting in its own right. For one, the shipwreck remains recorded in the rescue interventions strongly suggest a vessel of Basque origin possibly from the 16th century. There have been no identified shipwrecks of this nature in Latin American waters to this day. Comparisons of the timber dimensions with other shipwreck remains, specifically with the Red Bay shipwrecks, leads us to think that it was a minor wooden vessel. Thus, the hull design, the fastening elements, the employed materials, and the coincidences in various measurements, drive us to conclude it may be ascribed to the 16th-century Cantabric-Basque shipbuilding tradition. Following Parks Canada research, this particular construction method lays in the transition between the medieval and early colonial period "shell-first" and the renaissance or modern "skeleton-first" assemblage technique. The study of the cultural materials from Bajo Hornos permits us to plan new campaigns to comprehend the reef in its entirety and, with this, a wider understanding about the types of ships calling port, nautical activity in the area and the products that were once exchanged and consumed in New Spain and Mexico.

Acknowledgments

Filipe V. de Castro, Robert Grenier, Laura Carrillo Marquez, Pilar Luna, Flor Trejo, Jesús Alfaro, Pedro López, Mitzy Quinto, Colin Breen, Alasdair Brooks, Sarah Tarlow, David Ball, Delphine Tomes, Wes Forsythe, and Knic Pfost.

References

BARKER, DAVID AND TERESITA MAJEWSKI
2006 Ceramic studies in historical archaeology. *The Cambridge Companion to Historical Archaeology.* Hicks and Beaudry (eds.) Cambridge University Press, Cambridge.

BARKHAM, MICHAEL
1998 Las pequeñas embarcaciones costeras vascas en el siglo XVI: notas de investigación y documentos de archivo sobre el "galeón", la "chalupa" y la "pinaza". *Itsas memoria: revista de estudios marítimos del País Vasco.* No.2.

CARRILLO, LAURA.
2011 Propuesta de rescate arqueológico subacuático, Marina Veramar. Informe técnico parcial de actividades 2010-2011. Coordinación Nacional de Arqueología, Dirección De Estudios Arqueológicos, Subdirección De Arqueología Subacuática. Centro INAH Veracruz.

GAIZTARRO, CIRIQUIAN
1956 La pinaza en el litoral vasco. *Homenaje a Don Juan Mendizabal Cortazar*, Museo de San Telmo, San Sebastián, 98-102.

HARING, CLARENCE H
1918 Trade and Navigation between Spain and the Indies in the time of Hapsburgs. Cambridge University Press. London: Humphrey Milford. Oxford University Press.

JUNCO, ROBERTO
2012 La Ruta de Veracruz a la Habana en época colonial. *Arqueología marítima en México.* Vera Moya (ed.) Subdirección de Arqueología Subacuática, INAH.

LABURU, MIGUEL
1989 La Nao Ballenera Vasca del Siglo XVI. Caja de ahorros municipal, Donostia – San Sebastián.

LOEWEN, BRAD
1998 The Red Bay vessel: an example of a 16th-century Biscayan ship. *Itsas memoria: revista de estudios marítimos del País Vasco,* No.2. 193-199.

2007 Renaissance Hull Design: The Seeds of Moder Naval Architecture. In: Robert Grenier, Marc-André Bernier, and Willis Stevens (eds.). The Underwater. Archaeology of Red Bay: Basque Shipbuilding and Whaling in the 16th Century. Parks Canada, Ottawa, Vol. 3. 1-13.

LUNA, PILAR
2011 30 Years of Underwater Archaeology in Mexico: From vision to action. In: Filipe Castro and Lindsey Thomas (eds.) *ACUA Underwater Archaeology Proceedings.* 123-128.

Montero, Pablo
    1996   San Juan de Ulúa. Puerta de la Historia. Consejo Nacional para la Cultura y las Artes – Instituto Nacional de Antropología e Historia. México D.F.

Muckelroy, Keith
    1976   The Integration of historical and archaeological data concerning an historic wreck site: The 'Kennemerland'. *World Archaeology* Vol. 7, No. 3. 280–89.

Parker, A.J.
    1981   Stratification and contamination in ancient Mediterranean shipwrecks. *International Journal of Nautical Archaeology.* Vol. 10, No. 4. 309-335

Salas-Pérez, José and Alejandro Granados-Barba
    2008   Oceanographic characterization of the Veracruz reefs system. *Atmósfera.* Vol. 3, No. 21, 281-301.

Tuck, James A and Robert Grenier
    1989   Red Bay, Labrador –World Whaling Capital A.D.1550–1600. Atlantic Archaeology. St John´s, Newfoundland.

· · · · · · · · · · · · · · ·

Ricardo Borrero and Roberto Junco
Subdirección de Arqueología Subacuática INAH
Moneda 16
Col. Centro, Mexico D.F. 06070
ricardoborrero373@hotmail.com
robjunco@mac.com

The Formation of a West African Maritime Seascape: Atlantic Trade, Shipwrecks, and Formation Processes on the Coast of Ghana

Rachel L. Horlings

To combat rough seas and dangerous shorelines, vessels engaged in the Atlantic trade in West Africa generally anchored offshore in deeper water and used small vessels for trade and communication with trading establishments on shore. The intersection of ocean dynamics, dangerous seafloor and shoreline features, and shore-based trading centers formed the maritime seascape of the past and informs our understanding of it in the present. A shipwreck, other maritime sites, and coastal adaptations for trade in this zone illustrate these interrelated and tenuous relationships and the formation processes of historical maritime trade in Elmina, coastal Ghana.

Introduction

The entire history of maritime exploration and attendant international encounters is one of constant movement and change through a range of physical and cultural environments, with the sea as a key player. Interpreting this changing history on the sea and the regions that border it, however, is challenging. Recent work in coastal Ghana has demonstrated both that there is submerged heritage there and that it can provide immense amounts of data on historical maritime interactions in the region. Investigation of this submerged heritage is necessarily a holistic endeavor, encompassing the historical/cultural, the physical, and the environment/setting – here called the seascape – and engaging with both the heritage as it once was, for instance, a vessel before it sank, or a seashore modified for trade, and what it is today. The differential preservation and distortion of archaeological sites today is a direct result of both cultural and natural formation processes, and therefore any archaeological investigation must be deciphered and interpreted through the lens of formation processes (Ford 2011; Van de Noordt 2004, 2010; Westerdahl 1992).

Formation Processes

Rapp (2000:243) summarizes the premise of formation process research in noting that the "study of human cultures cannot be divorced from a study of their environment and the mutual interaction between human activities and environmental processes." This paper is an exploration of this within the historical maritime seascape of coastal Ghana during the era of the Atlantic trade, and for purposes here, site formation processes are defined as the historical circumstances of coastal maritime trade in the Atlantic era in Ghana (Figure 1), as well as those physical, chemical, and biological processes which create and transform archaeological sites through time (Horlings 2011). Historical formation processes frame the interpretation of heritage, including a mid-17th century shipwreck known as the Elmina Wreck and other submerged artifacts, in terms of their relationships to the historical trade and its seascape, and physical formation processes dictate the investigation and interpretation of physical remains. Encompassing both the sea and the adjacent shoreline, the seascape incorporates both African and European engagements with each other and with the sea.

Formation studies emphasize the "dynamic interactions between humans, the natural environment, and their depositional records" (Goldberg et al. 1993:vii) This presents a more complete picture of the processes that created, affected, and continue to impact historical submerged cultural resources, and of their interpretations concerning international maritime interactions of the past Atlantic world. Illustrative of these processes and their archaeological interpretation is maritime research at Elmina, located in coastal Ghana. Elmina's place is at the boundary of land and sea, historically a key juncture in the meeting and straddling of worlds, and a place now providing insights into the intricacies of maritime relationships, navigation within the complex seascape, and varying scales of history and archaeology.

The Elmina Seascape

The complex and intersecting historical processes that shaped the Elmina seascape included such factors as the Atlantic trade; international relations between Africans and Europeans or other foreigners trading at the coast; permanent presence of Europeans in Elmina Castle; resources of the Benya Lagoon; common sailing,

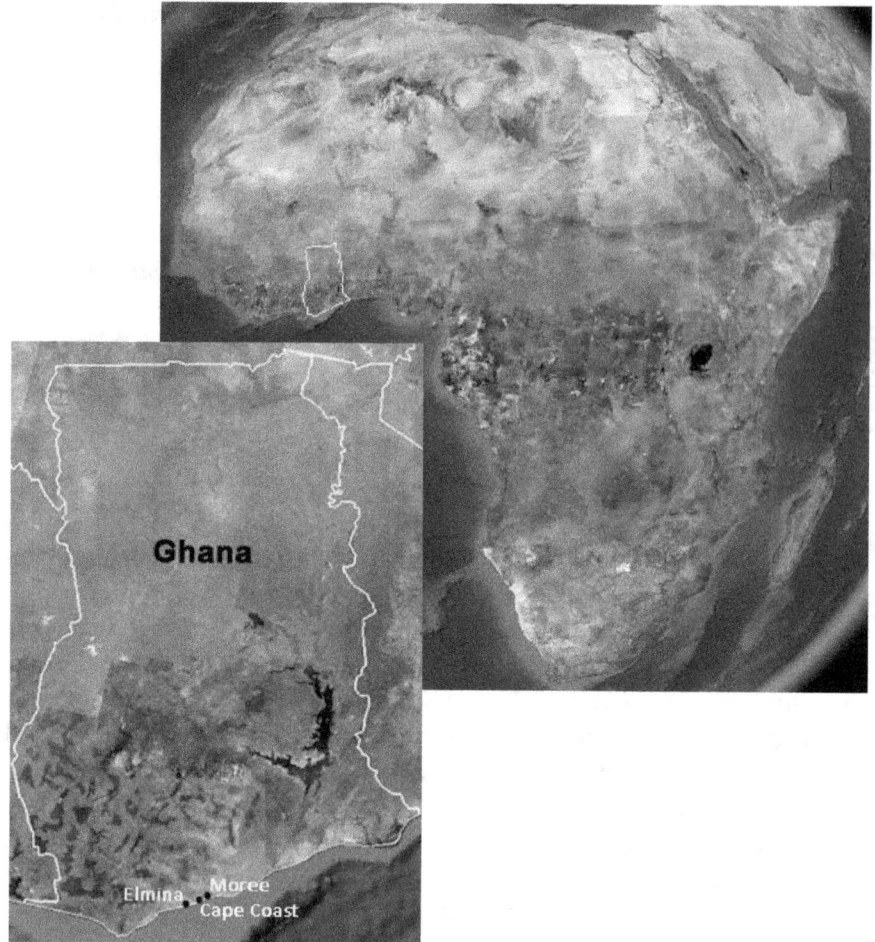

FIGURE 1. ELMINA IS LOCATED IN CENTRAL GHANA, WEST AFRICA (IMAGE BASED ON GOOGLE EARTH, 2012).

navigational and anchoring practices for international vessels; the central location of Elmina both in terms of the Ghanaian coast and in terms of the trade along the West African coast as a whole; and the weather and oceanographic patterns that dictated seasons of trade. The formation processes that determined the creation, destruction, and preservation of submerged cultural resources included all these factors and now affect the tangible remains of their presence across the submerged landscape and at the boundaries of land and sea, representing the intersection of all of these processes (Horlings 2011).

Originally called *São Jorge da Mina*, Elmina Castle (Figure 2) was established by the Portuguese in 1482 and was the first European trading post in sub-Saharan West Africa. In 1637, Elmina Castle was captured by the Dutch and remained in Dutch hands as a trading establishment until it was ceded to the British in 1872 (da Mota and Hair 1988:9; DeCorse 2001; Feinberg 1989; Yarak 2003). Not only was it the first permanent European establishment there, but the town and trading fort of Elmina was considered by many to be the most important trading center on the Ghanaian coast for at least two centuries (Blake 1967:40; Baesjou 1988:49-50; de Marees 1987:218-222; den Heijer 2003:149; DeCorse 2010; Feinberg 1989:v, 2; Van Den Boogaart 1992:373).

The principle advantages in the location of the castle were that it could be easily defended, had access to fresh water and already-established local networks of trade and resources (Feinberg 1989:41-42), and had a bay and beach area in which to careen, conduct trade, and protect small vessels and goods against storms (da Mota and Hair 1988:61; Hair 1994:16-17; Lawrence 1963:103). Elmina's location in the pseudo-harbor area of the Benya River and shallow Elmina Bay was all the more important because, with few exceptions, access to the coast of much of West Africa is difficult due to the lack of large river mouths and natural harbors, and the abundance of high waves (Allersma and Tilmans 1993:235; Bourret 1949:8; Dickson 1965; Rawley and Behrendt 2005:10; Zook 1919:183). This, in addition to the inherent dangers of sailing and navigation, dictated that merchant vessels would sail and anchor off the mouths of rivers or as far offshore as necessary to avoid dangers such as reefs or shoals (Adams 1966 [1823]:239, 243; Barbot's comments in Hair et al. 1992:382; Brooks 1970:235; Feinberg 1989:67-68; Martin 1837:228; Mitchell 2005:178-180; Smith 1970:516-517; Thomas 1969 [1860]:193). Vessels anchoring in these roadsteads used ships' boats or local canoes to transport people and goods from ship to shore.

Elmina's place straddling land and sea provided numerous opportunities for maritime trade and activities, but historical accounts of use and anchoring in and near the Benya River and Elmina harbor area are problematic in terms of reconstructing these practices (Horlings 2011). In general they provide only passing mentions of, for instance, changes made over time to the maritime

FIGURE 2. ELMINA CASTLE SITS ON A ROCKY PENINSULA. MODERN FISHING CANOES STILL ANCHOR IN THE SHALLOW ELMINA BAY IN CALM WEATHER (PHOTO BY THE AUTHOR, 2007).

the rainy season, optimal sailing to, from, and along the coast of West Africa was from September through April, during the dry season, as relatively predictable winds favored sailing and facilitated shipboard trading due to calmer seas and near-shore conditions (Adams 1966 [1823]:164; Awosika et al. 1993:31; Gu and Adler 2004:3366; Hopkins 1973:107; Opoku-Ankomah and Cordery 1993:552). Rainy season storms hammered the coast regularly and severely, posing dangers both at sea and in attempting to transition between ship and shore (Bold 1823:40-55). In addition, sitting for long periods of time also meant greater danger of being surprised and attacked by competitors (Mauny 1949 cited in Vogt 1979:15-16). For all these reasons any delays or other factors that caused vessels to remain on the coast for an extended period of time, including during the rainy season, had potentially serious deleterious effects on ships, as well as on crews and cargoes (particularly if the cargo was human captives).

infrastructure and modifications to the peninsula itself (DeCorse 2001; Hair et al. 1992:380), and in providing glimpses into how the maritime world was accessed, understood, and manipulated over time (Horlings 2011:80-91). It was within all of these historical formation processes that maritime trade occurred at Elmina, and within these and other processes that maritime cultural heritage is now interpreted and understood.

Physical Formation Processes

The physical environment played a significant role in the shaping and expansion of maritime trade. It affected trade patterns, provided the arena within which trade was enacted, and continues to play a dramatic role in the destruction and preservation of remaining traces of activity. Physical formation processes include currents, sedimentation, storms, benthic organisms, mechanisms that caused items to be submerged, such as a shipwrecking event, and any subsequent interactions with submerged sites (Horlings 2011).

Weather dictated both when the Ghanaian coast could be navigated as well as how it was navigated, particularly in the near-shore and roadstead zones (Bold 1823:39-42). Physical challenges to sailors included restricted visibility and extreme temperature and humidity changes that affected both the sailor and the integrity of wooden vessels. Because of the often violent weather in

Travel in any season was often difficult and erratic owing to hidden rocks and changing sedimentation rates, as well as weather and strong currents (de Marees 1987:86). Like ancient mariners, sailing along the coast depended heavily on the recognition of coastal or sea markers until well into the 19th century and later. The lack of charts and other navigational aids along the West African coast was a result of a lack of surveying, and was also due to different nations and traders hoarding information to prevent others from successfully trading in the region (Bold 1823:i-iv). Although Ghana's coasts may have been suitable for building forts and trade networks, it was not a kind place for ships, and these forces, combined with the political and economic struggles constantly at play, made the work of the sailor/merchant challenging indeed.

The Seascape: Sea-Land Interface

The sea was the connection between the disparate places of the Atlantic world, and the seascape was the theatre in which historical maritime interactions took place and which incorporated the physical, social,

FIGURE 3. SHOWN FROM THE PERSPECTIVE OF ST. JAGO HILL, LOCATED NORTHEAST OF THE PENINSULA, ELMINA CASTLE IS SHOWN HERE AT ITS PLACE BETWEEN LAND AND SEA; THE BENYA LAGOON IS ON THE SHOREWARD SIDE OF THE PENINSULA (PHOTOS BY D. KIPPING, 2009).

economic, and cultural interactions and embodiments of trade. The ship was the instrument that blurred continental boundaries (Ogundiran and Falola 2007:35). But ships and the sea could not sustain trade alone – it was its connection to the shore, with its attendant peoples, trade facilities, and resources that made it so important for the intersection of vastly different worlds and that provided transition points between the sea and land for both people and goods. The mutual shaping of seascape and trade provides the context for understanding submerged sites (Breen and Forsythe 2001) and views the past from outside the boundary of sea and land, because it encompasses both (Morgan and Greene 2009:12-13), including the blurred boundaries between peoples who met and lived and interacted and traded within the seascape setting. It is, therefore, impossible to understand international maritime interactions, cultures, and the archaeology of such, apart from the marine environment, seascape, or cultural maritime landscape in which they existed and exist today (Anuskiewicz 1998:224; Ash 2005; Breen and Lane 2003; Chapman and Chapman 2005; Cooney 2003; Dellino and Endere 2001:219; Dellino-Musgrave 2006:27; Flatman et al. 2005; Parker 2001; Van de Noort 2004, 2010; Westerdahl 1992), and this is especially true in the maritime Atlantic trade in Africa (Kelly and Norman 2007:173).

The seascape, then, is primarily the medium for action – for trade, social interactions, conflicts and exploration. The focal point on this stage of history is Elmina, spanning the boundary of land and sea. The location of Elmina Castle on shore was a place to which merchants came, but the coastal zone, the ocean, and the surrounding lands made up the larger landscape and seascape within which historical maritime trade actually took place (Branton 2009:52; Preucel and Meskell 2009:215). And it was within the constraints of the sea, within the context of the seascape, that vessels struggled and sank (Adams 2001:292; McCarthy 2008), leaving a concrete record of both physical and ephemeral events of the past. The event of the shipwreck or loss of other cultural material to the seascape serves to tie together the larger historical setting and context of trade and provides the tangible remains that may be studied, queried, and investigated (Adams 2001:299; Gould 2001:195; Green 2004). This material is then part of the "profoundly contextual" (van Dommelen 1999:283) seascape of historical coastal Elmina, articulating with what Preucel and Meskell (2009:216) call the "politics of location and the social construction of space and place" as it relates to the overarching historical formation processes of the region. A brief case study of submerged maritime heritage in Elmina, Ghana, serves to illustrate these complex interconnections.

The Elmina Wreck

The Elmina Wreck site is located approximately two kilometers southeast of the Elmina peninsula and is in 11-12 meters of water in a highly dynamic ocean environment (Anthony and Blivi 1999:165). The site appears to consist primarily of six cannon, an anchor, and trade items consisting of stacks of brass and pewter basins, barrels of brass manilas, lead rolls (which may or may not have been for trade), trade beads and cowry shells scattered throughout the site, as well as indications of cloth cargo, and a number of other objects (Cook 2012; Cook et al. [2013]; Horlings 2011; Pietruszka 2011). An additional object appears to be the remains of a birch tree that was likely live cargo on the vessel (Horlings 2011). The presence of wood from the hull was confirmed through collection of sediment core samples. There is extensive mixing across the site, and artifactual material within it spans a period of at least 400 years, from the 16th century through the 21st, making interpretation based on artifacts extremely difficult, although its nationality is most likely Dutch (Cook 2012; Pietruszka 2011). Radiocarbon dates taken from wood collected in sediment cores provides a mid-17th century date (Horlings 2011). Dramatic sedimentation on the site, monitored over the period of six years since its discovery, is illustrated by the fact that in 2009 more than two-thirds of the site was completely covered by sediments, dramatically changing its surface signature.

A possible candidate for the identity of the vessel, a Dutch Merchantman named *Groeningen* which sank near Elmina in 1647, has been proposed based on historical research (Furley Collection Notebook 1646-1647 pages 162-164, transcribed by C. R. DeCorse, August 2010; Pietruszka 2011), but this cannot be confirmed until more research is conducted, if ever.

Formation process research at the site, based primarily on material recovered in sediment cores (Horlings 2009, 2013), as well as assessment of the macro remains at the site, has provided insights into a range of topics, including causes of sinking and the vessel's subsequent tenure on the seafloor (Horlings 2011:293-294). A brief summary of the results of these investigations reads as follows:

> *Sometime in a dry season of the mid-17th century, a European trading vessel caught fire belowdecks, likely in the starboard bow. It sank on a relatively even keel, with decks just below the surface of the water, possibly providing opportunity for limited salvage. Over time the wreck was colonized by various biota, but the combined pressures of an active and dynamic seafloor environment and marine boring organisms caused the vessel to eventually accordion in on itself, preserving original lading even as the hull disintegrated. Cycles of burial and exposure served to trap and mix the original materials of the vessel with those of other centuries that were also in those waters. When discovered in 2003 the vessel once again became a part of the known seascape of coastal Ghana, and an active part of maritime history there.*

Other Submerged Heritage at Elmina

The single archaeological example presently known of European use of the Benya Lagoon for shipping-related activities may be found in the remains of a vessel discovered by dredgers in 2007 in the western or upper part of the lagoon (Pietruszka 2011). Found in material dredged from three meters below current sediment levels, most of the remains were broken and destroyed by the time archaeologists were called to investigate them. A total of 15 various hull elements and three cannon (originally four, but one disappeared, likely taken for scrap metal). Dendrochronological dating of timbers provides a date of the turn of the 18th century and a provenance of northern Europe; these clues, in addition to analysis of the cannon and historical documents, indicate a likely interpretation of the vessel having been Dutch. While a number of theories have been proposed, it is presently unknown what its purpose was so far up the lagoon (Horlings 2011; Pietruszka 2011), and since the site has now been likely completely obliterated (Horlings 2012), it is unlikely that a great deal more will be known from this vessel. Its presence in this intermediate zone between land and sea, however, provides another piece to the puzzle of understanding the historical maritime past of the coastal Ghanaian seascape.

Space does not allow for discussion of the Single Anchor Site, the Double Anchor site, the Chain site, or the shore wreck of a modern fishing vessel (Horlings 2011; Horlings et al 2011), but it is important to note here that these isolated objects also represent distinct facets of the historical and modern seascape, as well as

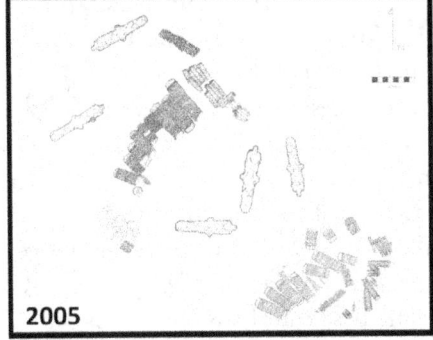
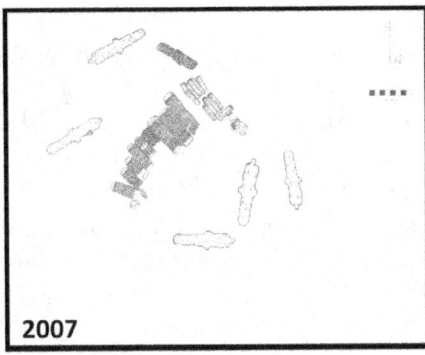
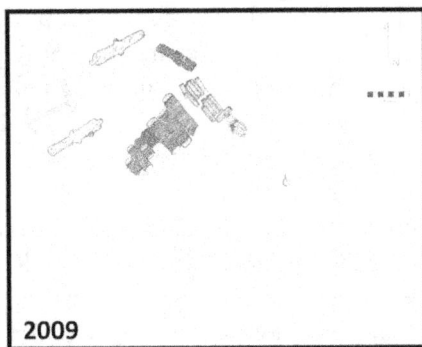

FIGURE 4. THIS COMPOSITE SITE PLAN OF THE ELMINA WRECK ILLUSTRATES WORK FROM THE 2005, 2007, AND 2009 FIELD SEASONS, INCLUDING LIMITED EXCAVATIONS AND EXTENSIVE SEDIMENT CORE COLLECTION (HORLINGS 2011).

historical and physical formation processes, and are all part of Ghana's maritime story.

Discussion and Conclusions: Seascape, Heritage, and Maritime Archaeology in Ghana

The historic African trade was notorious for its uncertainty, both in terms of profits and the very real possibility that those involved in the trade would never return from Africa due to mismanagement, illness, warfare, piracy, shipwreck, and any number of other mishaps (Eltis et al. 1999; Fage 1969; Hopkins 1973:92; Inikori 1996:58; Mancke 2004; Williams 1994 [1944]:38). The frequency with which historical vessels in general burned, were captured, sunk in storms, and suffered other mishaps, considered over a span of the nearly 400 years that Elmina was a major trading entrepôt, makes it likely that there are more shipwreck sites awaiting discovery in coastal Ghana. The integration of historical maritime practices and physical environmental processes allows for particular cultural remains to be interpreted as the remains of specific events in history, and even provides a means of conjecture for defining just what those events may have been. The locations of each site known to date within the historical seascape speak to navigational hazards, intentional use of the Benya Lagoon drainage, and possibly anchoring strategies, as well as the ever-present danger of sinking, and suggest that a majority of activity took place along the littoral margin, or the boundary between sea and land, with less activity in more seaward regions.

The investigations that have been conducted to date have only begun to scratch the surface of history. Future research into the events that occurred on this historically rich seascape holds the potential to offer insights into the historical maritime past that have yet to even be considered, and will undoubtedly impact future interpretations of history. As Murphy (1983:69) asserts, the archaeological investigation of shipwrecks and other submerged cultural resources should be "not merely the embellishment of the maritime historical record, but the elucidation of otherwise unattainable aspects of human behavior." While some insights have indeed been gained into these otherwise unattainable aspects of both human behavior and the environment in which evidence of that behavior remains, our understanding of the historic Ghanaian seascape is yet in its infancy.

Delgado (1988:3) once noted that "Not every shipwreck is old, not every old shipwreck is historic, not every shipwreck is significant." In all likelihood, the Elmina Wreck was never famous and was significant only to those who were directly affected by it. But, just as its discovery has once again placed it as an active part of Elmina's seascape, and quite apart from its intrinsic cultural and historical value, this site, along with others in the region, has been significant in demonstrating the potential for shipwreck and submerged cultural resource studies in Africa (Werz 1993:254). The application of the site formation processes framework has provided details concerning the physical remains and their tenure on the seafloor and situated those remains and the processes affecting them within the theoretical framework of larger formation processes, shedding light on the historical contexts of the past and the events that created and still affect the shipwreck site. Whether this wreck site represents the remains of the *Groningen* or not is still unknown, and perhaps will never be known, but it illustrates an event in the dramatic historical eventscape of coastal Elmina.

The presence of Elmina's 25,000 plus population living near the coast is having a significant and visible effect on submerged sites in several ways, most obviously visible in the extraordinary quantities of trash and debris in the water and along the coast. These items become entrapped in submerged sites, as illustrated in the Elmina Wreck site, as well as cause general pollution. In addition, the unintentional modification of the submerged environment by shoreline development and by those engaging in maritime activities, including extreme overfishing, is resulting in both the dramatic decline of marine resources, and unintentional disturbance of submerged heritage (Horlings 2011, 2012). Assisting the Ghanaian government in becoming effective stewards of submerged cultural history and the natural environment is vitally important for preservation of both.

Finally, research on submerged cultural resource site formation necessarily intersects both cultural and natural processes (Adams 2001; Gibbins and Adams 2001; Martin 2001; Murphy 1983, 1990; Oxley 1998a, b). While it is virtually impossible to account for all factors associated with these processes individually or in combination (Ward and Larcombe 2003:1233), characterizing formation processes and their effects is an invaluable archaeological tool for understanding the dynamic and subtle processes that convert submerged remains from articulated entities into dispersed sites, and which connect the past and the present. It is indeed the intersection of ocean dynamics, dangerous seafloor and shoreline features, and shore-based trading centers that formed the maritime seascape and eventscape of the past, and which informs our understanding of it in the present.

References

Adams, John
1966
[1823] *Remarks on the Country Extending from Cape Palmas to the River Congo with an Appendix containing an Account of the European trade with the West Coast of Africa.* Frank Cass & Co., Ltd, London.

Adams, Jonathan
2001 Ships and Boats as Archeological Source Material. *World Archaeology* 32:292-310.

Allersma, Egge and Wiel M. K. Tilmans
1993 Coastal Conditions in West Africa – A Review. *Ocean & Coastal Management* 19:199-240.

Anuskiewicz, Richard J.
1998 Technology, Theory, and Analysis: Using Remote Sensing as a Tool for Middle-Range Theory Building in Maritime and Nautical Archaeology. In *Maritime Archaeology: A Reader of Substantive and Theoretical Contributions*, edited by Lawrence E. Babits and Hans Van Tilburg, pp. 223-231. Plenum Press, New York.

Ash, Aiden
2007 *The Maritime Cultural Landscape of Port Willunga, South Australia.* Flinders University Monograph Series no. 4. Flinders University Department of Archaeology.

Awosika, L. F., A. C. Ibe and C. E. Ibe
1993 Anthropogenic Activities Affecting Sediment Load Balance along the West African Coastline. In *Coastlines of Western Africa*, edited by Awosika, L. F., A. Chidi Ibe, and P. Schroader, pp. 26-39. New York: American Society of Civil Engineers.

Baesjou, René
1988 The Historical Evidence in Old Maps and Charts of Africa with Special References to West Africa. *History in Africa* 15:1-83.

Blake, John W.
1967 *West Africa: Quest for God and Gold, 1454-1578.* Curzon Press, London.

Bold, Edward
1823
[1819] *The Merchant's and Mariner's African Guide: Containing an Accurate Description of the Coast, Bays, Harbours, and Adjacent Islands of West Africa, with Their Corrected Longitudinal Positions, Comprising a Statement of the Seasons, Winds, and Currents, Peculiar to Each Country, to which is added A Minute Explanation of the Various Systems of Traffic, that are Adopted on the Windward and Gold Coast, as well as the Principle Ports to Leeward, Also, A Few Hints to the Mercantile Navigator, Suggesting a Means of Securing More Rapid Passages, Both To and From the Coast, than have Hitherto been Practiced.* With additional observations by the Commander of a Boston vessel, and an English Gentleman, on the Coast in 1822. Cushing & Appleton, Salem.

Bourret, F. M.
1949 *The Gold Coast: A Survey of the Gold Coast and British Togoland.* Stanford University Press, Stanford.

Branton, Nicole
2009 Landscape Approaches in Historical Archaeology: The Archaeology of Place. In *International Handbook of Historical Archaeology*, edited by Teresita Majewski and David Gaimster, pp. 51-65. Springer, New York.

Breen, Colin and Wes Forsythe
2001 Management Protection of the Maritime Cultural Resource in Ireland. *Coastal Management* 29:41-51.

Breen, Colin and Paul J. Lane
2003 Archaeological Approaches to East Africa's Changing Seascapes. *World Archaeology* 35:469-489.

Brooks, George E. Jr.
1970 *Yankee Traders, Old Coasters and African Middlemen: A History of American Legitimate Trade with West Africa in the Nineteenth Century.* Boston University Press, Boston.

Chapman, Henry P. and Philip R. Chapman
2005 Seascapes and Landscapes – The Siting of the Ferriby Boat Finds in the Context of Prehistoric Pilotage. *International Journal of Nautical Archaeology* 34:43-50.

Cook, Gregory D.
2012 West Africa and the Atlantic World: Maritime Archaeological Investigations at Elmina, Ghana. Ph.D. dissertation, Department of Anthropology, Syracuse University.

Cook, Gregory. D., Rachel L. Horlings, and Andrew Pietruszka
[2013] Underwater archaeology and the Atlantic trade: Research at Elmina, Ghana. *International Journal of Nautical Archaeology.*

COONEY, GABRIEL
    2003   Introduction: Seeing Land from the Sea. *World Archaeology* 35:323-328.

DA MOTA, A TIEXEIRA AND PAUL. E. HAIR
    1988   *East of Mina: Afro-European Relations on the Gold Coast in the 1550s and 1560s*. African Studies Program, University of Wisconsin, Madison.

DE MAREES, PIETER
    1987   *Description and Historical Account of the Gold Kingdom of Guinea (1602)*. Translated from the Dutch and edited by Albert van Dantzig and Adam Jones. Oxford University Press, Oxford.

DECORSE, CHRISTOPHER R.
    2001   *An Archaeology of Elmina: Africans and Europeans on the Gold Coast. 1400-1900*. Smithsonian Institute Press, Washington.

    2010   Early Trade Posts and Forts of West Africa. In *First Forts: Essays on the Archaeology of Proto-colonial Fortifications*, edited by Eric Klingelhofer, pp. 209-233. Brill, Leiden.

DELGADO, JAMES P.
    1988   The Value of Shipwrecks. In *Historical shipwrecks: Issues in Management*, edited by Joy Waldron Murphy, pp.1-10. Partners for Livable Places and the National Trust for Historic Preservation Maritime Department, Washington, DC.

DELLINO, VIRGINIA AND MARÍA LUZ ENDERE
    2001   The HMS *Swift* Shipwreck: The Development of Underwater Heritage Protection in Argentina. *Conservation and Management of Archaeological Sites* 4:219-231.

DELLINO-MUSGRAVE, VIRGINIA E.
    2006   Maritime *Archaeology and Social Relations: British Action in the Southern Hemisphere*. Springer, New York.

DEN HEIJER, HENK
    2003   The West African Trade of the Dutch West India Company, 1674-1740. In 2003 *Riches from Atlantic Commerce: Dutch Transatlantic Trade and Shipping, 1585-1817*, edited by Johannes Postma and Victor Enthoven, pp. 139-169. Brill, Leiden.

DICKSON, K. B.
    1965   Evolution of Seaports in Ghana: 1800-1928. *Annals of the Association of American Geographers* 55:98-111.

ELTIS, DAVID, STEPHEN D. BEHRENDT, DAVID RICHARDSON AND HERBERT S. KLEIN
    1999   *The Atlantic Slave Trade: A Database on CD-ROM*. Cambridge University Press, Cambridge.

FAGE, J.D.
    1969   *A History of West Africa: An Introductory Survey*. 4th edition. Cambridge University Press, Cambridge.

FEINBERG, HARVEY M.
    1989   Africans and Europeans in West Africa: Elminans and Dutchmen on the Gold Coast During the Eighteenth Century. *Transactions of the American Philosophical Society* 79.

FLATMAN, JOE, MARK STANIFORTH, DAVID NUTLEY AND DEBRA SHEFI
    2005   Submerged Cultural Landscapes. Humanities Research Centre for Cultural Heritage and Cultural Exchange 'Understanding Cultural Landscapes' Symposium Report. http://wwwehlt.flinders.edu.au/humanities/exchange/asri/ucl_symp_pdf/2005_UCL_MS.pdf. Accessed 5/2009.

FORD, BEN (EDITOR)
    2012   *The Archaeology of Maritime Landscapes: When the Land Meets the Sea*. Springer, New York.

GIBBINS, DAVID AND JONATHAN ADAMS
    2001   Shipwrecks and Maritime Archaeology. *World Archaeology* 32:279-291.

GOLDBERG, PAUL, DAVID T. NASH AND MICHAEL D. PETRAGLIA
    1993   Preface. In *Formation Processes in Archaeological Context*. Monographs in World Archaeology No. 17, edited by Paul Goldberg, David T. Nash and Michael D. Petraglia, pp. vii-ix. Prehistory Press, Madison.

GOULD, RICHARD A.
    2001   From Sail to Steam at Sea in the Late Nineteenth Century. In *Anthropological Perspectives on Technology*, edited by Michael Brian Schiffer, pp. 193-213. University of New Mexico Press, Albuquerque.

GREEN, JEREMY
    2004   *Maritime Archaeology: A Technical Handbook*, 2nd edition. Academic Press, London.

GU, GUOJUN AND ROBERT F. ADLER
    2004   Seasonal Evolution and Variability Associated with the West African Monsoon System. *Journal of Climate* 17:3364-3377.

HAIR, PAUL E.
    1994   *The Founding of the Castelo de São Jorge da Mina: An Analysis of the Sources*. African Studies Program, University of Wisconsin, Madison.

HOPKINS, ANTHONY G.
    1973   *An Economic History of West Africa*. Columbia University Press, New York.

HORLINGS, RACHEL L.
    2013   Short Contribution: Archaeological Micro-Sampling by Means of Sediment Coring at Submerged Sites. *Geoarchaeology*.

2012 Maritime Cultural Resource Investigation, Management, and Mitigation in Coastal Ghana. *Journal of Maritime Archaeology* 7:141-164. DOI 10.1007/s11457-012-9086-9

2011 Of His Bones are Coral Made: Submerged Cultural Resources, Site Formation Processes, and Multiple Scales of Interpretation in Coastal Ghana. PhD dissertation, Department of Anthropology, Syracuse University, Syracuse, New York.

2009 Technical Brief: An Effective Diver-Operated Coring Device for Underwater Archaeology. *Technical Briefs in Historical Archaeology* 4:1-6.

Horlings, Rachel L., Darren Kipping, Casper Toftgaard Neilsen, and Kira Kaufmann
2011 Missing Shipwrecks, Methods or Imagining? A Preliminary Report on Maritime Archaeological Surveys in Coastal Ghana, 2009. *Nyame Akuma* 75:2-10.

Inikori, Joseph E.
1996 Measuring the Unmeasured Hazards of the Atlantic Slave Trade: Documents Relating to the British Trade. *Revue française d'histoire d'outre-mer* 312:53-92.

Kelly, Kenneth G. and Norman, Neil L.
2007 Historical Archaeology of Landscape in Atlantic Africa. In *Envisioning Landscape: Situations and Standpoints in Archaeology and Heritage*, edited by Dan Hicks, Laura McAtackney, Graham Fairclough. Left Coast Press, Walnut Creek, CA.

Lawrence, A. W.
1963 *Trade Castles & Forts of West Africa*. Stanford University Press, California.

Mancke, Elizabeth
2004 Oceanic Space and the Creation of at Global International System, 1450-1800. In *Maritime History as World History*, edited by Daniel Finamore, pp. 149-166. University of Florida, Gainesville.

Martin, Colin J. M.
2001 De-Particularizing the Particular: Approaches to the Investigation of Well-Documented Post-Medieval Shipwrecks. *World Archaeology* 32:383-399.

Martin, R. Montgomery
1837 *History of the British Possessions in the Indian & Atlantic Oceans; Comprising Ceylon, Penang, Malacca, Sincapore [sic], The Falkland Islands, St. Helena, Ascension, Sierra Leone, The Gambia, Cape Coast Castle, &c. &c*. Whitaker & Co., London.

McCarthy, Mike
2008 Boundaries and the Archaeology of Frontier Zones. In *Handbook of Landscape Archaeology*, edited by Bruno David and Julian Thomas, pp. 202-209. Left Coast Press, Walnut Creek, CA.

Mitchell, Peter
2005 *African Connections: Archaeological Perspectives on Africa and the Wider World*. AltaMira Press, Walnut Creek.

Morgan, Philip D. and Jack P. Greene
2009 Introduction: The Present State of the Atlantic History. In *Atlantic History: A Critical Appraisal*, edited by Jack P. Greene and Philip D. Morgan, pp. 3-33. Oxford University Press, Oxford.

Murphy, Larry E.
1983 Shipwrecks As Data Base for Human Behavioral Studies. In *Shipwreck Anthropology*, edited by Richard A. Gould, pp. 65-89. University of New Mexico Press, Albuquerque.

1990 *8SL17: Natural Site-Formation Processes of a Multiple-Component Underwater Site in Florida*. Southwest Cultural Resources Center Professional Papers, No. 39, Santa Fe, New Mexico.

Ogundiran, Akinwumi and Toyin Falola
2007 Pathways in the Archaeology of Transatlantic Africa. In *Archaeology of Atlantic Africa and the African Diaspora*, edited by Akinwumi Ogundiran and Toyin Falola, pp. 3-45. Indiana University Press, Bloomington.

Opoku-Ankomah, Yaw and Ian Cordery
1994 Atlantic Sea Surface Temperatures and Rainfall Variability in Ghana. *Journal of Climate* 7:551-558.

Oxley, Ian
1998a The Environment of Historical shipwreck Sites: A Review of the Presentation of Materials, Site Formation and Site Environmental Assessment. Unpublished Master's thesis. School of Geography and Geosciences, University of St Andrews, Fife, Scotland.

1998b The Investigation of Factors that Affect the Preservation of Underwater Archaeological Sites. In *Maritime Archaeology: A Reader of Substantive and Theoretical Contributions*, edited by Lawrence E. Babits and Hans Van Tilburg, pp. 523 – 529. Plenum Press, New York.

Parker, A.J.
2001 Maritime Landscapes. *Landscapes* 1:22-41.

Pietruszka, Andrew
2011 Artifacts of Exchange: A Multi-Scalar Approach to Maritime Archaeology at Elmina, Ghana. Ph.D. dissertation, Department of Anthropology, Syracuse University.

Preucel, Robert W. and Lynn Meskell
2009 Places. In *A Companion to Social Archaeology*, edited by Lynn Meskell and Robert W. Preucel, pp. 215-229.

Rapp, George R., Jr.
    2000   Geoarchaeology. In *Archaeological Method and Theory: An Encyclopedia*, edited by Linda Ellis, pp.237-244. Garland Publishing, Inc., New York.

Rawley, James A. and Stephen D. Behrendt
    2005   *The Atlantic Slave Trade: A History*. Revised edition. University of Nebraska Press, Lincoln.

Smith, Robert
    1970   The Canoe in West African History. *The Journal of African History* 11:515-533.

Thomas, Charles W.
    1969
    [1860]   *Adventures and Observations on the West Coast of Africa, and Its Islands. Historical and Descriptive Sketches of Madiera, Canary, Biafra and Cape Verd Islands; Their Climates, Inhabitants and productions. Accounts of Places, Peoples, Customs, Trade, Missionary Operations, Etc., Etc. On that Part of the African Coast Lying Between Tangier, Morocco and Benguela*. Negro Universities Press, New York.

Van de Noort, Robert
    2004   An Ancient Seascape: The Social Context of Seafaring in the Early Bronze Age. *World Archaeology* 35:404-415.

Van Den Boogaart
    1992   The Trade between Western Africa and the Atlantic World, 1600-90: Estimates of Trends in Composition and Value. *The Journal of African History* 33:369-385.

van Dommelen, Peter
    1999   Exploring Everyday Places and Cosmologies. In *Archaeologies of Landscape: Contemporary Perspectives*, edited by Wendy Ashmore and A. Bernard Knapp, pp. 277-285. Blackwell Publishers Ltd., Oxford.

Vogt, John
    1979   *Portuguese Rule on the Gold Coast, 1469-1682*. University of Georgia Press, Athens.

Ward, Ingrid and Piers Larcombe
    2003   A Process-Oriented Approach to Archaeological Site formation: Application to Semi-Arid Northern Australia. *Journal of Archaeological Science* 30:1223-1236.

Werz, Bruno E. J. S.
    1993   Shipwrecks of Robben Island, South Africa: An Exercise in Cultural Resource Management in the Underwater Environment. *The International Journal of Nautical Archaeology* 22:245-256.

Westerdahl, Christer
    1992   Maritime Cultural Landscape. International Journal of Nautical Archaeology 21:5-14.

Williams, Eric
    1994
    [1944]   *Capitalism & Slavery*. 2nd edition. The University of North Carolina Press, Chapel Hill.

Yarak, Larry W.
    2003   A West African Cosmopolis: Elmina (Ghana) in the Nineteenth Century. Paper presented at Seascapes, Littoral Cultures, and Trans-Oceanic Exchanges, Library of Congress, Washington D.C., February 12-15, 2003.

Zook, George Frederick
    1919   On the West Coast of Africa. *The Journal of Negro History* 4:163-205.

•••••••••••••••

[This paper is published posthumously, thus the author's address is not published here.]

The Maddalena Archipelago Maritime Target Survey: A Collaborative Effort toward the Enhancement of Maritime Cultural Heritage

Massimiliano Secci
Claudia Giarrusso
Giulia Nieddu
Alessandro Porqueddu
Pier Giorgio I. Spanu

The Maddalena Project attempted to verify information derived from archival research and local community reports through the employment of target dives. During the investigation, eight archaeologically significant sites dating from the Classical period (3rd century B.C.) to Modern times (19th century A.D.) were identified and documented. In addition to several scattered finds, six shipwrecks sites or ceramic concentrations have been identified as well as two harbour areas not previously documented. The information provides new insights on trading vectors through the Strait of Bonifacio, as well as internal routes within the Maddalena Archipelago. The value of the research, undertaken through the support and collaboration of various institutions, also extends to public outreach initiatives.

Introduction

The Strait of Bonifacio, a channel dividing Sardinia (Italy) from Corsica (France), and the Maddalena Archipelago, located along the north-eastern coast of Sardinia, has represented a crossroads for maritime trade in the central Mediterranean Sea throughout history. However, due to the scarcity of systematic underwater archaeological studies in the area, port and passage route dynamics have been difficult to understand.

To remedy this situation, a team of archaeologists from the Università degli Studi di Sassari (University), under the supervision of the Soprintendenza per i Beni Archeologici per le Provincie di Sassari e Nuoro (Superintendency) and the scientific direction of Pier Giorgio Spanu (Università degli Studi di Sassari), participated in the 'Maddalena Project' from 25 April 2012 to 6 June 2012. The involved institutions – who were not necessarily directly involved in the management of cultural heritage – recognised in the enhancement of cultural heritage a theme within their institutional duties providing the project with an inclusive and collaborative base. The founding concept of the Maddelena Project rests on the fundamental notion that archaeological research should participate, actively and effectively in the socio-cultural and economic dynamics of the local area (Secci 2013a). Archaeological research and, moreover, its reconstructive and interpretive efforts, can perfectly contribute to the socio-cultural and economic development of a highly depressed area.

Maddalena Project: Aims, Approach and Methodology

The Maddalena Project arose from a general necessity to create an archaeological chart of the Maddalena Archipelago that could be instrumental for any further research, outreach, or interpretive initiatives. The project developed through the systematic identification and documentation of known sites, the evaluation of site reports from local fishermen and scuba divers, and the investigation of specific areas such as emerging cliffs, bays, and coves potentially exploited as shelters or landing places. With these aims, underwater operations were preceded by a preliminary analysis of existing archaeological literature, verbal interviews with local community members, and a detailed study of historical sources and cartography, each essential for suitable dive planning.

During the second phase of the project, team members conducted almost 60 dives in a period of 40 days surveying areas previously identified. Once a site was located, the archaeological context and site characteristics (depth, site extension, bearings, seabed typology, etc.) were recorded with video and photography. Some 3D video footage was also taken at this time and was believed to be an interesting and useful tool for public interpretation and outreach activities. At a later date, thanks to a special permit granted by the Superintendency, some diagnostic artifacts were recovered and promptly processed in accordance with the 'First-Aid for underwater finds' approach (Bowens 2009:148–162). Following

FIGURE 1. SITE LOCATIONS WITHIN THE MADDALENA ARCHIPELAGO (IMAGE SETTING: ALESSANDRO PORQUEDDU).

daily diving operations, team members photographed, drew, and catalogued artifacts in order to provide a preliminary typology and related context.

A grant from the Municipality of La Maddalena and the technical support of the Arcipelago di La Maddalena National Park made the project possible. The collaboration between the institutions granted logistical and administrative support during project development. Park staff provided invaluable support to University archaeologists for all underwater activities. Each day a Park staff member – mainly Mr. Yuri Donno, a marine biologist and an expert on the Archipelago's waters – transported the archaeologists to sites, providing invaluable knowledge of winds, currents and weather dynamics which ensured the most effective planning of operations.

The Municipality of Maddalena is also responsible for the success of the project. Its staff provided outstanding support with administrative matters, speeding up the process of fieldwork planning and execution. Many locals offered valuable information regarding site locations and characteristics. Since the start of fieldwork, local community members were involved in the activities carried out by the Project staff and were willing to participate by offering valuable knowledge of areas of archaeological interest with usually precise information on site locations. This is an interesting outcome. In the past, the Archipelago has been damaged by looting and pillaging of significant archaeological sites. Nonetheless, during fieldwork the team noted an interest in the research being undertaken by archaeologists. Many local community members were passionate in both understanding what was being done and in participating in many ways, mostly reporting areas of archaeological interest.

The Associazione Culturale Castra Sardiniæ, a not-for-profit cultural organization established in 2009 in order to promote culture, history, archaeology, art, and architecture as well as the development of historical and archaeological research in Sardinia, provided research coordination. In relation to the bureaucratic/institutional aspects of the project, the Association signed some agreements with the Municipality and the Park, which allowed full independence in organizing and planning operations in order to capitalize on the time required for fieldwork. The agreement between the University and the Capitaneria di Porto di Cagliari (Coastguard) ensured high security standards during diving operations thanks to the technical and logistical support offered by the IV Nucleo Sommozzatori (4th Diving Department) commanded by Lieutenant Gianni Dessì. Professor Pier Giorgio Spanu provided didactic-formative support by allowing participating students to practice methodological approaches learnt during classes. Geologist Dr.

Fabrizio Antonioli (ENEA[1] First Researcher) and underwater archaeologist Emanuela Solinas also provided precious collaboration.

Historical and Archaeological Background

Due to its strategic position in Mediterranean, the Strait of Bonifacio has represented a crossroads for the movement of people and goods since the origins of maritime crossings in the Mediterranean basin. In the Neolithic Age, the strait acted as a passage for the diffusion of obsidian from Monte Arci, Sardinia – an extraction area for volcanic glass near modern Oristano (central-western Sardinia – Isola di Santo Stefano: Lilliu 1988:27; Mancini 2010:46; Cala Corsara: Ferrarese Ceruti and Pitzalis 1987:871ss; Caprara et al. 1996:501) – to the northwestern Mediterranean regions (Tykot 1996:43ss; Robb and Tykot 2003; Williams Thorpe et al. 1984:141), acting as an ideal route for the expansion of European proto-megalithic culture (Cesari and Leandri 2007:229–232).

During the 6th century BC, the *Periplus of Scylax* – one of the most ancient Greek geographical sources, described the voyage undertaken by Scylax of Caryanda to circumnavigate (clockwise) the Mediterranean and the Black Sea – it contains a brief description of the sea separating Sardinia from Corsica, 'from the island of Kyrnos to the island of Sardò is a distance of one third of a day; in the middle is an uninhabited island' (author's translation).

In ancient times, the Strait of Bonifacio was a military and trade route to the extreme western regions of the Mediterranean. Pliny the Elder (1st century A.D.) describes it as a strait – *fretum* or *Taphors* – dotted with small islands called Canicularia. The same name is quoted in the *Tabula Peutingeriana* (IV, 1) in the *Ravenna Cosmography* (V, 23) and in the *Passio SS. Gavini et Ianuarii* (Zichi and Accardo 1989:17, note 41). In the 2nd century AD, the Roman geographer Claudius Ptolemy, in his most famous work, describes two islands of the archipelago, Φίντωνος νῆσος (Caprera) and Ἰλούα νῆσος (La Maddalena) (*Geography*, III, 8).

Despite the collapse of the Western Roman Empire, the Strait of Bonifacio and its islands maintained a key role in the western Mediterranean navigation system, as indicated by several hagiographic, geographic, and historical sources. The island of Caprera is recalled with the entry Capraria in the *Ravenna Cosmography* (V, 26), appearing in the form Cravaira in the *Compasso de Navegare*; as Crapara in the *Carte Pisane* portolan; and, eventually, as Capraia in the *Tammar-Luxoro Atlas* (De Felice 1964:112). The island of La Maddalena has been known, since Medieval times, with variations of the toponym Bucina/Buzenare (Kretschmer 1909; Motzo 1936; Piloni 1974; Terrosu Asole 1987) and with the name Porcaria (Panedda 1978).

The *Compasso de Navegare,* a navigation chart from Pisa drawn in the 13th century, provides the most detailed source of information on the Maddalena Archipelago – providing not only the name of each one of its seven islands, but also an accurate description of their ports and a calculation of distances between the islands and the Northern Sardinian coast (Panedda 1978:90–93). Of similar value is another chart from Pisa, the *Grazia Pauli*, dating to the second half of the 14th century (Panedda 1978:97–98).

The centrality of the strait within Mediterranean maritime routes is echoed even as far as the Islamic world, as shown by the brief notices found in the work of the Muslim geographer Al-Idrisi. Commonly known as *The Book of Roger*, it was written in Palermo at the court of Norman King Roger II of Altavilla (Sicily) from 1139 to 1154. Mentions of the strait are also found in the work of Turkish Admiral Piri Muhi 'd-Din Re'is – one of the three most ill-famed Saracen pirates crossing the Mediterranean Sea during the 16th century.

Overall, Sardinia, and the archipelago specifically, was long valued as a strategic base for expansion within the western Mediterranean Sea. As late as the 19th century Admiral Lord Horatio Nelson – who spent a year and a half (1803-1805) riding at anchor near La Maddalena – wrote to the British Admiralty that Sardinia was to be strategically valued as 'the *summum bonum* of the Mediterranean Sea' (Brigaglia 2006:98–99).

Regarding the history of archaeological research in the area, apart from the fundamental work done by Nino Lamboglia on the *Spargi* shipwreck at Secca Corsara (Lamboglia 1971:205ss; Pallarés Salvador 1981:5–39; Ministero dei Beni Culturali e Ambientali, Soprintendenza ai Beni Archeologici per le Provincie di Sassari e Nuoro 1982); the waters around of the archipelago have never been thoroughly and systematically investigated, although occasional reporting and individual, non-systematic studies have contributed to the assessment of the area's main historical characteristics (D'Oriano and Pallarés Salvador 1988:43ss).

Identified Sites

During 60 dives, the Maddalena Project retrieved a great amount of data useful for clarifying the routes around the Maddalena Archipelago. Finds (Figure 2) are representative of a wide timeframe—from as early as the 3rd century B.C. to as late as the 19th century A.D.—allowing the project to pinpoint the leading maritime routes crossing the Southern part of the Strait of Bonifacio and to offer original data useful for understanding the locations of shelters and harbours among the islands.

The earliest shipwreck was located off the Northwestern coast of the Spargi Island, less than two nautical miles from the *Spargi* shipwreck (Secca Corsara; Figure 1, n. 5) excavated by Professor Nino Lamboglia during the 1960s. The shipwreck, christened *Spargiottello* (Figure 1, n. 3), lies near the islet of the same name, at a depth of about 24-34m. The ship seems to have been transporting a cargo of type D Late Graeco-Italic wine amphorae (Will 1982:341ss), produced in Tyrrhenian Italy between the dawn of the 3rd century and the second half of the 2nd century B.C. Site survey provided evidence of parasitic goods which are often associated with similar cargoes[2]. Archaeometric data analysis is underway at the Università degli Studi di Catania.[3] An autoptical analysis indicates that workshops located in Central Southern Italy likely produced the amphorae. Based on the morphological characteristics of recovered artifacts, the site probably dates to the central years of the 2nd century B.C. The Roman *oneraria* ship was thus sailing toward the west along the Southern passage of the Strait of Bonifacio, known in medieval times as the Bucinaria channel (Motzo 1947:90–93)[4]. In the same area, a few other archaeological contexts have been located and documented that are identifiable with a shipwreck site.

In Cala Corsara (Spargi Island; Figure 1, n. 6), a shipwreck has been located in the inner portion of the bay. Shipwreck remains at a depth of 4 m were identified in 2005 due to a storm that unveiled part of the hull structure (Figure 3). Today, some remains of the hull – possibly the keelson – are visible on the seabed. Underneath a layer of sandy sediment, what appear to be planking frames joined by the mortise and tenon technique are also visible. Unfortunately, a thick layer of sediment covers the remains and the limitations of the project have not allowed further investigation. In addition, due to shallow waters and the short distance from shore, few artifacts have been preserved *in situ* – possible proof of salvage operation undertaken soon after the wreckage. Rare artifact fragments have nonetheless allowed the project members to identify the shipwreck

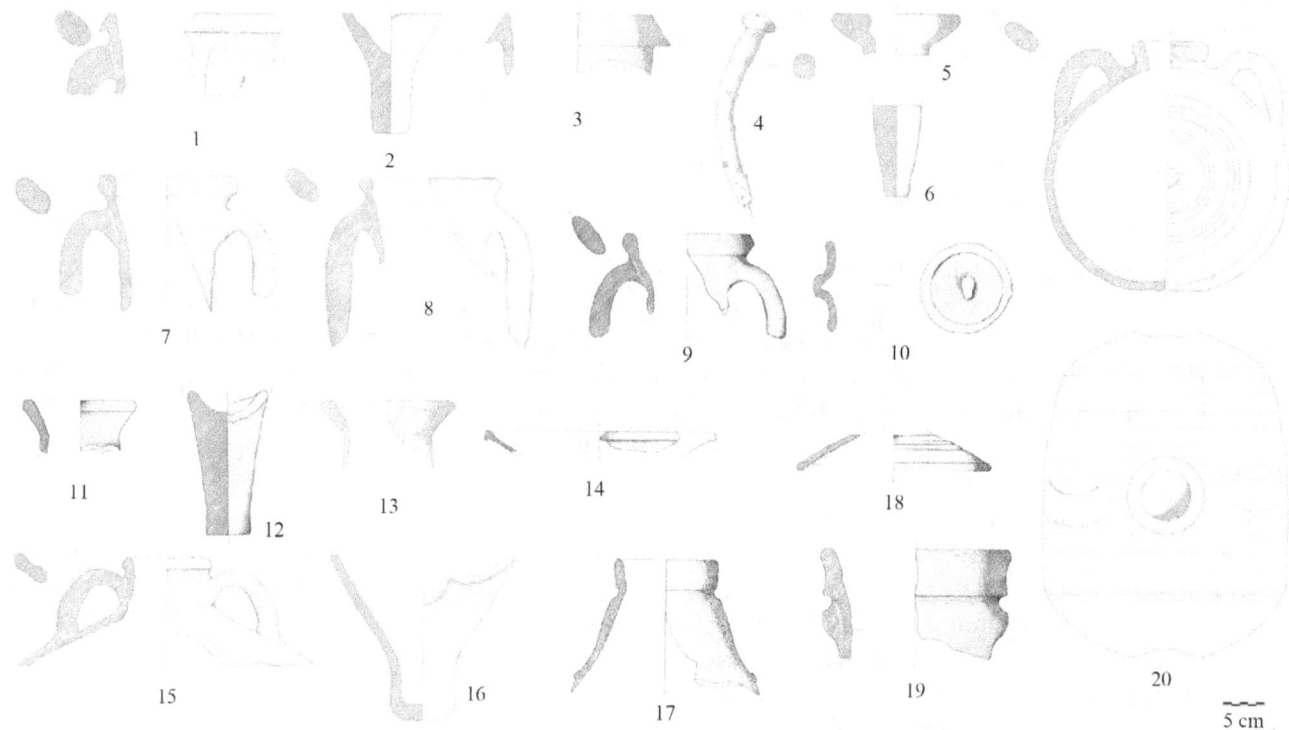

FIGURE 2. SOME OF THE ARTIFACTS RECOVERED FROM THE INVESTIGATED SITES (DRAWINGS: CLAUDIA GIARRUSSO; IMAGE SETTING: ALESSANDRO PORQUEDDU).

Figure 3. Archaeologists hand fanning and documenting the visible shipwreck wooden structure at Cala Corsara (photo courtesy: Dr. Fabrizio Antonioli).

as a Roman *oneraria* transporting oil (Dressel 20; Figure 2, n. 5), *defrutum* (Haltern 70; Figure 2, n. 6), and fish sauce (Dressel 7-11 and Beltran II) hailing from *Hispania Baetica* (Southwest Spain). Based on available data, the wreckage can be dated to around the second or third quarter of the 1st century A.D.

Within La Maddalena Island's broad Cala Francese Bay (Figure 1, n. 7), a shipwreck transporting *dolia* has been noted previously (Parker 1992:88, n. 146; Mastino et al. 2005:235, n. 90). The uncertain location of this shipwreck did not allow the project to relocate the site but, nonetheless, the team documented a site lying along a slope at the foot of an emerging cliff in 4-8m. The bricks on site were identified, documented, and ascribed to the Roman period on the basis of their correspondence with Roman measurements (29.6 cm = 1 *pedalis*).

Roman Sardinia represented a secondary market for construction materials (Zucca 1987:662–663), and such a cargo may have been intended for a construction of considerable importance and/or of public interest. This structure may have been thermal baths (as indicated by the characteristics of some associated artifacts) but may have been commissioned for another market. Again, the nature of the survey has not allowed the project to acquire sufficient data to better define the chronological context. Recovered artifacts tend to indicate local visits dating to the Late-Republican period, specifically late Graeco-Italic amphorae and the foot of a Brindisi amphora. Imperial amphorae, however, are present – including the rim of an Agora M254/Ostia I 453-4 amphora (Bertoldi 2012:109; Panella 1973:469–471; Peacock and Williams 1986:175; Rizzo 2003:157; Sciallano and Sibella 1991) – and characterize the site as very complex and in need of further research.

Two Roman shipwrecks have been located off Punta Sardegna and Capo d'Orso, along the Northern Sardinian coast. Nearby Punta Sardegna (Figure 1, n. 16), at a depth of 5-8 m, the project located a known concentration of fragmentary amphorae bodies (Parker 1992:359; Zucca 2003:177). Site recording further defined cargo typology, origin, and date. Recovered artifact fragments mainly belong to amphorae from Lusitania (Dressel 14b: Panella 1973:519ss; Parker 1977:37ss; Figure 2, nn. 7–9), from Baetica (Dressel 7-11 and Dressel 20: Peacock and Williams 1986:118,136) and, to a lesser extent, from Italy (a foot of a Dressel 2-4: Peacock and Williams 1986:105). Also recovered were two opercula (Bernal Casasola and Saéz Romero 2007; Figure 2, n. 10) and common ware in poor state of preservation. The ship, potentially departing from Lusitania with a cargo of fish sauce, may have stopped in a harbor in Baetica before attempting to cross the Strait of Bonifacio toward the Italian coast. Artifacts were analyzed and dated between the end of the 1st century and the first half of the 2nd century AD. Among other recovered material was a human bone (possibly a radius) which, related to similar findings from the same context (De Marzo 2010), could indicate the likelihood of a violent wreckage.

In the waters off Capo d'Orso (Figure 1, n. 14), at a depth of about 3m, a high concentration of Late Antique African amphorae bodies has also been located, all fragmentary. Rare diagnostic fragments suggest the ship was transporting African III amphorae of types A, B, and C (Bonifay 2004:119ss; Keay 1984:184–212; Manacorda 1977:171–85; Figure 2, nn. 11–13), as well as Dressel 30 amphorae of uncertain identification (Keay 1984:95; Peacock and Williams 1986:171). A rim fragment of African Red Slip ware, possibly belonging to 72 or 76 Hayes typology (Istituto della Enciclopedia italiana 1981:89–90, table 38, figure 6; Figure 2, n. 14) and dating from A.D. 425 to 475, is of uncertain identification due to the poor state of preservation. Considering the analyzed material culture, the shipwreck can be dated to the first half of the 5th century AD, most likely within the second quarter.

Among the identified shipwreck sites, only one was travelling the route through the Bocca Grande channel. Part of the cargo, composed of African amphorae and common wares and possibly associated with on-board facilities, is scattered at a depth of 6.8-9.3m within a large creek formed by the islands of Santa Maria and Razzoli (Figure 1, n. 1). This location is in immediate proximity to the rocky coast at the foot of a cliff. The cargo was mainly composed of Dressel 30 amphorae from *Mauretania Caesarensis* (Keay 1984:95; Peacock and Williams 1986:171; Figure 2, nn. 15–16), African IID from *Byzacena* (Bonifay 2004:117; Figure 2, n. 17), and a not clearly identifiable variation of African III. The ship, possibly departing from a North African port, could have stopped in a Sardinian port – ostensibly *Turris Libisonis* (ancient name of Porto Torres), an influential port settlement in northwestern Sardinia where this amphora typology is well attested (Villedieu 1984:178,183) – prior to crossing the strait and lying up in a port in central Italy (Panella 2001:207, note 231; Gibbins 2001:314). According to amphora typologies, the shipwreck site could be dated to the first half of the 4th century A.D.

Apart from shipwreck sites, survey has allowed La Maddalena Project members to identify three areas of scattered ceramic artifacts, all of which are inconclusive from chronological and provenance perspectives. Archaeological contexts located in areas sheltered by prevailing winds can likely be interpreted as docking or sheltering sites. In Budelli (Figure 1, n. 2), one of the three northern islands of the archipelago, a massive concentration of Roman ceramic material embedded in a section of dry land progressively eroded by rising sea levels was located and documented (Antonioli et al. 2012). Near two spring-puddles team members discovered Dressel 1 A and B amphora fragments (Figure 2, n. 19). A few artifacts have also been collected from the beach. Unfortunately, the acidic nature of the soil has compromised the fragments' state of preservation. However, some more intact artifacts have allowed a chronological range for site to be established. The earliest artifact is a Dressel 1 rim dating to A.D. 120 to A.D. 150, while the latest is a fragment of an African cooking ware dish/lid with a blackened rim dating from between the first half of the 3rd century and the 4th century A.D. (Carandini et al. 1968: figure 261, table 32, number 5; Figure 2, n. 18).

Baia di Spalmatore in La Maddalena Island, one of the best-protected bays in the whole archipelago, produced a generally later assemblage of material (Figure 1, n. 9). Within the bay, the survey found evidence for the existence of at least two important sites. The first, located at a depth of about 10m, is characterized by various ceramics embedded within an eroding root system. Among these were a *spatheion* dating to the first half of the 5th century A.D. (Bonifay 2004:124, figure 67), a barrel amphora of uncertain dating (Purpura 1986:148–150; Figure 2, n. 20), an amphora of unknown type and various artifacts from the Post-Medieval period up to the 17th century A.D. The second site, located in very shallow water near the beach, provided a large concentration of fragmentary ceramics suggesting a date in the late Middle Ages. This was a period of instability when Islamic people, the Mariner Republics of Pisa and Genoa, the Crown of Aragon, and the Saracen pirates competed for a strategic sea passage controlling trade routes. The bay, totally hidden from the open sea, may have appealed to those seeking control in the Medieval and Post-Medieval periods.

Collaborative Archaeology: a Joined Effort for the Management and Enhancement of Maritime Cultural Heritage

As noted in the introduction, the main objective of the Maddalena Project was to generate an archaeological chart of the waters in the Maddalena archipelago as a basis to promote further studies and to understand the archaeological potential of the archipelagic waters. The project also aimed to enhance public interpretation of maritime cultural heritage through planning and establishing public outreach and access activities (underwater cultural heritage trails, outreach activities, seminars, etc.). Geographic, socio-economic and, *lato sensu*, cultural characteristics adapt well to the planning and development of a structured public interpretation and access program which could – thanks to the already substantial influx of tourists – bolster the cultural tourism sector. This kind of tourism could be, in a structured and varied program, an appealing catalyst for national and international tourist operators, acting at the same time as a flywheel for the promotion, enhancement, and protection of the maritime cultural heritage in the area. Such structured programs have been implemented elsewhere. Notable successes include Florida, USA (Scott-Ireton 2005, 2006, 2007, 2008; McKinnon 2007), and Australia (Anderson et al. 2006; Nutley 1987, 2006; Souter 2006; Staniforth 1994). The Cayman Islands are of particular interest with similar geographical characteristics and an elaborate and appealing public outreach experience (Leshikar-Denton 2006, 2010; Scott-Ireton 2005; Leshikar-Denton and Scott-Ireton 2007).

Cultural and historical diversity and relatively accessible sites within the Maddalena Archipelago could facilitate the establishment of a structured program. The extended and enduring collaboration between different stakeholders – as it is in the case of the Maddalena Project – can aid in the management and fostering of different but complementary sectors of public life. Sectors that may be key are the territorial management and development (Municipality), the research, protection and management of the natural and cultural heritage (National Park), and the protection and management of cultural heritage (Superintendency and, to a lesser extent, the University). These shared benefits could and should allow for the structuring of a coherent and proactive public outreach program. The participation of the National Park will foster the value of protecting submerged archaeological heritage, but also one that includes landscape heritage as well. As specified elsewhere (Lekishar-Denton 2010), a collaborative effort is key for a successful interpretation, protection, and management of heritage activities.

Logically, by the definition of cultural heritage proposed by the *Codice dei Beni Culturali e Paesaggistici* (Code of Cultural and Landscape Heritage: Ainis, Fiorillo 2008; Cammelli 2006; Corso 2004; Sciullo 2008; Severini 2004, 2006) where cultural heritage is characterized by both cultural property and landscape property (art. 2, commas 1-3, *Code*), institutional collaboration – dictated and stimulated by legislation in Italy (Frigerio 2010; Secci 2011) – seems to be the most feasible and consistent way to accomplish protection, management, and promotion efforts. In addition, a collaborative allegiance appears far more holistic in scope and incisive in facilitating the consideration of an issue from different points of view, offering a more comprehensive and complete final historical and archaeological reconstruction.

At the end of fieldwork, in cooperation with the Municipality, the Maddalena Project team produced a series of posters and an afternoon lecture to present the final project to the local and tourist community. The lecture fulfilled part of the original objective of the project – communicating to the public and raising awareness of the value of intact and protected underwater cultural heritage. The posters, permanently displayed inside the Municipality's buildings, have provided the opportunity to communicate archaeological ethics and practices in a consistent and effective manner. They also present reasons, statements, and legislative references regarding the protection of underwater cultural heritage in Italy, while placing value on supporting site protection and archaeological research in view of potential responsible exploitation of such heritage for tourist and sustainable local development purposes.

Conclusions

The maritime archaeological sites of the Maddalena Archipelago – in terms of the variety of site typology, chronological range – represent a valuable yet underestimated resource for the advancement of research on ancient trade through the Strait of Bonifacio. Equally

Figure 4. One of the 4 posters produced for the Municipality of La Maddalena, offering a summary of investigated sites and their characteristics (poster setting: Alessandro Porqueddu, Massimiliano Secci).

important is public interpretation of maritime cultural heritage in an archipelago that is currently undergoing economic depression and depopulation. Tourism still plays a relevant role in the economy of the archipelago and, as proved by the Garibaldi Museum, cultural assets should and could play a distinctive role in the development of the islands' economy.[5]

In order to achieve this goal, major efforts are necessary not only with regards to the creation of cultural attractions that can appeal tourists but also to changing the local community's attitude towards maritime cultural heritage – commonly seen as monetary profit when sold in the black market. Maritime cultural heritage is and should be a financial resource. However profits should generated by the understanding of the value of maritime cultural heritage in terms of strengthening personal identities and sense of belonging and (Secci 2013a, b) by the effect that a land (and its people) proud of its past can have in fascinating and attracting tourists. The preliminary survey and distribution chart produced by the Maddalena Project could therefore potentially be a strong and valuable basis for further research, for the identification of sites of major interest for public interpretive purposes, and for the organization of a regulated system dedicated to the protection and the enhancement of the local maritime cultural heritage.

Acknowledgments

Authors would like to thank the Municipality of La Maddalena, the Parco Nazionale dell'Arcipelago di La Maddalena, the Soprintendenza ai Beni Archeologici per le Province di Sassari e Nuoro, the IV Nucleo Sommozzatori of the Capitaneria di Porto in Cagliari, the Diving Center La Maddalena, and the Associazione Culturale Castra Sardiniæ. Many thanks also go to colleagues Dr. Fabrizio Antonioli, Dr. Emanuela Solinas, Prof. Raimondo Zucca and Dr. Rubens D'Oriano for their precious scientific consultancy. A special thank you goes to all students and researchers at the Università degli Studi di Sassari for their valid and substantial commitment.

Notes

1. *Italian National Agency for New Technologies, Energy and Sustainable Economic Development*

2. *These items were often represented by small marketable goods stowed in the interstice between amphoras. Mostly associated with Graeco-Italic amphoras were Campana wares.*

3. *Dipartimento di Chimica, Corso di Tecnologie Applicate ai Beni Culturali, under the scientific direction of Prof. E. Ciliberto.*

4. *Name offered by the Compasso de Navegare, Medieval navigation chart from Pisa, defining the sea between Capo della Vite and Isola delle Bisce.*

5. *The exceptional historical value of the house of Garibaldi does not allow a full and direct comparison, but rather a touchstone based on the idea of cultural and historical heritage interpretation, promotion, and access.*

References

AINIS, MICHELE AND FIORILLO MARCO
2008   *L'ordinamento della cultura: Manuale di legislazione dei beni culturali*, Giuffrè, Milano.

ANDERSON, ROSS, CASSANDRA PHILIPPOU, AND PETER HARVEY
2006   Innovative Approaches in Underwater Cultural Heritage Management. In *Maritime Archaeology: Australian Approaches*, Mark Staniforth, Mike Nash, editors, pp. 137–150. Springer, New York.

ANTONIOLI, FABRIZIO, PAOLO E. ORRÙ, ALESSANDRO PORQUEDDU, AND EMANUELA SOLINAS
2012   *Variazioni del livello marino in Sardegna durante gli ultimi millenni sulla base di indicatori geo-archeologici costieri*. In L'Africa romana, Atti del XIX Convegno di Studi (Sassari 16-19 dicembre 2010), Vol. 3, Cocco M. B., Alberto Gavini, and Ibba A. (a cura di), pp. 296–2972. Carocci, Roma.

BERNAL CASASOLA, DARIO AND SÁEZ ROMERO ANTONIO
2007   *Opérculos y ánforas romanas es el Círculo del Estrecho. Precisiones tipológicas, cronológicas y funcionales*, in Rei Cretariæ Romanæ Fautorum Acta 40, Susanne Biegert, editor, pp. 1–18. Prime Rate kft., Budapest.

BERTOLDI, TOMMASO
2012   *Guida alle anfore romane di età imperiale. Forme, impasti e distribuzione*. Espera, Roma.

BONIFAY, MICHEL
2004   *Études sur la céramique romaine tardive d'Afrique*. British Archaeological Reports International Series 1301, Oxford.

BOWENS, AMANDA (EDITOR)
2009   *Underwater Archaeology: the NAS Guide to Principles and Practice*. Nautical Archaeology Society, Blackwell Publishing, Portsmouth.

CAMMELLI, MARCO
2006 *Introduzione*. In *Il diritto dei beni culturali (2nd edition)*, Carla Barbati, Marco Cammelli, Girolamo Sciullo, editors, pp. XI – XXVII. Il Mulino, Bologna.

CAPRARA, ROBERTO, ALBERTO LUCIANO, AND GIOVANNI MACIOCCO (EDITORS)
1996 *Archeologia del territorio, territorio dell'archeologia*. Delfino, Sassari.

CARANDINI, ANDREA, EMANUELA FABBRICOTTI, AND CARLO GASPARRI (EDITORS)
1968 Le Terme del Nuotatore. Scavo dell'Ambiente IV. Ostia I. *Studi Miscellanei 13*, Roma.

CESARI, JOSEPH. AND LEANDRI FRANK
2007 Le mégalithisme de la Corse. In *Patrimonio Archeologico e Architettonico Sardo-Corso: Affinità e differenze*, pp. 217–288. EDES, Sassari.

CORSO, GUIDO
2004 *Articoli 1. Principi*. In *Il Codice dei beni culturali e del paesaggio. Commento al decreto legislativo 22 gennaio 2004, n. 42*, Marco Cammelli, editor, pp. 55–58. Il Mulino, Bologna 2004.

D'ORIANO, RUBENS AND PALLARÉS SALVADOR FRANCISCA
1988 La Maddalena. in *L'Antiquarium arborense e i civici musei archeologici della Sardegna*, Giovanni Lilliu, editor, pp. 43-54. Banco di Sardegna, Sassari.

DE FELICE, EMIDIO
1964 *Le coste della Sardegna: saggio toponomastico storico-descrittivo*.Ed. Sarda Fossataro, Cagliari.

DE MARZO, ROBERTA
2010 *Storia e commerci del Fretum Gallicum romano attraverso i relitti. Il relitto di Cala Corsara*, Thesis, Dipartimento di Storia, Università di Sassari, Sassari, Italy.

FERRARESE CERUTI, MARIA. LUISA AND PITZALIS GIUSEPPE
1987 Il tafone di Cala Corsara nell'isola di Spargi (La Maddalena). In *Il Neolitico in Italia, Atti della XXVI Riunione Scientifica (Firenze 7-10 novembre 1985)*, pp. 871-886. Firenze.

FRIGERIO, ALBERTO
2010 L'entrata in vigore in Italia della Convenzione UNESCO 2001 sulla protezione del patrimonio culturale subacqueo. *Aedon* 2. www.aedon.mulino.it (last access 01 March 2013).

GIBBINS, DAVID
2001 A Roman Shipwreck of c. AD 200 at Plemmirio, Sicily: Evidence for North African Amphora Production during the Severan Period. *World archaeology* 32(3):311-334.

ISTITUTO DELLA ENCICLOPEDIA ITALIANA
1981 *Atlante delle forme ceramiche I*. In *Enciclopedia dell'Arte antica classica e orientale* Carandini Andrea, editore. Istituto della Enciclopedia italiana, Roma.

KEAY, SIMON J.
1984 *Late roman amphorae in the western Mediterranean*. British Archaeological Reports International Series 196 (I), Oxford.

KRETSCHMER, KONRAD
1909 *Die Italianischen Portolane des Mittelalters. Ein Beitraghe zur Geschichte der Kartographie und Nautik*. Berlin.

LAMBOGLIA, NINO
1971 La seconda campagna di scavo sulla nave romana di Spargi (1959). In *Atti III Congresso Internazionale di Archeologia sottomarina, Barcellona 1961*, pp. 205-ss. Bordighera.

LESHIKAR-DENTON, MARGARET E.
2006 Foundations in Management of Maritime Cultural Heritage in the Cayman Islands. In *Underwater Cultural Heritage at Risk: Managing Natural and Human Impacts*, Robert Grenier, David Nutley, and Ian Cochran, editors, pp. 23–25, Biedermann Offsetdruck, München.

LESHIKAR-DENTON, MARGARET E.
2010 Cooperation is the Key: We Can Protect the Underwater Cultural Heritage. *Journal of Maritime Archaeology* 5:85–95.

LESHIKAR-DENTON, MARGARET E. AND SCOTT-IRETON DELLA A.
2007 A Maritime Heritage Trail and Shipwreck Preserves for the Cayman Islands. In *Out of the blue: public interpretation of maritime cultural resources*. John H. Jameson, Della A. Scott-Ireton, editors, pp. 64–94, Springer, New York.

LILLIU, GIOVANNI
1988 *La civiltà dei Sardi dal Paleolitico all'età dei nuraghi*. Nuova ERI, Torino (I ed. 1967).

MANCINI, PAOLA
2010 *Gallura orientale: preistoria e protostoria*. Taphros, Olbia.

MASTINO ATTILIO, PIER GIORGIO SPANU, AND RAIMONDO ZUCCA
2005 *Mare Sardvm. Merci, mercati e scambi della Sardegna antica*. Carocci, Roma.

MCKINNON, JENNIFER F.
2007 Creating a Shipwreck Trail: Documenting the 1733 Spanish Plate Fleet Wrecks. In *Out of the blue: public interpretation of maritime cultural resources*. John H. Jameson, Della A. Scott-Ireton, editors, pp. 85–94, Springer, New York.

Ministero dei Beni Culturali e Ambientali, Soprintendenza ai Beni Archeologici per le province di Sassari e Nuoro
1982   *La Maddalena: Museo Archeologico Navale "Nino Lamboglia": guida breve*. Chiarella, Sassari.

Motzo, Bachisio R.
1936   La Sardegna nel Compasso de Navegare. *Archivio Storico Sardo 20*.

Motzo, Bachisio R.
1947   *Il Compasso da Navigare. Opera italiana della metà del secolo 13*. Università, Cagliari.

Nutley, David
1987   Maritime archaeology: education as the long arm of the law. *Bulletin of the Austalian Institute for Maritime Archaeology* 11(1):29–33.

2006   Protected Zones and Partnerships: Their Application and Importance to Underwater Cultural Heritage Management. In *Underwater Cultural Heritage at Risk: Managing Natural and Human Impacts*, Robert Grenier, David Nutley, and Ian Cochran, editors, pp. 32–34, Biedermann Offsetdruck, München.

Pallarés Salvador, Francisca
1981   Il relitto romano di Spargi (La Maddalena, Sardegna). *Rivista di Studi Liguri* 1977-1981:5–39.

Panedda, Dionici
1978   *Il Giudicato di Gallura:curatorie e centri abitati*. Editrice libreria Dessi, Sassari.

Panella, Clementina
1973   *Appunti su un gruppo di anfore della prima, media e tarda età imperiale*. In *Ostia III, Studi Miscellanei 21*, Andrea Carandini, Clementina Panella, editors, pp. 460–633. Roma.

2001   *Le anfore di età imperiale nel Mediterraneo occidentale*. In *Céramiques hellénistique et romaines III*, Pierre Lévêque, Jean P. Morel and Evelyne Geny, editors, pp. 177 – 275. Presses Univ. Franche-Comté, Paris.

Parker, Anthony J.
1977   Lusitanian Amphorae, In *Méthodes classiques et méthodes formelles dans l'étude des amphores*. Collection de l'École française de Rome 32:35–47.

1992   *Ancient Shipwrecks of the Mediterranean and the Roman provinces*. British Aarchaeological Reports International Series, Oxford.

Peacock, David P. S. and Williams David F.
1986   *Amphorae and the Roman economy. An introductory guide*. Longman, London and New York.

Piloni, Luigi
1974   *Carte geografiche della Sardegna*, Edizioni della Torre, Cagliari.

Rizzo, Giorgio
2003   Instrumenta Urbis I. Ceramiche fini da mensa, lucerne e anfore a Roma nei primi due secoli dell'Impero. *Collection de l'École française de Rome* 307. École française de Rome, Roma.

Robb, John and Tykot Robert H.
2003   Ricostruzione tramite analisi Gis di aspetti marittimi e sociali nello scambio di ossidiana durante il Neolitico. In *Atti della XXXV Riunione Scientifica: Le comunità della Preistoria Italiana*, Firenze, pp. 1021–1025.

Sciallano, Martine and Sibella Patricia
1991   *Amphores. Comment les identifier?*. Edisud, Aix-en-Provence.

Sciullo, Girolamo
2008   La tutela: gli artt. 1–15. *Aedon* 3. http://www.aedon.mulino.it/archivio/2008/3/sciullo.htm (last access 01 March 2013).

Scott-Ireton, Della A.
2005   Preserves parks and trails: strategy and response in maritime cultural resource. Unpublished Doctoral dissertation, The Florida State University, Tallahassee. Florida.

2006   Florida's Underwater Archaeological Preserves: Preservation through Education. In *Underwater Cultural Heritage at Risk: Managing Natural and Human Impacts*, Robert Grenier, David Nutley, and Ian Cochran, editors, pp. 5–7, Biedermann Offsetdruck, München.

2007   The value of public education and interpretation in Submerged Cultural Resource Management. In *Out of the blue: public interpretation of maritime cultural resources*. John H. Jameson, Della A. Scott-Ireton, editors, pp 19–32, Springer, New York.

2008   Teaching 'heritage awareness' rather than 'skills' to sports diving community. *Journal of Maritime Archaeology* 3:119–120.

Secci, Massimiliano
2011   Protection vs. Public Access: two concepts compared within the Italian underwater cultural heritage management system. *Journal of Maritime Archaeology* 6(2):113–128.

2013a   Public interpretation of maritime cultural heritage in Sardinia: the value of outreach activities within the socio-cultural and economic fabric. In *Identity & Connectivity, Proceedings of the 16th Symposium on Mediterranean Archaeology (Florence, 1-3 March 2012)*, Bombardieri L., D'Agostino A., Guido Guarducci, Orsi V. and Stefano Valentini, editors. British Archaeological Reports, Oxford, (in print).

2013b "Public" and "the Public" in Italian Underwater Archaeology: A Sardinian Perspective. In Della A. Scott-Ireton, editors, *Meeting Challenges in the Public Interpretation of Maritime Cultural Heritage – Between the Devil and the Deep*, Annalies Corbin, Joe W. Joseph, editors, *When the Land Meets the Sea Series*. Springer, New York, pp. 73 – 84.

SEVERINI, GIUSEPPE
2004 *I principi del Codice dei beni culturali e del paesaggio*. In *Giornale Diritto Amministrativo* 5.

2006 *Disposizioni Generali*. In *Codice dei Beni Culturali e del Paesaggio*, Maria Alessandra Sandulli, editor, pp. 1 – 33, Giuffré, Milano.

SOUTER, CORIOLI
2006 Cultural Tourism and Diver Education. In *Maritime Archaeology: Australian Approaches*, Mark Staniforth, Mike Nash, editors, pp.163–176. Springer, New York.

STANIFORTH, MARK
1994 Public Access to Maritime Archaeology. *Bulletin of the Austalian Institute for Maritime Archaeology* 18(1):13–16.

TERROSU ASOLE, ANGELA
1987 *Il Portolano di Grazia Pauli:opera italiana del secolo 14*. CNR, Cagliari.

TYKOT, ROBERT H.
1996 Obsidian procurement and distribution in the Central and Western Mediterranean. *Journal of Mediterranean Archeology* 9(1):39–82.

VILLEDIEU, FRANÇOISE
1984 *Turris Libisonis. Fouille d'un site romain tardif à Porto Torres, Sardaigne*. British Aarchaelogical Reports International Series, Oxford.

WILLIAMS THORPE, OLWEN, STANLEY E. WARREN, AND JEAN COURTIN
1984 The distribution and sources of archeological obsidian from southern France. *Journal of archeological Science* 11(2):135–146.

ZICHI, GIANCARLO AND ACCARDO KATIE
1989 *Passio sanctorum martyrum Gavini, Proti et Januarii*. Chiarella, Sassari.

ZUCCA, RAIMONDO
1987 *L'opus doliare urbano in Africa ed in Sardinia*, in Mastino A., (a cura di), L'Africa romana, Atti del IV convegno di studio, 2, Sassari 12-14 dicembre 1986, pp. 665 – 673.

2003 *Insulae Sardiniae et Corsicae. Le isole minori della Sardegna e della Corsica nell'antichità*. Carocci, Roma.

· · · · · · · · · · · · · · · ·

Massimiliano Secci
Dipartimento di Storia
Scienze dell'Uomo e della Formazione
Università degli Studi diSassari
Via Zanfarino, 62
07100 - Sassari

Ports and Settlements in the Gulf of Oristano: A Coastal and Underwater Archaeological Approach

Paolo Orrù
Emanuela Solinas
Pier Giorgio I. Spanu
Raimondo Zucca

A multidisciplinary team from the universities of Cagliari and Sassari (Sardinia, Italy) has, in recent years, undertaken a series of global archaeology research campaigns. Major attention has been placed on the area surrounding Oristano. Studies have focused on maritime sites and port facilities but also on settlement dynamics in a territory characterized by wetlands and large lagoons. A high concentration of ancient cities and a high number of rural settlements connected to road networks, resource exploitation and port infrastructures characterize the area. Geomorphologic dynamics have also been considered in order to re-construct the ancient natural and cultural landscape.

Introduction

Tharros is located in Central Western Sardinia (Italy), at the Southern end of the Sinis Peninsula delimitating the Northern end of the wide Oristano Bay. Tharros was founded by Phoenicians around the last quarter of the 7th century B.C., following a Nuragic settlement of the Bronze Age dating back to the 15th century B.C. The city was monumentalized in Punic (end of 6th century B.C. – 238 B.C.) and Roman times (238 B.C. – middle of the 5th century A.D.). The urban settlement declines in Early Medieval times until a complete abandonment near A.D. 1070 for the benefit of the town of Oristano. Excavation campaigns started in the 19th century in the Phoenician and Punic funeral areas and have been resumed in 1956 with regular campaigns by the Sorpintendenza Archeologica di Cagliari (Superintendency), in collaboration with the National Centre for Research (CNR), and the Universities of Roma "La Sapienza", Bologna, Cagliari, and Sassari.

The aim of the present paper is to underline the intense interaction between natural processes and human settlement dynamics, with a particular reference to confronting archaeological, geomorphologic, and isotopic C14 dating data of littoral ribbons. Such interpretation allows, firstly, for the revocation of any doubt on the reconstruction of the Sinis peninsula landscape proposed by Fedele in 1980 (1980:52, figure 40), where isobaths of – 5 m were used to reconstruct the coastline between the end of the 2nd millennium and the first half of the 1st millennium B.C. Fedele's reconstruction places the former coastline about 2 km east of the modern Su Siccu-Sa Mistra Manna's ribbon.

Geomorphologic studies and coastal landscape archaeology research produced in the coastal area known as Mare Morto, or Dead Sea, facing the Western Sardinia's Oristano Bay and the inland marshes beyond it, have overlooked the urban area at the feet of the Tower of San Giovanni as the hypothetical location for the town of Tharros' harbor infrastructures. Since the first underwater survey of Tharros sea floor produced by Luigi Fozzati and Piero Bartoloni, these studies have instead advanced a location for port in the area known as *Porto Vecchio*, or Ancient Harbor, north of Murru Mannu, the Big Face Hill (Fozzati 1980:99–109; Acquaro et al. 1999).

During the last two years, the congruent development of research produced by the Soprintendenza per i Beni Archeologici di Cagliari e di Oristano (the local Superintendency) and the University of Cagliari and Sassari has endorsed an hypothesis first proposed by Raimondo Zucca in 1993 (1993:45,48,80) on the location of the Tharros harbor, partially mired and buried, within the swampy Mistras area. Such speculation was initially based on photographic interpretation of ancient coastline presented in 1985 by Alessandro Fioravanti (1985:87–92) who denounced a recent formation of the Mistras area while he hypothesized that "the ancient harbour of Tharros" lay in a hollow north of the highest sand dune (7.4 m) of the Bidda de is Piscadoris ("Town of Fishermen"). Most relevant in the formulation of his hypothesis was the connection between the extended Archaic and Punic Necropolis of Santu Marcu – San Giovanni di Sinis with settlement revolving around the harbor. Finally, the discovery of the Punic Tharros *Keramikòs* in 1981, located in the area between the Santu Marcu necropolis and the San Giovanni di Sinis church, documented the existence of a "handcrafting" center

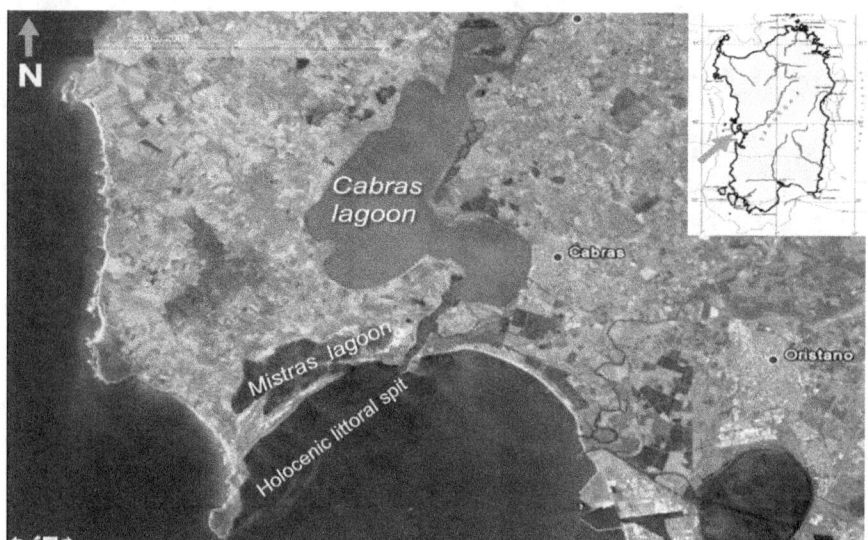

FIGURE 1. ORTHOGONAL PHOTO OF THE MISTRAS LAGOON AREA (IMAGE ELABORATION: PAOLO ORRÙ).

undoubtedly functional to the production of containers for food supplies allocated for local consumption and maritime export.

Geomorphologic and Archaeological Considerations

A better analysis of Mistras coastal landscape dynamics is bound to a preliminary interpretation of the area geomorphology. Marine ingression during the latest interglacial MIS 5e (Tyrrhenian auct.) has resulted in the partial submersion of the Campidano di Oristano – a coastal plain surrounding the town of Oristano – up to the present 7.5 m above sea level, and the formation of an ample bay subsequently closed by a great littoral ribbon creating present-day Cabras Lagoon. Evidence of this littoral ribbon survives in the extensive fossiliferous calcarenites outcrops often used in ancient times as construction materials. Gradually, cold climate phases characterized by levels of low eustatic change produced prevailing erosive processes, engraving deep palaeo-valleys often in correspondence with the mouths of "Tyrrhenian" palaeo-lagoons (MIS 2 – Würm). A return of the Holocene sea has re-elaborated and re-distributed alluvial contribution of the Tirso River, erecting littoral ribbons organized in different orders, again transforming coastal inlets into lagoons and ponds.

Geomorphologic evidences testify to how the genesis of the current Mistras Lagoon (with the Northeastern appendix of Sa Mardini) is distinct from the *Mare Pontis* (or Cabras) pond's origin. The latter is recognizable as an ancient Würmian (MIS 2) fluvial valley excavated by the Mare Foghe stream into the MIS 5 calcarenites. Tyrrhenian sandstone bed deposits separate the Southern coast of the Cabras Lagoon from the complex Mistras – Sa Mardini. A recent study from the University of Cagliari suggests (Del Vais et al. 2008), that the Mistras lagoon "appears partially closed by the current littoral ribbons of *Su Siccu* and *Mare Morto* [Su Siccu and Sa Mistra Manna]," nonetheless "evidences of littoral ribbons and lagoons associated with the last transgression have been observed", as already highlighted in the past by Acquaro (Acquaro, et al. 1999). Our analysis allows for a more precise final return phase of the Holocene sea that has taken in the external part of a large bay and partially closed it by patches of wrecked ribbons, forming the current rear-littoral Mistras Lagoon allowing a structuring and growing of today's littoral ribbon.

The evaluation of shoreline variations in lagoon areas is extremely problematic (Solinas and Orrù 2006; Auriemma and Solinas 2009). Beside eustatic sea level

FIGURE 2. AERIAL PHOTOGRAPH OF THE MISTRAS LAGOON BASIN. 1) THARROS PUNIC HARBOR QUAY; 2) BASIS OF A TOWER OR LIGHTHOUSE (PROVINCIA DI ORISTANO. PHOTO: FRANCESCO CUBEDDU).

rise trends, evaluations require the calculation of the dynamism of a coastal area that is often subsiding (due to tectonic reasons or to sedimentary compression), (Antonioli et al. 2007) as well as the incidence of the regional isostatic glacial-hydro degree (Lambeck et al. 2005). To this purpose, three stratigraphic probes – still undergoing in-depth analysis – have been utilized in the coastal plain of the Tirso River.

Analysis does not seem to confirm the most recent studies on sea level change that determined a level of – 1.98 m for the period comprised between the 1st century B.C. and the 1st century A.D. (Del Vais et al. 2008:408–412). In fact, such data is not applicable to any coastal area of the Mediterranean, as elaborate interactions between human and natural factors could produce far vaster variations compared to data that are more general.

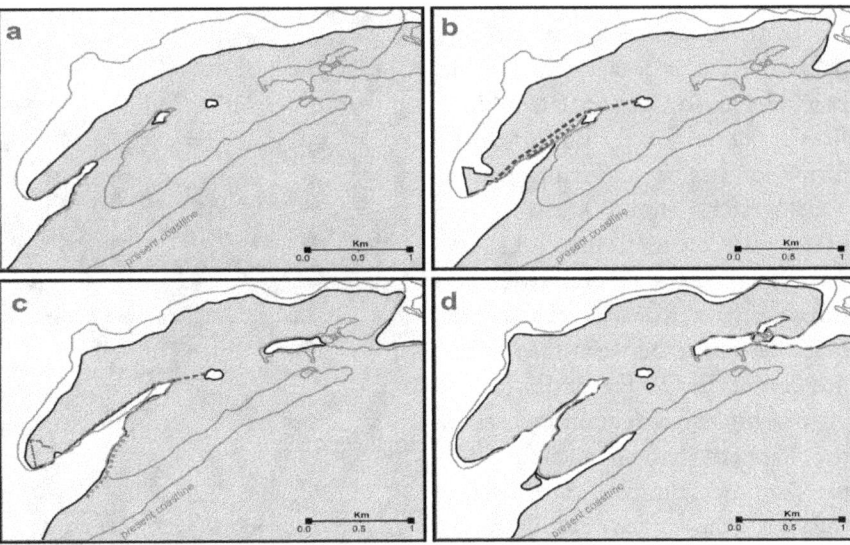

FIGURE 3. GEOMORPHOLOGIC EVOLUTION OF THE MISTRAS LAGOON (ELABORATION: PAOLO ORRÙ).

Regarding Mistras, some geo-archaeological indicators lead to the dating of the progressive formation of Mistras's internal dune ribbons between the 8th century B.C., the Imperial Roman period, and the Late Medieval period. References to variations in extensions of ponds – particularly that of Mistras (despite wrongly referred to as "of Cabras") – were made by both an anonymous scholar in 1833 and by archaeologist Giovanni Spano (1851:12–13, n. 2; 1861:179–180, n. 4) when referring to a "long section of a Roman road" (Figure 2).

As has been maintained by Carla Del Vais et al. (2008:408–412), these 19th-century references represent the first attestation (despite a misleading interpretation) of a monumental submerged structure recognized, *ex novo*, by Giuseppe Pisanu and preliminarily published by the University of Cagliari team. Probing carried out near the submerged structure has offered a twelve-meter stratigraphy with "an interchange of sandy and silt-clay layers, very rich in Posidonia and brackish fauna" (Del Vais 2008). This, however, does not add any clarifying information to the palaeo-environmental character of the area.

Our hypothesis of a marine bay open toward the Gulf of Oristano, thus requiring a protective port infrastructure, fits perfectly with a harbor characterization defined by a natural shelter protected from winds and billows immediately inland of the Archaic and Punic settlement of San Giovanni – Santu Marcu. Starting from the creek, the lagoon formation appears connected to a remarkable supply of sand by the Tirso River, the predominant wind flow, and the internal gulf currents. Such a combination of factors could well explain recurring formation of progressive littoral ribbons and silting of the borders of the original body of water of Mistras. The primeval ribbon could be identified with the strip of Sa Mistraredda where the above-mentioned submerged structure is grafted connecting the dune ribbon with an oxbow. A survey of the dune ribbon has revealed silted beachrock (Kelletat 2006) containing washed archaeological material, particularly amphorae fragments, useful for a chronological definition of the beachrock formation.

The Soprintendenza per I Beni Archeologici di Cagliari e Oristano and the University of Sassari have produced four archaeological campaigns in the Mistras Lagoon area between 2008 and 2011. Several test trenches have been excavated along the beachrock formation that provided evidence of washed archaeological artifacts alternating to a sandy lens and ending in a layer with a high water infiltration percentage. Composed of Nuragic amphorae of Sant'Imbenia typology, Phoenician and Carthaginian amphorae, Corinthian amphorae of the Koehler A type, Ionic-Massaliots amphorae produced in Magna Graecia, and Attic ceramics, the artifacts assemblage fits chronologically between the first half of the 7th century and the end of the 4th century B.C. (Figure 3a). Survey has also revealed beachrock related to the current Western basin shoreline of the Mistras Lagoon. This second beachrock formation has returned archaeological artifacts, particularly amphorae, dating to the Late Hellenistic period (Republican Rome; Figure 3b). A third beachrock formation has been identified on the Southwestern shore of the second basin, east of the Mistras Lagoon. This last beachrock exclusively featured Imperial Roman archaeological material dating between the 1st and 3rd century A.D. (Figure 3c).

A second investigation focused on the Western basin's ancient structures submersion, connected both to the rise of the sea level during the last 3000 years and to subsiding phenomenon. Ancient structures particularly are represented by "a wall clear for over 150 meters, with a South-West/North-East orientation; the work is formed by two hangings of squared sandstone blocks, well worked and regularly tangentially aligned on the long-side, in few cases slice-placed" (Del Vais et al. 2008; Figure 2, n. 1; Figure 4).

The Cagliari research team (Del Vais et al. 2008) also proposes the interpretation of the wall as:

> ...a structure functional to supporting a free quay, that is a docking place nearby the sandy moorings for unloading fishing cargoes or other reasons; or else an embankment addressed to partially close the basin, for reasons tied to offering shelter for fishing boats – a sort of rudimental kleistos limen [closed harbor] – or to diverse manufacturing practices connected to auletica ruling and enregimentation, which remains an activity vivaciously dynamic in Cabras' lagoon...

Concerning chronology, the authors supposed a Late Punic timeframe that does not exclude a later Roman date when Punic techniques persisted. Cagliari's research team has nonetheless overlooked the characteristics of the groundwork for such a tremendous structure, which

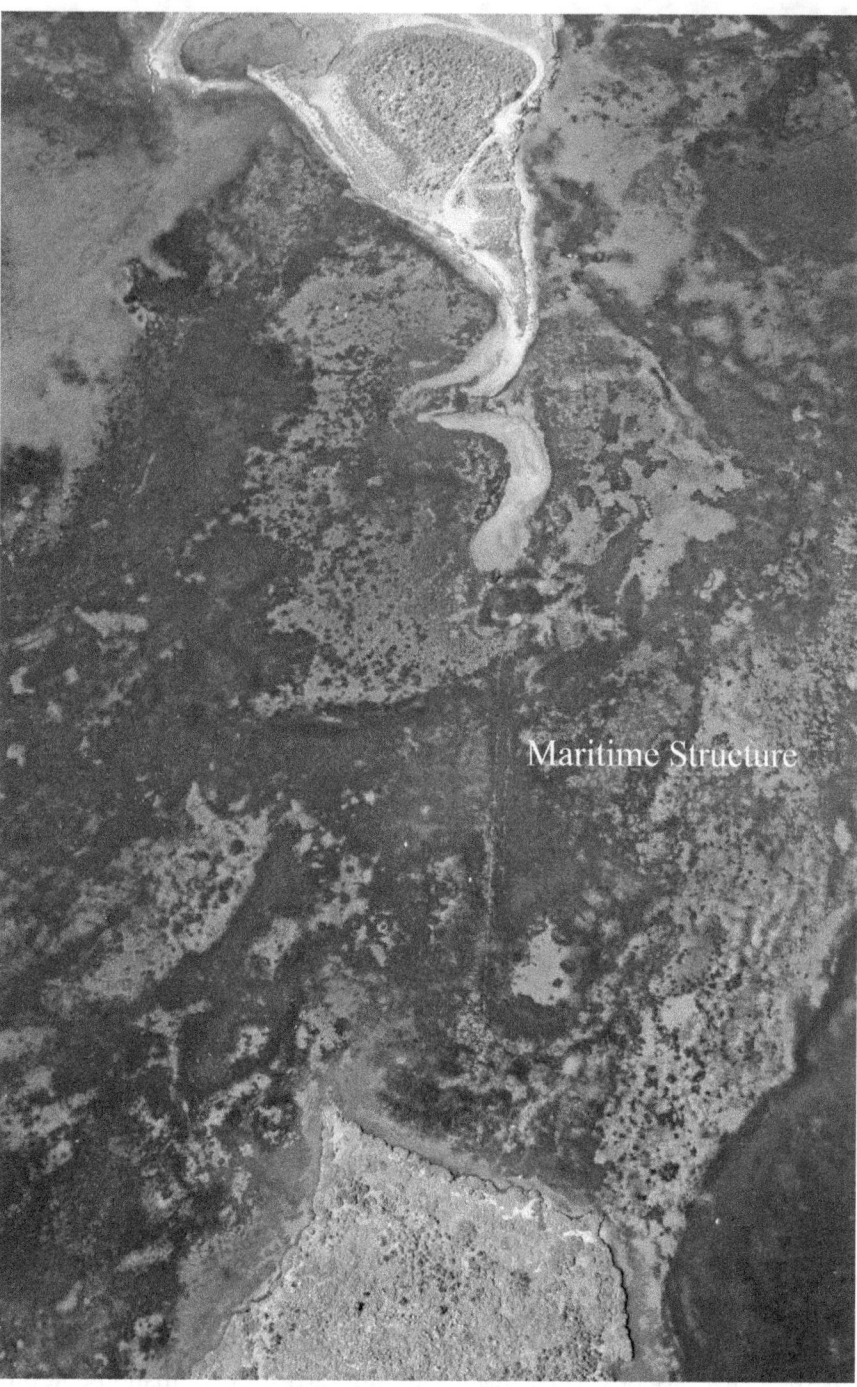

FIGURE 4. LOCATION OF THE MARITIME STRUCTURE (PROVINCIA DI ORISTANO. PHOTO: FRANCESCO CUBEDDU).

must be unique when taking into account the humble consistency of soils and, above all, the modifications that the work must have undergone due to vertical shakedown and partial dismantling caused by wave action (Orrù et al. 2009).

Simultaneous research by the Soprintendenza per i Beni Archeologici di Cagliari and the University of Sassari, with the collaboration of Prof. Paolo Orrù of the University of Cagliari and underwater archaeologist Dott.ssa Emanuela Solinas, allowed for the proposal of an evolutionary process for the Mistras landscape different from that put forth by Cagliari's colleagues. Archaeological investigations perfectly matched with C14 isotopic dating performed by Prof. Paolo Orrù of the University of Cagliari.

C14 Isotopic Samples and Analysis

Sample points have been located through a DGPS LEICA 2010 Total Station assaying high beach and dune sediments that have been analyzed both for granulometry and mineralogic characteristics. Analysis revealed that these sediments are composed of thin and very thin sands with a humble, silty fraction; composition is mainly biogenic, while quartz prevails within the crystalline particles. Stratigraphic basins, about 50 cm deep, have revealed layers with gastropods and clams. From these levels, shells have been collected and analyzed with C14 isotopic analysis, revealing samples belonging to gastropods *turriculata* of the family of *Rissoidae*.

C14 isotopic analysis has been realized with the AMS (Accelerator Mass Spectrometry) method at the Beta Analytic Radiocarbon Dating Laboratory in Miami, Florida, USA.

Geomorphologic Evolution of the Mistras Lagoon in Historical Times

Based on geo-chronological data and the integrated analysis of geomorphologic survey and archaeological data, it is possible to reconstruct some elements of the evolutionary processes of the Mistras Lagoon in historical times.

Beginning with the Neolithic Age, the initial landscape is represented by a coastal plane possibly articulated with hollows and swamps from where some dune ribbon emerges. Gradually, since the First Iron Age and following eustatic sea level rise, an almost completely open bay formed with some residual strips of ancient dune ribbons likely protected from erosion by a limestone nucleus (MIS 5 – Tyrrhenian auct.). A full correspondence exists between the radiocarbon data and the shoreline of the first Phoenician appearance (located facing the open sea and not facing the lagoon). During the Phoenician period, a monumental maritime structure was constructed which, starting from a residual strip of the "ancient" ribbon, placed two isolated strips in communication one another (Spanu and Zucca 2011:15–103). Again, the evolution of the inner ribbon proceeded because of the interference between maritime work and sedimentary dynamics, as testified to by the Roman shoreline in a facies of beachrock with embedded ceramic fragments that represent a palaeo-beach facing the open sea. The second ribbon began to evolve in the Byzantine period and was fully structured by the Medieval period (Figure 3d).

Conclusion

Based on acquired data, the authors believe that the submerged structure most likely dates to the Late Punic period, realizing the connection between a primeval

Sample	N° Beta	Misured Radiocarbon Age	Calibrated Age	Conventional Radiocarbon Age	Geo. Cord.
C1	307732	3240 +/- 30 BP	**Cal BC 1720 to 1590**	3690 +/- 30 BP	39°53'27,9 N
			(Cal BP 3640 to 3540)		8° 26'31,3 E
C2	307733	3820 +/- 30 BP	**Cal BC 2250 to 2060**	4070 +/- 30 BP	39°53'24,5 N
			(Cal BP 4200 to 4070)		8° 26'36,1 E
C3	307734	2370 +/- 30 BP	**Cal BC 730 to 500**	2810 +/- 30 BP	39°53'22,3 N
			(Cal BP 2680 to 2450)		8° 26'26,35 E
C3B	307735	2050+/- 30 BP	**Cal BC 320 to 140**	2500+/- 30 BP	39°53'21,1 N
			(Cal BP 2270 to 2090)		8° 26'41,6 E
C4	307736	1200+/- 30 BP	**Cal AC 690 to 800**	1640+/- 30 BP	39°53'18,3 N
			(Cal BP 1260 to 1140)		8° 26'51,8 E

Table 1. Data related to the analysis AMS – C14, Beta Analytic USA.

dune ribbon of the Western basin of the lagoon to the quadrangular oxbow. The preliminary suggestion for interpretation envisions the Nuragic and Phoenician Tárrai, or Tharros, first harbor in the Mistras inlet with the shoreline located in San Giovanni di Sinis, Prei Sinnis, Matta Tramatza in correspondence with polygenetic conglomerate, Middle-Superior Pleistocene stratified conglomeratic, calcarenites sandstones, and Holocene sands, silt, and clays. Explanation of the formation of the first dune ribbon, in the historical phase, will have to await chronological clarifications connected to climate conditions and human factors that could have determined, for certain periods, an increase in the Tirso River's flow rate with consequential deposits along the coastal zone of Mare Morto. A progressive silting in the Southeastern sector of the Western Mistras basin is nevertheless discernible, following the formation of the original ribbon, creating the neo-formation of beachrock containing archaeological material no later than the Hellenistic period. The wall structure, with a double hanging in sandstone blocks and probably better interpreted as a "headers" dam, likely functioned as a ship shelter from swell produced by winds from the West and Southwest.

The head of Tárrai harbor is likely located in the Southern sector of the Western Mistras basin based on the presence of additional dockings along Eastern banks of the lagoon basin represented by amphorae fragments and other ceramic material stacks, an outcome of typical material toss, as well as loading and unloading operations in port areas. It is in fact presumable that the port was in strict relation both with Tárrai settlements (those of the Tower of San Giovanni – Murru Mannu and Santu Marcu – San Giovanni di Sinis) and with the inland settlements of Sinis – Campidano di Milis. The harbor must have taken resource surpluses allocated by these settlements for international export.

Upon analysis of aerial and satellite photographs, research produced under supervision of Emanuela Solinas has provided particular evidence for a possible submerged "basin" of trapezoidal shape characterized by a long internal side, oriented NNW-SSE of 224 m, and a short internal side, oriented W-E of 138 m, at the Southern end of the Western basin. The basin also has another arm orthogonal to the previous measurements that is 25 m long and 52 m wide.

In correspondence to the regular shape as defined by aerial photographs, survey has revealed a hard and solid layer possibly made of stone underneath an uneven layer of silt. Within the delimited area, probes descended through a silt layer to a depth of 4 m underneath the current lagoon level. The interpretation of the "basin" is problematic and in need of further research, but further geo-archaeological investigations may suggest that the existence of in situ levels of Tyrrhenian sandstone bed and a now-submerged quarry could have allowed for the exploitation of stone material for the dam structure. Additionally, cutting the extreme Northern diaphragm at the end of mining operations may have also provided Tharros inhabitants with a *cothon* comparable to later examples located in Carthage and Mahdia.

The basin was protected on the Eastern side by a breakwater lying on the original dune ribbon, with a length of about 1400 m, cloaked with sandstone squared blocks, and whose better preserved sector is the one identified by Cagliari's research team. About 700 m from the possible *cothon,* a tower or lighthouse – whose quadrangular base can be identified by structure of large sandstone squared blocks – probably protruded from the dam toward the West.

A harbor thus conceived would have certainly been appropriate for Tharros, the Punic QRTHDSHT (New Capital) in Sardinia. The harbor may have housed Annone's fleet sent by Carthage for assisting the town kept in check by mercenaries in 240 B.C.; it may have also been the landing site, in 215 B.C., for the *classis punica cum duce Hasdrubale* – a Punic army conducted by Hasdrubal – which the Carthaginian Senate sent to support Amsicora's uprising. In any case, the harbor should have been located on the road that, following the Western Mistras basin shore, steers North in the Tharros *chora*, splitting nearby Murru Zoppu in two arterial roads respectively heading towards Cornus and Othoca.

For the Roman and Medieval periods, the area characterization will have persisted unchanged. In fact, preliminary chronological sequences of the shorelines examined above suggest that the Western Mistras basin represented the main Tárrai docking during Archaic and Hellenistic epochs. In the Roman period, possibly following a sea/lagoon level change and/or subsiding phenomena, the docking in the Eastern Mistras basin was built up again and eventually closed by Eastern dune ribbons formations during the Early Medieval period (Spanu and Zucca 2011:15–103).

Moreover, it is still possible that Medieval and Post-Medieval references of the *portus sancti Marci* could refer to the Porto Vecchio in the Mare Morto with quays located by investigations produced by Luigi Fozzati or the sea cliff quoted in the Kitab-i Bahriyye by the geographer Piri Muhi 'd-Din Re'is, likely a breakwater dike identified by Elisha Linder (Linder 1987:47–53).

References

Acquaro, Enrico, Bruno Marcolongo, Fabio Vangelista, and Flaminia Verga (editors)
    1999   *Il porto buono di Tharros*. Agorà, La Spezia.

Antonioli, Fabrizio, Marco Anzidei, , Kurt Lambeck, Rita Auriemma, Dario Gaddi, Stefano Furlani, Paolo E. Orrù, Emanuela Solinas, Andrej Gaspari, Snjezana Karinja, Vlasta Tari Kovačić, and Luciano Surace
    2007   Sea level change during the Holocene in Sardinia and in the North-eastern Adriatic (Central Mediterranean sea) from archaeological and geomorphological data. *Quarternary Science Review* 26:2463–2486.

Del Vais, Carla, Anna De Palmas, Anna Chiara Fariselli, Rita T. Melis, and Giuseppe Pisanu
    2008   Ricerche geo-archeologiche nella penisola del Sinis (OR): aspetti e modificazioni del paesaggio tra Preistoria e Storia. In *Atti del Secondo Simposio Internazionale "Il Monitoraggio Costiero Mediterraneo: problematiche e tecniche di misura"*, Napoli 4-6 giugno 2008, Firenze 2008, pp. 403–414.

Fedele, Francesco
    1980   Il luogo e il tempo della vicenda Nur. I boschi, gli animali. In *Nur. La misteriosa civiltà dei Sardi*, Dino Sanna, editor, pp. 45–47 Cariplo, Milano.

Fioravanti, Alessandro
    1985   The contribution of Geomorphology and Photointerpretation to the Definition of the Port Installation at Tharros (Sardegna). In *Harbour Archaeology*, Avner Raban, editor, pp. 87–92, BAR International Series 257, London.

Fozzati, Luigi
    1980   Archeologia marina di Tharros. *Rivista di Studi Fenici* 8:99–109.

Kelletat, Dieter
    2006   Beachrock as sea-level indicator? Remarks from a geomorphological point of view. *Journal of Coastal Research* 22:1558–1564.

Lambeck, Kurt and Anthony Purcell
    2005   Sea-level change in the Mediterranean Sea since the LGM: model prediction for tectonically stable areas. *Quaternary Science Reviews* 24:1969–1988.

Linder, Elisha
    1987   The maritime installation of Tharros (Sardinia). A recent discovery. *Rivista di Studi Fenici* 15:47–53.

Orrù, Paolo E., Emanuela Solinas, and Elisabetta Frau
    2009   Modificazioni della linea di costa nella laguna di Sulki in epoca punico – romana (Isola di sant'Antioco, Sardegna sud-occidentale). In *Terre di Mare. L'archeologia dei paesaggi costieri e le variazioni climatiche*, Atti del Convegno Internazionale di Studi (Trieste, 8 – 10 novembre 2007), Rita Auriemma and Snjezana Karinja, editors, 247–256, Università degli Studi di Trieste-Pomorski muzej, Trieste-Pirano.

Solinas, Emanuela, and Paolo E. Orrù
    2006   Santa Gilla: spiagge sommerse e frequentazioni di epoca punica. In *Aequora, pontos, jam, mare... Mare, uomini e merci nel Mediterraneo Antico*, Atti del Convegno Internazionale (Genova 9-10 dicembre 2004), Giannattasio Bianca M., editor, pp. 249–252, All'Insegna del Giglio, Firenze.

Spano, Giovanni
    1851   *Notizie sull'antica città di Tarros*, Cagliari.
    1861   Notizie sull'antica città di Tharros. *Bullettino Archeologico Sardo* 7 .

Spanu, Pier Giorgio, and Raimondo Zucca
    2011   Da Tarrai polis al portus sancti Marci. Storia e archeologia di una città portuale dall' antichità al medioevo. In *Tharros Felix 5*, Attilio Mastino, Pier Giorgio I. Spanu, Alessandro Usai, Raimondo Zucca, editors, pp. 15–103, Carocci, Roma.

Zucca, Raimondo
    1993   *Tharros*, Corrias, Oristano.

• • • • • • • • • • • • • • •

Paolo Orrù:
Dipartimento di Scienze della Terra
Università degli
Studi di Cagliari
Via Trentino, 51
09127 Cagliari

Emanuela Solinas, Pier Giorgio I. Spanu,
    and Raimondo Zucca:
Dipartimento di Storia, Scienze
    dell'Uomo e della Formazione
Università degli
Studi di Sassari
Via Zanfarino, 62
07100 Sassari

Edward Rhodes – His Booke: Examining Trade Routes, Functions, and Vessel Performance in the 17th Century Through Primary Source Documents

Scott A. Tucker

Edward Rhodes was a seventeenth-century sailor involved in the English-Chesapeake tobacco trade. From 1670-1676, he kept a book describing his journeys back and forth across the Atlantic in four different ships, keeping information on daily positions and weather, functional aspects of trade, deaths aboard the ship, and other relevant information. Daily position is described with latitude and a relative longitude, showing a very early and curious attempt at lateral navigation. This record is used to examine many of the unknown maritime aspects of the early English tobacco trade including mapping routes and clarifying some functional aspects of shipping this commodity.

Introduction

Understanding ship performance from past periods is perhaps one of the most fundamental aims of maritime archaeology, but also one of the most elusive. Studies of this topic are further useful for maritime and economic historians and those studying technologies in antiquity. The material record can reveal much of hull design, but differential preservation often leaves very little evidence of rigging, this being a necessary factor in modeling ship performance. Additionally, tracking trade routes across oceans is especially problematic through the material record. One way to bridge these gaps is through archaeological documentary research. This term, as defined by Ahlström, describes the "combined use of written and artifactual sources to improve opportunities for interpretation and to impart more clarity to the archaeological record" (1997:32). Barbara Little points out that archaeological evidence consists not only of artifacts, ecofacts, physical remains, and features traditionally used as source materials, but of historical documents and oral histories as well, highlighting the archaeological significance of some historical studies (2007:60). Topics of archaeological significance should be examined with all available evidence, not simply the materials we customarily consider.

Some recent research using contemporary accounts of shipping in the 17th century is beginning to clarify questions of the performance capabilities of English ships, particularly through the use of merchant logbooks. The logbook of Edward Rhodes, dating from 1670-1676, describes six round-trip voyages from London to the Virginia and Maryland colonies aboard tobacco trading vessels. Through this log, recent work has enhanced knowledge of 17th-century merchant trade between England and the Chesapeake, and raised new questions about conventionally held principles of the tobacco trade. The Rhodes log and others like it are being used to plot trade routes with surprising accuracy. Preliminary averages on velocity made good (Vmg) have been established with continuing work promising to provide sound data on this topic, and some indication of performance to windward have been gained. Calculating performance to windward accurately through these methods still requires reconstructions or computer-aided modeling, but where unavailable, as shown herein, such methods remain a useful exercise. This paper will describe the research and methods being performed on these themes and demonstrate the usefulness of engaging these sources where available.

Firstly, this paper will examine changes in trade routes throughout the 17th century. Routes between England and the Chesapeake colonies have been said to have shifted north throughout the period in question, with specific dates given by previous scholars for the variation. According to Middleton, throughout the first half of the 17th century, ships voyaged along a southerly route to the Chesapeake, utilizing the clockwise trade winds in the north Atlantic (1984:7-8) (Figure 1). Ships on this route would sail south from England, past the coast of Spain and further, perhaps as far south as Angola before heading west and sailing a direct line to Barbados. After about 1650, Middleton writes that English merchant ships began using a northern passage; the signature of this route being a northern arc from England to Newfoundland. Ships would then head south along the North American coast to the Chesapeake Bay (1984:7-8). Bruce further points to attempts to cross the Atlantic as early as 1609 utilizing what he termed a northern passage, traveling south along the Spanish coast to the Canary Islands before turning west and sailing near Bermuda, then sighting land near what is

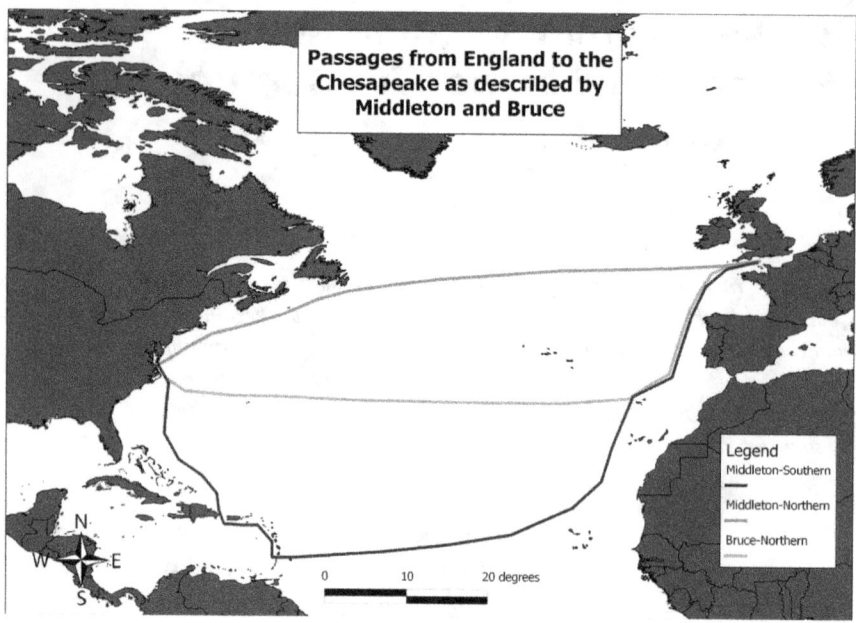

FIGURE 1: PASSAGES FROM ENGLAND TO THE CHESAPEAKE COLONIES AS DESCRIBED BY BRUCE (1896 VOL. 1: 623-624) AND DEPICTED BY MIDDLETON (1952/1984: 7-8). MAP BY SCOTT TUCKER.

the eastbound voyage until reaching Land's End. While these six voyages do not in themselves discount Middleton's assertion of a northward arching passage, it does call into question the date by which ships were taking this route. It is quite possible that Middleton's northern route is actually not in use until the 18th century, which is of particular concern in the broader context of this research. As more similar documents are discovered and analyzed, it is likely that this issue will be clarified.

From a perspective examining only wind and currents, the southern passage is perhaps the most sensible. Each of the other routes described herein from England to the Chesapeake are against the prevailing winds, and the route taken by *Sea Venture* and other early ships to

now North Carolina (1896[1]:623-625). Indeed, this was the route intended by the ill-fated ship, *Sea Venture*, which famously wrecked on a reef near Bermuda. These general routes have been continuously pointed to as the trade routes between England and the Chesapeake colonies, but as will be shown, a fourth passage was in use, perhaps pushing back the date of Middleton's northern route. With each day's entry, Rhodes provides the coordinates reached in the previous 24 hours, citing latitude and a longitude relative to the starting location, always set to zero degrees. While latitude could be described in the 17th century quite accurately, it would be another century before lateral navigation could be accurately measured. It is unclear what methods Rhodes used to ascertain his daily longitude, but the ending longitudes given for each voyage are generally quite close, allowing for corrections to be made and routes plotted with a reasonable assumption of accuracy.

Using the vertical positions described by Rhodes each day, and the corrected horizontal locations, each voyage has been plotted. The results show that rather than taking a northern arc from England as shown by Middleton for this time period, these ships were sailing south-west, likely making sighting of the Azores, and heading from there directly west along the 38th parallel to reach the capes of the Chesapeake Bay (Figure 2). On the reverse, it appears that a direct line north-east across the Atlantic was attempted. No land would be sighted throughout

Virginia would go directly through a large mid-ocean gyre known as the Sargasso Sea. The Rhodes voyages seem to be meant to remain just to the north of this, but combining the data from Rhodes' logbook with a map of prevailing ocean currents indicates that traveling too far south within this oceanographic feature is of factor in the difficulties experienced in the voyages. Sailing Middleton's northern route would put a ship in potential danger of icebergs in the northern stretches of the Atlantic, and then by rocks and sandbars as it travels southward along the North-American coast. The southern passage placed the mariners in danger of tropical disease, along with the threat of hostile nations and pirates. Bruce's northern passage again required ships to sail by Spain and northern Africa before heading directly west through the Sargasso Sea. Upon reaching the North American coast, they would need to sail northward by Cape Hatteras, which was known to be a troublesome spot for mariners. The general path of the Rhodes voyages avoids each of these dangers, with its major fault being that it too is against prevailing winds.

Contemporary maps from the period may shed some light on the choice of the route taken. Rhumb lines are features on Mercator navigational maps to help mariners manage their way along a flat map of a spherical earth. Several popular maps of this period, including the 1660 Jan Janssen map of the North Atlantic display Rhumb lines along similar points to average points along Rhodes'

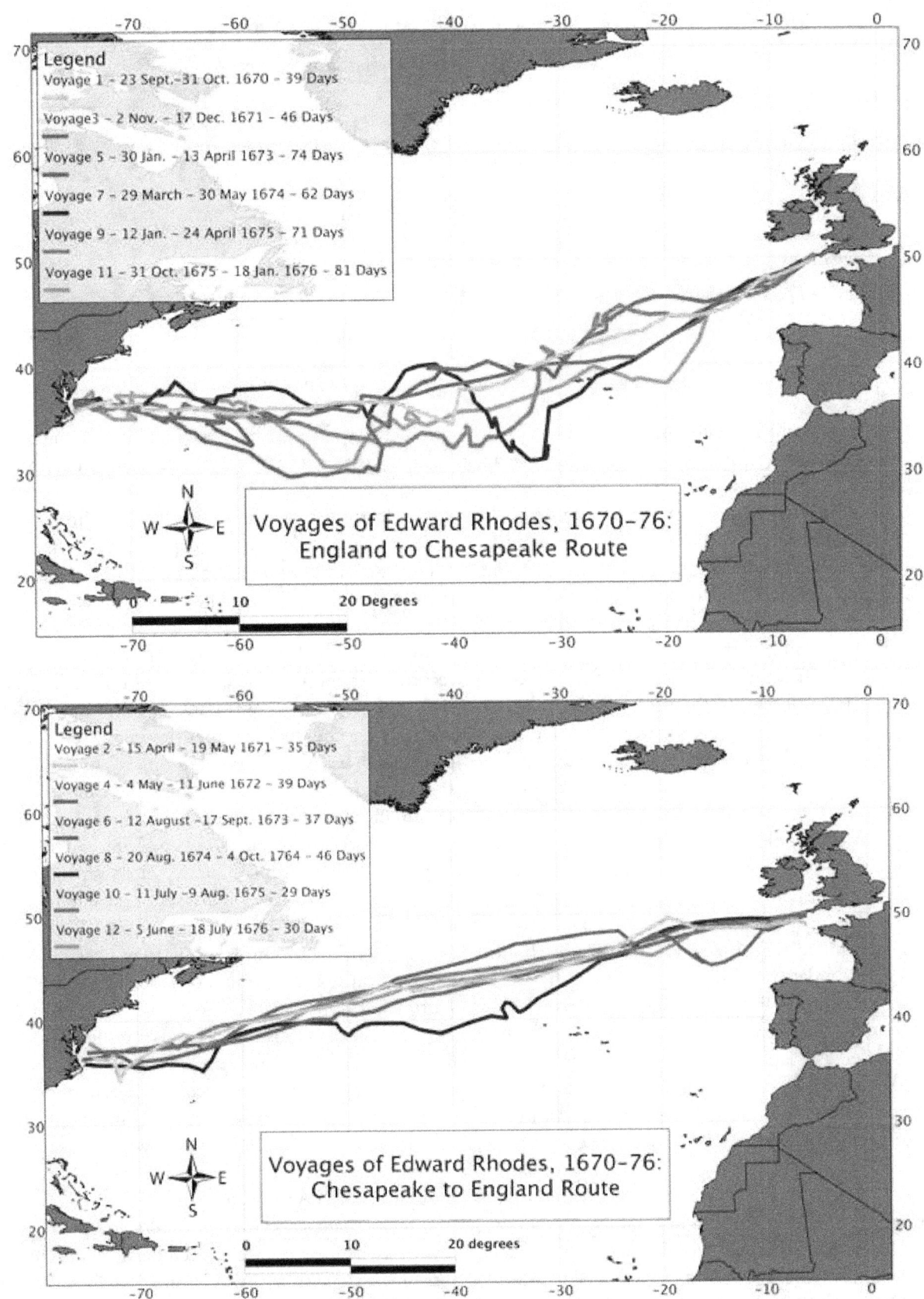

FIGURE 2: EAST AND WESTBOUND PASSAGES OF EDWARD RHODES, BETWEEN ENGLAND AND THE CHESAPEAKE, 1670-1676. MAP BY SCOTT TUCKER AND SCOTT STRICKLAND.

Edward Rhodes' Voyages, England to Chesapeake, ca. 3,400 nautical miles

Ship	Days spent at sea	Average distance per day (NM)	Vmg
Duke of York	39	87.17	3.63
Constant Friendship	46	73.91	3.08
Baltimore	74	45.94	1.91
Johanna	62	54.83	2.28
Johanna	71	47.88	1.99
Johanna	81	41.97	1.75
Averages	62.16	54.69	2.44

TABLE 1: PERFORMANCE OF THE WESTBOUND SHIPS FROM THE LOGBOOK OF EDWARD RHODES.

voyages. Indeed, "sailing on a Rhumb" was a common expression at the time. This practice would provide an easy and direct route of navigation.

The answers to what triggered the shift in route likely lie within several interrelated causes. One of these causes being a desire to avoid hostile nations and a growing threat of piracy. As stated, the coasts of Spain and Africa, and the Caribbean Islands were hotbeds of piracy during this period. The timing of the shift may be also have required a certain infrastructural maturity not achieved in the New World until post 1650, when the multi-lateral trade route for tobacco, sugar, and other staples could be replaced by several uni-lateral routes; however, further research is required to determine this to any degree of certainty.

The Rhodes logbook can also be used as a tool for examining ship performance. This will be examined through two themes: Velocity made good and performance to windward. Previously, several economic historians examined shipping productivity in 17th and 18th-century England using port records as their primary source (Walton 1966; Walton 1967; North 1968; Walton 1968; Shepherd and Walton 1972; French 1987). Walton, and later Shepherd, found that between the 1680s and 1770s, there was no trend toward increased speed in voyages between New England and the Caribbean colonies (Walton 1967:73-74; Shepherd and Walton 1972:77-78). Their data shows Vmg to range between 1.31 and 2.09 knots from the Caribbean to New England and New York, and 1.6 and 1.97 knots on the reverse leg. These figures do show an increase of speed between the 1680s and the second decade of the 18th century, but then a long period of decrease until 1770. They argue that technological innovation in shipbuilding was not a factor in increased shipping productivity during this period. This statement clearly ignores decreases in necessary crew members for these ships, likely caused by a simplification of rigging, and design features on the interior of a ship diminishing the necessary materials needed to produce these ships in a time at which shipbuilding materials were becoming increasingly expensive and hard to acquire.

Port records are, however, not the most appropriate source from which to calculate Vmg. Simply stated, port records describe a vessel's entry into or out of port, along with some other relevant data. Shepherd and Walton's research use the documents to examine well connected ports, such as New York and Boston to Jamaica and Barbados, marking when a ship would depart one location and arrive at another. From these data, distance between ports can be measured and Vmg can be presumably calculated. Unfortunately, ships were not always registered as arriving or departing on the dates when this actually occurred, as even Shepherd and Walton admit (1972:197). For instance, a ship may register its intent to depart on a particular day, but then be kept in *harbour* waiting for appropriate winds to advance out of port. This introduces a possible degree of error to their data. For a journey taking on average five days, the addition of a single day will significantly affect a calculation of Vmg for the voyage. Naturally, longer voyages would be less affected by these clerical errors; however, Shepherd and Walton apply them only to the relatively short voyages along the North American coast.

Velocity made good on the Rhodes voyages show high variability in average speeds, even between different voyages of the same ship. This volume describes four different ships: *Duke of York, Constant Friendship, Baltimore,* and *Johanna*. No detail is given of any of size, tonnage, or rigging of these four vessels, so they cannot perhaps

Edward Rhodes' Voyages, Chesapeake to England, ca. 3,000 nautical miles

Ship	Days spent at sea	Average distance per day (NM)	Vmg
Duke of York	35	85.71	3.57
Constant Friendship	39	76.92	3.20
Baltimore	37	81.08	3.37
Johanna	46	65.21	2.71
Johanna	29	103.44	4.31
Johanna	30	100.00	4.16
Averages	36	83.33	3.55

TABLE 2: PERFORMANCE OF THE EASTBOUND SHIPS FROM THE LOGBOOK OF EDWARD RHODES

be adequately compared, save for *Johanna* where six voyages are given. The cargo of the *Constant Friendship*, given as 724 hogsheads of tobacco, does nonetheless allow for a possible tonnage to be ascertained. Wing, who has worked with this voyage, suggests that based on this ship's cargo, using Wyckoff's study of port records as comparison, the *Constant Friendship* would be approximately 215 tonnes (Wyckoff 1938-1939; Wing 1999:12). Established research shows that registered tonnages of ships in the first three quarters of the 18th century were commonly reported at an average of two thirds actual measured tonnage (McCusker 1967:86-90; Walton 1967:395-397; French 1973:495). This was indeed noted by a contemporary observer, Thomas Irving, perhaps leading to the changes in tonnage registration in the last quarter of the eighteenth century (McCusker 1967:82). French asserts that understating tonnage became common practice as a means of reducing duties paid at ports and lighthouses (1973:434). If this is indeed a feature of 17th-century shipping as well, the *Constant Friendship* would likely have an actual tonnage of approximately 285 tonnes. Recent work by this author suggests that a ship of this period could store approximately 1.5 tobacco hogsheads for each tonne to which it could be measured. As such, that would place the vessel at approximately 280 tonnes.

Calculations of Vmg for each of the voyages in the Rhodes logbook show compelling results. These journeys range between 1.75 and 3.63 knots on the outward bound, averaging 2.44 knots (table 1), and achieving 2.71 to 4.31 knots on the return, averaging 3.55 knots (table 2). Seasonality seems to be a key factor in voyage times, with those outward bound voyages departing in late autumn and early winter being the most problematic. The homeward bound departures are much more regular in date taken to sea, limiting what can be said of seasonality for eastward-bound voyages; however, as these journeys are with the prevailing winds it is unlikely that season plays much of a role in this direction of travel. The voyages of *Johanna* are perhaps the most significant with six voyages accounted for. Through *Johanna*, one can observe both the slowest and fastest crossings of the log, giving strong indication that a ship of the time was only as quick as the winds that drove it. The merchant fleet's choice to sail against prevailing winds or out of season suggest that time spent in transit was of little consequence in the productivity in the trade, as only one tobacco crop was produced annually. Further, the lack of centrality in the tobacco trade at the time required extended times to be spent in port collecting tobacco and distributing the trade goods brought across the Atlantic, meaning two voyages per year were both not possible and unnecessary. The voyage of the *Constant Friendship* serves as an example of the amount of time necessary in port. The mariners aboard this ship spent 85 days collecting the 724 hogsheads of tobacco that they transported back to England. Without established ports and towns in the region, the ships were required to sail to each plantation and load hogsheads onto small "shallups" before bringing them to the ship for storage in the hold (Rhodes 1670-1676: entry dated 25 March, 1672).

Performance to windward can be to some degree examined through the Rhodes log. It should be noted that there are severe limitations in doing this, as Rhodes gives only a general bearing to the wind each day. Occasionally a qualifier is added to a day's description of wind, although this is usually no more than a term such

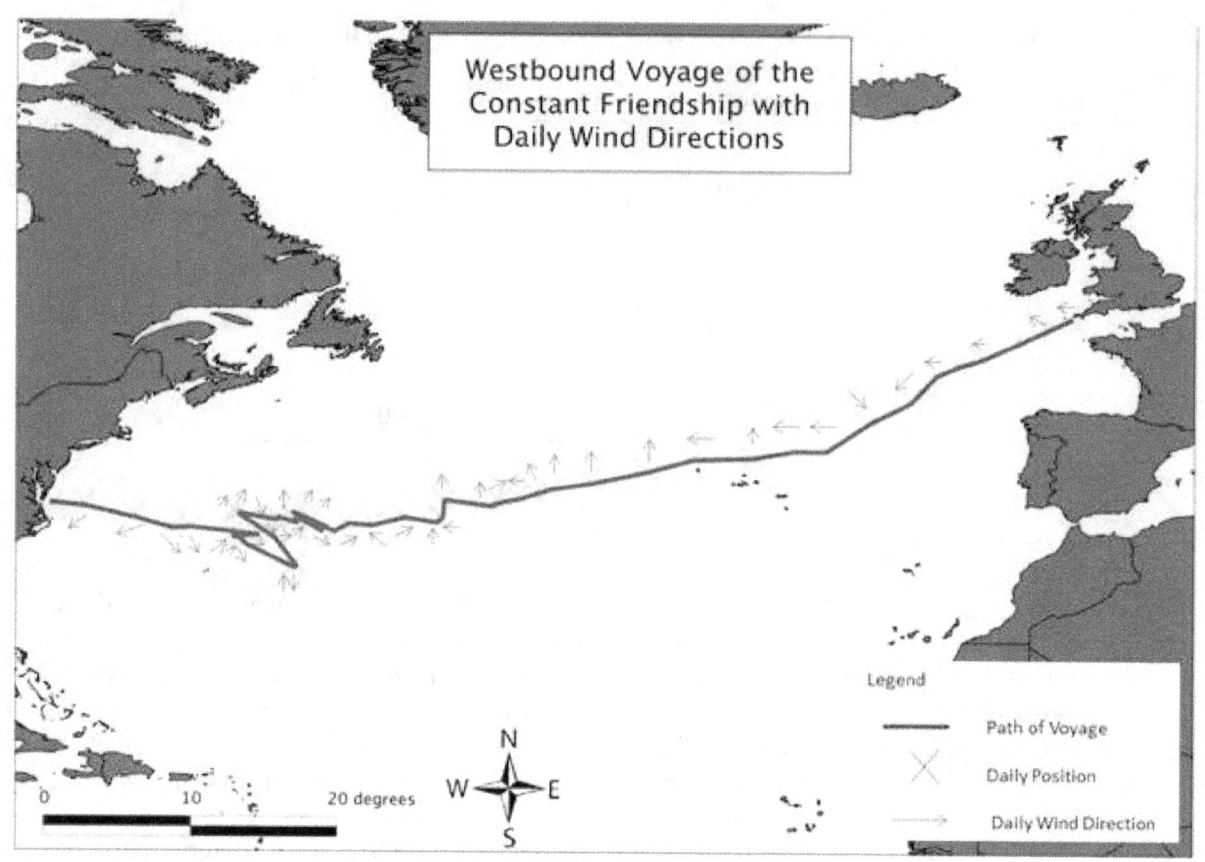
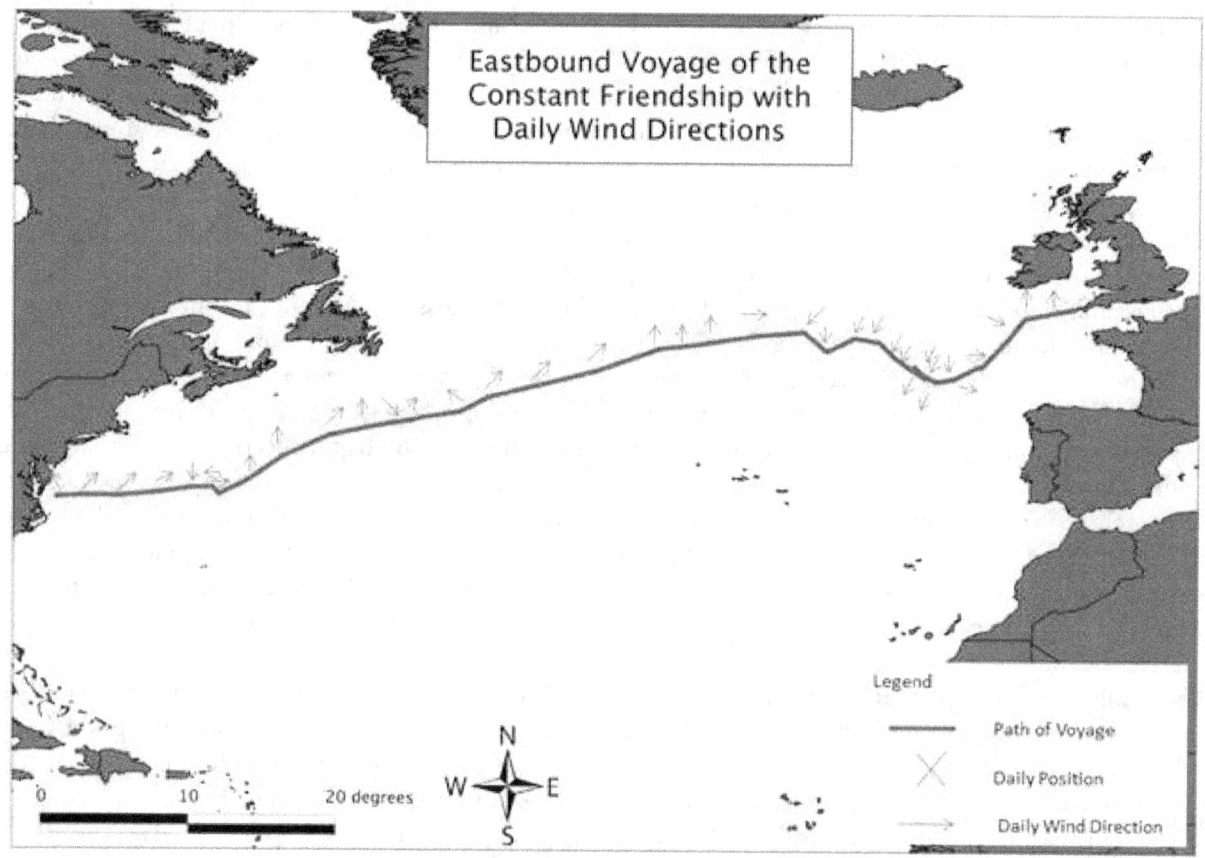

FIGURE 3: VOYAGES OF CONSTANT FRIENDSHIP, WITH DAILY WIND DIRECTIONS, 1672. MAP BY SCOTT TUCKER.

as "gaile." Much as maximum speed of a ship cannot be seen through this source, but rather only a speed made good, windward performance can also be examined within similar parameters. That is, a ship's ability to sail to windward will be over-stated using this method as tacking back and forth across the wind will allow a ship to make some forward motion to the prevailing winds. Some data comparing one of Rhodes' voyages to trials of *Maryland Dove*, the reconstructed 17th-century trade ship at the Historic St. Mary's City Museum, will be included for comparison.

As wind direction is given daily, one can observe this data combined with the distance covered each day. Through this, it becomes apparent which directions allow for the greatest distances covered. Using the voyage of *Constant Friendship* as an example, performance to windward has been examined (Figure 3). Based on these data of daily wind direction, it can be seen that this vessel, in the simplest of terms, could not sail into the wind or close-hauled. Sailing with a beam reach to a broad reach are the most effective winds for this ship. The performance of this ship appears to be hindered when running with the wind. These figures are consistent with other such studies, such as that of the *Benzai* ship (Palmer 2009b:324).

Personal correspondence with Captain Will Gates of *Maryland Dove* has given greater insight into a square-rigged vessel's windward capability with more exact terms. *Maryland Dove* is a modern reconstruction of a 17th-century trade ship, rated at 42 tonnes. The ship's sailing rig is similar to that of what would have been aboard *Constant Friendship*, although *Constant Friendship* would have likely carried three fully rigged masts whereas *Maryland Dove* carries only two. *Maryland Dove* is also rigged with taller masts than a typical 17th-century ship, allowing for better performance

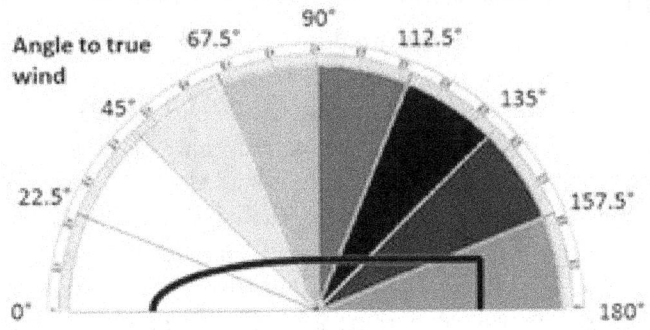

FIGURE 4: PERFORMANCE TO WINDWARD AS OBSERVED ON CONSTANT FRIENDSHIP AND MARYLAND DOVE. IMAGE BY SCOTT TUCKER.

within the calm, flat waters of the Chesapeake Bay, but decreasing the vessel's ability to sail in open water conditions. Information for both calm water and open water sailing conditions are therefore provided (Figure 4).

In comparison to the windward capabilities of the *Maryland Dove*, it can be observed that *Constant Friendship* shows better performance to windward. This can be accounted for as from the log one can only ascertain daily progress made good rather than the actual path taken between the two points, although a hull fully weighted with cargo would have a positive effect on a vessels performance to windward (Palmer 2009a:91; Steffy 2006:9). While the winds may have been near head-on certain days, sailing close-hauled would result in the minimal progress seen on the days with such an unfavorable wind. *Maryland Dove* requires a minimum angle of 67.5 degrees to windward to achieve forward progress under ideal conditions, and has been observed as needing an angle as high as 80 degrees for this on open seas, but could likely make some progress to windward over a period of time by making skilled use of the wind.

Ideally, data such as these on *Maryland Dove* would be more abundant, allowing for a more complete data set to be compiled on the topic. The sheer costs involved in building a ship to such specifications for sea-trials is a limiting factor. Of those ships already built, these provide the best comparative data available, but research is therefore restricted by the ships' size and design. Computer modeling programs will in all likelihood aid such studies in the future, but this can be expected to prove costly for some time. While ships' logs are equally limited by a lack of ability to accurately calculate minimum angles to the wind needed for forward progress, they give a different type of data that is perhaps more practical to studies of vessel performance. Much as a ship's top speed is unimportant to the aims of archaeology, as ships do not travel in a straight path between two points (Englert 2007:121-122), perhaps the exact angle to windward at which a ship can sail forward is here similarly moot, although for studies of technological change, performance to windward remains an important area of concern. While the comparative data makes it quite clear that ships in this period could not sail to windward or close-hauled, examination of the Rhodes log indicates that some forward progress could in reality be made through the practice of tacking.

Logbooks such as this are quite rare in the 17th century, but become increasingly abundant in subsequent centuries. Of those that do exist, they can provide extremely useful data into many of the topics with which maritime archaeologists concern themselves. Other primary source documents can also provide similar data, albeit often with less detail. Passenger and crew journals allow for comparable analysis, although these are highly difficult to come by due to the age and personal nature of such books. Narratives of voyages, such Father Andrew White's relation of the 1634 founding voyage to Maryland aboard the *Ark* allow for routes to be plotted and Vmg to be calculated (White 1910). Through archaeological documentary investigations such as this, information only available through very expensive and often limiting means become widely available. Additionally, establishing trade routes would be almost impossible through any other means, save for extensive examination of wrecks from this period, of which very few are currently known. The logbooks left by Rhodes and other mariners provide perhaps the simplest and most cost-effective means of investigation of ship performance and trade routes in the historical period, and deserve more attention within the archaeological community.

References

AHLSTRÖM, CHRISTIAN
1997 *Looking for Leads: Shipwrecks of the past revealed by contemporary documents and the archaeological record*, The Finnish Academy of Science and Letters, Helsinki.

BRUCE, PHILLIP A.,
1896 *Economic History of Virginia in the Seventeenth Century: An inquiry into the material condition of the people, based upon original and contemporaneous records*, McMillan and Co., New York and London

ENGLERT, ANTON
2007 Othere's voyages seen from a nautical angle. In *Othere's Voyages: A late 9th-century account of voyages along the coasts of Norway and Denmark and its cultural context*, J. Bately and A. Englert, editors, pp. 117-129. Viking Ship Museum, Roskilde.

FRENCH, C. J.
1987 Productivity in the Atlantic Shipping Industry: A Quantitative Study. *The Journal of Interdisciplinary History* 17(3):613-638.

LITTLE, BARBARA J.
2007 *Historical Archaeology: Why the Past Matters*, Left Coast Press, Walnut Creek, CA.

MCCUSKER, JOHN J.
1967 Colonial Tonnage Measurement: Five Philadelphia Merchant Ships as Sample. *The Journal of Economic History* 27(1):82-91.

MIDDLETON, ARTHUR P.
1984 Tobacco Coast: A Maritime History of the Chesapeake Bay in the Colonial Era, reprinted and expanded from 1953 edition. The Johns Hopkins University Press, Baltimore, MD.

North, Douglass. C.
    1968   Sources of Productivity Change in Ocean Shipping, 1600-1850. *Journal of Political Economy* 76(5):953-970.

Palmer, Colin
    2009a   Reflections on the Balance of Traditional Sailing Vessels. *International Journal of Nautical Archaeology* 38(1):90-96.

    2009b   Windward Sailing Capabilities of Ancient Vessels. *International Journal of Nautical Archaeology* 38(2):314-330.

Rhodes, Edward
    1670-1676   *Edward Rhodes, His Booke.* Mariner's logbook, Special Collections, MS. Rawl, D. 702. Bodleian Library, Oxford.

Shepherd, James F. and Gary M. Walton
    1972   *Shipping, Maritime Trade, and the Economic Development of Colonial North America*, Cambridge University Press, Cambridge.

Steffy, R. J.
    2006   *Wooden Ship Building and the Interpretation of Shipwrecks*, expanded and revised from 1994 edition. Texas A&M University Press, College Station.

Walton, Gary. M.
    1966   A Quantitative Study of American Colonial Shipping: A Summary. *The Journal of Economic History* 26(4):595-598.

    1967   Colonial Tonnage Measurements: A Comment. *Journal of Economic History*. 27(3):392-397.

    1968   A Measure of Productivity Change in American Colonial Shipping. *The Economic History Review* 21(2):268-282.

White, Andrew, S.J.
    1910   A Brief Relation of the Voyage Unto Maryland. In *Narratives of Early Maryland, 1633-1684*, Clayton Colman Hall, editor, pp. 29-45. Charles Scribner's Sons: New York.

Wing, John. F.
    1999   *Bound by God… For Merryland: The Voyage of the Constant Friendship, 1671-1672*, The Maryland State Archives & The Maryland Historical Trust, Annapolis & Crownsville.

Wyckoff, V. J.
    1938-1939   Ships and Shipping of Seventeenth Century Maryland. *Maryland Historical Magazine* 33(4):334-342, 34(1):46-63, 34(3): 270-283, 34(4): 349-361.

Scott A. Tucker
Postgraduate Researcher
Centre for Maritime Archaeology
University of Southampton
Avenue Campus
Southampton
SO17 1BF
UK

Digitally Reconstructing the Newport Medieval Ship: 3D Designs and Dynamic Visualisations for Recreating the Original Hull Form, Loading Factors, Displacement, and Sailing Characteristics

Toby Jones
Nigel Nayling
Pat Tanner

Since its discovery in 2002, the remains of the mid 15th-century clinker built Newport Medieval Ship have been excavated, cleaned, documented, modelled, and are now midway through conservation treatment. Digital documentation methods, including laser scanning and contact digitising, were used extensively to record the hull timbers. The manufacture and assembly of a 1:10 scale physical model of the vessel remains has provided both construction sequence information and a suitable foundation from which to reconstruct the missing or damaged areas. The physical model was then digitised and a set of lines extracted and faired using Rhinoceros3D software. The lines were turned into a digital model representing the original hull form and analysed in a related modelling software plug-in called Orca3D, which has been used to determine the hydrostatic and hydrodynamic characteristics of the modelled hull form. The use of the abovementioned advanced digital modelling software has allowed archaeologists to accurately characterise the capabilities, capacity, and seaworthiness of the original vessel.

Introduction

The following paper outlines the process for creating a definitive digital and physical reconstruction of the Newport Medieval Ship using advanced modelling software coupled with detailed archaeological evidence, traditional shipbuilding knowledge and historical research. The Newport Ship hull timbers have been comprehensively digitally documented using three dimensional contact digitisers and laser scanners (Jones 2009a, 2009b, Nayling and Jones 2012). The resulting data, captured as 3D wire frame drawings of each timber, was then converted to digital solid models and finally physically manufactured using an additive manufacturing process called selective laser sintering (Jones and Nayling 2011: 54-60, Soe *et. al.* 2012, 443 – 450). The resulting individual model parts strong, light and flexible, and, when fastened together, formed a 1:10 scale model representing the recovered structural hull remains (Figure 1).

Recording the Physical Scale Model

The reconstructed 1:10 scale physical scale model of the hull remains was laser scanned using a Faro Platinum Arm and Laser-line Probe to capture a three dimensional point cloud. The scanning was carried out in three stages, the exterior scan consisting of 112.8 million points, the interior scan consisting of 15.6 million points, and the disarticulated bow portion consisting of 3 million points, giving a combined total of 131.4 million points recorded at an accuracy of ± 0.08 mm. These point clouds were individually processed and aligned using a best fit algorithm with Geomagic Studio software. A polygon mesh surface was then fitted to the scanned point cloud and deviations checked to maintain the desired ± 0.08 mm accuracy, actual deviation achieved was ± 0.054 mm (Tanner this vol.).

The reconstructed physical scale model was assembled in the perceived order of construction using only recovered material with the emphasis on allowing the hull planking to determine the original hull form. No attempt was made to flatten distorted timbers. This process created a unique object or shape state, that is neither the original as-built vessel nor the vessel shape at time of sinking but a "post-deposition" shape state.

Reconstructing the Hull Shape

Once the scanned model has been processed and the polygon mesh surface fitted it was exported to Rhinoceros3D and the required lines plan, main and additional dimensions, hydrostatic data, and form coefficients could be extracted. This methodology was similar to the one used in reconstructing the Drogheda boat original hull form (Tanner, this vol.).

It quickly became apparent that this reconstructed physical scale model had significant amounts of twist and distortion due to incomplete framing and the asymmetric quantity of materials recovered, as well as

FIGURE 1. THE PHYSICAL SCALE MODEL TWISTED TO MATCH THE FAIRED DIGITAL HULL SHAPE WITH FAIRING RIBBANDS FITTED AT EVERY 4TH STRAKE RUN.

the uneven nature of the ground the vessel came to rest on, coupled with the compressive forces of the 5 to 7m of overburden. A longitudinal symmetry plane was fitted along the vessel centre line, with the scanned mesh orientated to suit. A substantial amount of distortion or twist towards the starboard was readily visible, measuring 8.4° in the bow and 4.2° in the stern.

A series of curves were projected onto the oriented polygon mesh to coincide with every fifth frame station and, using data from each solid model/wireframe from the recording phase, the actual strake cross sections (as recorded) was best fit to these curves.

A second series of curves was projected onto the scanned mesh to create longitudinal fairing ribbands coinciding with every fourth strake run. Site sections and photogrammetric records were then examined to reveal any localised distortion which may have resulted from post-deposition distortion of individual elements at these frame stations.

As the recovered materials included the bottom edge of a 35th strake on the starboard side, a decision was made to attempt a "minimum reconstruction" as defined by Crumlin-Pedersen and McGrail (2006:57), to at least this level. The first step in the reconstruction process was to determine a preliminary hull form, including stem and stern shape and sheer line. For the hull form shape, this sheer line was exclusive of any bow or stern castles. In order to determine a sheer line, each framing station was examined and the height extended using faired curves to coincide with 35 strakes.

In order to determine the sheer height at each of these framing stations, an average strake width at each station was required. Initially the strake widths were measured at the visible external widths, that is from the bottom edge of a strake to the bottom edge of the strake above. However these widths varied to such an extent that it proved impossible to determine accurate average widths. The internal visible widths (the upper inboard edge of a strake to the upper inboard edge of the strake above) were examined and this produced a more consistent average width (Table 1 column 2). This observation would also indicate the plank widths were not overworked until the complete strake was hung and the upper edge was then trimmed to a fair run.

A faired curve was then created at each of these frame stations, with a curve length set to the relevant average strake widths. It should be noted that all "faired curves" used from this point onwards are degree three curves, degree one curves were used in the recording phase, but as the intended output is to represent a faired hull shape, degree three curves are required. A degree one curve comprises a succession of straight lines from control point to control point, whereas higher degree curves comprise continuous curves influenced by, but not necessarily passing through, their control points. A curve was then created passing fore and aft through the top of these extended frame stations. This three dimensional curve represents a preliminary sheer line, and was analysed using the curvature graph feature in Rhinoceros3D. The preliminary sheer line was then faired, and the corresponding station curves modified to suit. The station curves were then subdivided to fit 35 strakes giving a corrected average strake width (Table 1 column 4). The fairing ribbands were then checked longitudinally and transversely to repair any global distortion.

Once the sheer line has been created, the next stage was to determine the form of the two ends of the vessel. The recovered portions of the stem revealed that from the garboard strake up to strake eight, the planks had hood ends which terminated into a stepped rebate. From strake nine upwards, there was a change to a continuous smooth curved rebate along the stem. The recovered stem fragments also indicated a curved stem post, which was recreated using Rhinoceros3D and extended to meet the sheer line (Figure 2).

As no part of the stern was recovered, the model needed to be examined in more detail in order to extrapolate

Frame Station	Avg. internal strake width, measured	No. of strakes recovered	Corrected avg. strake widths from fairing
1	146.8 mm	4 strakes	142.5 mm
5	149.8 mm	20 strakes	144.5 mm
10	155.2 mm	24 strakes	149.0 mm
15	160.6 mm	26 strakes	157.3 mm
20	167.9 mm	31 strakes	165.6 mm
25	172.6 mm	34 strakes / partial 35th	172.9 mm
30	176.1 mm	32 strakes	175.7 mm
35	171.9 mm	32 strakes	174.0 mm
40	167.4 mm	28 strakes	169.5 mm
45	159.5 mm	25 strakes	164.7 mm
50	153.3 mm	19 strakes	159.6 mm
55	149.9 mm	16 strakes	156.5 mm
60	147.3 mm	8 strakes	152.6 mm

TABLE 1. AVERAGE INTERNAL VISIBLE STRAKE WIDTHS. THESE STRAKE WIDTHS ARE A STATISTICAL CONSTRUCT AS OPPOSED TO REPRESENTING ACTUAL STRAKE WIDTHS.

Visible Length [†]	Port Side	Starboard Side	Total Number
< 1 m	0	1	1
1 - 1.5 m	3	8	11
1.5 - 2 m	12	19	31
2 - 2.5 m	28	37	65
2.5 - 3 m	28	50	78
3 - 3.5 m	23	42	65
3.5 - 4 m	1	15	16
> 4 m	0	3	3

TABLE 2. VISIBLE PLANK LENGTHS. [†]VISIBLE LENGTH IS FROM AFT END OF FORWARD SCARF TO AFT END OF PLANK, ALL DIMENSIONS ARE IN MM. INCOMPLETE, DAMAGED OR FRAGMENTED PLANKS HAVE NOT BEEN INCLUDED.

the structure of the aft end. Firstly the plank lengths making up each strake were examined to determine both shortest and longest lengths used in the building of the vessel (Table 2). These lengths were then overlaid on the existing strake from the preceding complete scarf end. Taking a maximum and minimum plank length created a probability box inside which the final plank hood end should lay (Figure 2). When this procedure was repeated for each strake run an overlapping region within these probability areas would indicate a probable location for the aft hood ends. A stern post angle (taken from archaeological and historical parallels) was then created to fit within this probability box. With all of these curves faired a preliminary faired surface was generated to represent the outer hull form of the vessel corrected for global distortion. The scanned polygon mesh was then rectified to match this repaired hull shape.

The project then returned to the physical world, where a combination of screws, braces, and cable ties were used to "force" the physical scale model into a more faired shape, closely matching the digital model. The locations of the fairing ribbands on the digital model were measured and then physically fitted as plastic ribbands to the scale model (Figure 1).

At this stage the digital model still did not represent a complete vessel so the missing parts would need to be extrapolated and recreated. For the purposes of this reconstruction it is assumed that the hull is generally symmetrical.

Establishing a Floatation Condition

In order to establish a floatation condition for the vessel, three key facts are required:

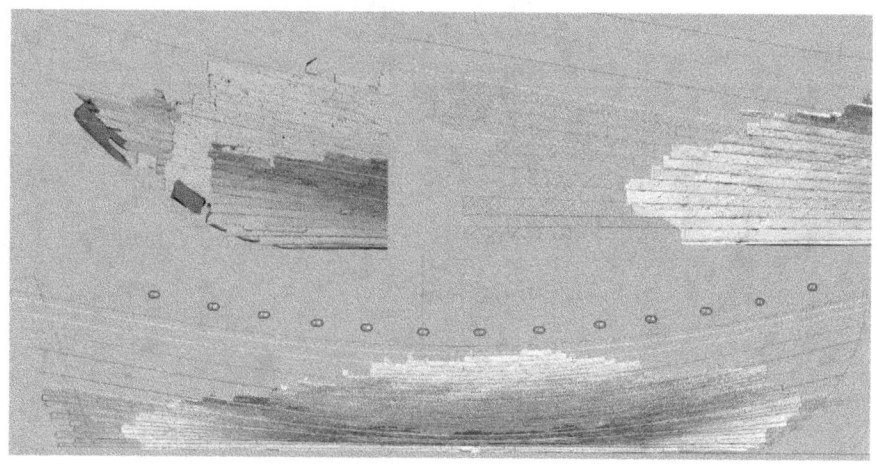

FIGURE 2. PLANK LENGTHS EXTRAPOLATED TO FIND STEM AND STERN POSTS.

1. Vessel hull shape in order to establish the centre of buoyancy 'B'.

2. Vessel centre of gravity 'G' to establish floatation trim.

3. Vessel weight in order to establish displacement.

The Newport Ship hull shape had been established based on the reconstruction methods already employed, but a vessel weight and centre of gravity had not yet been established.

The most accurate method of determining the weight of a vessel is to weigh it in air and then carry out an inclining test to establish the position of centre of gravity (McKee 1974:11–13). In order to weigh the vessel and perform an inclining test, a complete, rebuilt vessel would be required. As this was not practical, and the fact that various hypothetical reconstructions are still being examined, an alternative approach was used (Institute for Archaeologists 2008, 8-9). Every constituent part of the vessel was accurately modelled using Rhinoceros3D solid modelling techniques and, using the Orca3D plug-in for Rhinoceros3D, a material is assigned to each part and Orca3D used to calculate the weight, as well as the longitudinal, transverse and vertical centres of gravity (Tanner, this vol.).

As the flotation plane is calculated from the total weight, it is important to reconstruct as much of the overall vessel as possible by solid modelling each of the constituent parts and mirroring where necessary. The reconstructed physical scale model used as the basis for the digital reconstruction consisted of the keel, hull planking, framing, keelson, braces and stringers as recovered, but excluded items such as ceilings and the

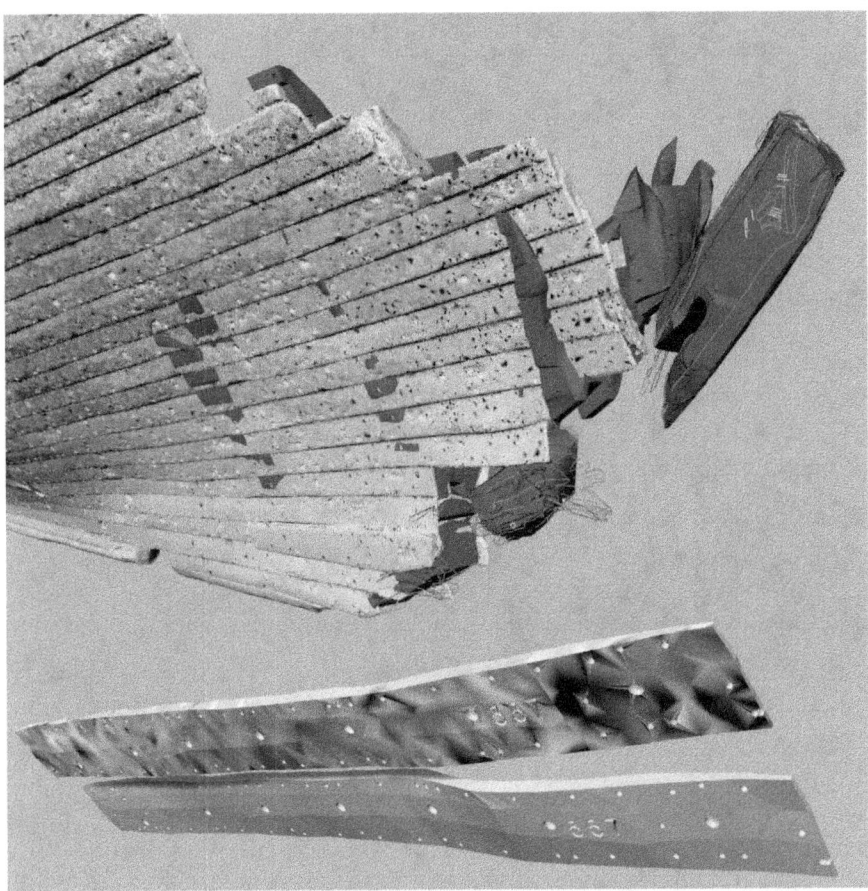

FIGURE 3: DIGITAL SOLID FRAMES AND STEM ADDED TO THE LASER SCANNED DATA SHOWING THAT THE SHAPE IS STILL INCORRECT AS RECORDED FROM THE PHYSICAL SCALE MODEL, IN THE FOREGROUND THE "REPAIRED" PLANK (TOP) AND ORIGINAL AS RECORDED STRAKE (BOTTOM). THE ORIGINAL STRAKE HAS A VOLUME OF 0.017163 M^3. THE REPAIRED STRAKE (BENT TO REMOVE LOCALISED DISTORTION) HAS A VOLUME OF 0.017166 M^3, A CHANGE OF LESS THAN 0.02%.

shipwright: twist and bend, have not been widely used.

One approach has been to flatten the digital data prior to printing on cardboard and then re-bending to create a physical scale model (Ravn 2012:316). Ravn has also suggested that the deformed and broken parts should be digitally repaired to their original design state prior to manufacturing solid components. This process could prove problematic when dealing with a component part in isolation as opposed to that component being a constituent part of the entire vessel.

Preliminary investigations using the bend and twist commands to "transform" the recorded shape state back to a shape approximating its original design have proved promising. To assess and quantify the effects of these powerful transformation tools, a number of typical planks were firstly measured in their original recorded shape state using the Analyze/Mass Properties/Volume feature in Rhinoceros3D. Then the digital solid was twisted to conform to the emerging hull shape, as a shipbuilder would the actual plank when building the vessel, and the resulting "repaired" plank again measured with the Analyze/Mass Properties/Volume command. Results to date indicate changes in the repaired component's volume of 0.02% or less when compared to the original volume (Figure 3).

Advances in computing power, and the relatively low cost of hardware and software have enabled the combining of the vast quantities of digitally recorded data into single files which can be modified in unison rather that working on isolated elements or sections of the vessel. As a result, when an individual component is twisted or reshaped, the associated original wireframe can be grouped or linked to the digital solid component and modified in tandem, thereby repositioning recorded items, such as fastening locations, tool marks, intentional marks, and any other relevant data which would be beneficial in the reconstruction process (Figure 4).

The end result of this methodology is the delivery, through an iterative process alternating between digital

many disarticulated timbers that were recovered during the excavation. In order to recreate a more complete vessel, including items which could not be fitted to the physical scale model, the next stage was to import and align the individual recorded components into the digital reconstruction. This information was used as the basis for positioning disarticulated timbers and recreating missing components. Initial attempts at this procedure proved difficult, due to the distorted nature of the individual recorded components.

Colleagues from across Europe, using similar digital recording and modelling methods, and collectively known as the Faro Rhino Archaeology Users Group (FRAUG), have been cautious to use the powerful transform tools in the Rhinoceros 3D software. The common transform tools such as rotate and move are well understood and frequently used, however two other transform commands, which are part of the daily language of every

FIGURE 4: EACH INDIVIDUAL DIGITAL SOLID AND ITS ASSOCIATED WIREFRAME IS FITTED TO THE RECONSTRUCTED SHAPE.

and physical environments, of a more definitive, synthetic reconstruction bringing together many data sets (including site records of the *in situ* ship, individual timber wireframe records and their subsequent digital solid models; scans of scaled physical models from assembled, rapid-prototype manufactured 'timbers'; repaired digital timbers where localised deformation has been removed; computer generated faired surface models). The ability to include the original recorded data, including items such as additional nail holes, intentional marks, or unexplained features in the synthetic reconstruction leads to the production of a research tool which can provide insight into a wide range of potential analyses beyond original hull form and ship performance such as construction sequence and design intent.

The oft quoted archaeological truism "absence of evidence is not evidence of absence" can be reversed to read "presence of evidence, (such as a seemingly unexplained fastening or feature) is evidence of absence". This can be applied to seemingly unexplained fastenings or features present in the reconstruction, encouraging further investigation. This may lead to the identification of missing elements in the ship, leading to an "as complete as possible" reconstruction. This will aid in the analysis of the reconstructed vessel for seaworthiness, performance, propulsion and cargo capacity (Tanner, this vol.).

Conclusion

The methods of documentation and subsequent analysis of the Newport Ship have been unashamedly experimental, combining well-established methods with new approaches, while taking advantage of developments in digital technologies and relatively accessible computing power. Such methodological development is not without its risks and the efficacy of new procedures in meeting the rigorous requirements of ship reconstruction will need to be critically assessed by the wider nautical archaeology community. The purpose of the digital approaches in nautical archaeology session at the 2013 Society of Historical Archaeology conference was to encourage exchange of ideas between projects working, at least in part, in a digital environment. While the research objectives of these projects are likely to be closely aligned, focusing on reconstruction of original hull form and examination of ship performance, the specifics of the methods employed will necessarily be optimised to meet the circumstances of individual ship finds addressing specific characteristics of shipbuilding tradition and the nature and extent of archaeological survival.

As experience with the use of digital approaches grows, methods may become more formalised. In the present developmental stage, the philosophy of research networks such as FRAUG, and of the SHA session has been to exchange experience without seeking primacy for any particular method. Constructive criticism within a supportive environment offers the opportunity to pool the hard won experience of nautical archaeologists optimising development of credible alternatives to traditional techniques. In a digital media age, other gains beyond academic research outcomes should also be considered in research designs. At the Newport Ship, the aim is to use its digital reconstructions to help guide the reassembly and reshaping of the conserved hull, as well as providing versatile content for the final publication, interim articles and future interactive museum displays, including games and animations. It is envisioned that the digital hull form will be used in complex visualisations depicting the ship in dynamic medieval settings, allowing the public the gain insight and understanding of many aspects of life in the medieval period. When successfully realised, the digital models will enable increased public access to a unique archaeological find.

Acknowledgments:

The research outlined in this paper has been made possible by a CyMAL-Museums, Archives and Libraries Wales Innovation and Development Grant (Project No. 2012-m-027-023). Additional research funding and support was provided by the Newport Museum, the Friends of the Newport Medieval Ship, University of Wales Trinity Saint David, and the Arts and Humanities Research Council. Special thanks to Erica McCarthy for working on many aspects of the digital and physical modelling program and related archaeological research. We would also like to acknowledge the support of the FRAUG (Faro Rhino Archaeological Users Group) members from across Europe who meets annually to discuss and compare projects, templates and methodologies.

References

CRUMLIN-PEDERSEN, O., AND MCGRAIL, S.
    2006   "Some Principles for the Reconstruction of Ancient Boat Structures." *International Journal of Nautical Archaeology* 35(1):53–57.

INSTITUTE FOR ARCHAEOLOGISTS
    2008   *Standards and Guidance for Nautical Archaeological Recording and Reconstruction.* http://www.archaeologists.net/sites/default/files/node-files/ifa_standards_nautical.pdf (accessed 28/2/2013).

JONES, T.
    2009a   "The Three-Dimensional Recording and Digital Modeling of the Newport Medieval Ship." In *ACUA Underwater Archaeology Proceedings* 2009, Laanela, E., and Moore, J., (eds.). Columbus, Ohio: PAST Foundation. pp. 111-116.

    2009b   'The Newport Medieval Ship: Her Three-Dimensional Digital Recording and Analysis.' *SKYLLIS Journal: Zeitshrift für Unterwasserarchäologie.* 9. Jahrgang 2009, Heft 1.

JONES, T., AND NAYLING, N.
    2011   "ShipShape: Creating a 3D Solid Model of the Newport Medieval Ship." In *ACUA Underwater Archaeology Proceedings* 2011, Castro, F., and Thomas, L.(eds.). Tucson, Arizona: Society for Historical Archaeology. pp. 54-60.

MCKEE, E.
    1974   *Building and Trials of the Replica of an Ancient Boat: The Gokstad Faering, Part 2: The Sea Trials.* National Maritime Museum, Greenwich.

NAYLING, N., AND JONES, T.
    2012   "Three-dimensional Recording and Hull Form Modelling of the Newport Medieval Ship (Wales, UK)," In N. Gunsenin (ed.), *Between Continents: Proceedings of the 12th international symposium on boat and ship archaeology,* Istanbul 2009 (ISBSA12) pp. 319–324.

RAVN, M.
    2012   "Recent Advances in Post-Excavation Documentation: Roskilde Method," In N. Günsenin (ed.), *Between Continents: Proceedings of the 12th international symposium on boat and ship archaeology,* Istanbul 2009 (ISBSA12) pp. 313–317.

SOE, S., EYERS, D., JONES, T., AND NAYLING, N.
    2012   "Additive manufacturing for archaeological reconstruction of a medieval ship," *Rapid Prototyping Journal,* Vol. 18, Issue 6, pp. 443 – 450

• • • • • • • • • • • • • • • •

Toby Jones
Newport Medieval Ship Project
Newport Museum and Heritage Service
Unit 22, Maesglas Industrial Estate
Newport, Wales
United Kingdom
NP20 2NN
toby.jones@newport.gov.uk

Nigel Nayling
School of Archaeology, History and Anthropology
University of Wales: Trinity Saint David
Lampeter, Ceredigion, Wales
United Kingdom
SA48 7ED
n.nayling@tsd.ac.uk

Pat Tanner
Traditional Boats of Ireland Project
32 Rowan Court,
Ballea Woods, Carrigaline,
Co. Cork.
Ireland
Email: pattanner@eircom.net

Ship Reconstruction and Digital Modeling: the Example of the Aber Wrac'h 1 Wreck (France)

Alexandra Grille

The reconstruction of the Aber Wrac'h 1 ship was carried out from documentation recorded at the end of the 1980's, when only two-dimensional recording were available. The process includes the realisation of a wooden 1:10 scale model in order to reconstruct the missing bow and stern. A three-dimensional digital model was done in the modeling software Rhinoceros. It completed the process to verify the physical model by reconstructing the original timbers of the ship. It allows calculation of hydrostatic properties and offers a better visualisation as well as a comprehension of the ship and its construction within its socio-economic context.

Introduction

The Aber Wrac'h 1 wreck was found in October 1985 in the north-western part of Brittany near the town of Brest. Two excavation seasons were organised in 1987 and 1988 by the DRASSM under the direction of Michel L'Hour. In 2004, a reconstruction of the shipwreck was carried out with a physical wooden model to reconstruct missing parts. This latter was converted into a digital model to analyse the ship building sequence after the reconstruction of each individual timbers and allow calculation of hydrostatics properties.

The Wreck

The hull portion preserved was 18 m long, 5 m wide and essentially of oak, except for the deep keel made of beech (Fagus sylvatica). A fragment of the stem was preserved with the imprints of 3 hood-ends. 24 overlapping strakes, averaging 23 cm wide and 3 cm thick, were luted with moss and riveted. A heavy framing was inserted into the planking shell. The frames were 20-25 cm wide with 13 cm average space between them. A ceiling was treenailed in place and closed by filling timbers. Two additional stringers were placed higher in the hull. The highest helped to support some of the beams. Three through beam heads were found in the middle and forward part of the wreck. Half-cone shaped (cuneiform) fenders were located at the beam ends, pointing toward the stem. (L'Hour and Veyrat: 169-174).

The ship is dated to the period 1380-1440 by archaeological finds: coins and shoes (L'Hour and Veyrat 1994: 166). Unfortunately, all attempts to date the ship by dendrochronology failed, as the Aber Wrac'h 1 curve composed from the planking does not match the master curve from North-Western Europe.

Reconstruction Process

Physical modeling

The initial reconstruction was based on the frames and keel, as the plank shapes were not recorded. Two distinct types of information were available about the frames: cross-sections and 1:1 scale drawings. After the reassembly of each frame, a line linking up the upper inboard edge of each plank joggle (the neckline) was traced. It served as a distorted foundation of a hull plan of the middle part of the ship. These lines were carefully faired.

Each frame served as a mould in a 1:10 scale wooden model. The planking was reconstructed according to the width of the strakes, recorded in the frame drawings and site cross sections, and the natural development of the wood following the shell-based construction principle. In order to find the bow and stern of the ship, the patterns of stem and sternpost were placed on a device moving horizontally and vertically. The stem and sternpost were placed in their minimal position first, according to the preserved length of the strakes, and moved according to the planks run. This allowed the determination of the rake of the stem and sternpost by controlling the distortions in the hull. Three principal iterations were necessary to find the best balance (Figure 1).

Due to software interoperability problems, a first reconstruction of the ship failed. It was necessary to repeat all the process from the early stage.

Digital modeling

<u>Surviving part of the ship</u>

As the second physical model was finished in 2007, the digital modeling had appeared as a solution to achieve the hull shape reconstruction process and verify the physical model by reconstructing each timber.

FIGURE 1. THE PHYSICAL MODEL IN ITS FINAL STAGE.

An attempt of digital recording of the model was done with a 3d scanner. The method was relatively new. The scanner recorded more points than the computer, except workstation, were able to treat. The point cloud was about 4 Gb. To reduce the weight of the file, some points were digitally removed without taking into consideration their position in regards to the required data. At the end, the file was totally inexploitable, as the edges of the planks were not recorded properly and impossible to reconstruct.

A digital model was created from the physical model by manual measurement. The inside edge of each plank was recorded at regular station and transferred into Rhinoceros software. As soon as the planking was modeled, the framing, ceiling and beams were reconstructed according to the original data coming from cross section, plan and 1:1 scale drawing.

In missing parts of the bow and stern, the digital modeling allowed to test different possibilities and clarify the construction mode. In the bow, two loose V-shaped floor timbers found forward of the wreck were replaced. To do this, the deadrise and plank bevels were taken into consideration, as no cross-section was recorded. The floor timbers were replaced on the stem: one in the bottom and the other higher up. Considering that their original position was unknown, they were not used in the hull shape reconstruction process and enabled to check the physical model. Their molded dimension was also very useful to reconstruct other missing floor timbers, as only treenails were recorded in the planking of the bow. After having plotted the position of these treenails in the digital model, it was possible to reconstruct the approximate framing positions and shapes in this area, using the average frame width and centering it on the line of treenails.

In the stern, no information was preserved. The reconstruction is purely hypothetical, based on the preserved frames. Due to the hull shape and according to the construction process in the bow, it was decided to reconstruct floor timbers and futtocks as in the bow and to keep the same spacing and dimensions than the preserved frames of the stern. This allowed to get a maximum accuracy for the hydrostatics properties (Figure 2).

Finally, the keelson was reconstructed following the buttressing timbers and futtock heels data. It stops when the frames begin to be deeper.

Comparison between the original and the modeled timbers

The comparison between the original timbers drawings reassembled and the modeled one showed that the first and last recorded frames respectively in the bow and stern only have a difference of 4 cm. In the middle part of the ship where the futtocks were very distorted and bent outwards by the weight of the ballast, the difference is of about 40 cm. The angles recorded on the original beam head from the middle part and the bow, M116 and M107, are at 1-2° the same than those of the model. Finally according to the planks angle running into the stem between the original and modeled stem part, there is a light modification of about 2°, but the inside and outside face of the stem were not well preserved.

Reconstruction of the upper work

The reconstruction of the upper work is primarily based on the first results of hydrostatic calculations for the underwater hull. Due to the fine entrance and run as well as the relatively low volume of the ship, the upper works were reconstructed as minimal as possible to avoid instability. It is based on timbers considered as structurally necessary for the ship construction and known from contemporary or earlier shipwrecks.

The distance between the beams required the establishment of longitudinal beams to support the deck planking, following the example of the Bremen cog. Eight strakes above the 23rd strakes form a bulwark 1.30 m high. This is sufficient to protect the crew when the ship is heeling without overloading the upper works. No bevels in the overlap were recorded on the 23rd and 24th strakes. This suggests that the original sides continued in the line of the planking below. There is no change of the hull shape. Standing knees are reconstructed as directly fastened to the planking, as suggested by a very damaged loose timbers found in the middle part of the wreck.

Finally, the larger volume of the stern as well as contemporary ship finds leads us to reconstruct a stern castle. As the hull shape is very fine in this area, it was not possible to integrate and fair the castle into the ship side below. The hull shape is too fine and there is no space with the passage of the helm. The integration of the stern castle in 16th-century ships seems to be tied to the introduction of the transom which allows ensuring the continuity of the hull shape higher. Due to its shape, reconstructed according to the frame recorded in the stern area, the Aber Wrac'h 1 ship would not support such a structure. The stern castle is then reconstructed as a separate structure, based on the Bremen cog principle, but adapted to the Aber Wrac'h 1 hull shape.

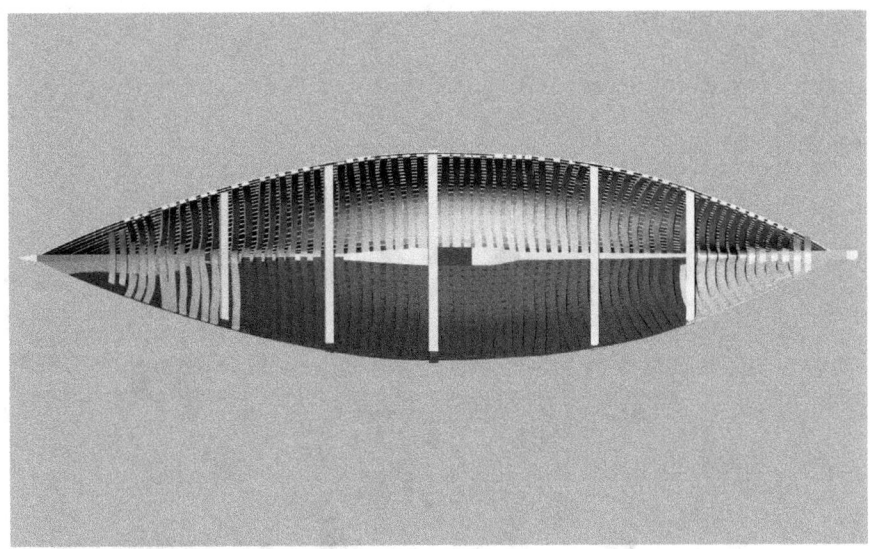

FIGURE 2. RECONSTRUCTION OF THE PRESERVED PART OF THE SHIP. THE PRESERVED TIMBERS ARE IN BLUE AND THE RECONSTRUCTED IN GRAY.

Reconstruction of the rudder

As the stern part was missing, no evidence of a rudder was found. For modeling purpose, an hypothetical reconstruction of a rudder was done. 16th century ship finds, such as Mary Rose, have completely different hull shape and rigging, and do not have the same steering constraints. An attempt to use 18th century treatise rules gives no results for the same reason. So the rudder reconstruction is based on the Bremen cog, as no contemporary rudder of large 15th century clinker ship is known.

The model and its application

Design and construction sequence

Bottom

The reconstruction helps to understand the construction sequence and the design behind it. The keel is already shaped to accommodate the twist in the garboard, which is flatter amidships. It tapers towards both ends from a maximum width near the middle of its length.

The first 3 strakes form the hollow below the bottom and establish the hull shape. The garboard itself was carved to shape. The second and third strakes were beveled before they were placed. The 4th to 6th strakes make up the narrow bottom. Their bevels are less substantial and served to seal the overlap. The 7th to 9th strakes composed the turn of the bilge. The former strakes were beveled before they were placed.

This first sequence of the construction may also be recognized by the insertion of all the floor timbers. The first could have been placed in the stern once the 5th strake was complete (M130). A second floor timber is located in the stem which could have been inserted once the 6th strake was in place (M105). The first substantial floortimbers had to wait for the 7th strake. Most of the floor timbers likely reached the 8th and 9th strake, with short and long ends alternating to avoid creating a breaking line (except those crossing the stem and sternpost).

Sides: a second independent sequence.

The planking of the sides was hung without beveling the strakes. The sides are vertically straight without any real complexity of curvature. As preserved and recorded, the first futtocks reach at least to the 19th strake, as in the middle part of the ship (M114-118-124). But the irregular preservation of the futtocks in the bow and stern give a limited image. Most of the first futtocks reached the 21st and 22nd strakes.

FIGURE 3. RECONSTRUCTION OF THE PRESERVED PART OF THE SHIP. ALL TIMBERS PRESERVED ARE RECONSTRUCTED.

The surviving throughbeams are integral to the construction process. The forward beam is placed a strake lower than the other, probably to limit the sheer of the deck and then the efforts of the crew. The construction sequence follows the same principle as the other beams placed in the 21st strake. The plank is notched to receive the lower face of the beam, which is rabbeted to receive the plank. A local reinforcing plank is placed inside of the strakes in the area of the beam. A notch made on the underside of the beam receives the futtock head, narrowed from 25 cm to 10-12 cm. Then the 22nd strake was placed. It is cut at each beam, ending and beginning in the vertical rabbet in the side of the beam. And finally the 23rd strake was placed in the upper rabbet of the beam and reinforced with another short interior plank. This strake is not beveled which suggests that the upper part of the side continued in line with the 22nd strake.

Reversed futtock scarfs, where the second futtock was laid before the first one, are found in some locations. Their original extent is unknown, but their heels reach the 12th–14th strakes. Nine of the reversed futtocks survived. They are set symmetrically from the beam M116, acting as a mast partner. This beam is framed by two reversed futtocks (M115 and M117). The rhythm of others varies: a first set very close in the middle part (two then one normal futtock separating the reversed ones) and a second set in the bow and stern separated by seven to eight frames.

The pattern of these futtocks shows that their position was intentionally defined, probably since the very beginning of the construction and before the introduction of the beams. As reversed futtocks are not preserved in their original length, it is difficult to have a clear understanding of their role. The symmetrical distribution suggests that they were placed to spread stress on the hull. As they reached the 12th–14th strakes, they avoided having the first futtock—top timber scarfs in the same strakes and maybe counteracted the pressure on the hull by reversed scarfs. Note that the intermediate stringer above the ceiling is placed to reinforce the joinery of these frames.

Stringers were then placed. The lowest one is notched over the floor-timbers—first futtock overlap. The second is placed in the turn of the bilge. The highest served as an additional support for the beams.

A ceiling completes the space between the lowest stringers and protects the frames. It is closed by filling timbers placed along the bilge stringer (Figure 3).

Preliminary calculation of hydrostatic properties

Although this work is still in progress, some preliminary analysis of the hydrostatic properties may be presented. They were done with Orca, a complementary module of Rhinoceros.

General hydrostatics data

As reconstructed, the overall dimensions of the ship are 25.850 m in length, 6.95 m in beam and 4.45 m in depth (8.26 m as an overall depth at the stem). The hold space is estimated, under the beam, at 96 m^3.

Although it is founded on a minimal reconstruction of the upper work of the ship, the weight may be estimated on the reconstructed timbers modeled under Rhinoceros. The software gives a very accurate volume of individual timbers. Considering a density of 800 kg/m^{-3} for oak wood and 700 kg/m^{-3} for beech wood, the ship weighs about 35 tons.

Through beams give a theoretical maximum waterline. Considering the weight distribution, the waterline appears to be parallel to the underside of the keel. At this maximum limit, the lowest beam is placed 2.88 m higher than the baseline. The displacement is then 115 t. But the beams were not permanently underwater, so it is certain that this limit should not be reached. The normal loaded draft is probably somewhat less.

Hydrostatics properties without the rigging

The center of gravity of the ship may be defined from the weight and position of individual timbers. Rhinoceros calculates the position of the center of the volume of individual timbers. The moment of mass corresponds to the center of this volume multiplied by the mass of the timbers. The position of the center of gravity is given by the sum of these centers of mass divided by the total mass of the ship (Kemp 1896, p. 200). In this condition, the position of the longitudinal center of gravity is 14,319 m from the forward perpendicular and vertical center of gravity is 2.90 m.

Due to its shape, the empty hull is not stable, as its transverse metacentric height is negative. A minimal ballast is then required. Some analyses were carried out on the stones found on the wreck, which at least a part came from the ballast. This showed that the ballast was mainly composed of granite.

It was considered that the ceiling in the bottom of the ship, closed by filling timbers, was also placed to help in stowing ballast in the hull. The volume of this part of the ship, 14 m³, was then lowered progressively to determine the minimal ballast. With a ballasted space of 5m³, corresponding to a weight of 11.7 t of granite, the ship without its rigging is stable. The righting arm is sufficient to 45°, where most of the ship side is underwater (inwale, stem, and sternpost).

In this minimal configuration, the draft is 1.756 m, more than a meter below the beam heads.

Hydrostatics properties with the rigging

<u>Reconstruction of the mast and yard</u>
The mast step, which is part of the keelson, is the only evidence preserved of the rig. It is 2.13 m long, 50 m wide and 25 cm deep. The rebate for the mast heel is 90 cm long, 34 cm wide and 14 cm deep.

According to the contemporary iconography, it is possible to guess that the mast length was close to the ship

Figure 4. Hypothetical reconstruction of the ship under sail. Left: hull reconstructed with the stern castle. Right: The ship close to its maximum sinkage.

length. As the mast tenon would not have exceeded the keelson width in this area, its maximum diameter would have been 50 cm. The reconstructed mast is then about 25 m long and 50 cm in diameter at the heel. The yard is estimated to be about 13 m wide. Mast and yard weigh 2,748 t (Figure 4). The longitudinal center of gravity is then 14,108 m from the forward perpendicular and the vertical center of gravity is 3,625 m.

A first approach of fully loaded stability was carried out with a bulk grain cargo. Its weight reaches almost 75 t. The displacement is then 112 t. The draft is 2.84 m, 4 cm below the beam head. In this excessive condition, where the waterline is placed too high, the righting arm is efficient up to a heeling angle of 52°. At a heeling angle of 30.5°, downflooding results. A ship without a watertight deck needs more stability than this, so the actual loaded draft is probably even less.

Despite its specificity, the reconstructed hull shape of the Aber Wrac'h 1 ship is stable. It remains to perform its real cargo capacity, avoiding a regular immersion of the beams. Different types of cargo need to be modeled to correspond to the medieval context: load in barrels or mixt cargoes as mentioned in the archives. Digital modeling will help to define the best position of different type of cargoes, and check the stability according to them.

Acknowledgments

I would like to thank especially Pierre Lotodé and Dr Fred Hocker for their help and guidance throughout this project. Without their presence and advices, this reconstruction would never have come true. Thanks also to Dr Eric Rieth, Michel L'Hour and Elisabeth Veyrat for the opportunity of this study. Thanks, finally, to my son for his love and patience.

References

L'Hour M., and Veyrat E.
    1994   The French medieval clinker wreck from Aber Wrac'h. *In Crossroads in ancient shipbuilding, Proceedings of the Sixth Symposium on Boat and Ship Archaeology, Roskilde 1991, ISBSA 6,* C. Westerdahl, editor, pp. 165-180. Oxbow Monograph 40, 1994.

Kemp, Dixon
    1896   *Yacht and boat sailing. Editon française traduite, annotée et augmentée par MM. Boyn & Martinenq.* Vol. 2. Paris.

• • • • • • • • • • • • • • • •

Alexandra Grille
5 rue Henri Barnoin,
F-56400 Le Bono
France
alexandra.grille@sfr.fr

3D Laser Scanning for the Digital Reconstruction and Analysis of a 16th-Century Clinker Built Sailing Vessel

Pat Tanner

The following methodology has been developed to model and analyse the hydrostatic and hydrodynamic characteristics of a reconstructed hull. The Drogheda boat physical scale model was 3D laser scanned and processed using Geomagic Studio software. Each individual component is solid modelled using Rhinoceros 3D software and assigned a material. This enables the Orca 3D software, a plug-in for Rhinoceros 3D to calculate important factors such as centre of gravity and density and establish a floatation condition for the vessel, and examine external influences such as ballast, cargo, crew, and wind loading. Using this digital approach quickly allows for multiple variables to be tested and modified in order to reach a definitive original hull form.

Introduction

This project follows on from the discovery and recording of the Drogheda Boat, a 16th century clinker built sailing vessel discovered 1.5 km east of Drogheda on the River Boyne, Ireland, during a capital dredging project on behalf of Drogheda Port Company in 2006. The remains, with an overall preserved length of circa 9 m and circa 3 m in width, partial stem and stern post, 11 frames stations and 2 mast steps represents almost the entire original length of the boat. Since the remains were located within the footprint of the dredging works, in-situ preservation was not possible and an excavation was carried out by the Underwater Archaeology Unit of the National Monuments Service between February and July 2007.

All boat timbers were recorded by written description, digital photography, and detailed digital recording using a Faro Arm coordinate measuring machine and Rhinoceros 3D software, following the recording guidelines devised by the Viking Ship Museum, Roskilde and the Newport Medieval Ship project. A 1:10 scale model of all the structural elements found during the excavation was created using contact digitising, digital solid modelling and selective laser sintering techniques (Schweitzer 2012:225–234). This modelling approach was developed for use on the Newport Medieval Ship scale model (Nayling and Jones 2012). This particular scale model represents a unique object in that it is neither the original as-built vessel nor the vessel shape at time of sinking, but a "post deposition" shape state (Jones and Nayling 2011). The project is broadly divided into two separate phases. Phase one is the digital recording of the physical scale model, with attempts at a minimum or complete reconstruction, while phase two deals with the analysis of that reconstruction.

The aim in reconstructing the hull shape is to generate a floating hypothesis for the vessel in order to arrive at lines plans and hydrostatic data, such as displacement, sailing characteristics, and cargo carrying capabilities. "Principles for the Reconstruction of Ancient Boat Structures"(Crumlin-Pedersen and McGrail 2006) recommends general principles that should be observed and considered under five headings: (1) deformation and its effects on the hull shape, (2) the impact of modem naval architectural standards, (3) the introduction of alien elements to complete the hull, (4) the consideration of propulsion, steering and seaworthiness, and (5) the concept of minimum reconstruction.

The issue of deformation is dealt with by laser scanning the reconstructed 1:10 scale model of the vessel, and using Rhinoceros 3D CAD software to examine and analyse the recorded shape. This scanned digital model is then examined for any twist or hogging and repaired as necessary.

The impact of modern naval architectural standards are noted,

> *Since ships and boats are three-dimensionally curved bodies of varying complexity, a naval architect, developing drawings for a ship or a boat will inevitably apply a rectilinear system of sections in order to 'cut up' the hull into manageable slices which can be represented in two-dimensional drawings. These lines-drawings provide the basis for strength and performance calculations, and also for the plans needed for the construction of a vessel.* (Crumlin-Pedersen and McGrail 2006:54)

This was achieved by combining the 3D laser scan of the reconstructed physical scale model, repaired to remove deformation, with the digitally reconstructed

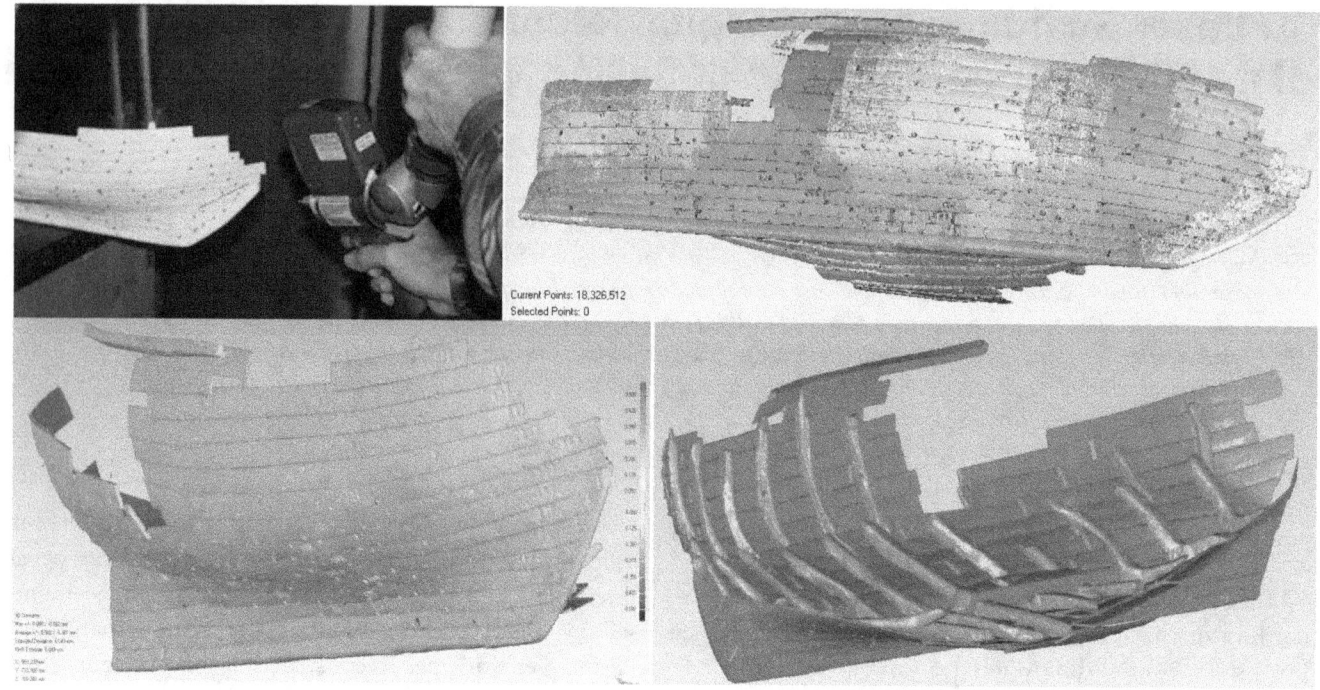

FIGURE 1. THE RECORDING PROCESS: CLOCKWISE FROM TOP LEFT: 3D LASER SCANNING THE PHYSICAL SCALE MODEL, 41 SCANS OF THE EXTERIOR SURFACE BEING ALIGNED, COMPARING DEVIATION BETWEEN GENERATED SURFACES AND SCAN DATA, SCAN DATA CONVERTED TO A POLYGON MESH MODEL.

missing portions to create a floating hypothesis, which could then be analysed using the Orca 3D software to produce lines plans and the various hydrostatic calculation results.

The introduction of alien elements to complete the hull has been kept to the absolute minimum, and the reconstructed hull has been primarily created by mirroring existing parts, or extrapolation from the preserved majority of the hull. Any elements added to the hull, for which no distinctive evidence has been found, are in all cases clearly identified and reasons or explanations for their inclusion are given.

Steering, propulsion and seaworthiness are all dealt with in detail in both the reconstruction and analysis phases of this project.

The concept of minimum reconstruction is now used to describe one or more (partial) reconstructions based on the excavated evidence (Crumlin-Pedersen and McGrail 2006:57). This methodology uses an iterative process to analyse several potential reconstructions and allows for multiple variables to be tested and modified in order to reach a more definitive original hull form.

Digital Reconstruction

Recording the Physical Scale Model

As the component parts were recorded, after lifting and prior to conservation, they were reassembled into the physical scale model and aligned using their original recorded fastenings. This created an accurate model of the post deposition vessel shape using only the recovered materials. The next stage in analysing the overall vessel was to record this reassembled hull shape and generate lines, plans, and hydrostatic data. As the scale model is still relatively delicate, especially in the areas such as unfastened strake ends, touch probing would not provide as accurate a recording as a non contact form of measurement such as 3D laser scanning. The reconstructed 1:10 scale model was laser scanned using a Faro Platinum Arm and Laser-line Probe (Figure 1 top left) to capture a 3 dimensional point cloud.

The point cloud data for the Drogheda boat consists of 46.63 million points recorded at an accuracy of ± 0.076mm (Figure 1 bottom right).

Processing the Scan Data

The scan data consists of many individual scans, 41 scans for the exterior surface, which are aligned into a single point cloud using Geomagic Studio software

(Figure 1 top right). The software is then used to clean the scan data and a usable surface model is generated by fitting a polygon mesh to the underlying point cloud data, followed by a smooth NURB'S (Non Uniform Rational B-Splines) surface fitted to the polygon mesh. At all stages of this process the deviation between the generated surfaces and the original scanned point cloud data is checked to remain within the desired 0.080 mm tolerances (Figure 1 bottom right). By maintaining a tolerance of 0.080 mm (80 microns) with the 1:10 scale model, the resultant full size vessel measurements will be accurate to within 0.8 mm, twice as accurate as traditional naval architecture surveys for taking lines plan, which were typically carried out to 1/16 in. (1.58 mm).

This is where the current methodology differs from others to date where the recorded polygon mesh data has been used to produce a profile, longitudinal sections, plan sections, and cross sections and group these together as futtocks, waterlines, and stations to become a lines plan (Moreton, et al. 2000,466). In the present process, the scanned data is used to generate an exact replica computer model of the item scanned, in this instance a boat hull, and continues to treat it as such. Once the scanned model has been processed, the polygon mesh (Figure 1 bottom left) and NURB's surface fitted, it is exported to Rhino and the required lines plan, main and additional dimensions, hydrostatic data, and form coefficients can be extracted.

In the case of the Drogheda boat the design water line (DWL) was not clearly known, and to begin with, the model was orientated along its keel, the model was re-scaled back to full size, by a factor of 10 in this case, and a basic lines plan generated as a starting reference point. As the model is incomplete and there is no datum or waterline, this set of lines plans is of little value and is created solely to record the shape and form of the reconstructed model.

Reconstructing the Hull Shape

At this stage the remodelled vessel still did not represent a complete vessel so the missing parts would need to be extrapolated and recreated. For the purposes of this reconstruction it is assumed that the hull is generally symmetrical. The reconstructed model was broken down into four main categories:

1. Recovered material, (coloured brown on the reconstructed model).

2. Parts which are critical to creating a watertight hull which can function properly in the water. These include the stem extended up to gunwale level, the sternpost extended up to gunwale level, and the remainder of the hull planking up to and including the gunwale (coloured blue on the reconstructed model).

3. Items which would be considered necessary for the construction of the vessel, where some evidence of their existence remains even though the component part was not recovered. These items include the top or futtock sections of frames 7, 8, 9, 10, and 11, as well as frame 0 which was added between frame 1 and the stem post, in order to maintain frame spacing. Additional evidence for frame 0 includes treenail holes at this position, a sheer clamp or inwale has also been added along the tops of the frames, the tops of frames 1,4 and 5 have a scarf or rebate cut in to take this sheer clamp. A main mast, foremast, yards and rudder have also been added and these will be dealt with in more detail under considerations of propulsion and steering (coloured green on the reconstructed model).

4. Items which were probably part of the complete vessel but no evidence of their existence was recovered. This includes frame 11a, which has been added between frame 11 and the sternpost, in order to maintain frame spacing, although no evidence can be found for this frame as the hull planking in this area was not recovered. Two thwarts have also been added to coincide with the mast positions to provide transverse strength to the hull and support to both masts. A cockpit sole has also been added in order to enable the helmsman reach the tiller (coloured red on the reconstructed model).

Shown in gray are items which have been mirrored. As the starboard side of the vessel was more complete, this side was recreated and then mirrored to the missing port side.

The first stage was to check the digital model as recorded during 3D scanning for fairness as the re-scaling to full size will have increased any errors or unfair regions by a factor of 10. "Fair" is a term that is used whenever a boat is built. When wood is bent or curved or cut, or a line drawn, a boat builder must be concerned about fairness. A "fair curve" or line is one that is as smooth as

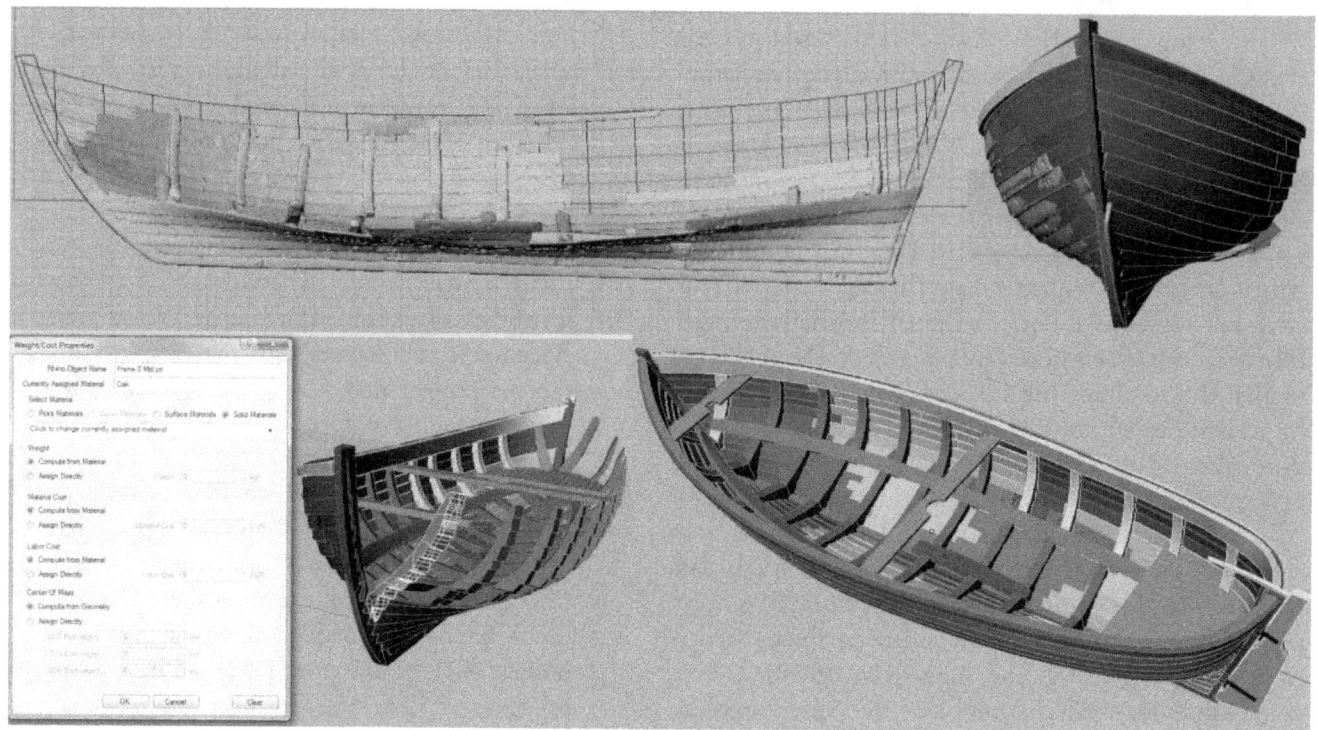

FIGURE 2. RECONSTRUCTING THE HULL SHAPE: CLOCKWISE FROM TOP LEFT: PROJECTING FAIR CURVES ONTO THE MESH MODEL TO COINCIDE WITH STRAKE RUNS AND OTHER PROMINENT FEATURES, FAIRED SURFACE OVERLAID ON THE SCANNED MODEL TO DETERMINE VARIATIONS, RECONSTRUCTED MODEL COLOUR CODED TO DIFFERENTIATE RECOVERED MATERIAL FROM INTRODUCED ELEMENTS, A MATERIAL IS ASSIGNED TO EACH CONSTITUENT PART USING ORCA 3D PLUG-IN.

it can be as it follows the path it must take around the hull of a boat. A fair line is free of extraneous bumps or hollows, and an unfair line needs to be faired, or smoothed out.

The recovered materials included 7 complete hull strakes and partial strakes up to a 15th strake on the starboard side. Curves are projected onto the mesh model to coincide with strake runs and other prominent features (Figure 2 top left). A curve representing the existing portion of the stem was created and extended as a fair curve to represent the missing portion. The sternpost was extrapolated by examining the recovered sternhook and in particular the scarf joint at the top section, which indicated that the missing sternpost extended in a straight line continuing from the top of the sternhook up to gunwale level. These curves are then extended to complete the hull shape and checked with the curvature graph feature in Rhinoceros 3D. A faired surface is then created using these curves and overlaid on the scanned model to determine variations between the actual vessel and a faired surface (Figure 2 top right). Once the existing surfaces were checked and faired, they were then mirrored in order to create a more complete hull shape. At this point the process of recreating the vessel shape up to the level of the 15th strake was completed, which provides a basic hull shape for the reconstructed vessel. In order to continue to examine the vessel and proceed to a full reconstruction, it will be necessary to establish how the vessel was intended to (or actually) floated.

Establishing Floatation Condition

In order to establish a floatation condition for the vessel, three key facts are required, (1) vessel hull shape in order to establish the centre of buoyancy (B), (2) vessel centre of gravity (G) to establish floatation trim and (3) vessel weight in order to establish displacement. The vessel hull shape has been established based on the reconstruction methods already employed, but a vessel weight and centre of gravity have not yet been established.

The most accurate method of determining the weight of a vessel is to weigh it in air and then carry out an inclining test to establish the position of centre of gravity (G) (McKee 1974:11–13). In order to weigh the vessel and perform an inclining test, a complete, rebuilt vessel would be required. As this is not practical, and the fact that various hypothetical reconstructions are still being examined, an alternative approach is used.

Every constituent part of the vessel is accurately modelled using Rhinoceros 3D solid modelling techniques and, using the Orca 3D plug-in for Rhinoceros 3D, a material is assigned to each part (Figure 2 bottom left). Orca 3D can use each constituent part's dimensions and assigned material, to calculate the weight, longitudinal, transverse and vertical centre of gravity. When all of these constituent parts are combined an overall weight, centre of gravity and centre of buoyancy for the entire vessel is produced. As the floatation plane is calculated from the total weight, it is important to reconstruct as much of the overall vessel as possible by solid modelling each of the constituent parts and mirroring where necessary. With regard to the materials assigned for each element, as the density of timber varies, an average density is used. All of the timbers recovered with the exception of the forward mast step were oak, which can vary between 600 and 900 kg per m^3, and in this case 750 kg per m^3 was used. Similarly, the barrels had a mass of between 193.5 and 245.65 kg, so an average of 219.5 kg was used for modelling purposes. The iron nails and roves were not individually modelled in the boat but have been included in the weight calculations on the basis of approx 40 nails per strake giving a total of 1360 nails at an approx total weight of 227 kg. The treenails have not been modelled, as these are basically a wooden dowel fitted to a pre drilled hole and would have no effect on the overall weight.

When the entire vessel has been solid modelled in this fashion a total weight and centre of floatation for the vessel is calculated. When this is applied to the model it has the effect of orientating the vessel to its flotation condition. The Drogheda Boat excluding any cargo or ballast (as built condition) weighs 2,909 kg, with longitudinal centre of gravity (LCG) located 4,322.5 mm aft of the Forward Perpendicular (FP), and the vertical centre of gravity (VCG) located 516 mm above the DWL, transverse centre of gravity (TCG) is 0 mm, located on the centre line as it is assumed the vessel is symmetrical. Additional influences such as crew number and position, ballast quantity and location can also be modelled and used to analyse various floatation conditions.

Spars and Rigging

As little evidence of rig types or sails exists and no masts were recovered, they will have to be extrapolated from contemporary iconography combined with the use of modern calculations and formulas. Evidence recovered included a mainmast heel block and a foremast heel block, indicating that the vessel carried two masts for sailing purposes.

The dimensions of the two mast steps are: Mainmast step 180 mm moulded by 220 mm sided and 1,860 mm in length with a rectangular mast heel socket of 140 by 110 mm and a depth of 85 mm: Foremast step 130 mm moulded by 90 mm sided and 510 mm length with a square mast heel socket of 80 x 80 mm and a depth of 40mm. This would suggest the foremast was smaller than the mainmast.

A relatively small block was found broken but almost complete underneath a stringer and would appear to be a clew garnet block. A possible parrel truck from the Drogheda Boat was found amongst material which had collapsed into Cask 8, which was located immediately next to the starboard side of the mast step.

The method of estimating the rig size examines the two mast steps recovered, which gives a mast tenon size for the main mast of 140 x 110 x 85 mm and the mast heel block is 180 mm sided dimension. If you take it that the mast base diameter is unlikely to be wider than the mast step, and also unlikely to be less than the longest dimension of the tenon, one can estimate the diameter at heel and hence the probable length (as these are usually related). Probable mainmast length is circa LOA 9.795 m (32 ft.). Using the "old rule" Dixon Kemp et al quote (Kemp 1897), of 7/32 inch per ft., this would give a diameter of 7 inches (180 mm) which matches the mast step. Then the logic is reversed for the foremast. On the basis of the mast step width of 90 mm one would predict a mast length of 5 m. The yard length is usually between 7/8 and 3/5 of the mast length, giving average lengths of 8.5 m and 4.3 m respectively. The corresponding total sail area is approx. 51 m^2.

Steering

Evidence was found of a rectangular rebate on either side of the sternhook as well as a groove on the aft face, which confirm the existence of an iron gudgeon fitted to receive the mating pintle of a transom hung rudder. No evidence of the rudder was found so a basic representation has been used for modelling purposes.

A typical modern-day formula for calculating rudder area for a traditional shape long keel sailing vessel would be 0.068 x waterline length x draft. This formula would give

$$0.068 \times 8.5 \times 0.84 = 0.485 \text{ m}^2.$$

The actual rudder used has an area of 0.485 m^2.

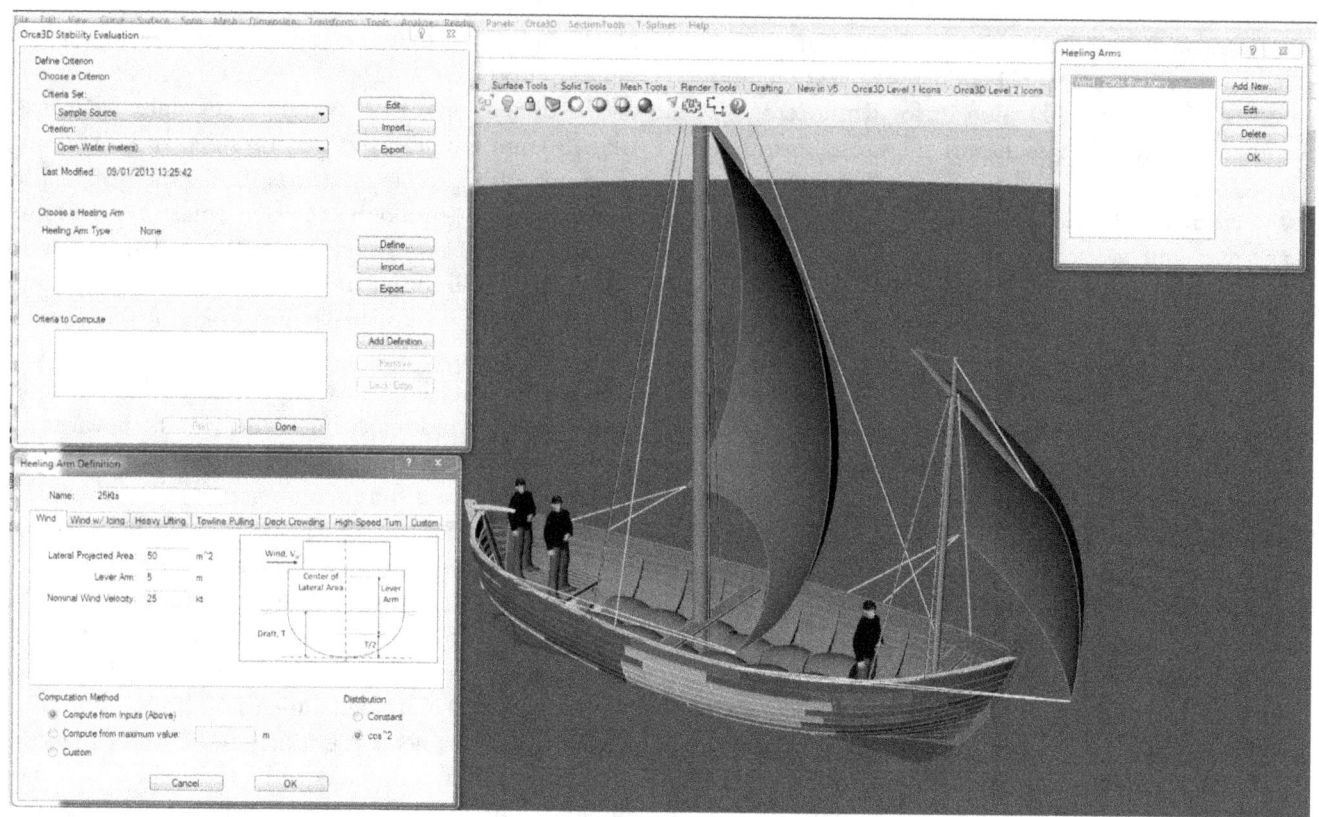

FIGURE 3. EXAMINING EXTERNAL INFLUENCES: CARGO IS ADDED IN THE FORM OF THE RECOVERED CASKS, CREW ARE PLACED AND THE ORCA SOFTWARE IS CONFIGURED FOR WIND LOADING ANALYSIS.

Analysis of the Reconstructed Vessel

Seaworthiness

The term seaworthiness is a very broad one, as it not only includes the physical state of the vessel, but also extends to other aspects and factors. Consequently, it is not easy to define seaworthiness in rigorous terms. A 13th century law defined a ship as seaworthy if she did not need to be bailed more than three times in 24 hours (Christensen 1968,138-9). The Marine Insurance Act (1906) states 'A ship is deemed to be seaworthy when she is reasonably fit in all respects to encounter the ordinary perils of the seas of the adventure insured' (Chalmers and Ivamy 1976). Consequently seaworthiness can be defined as the following: the fitness of the vessel in all respects, to encounter the ordinary perils of the sea, that could be expected on her voyage, and deliver the cargo safely to its destination.

Evaluating whether a vessel would have been seagoing is an art as well as a science, since a number of interacting factors have to be considered, including the strength, durability and integrity of the hull, the freeboard at operational drafts, the stability and reserves of buoyancy (McGrail 2001:6). McGrail also states that an open boat below a certain size is unlikely to have been seagoing while a boat-shaped underwater hull and a sheerline rising towards the ends suggest a seagoing vessel (McGrail 2001:6).

In order to determine seaworthiness, the vessel must be examined in varying floatation conditions. These conditions are suggested as being influenced by the following four main factors (McGrail 1998:13)

Weight and centre of gravity of the vessel, this has been calculated in the previous section for the as built or lightship condition

Number and normal station of crew, no evidence was recovered, but there is evidence of similar sized vessels being operated by 2 crew, (One man and a boy) (Scott 2004:58).

Bulk density of cargo, evidence of cargo recovered was in the form of 12 casks which have been included in the weight analysis, and the vessel will be assessed using these casks as the main cargo, with various quantities to determine load carrying capabilities.

Freeboard, the distance between the gunwale or top edge, and the operational waterplane, will need to be examined. Ethnographic evidence suggests that for inland

Vessel Condition	As Built	Lightship	As Found	Fully Laden
Length Overall	9,795 mm	9,795 mm	9,795 mm	9,795 mm
Beam Overall	3,095 mm	3,095 mm	3,095 mm	3,095 mm
Waterline Length	8,388 mm	8,372 mm	8,587 mm	8,955 mm
Waterline Beam	2,306 mm	2,320 mm	2,627 mm	2,964 mm
Displacement	2900 kg	3,084 kg	5,718 kg	12,418 kg
Draft	622.5 mm	684.5 mm	839.5 mm	1,171 mm
Freeboard	1117 mm	1095 mm	921 mm	568 mm
Waterplane Area	12.56 m²	12.84 m²	16.04 m²	20.06 m²
Wetted Surface Area	19.55 m²	19.89 m²	24.68 m²	33.0 m²
Sinkage	-194 mm	-152 mm	11 mm	397 mm
Prismatic Co-Efficient	0.666	0.675	0.679	0.698

TABLE 1. FLOATATION CONDITION FOR VARIOUS LOADING STATES.

Vessel Condition	Lightship	As Found	75% Loading
Length Overall	9,795 mm	9,795 mm	9,795 mm
Beam Overall	3,095 mm	3,095 mm	3,095 mm
Waterline Length	8,372 mm	8,587 mm	8,822 mm
Waterline Beam	2,320 mm	2,627 mm	2,880 mm
Displacement	3,084 kg	5,718 kg	10,223 kg
Draft	684.5 mm	839.5 mm	1,139 mm
Freeboard	1,095 mm	922 mm	662 mm
Waterplane Area	12.84 m²	16.04 m²	19.03 m²
Wetted Surface Area	19.89 m²	24.68 m²	30.49 m²
Sinkage	-152 mm	11 mm	205 mm
Prismatic Co-Efficient	0.675	0.678	0.700
Downflooding angle df	46.2°	38°	26°
Righting moment @ df	823 kgf/m	1953 kgf/m	2124.6 kgf/m

TABLE 2. HYDROSTATIC AND STATIC STABILITY FOR VARIOUS LOADING STATES.

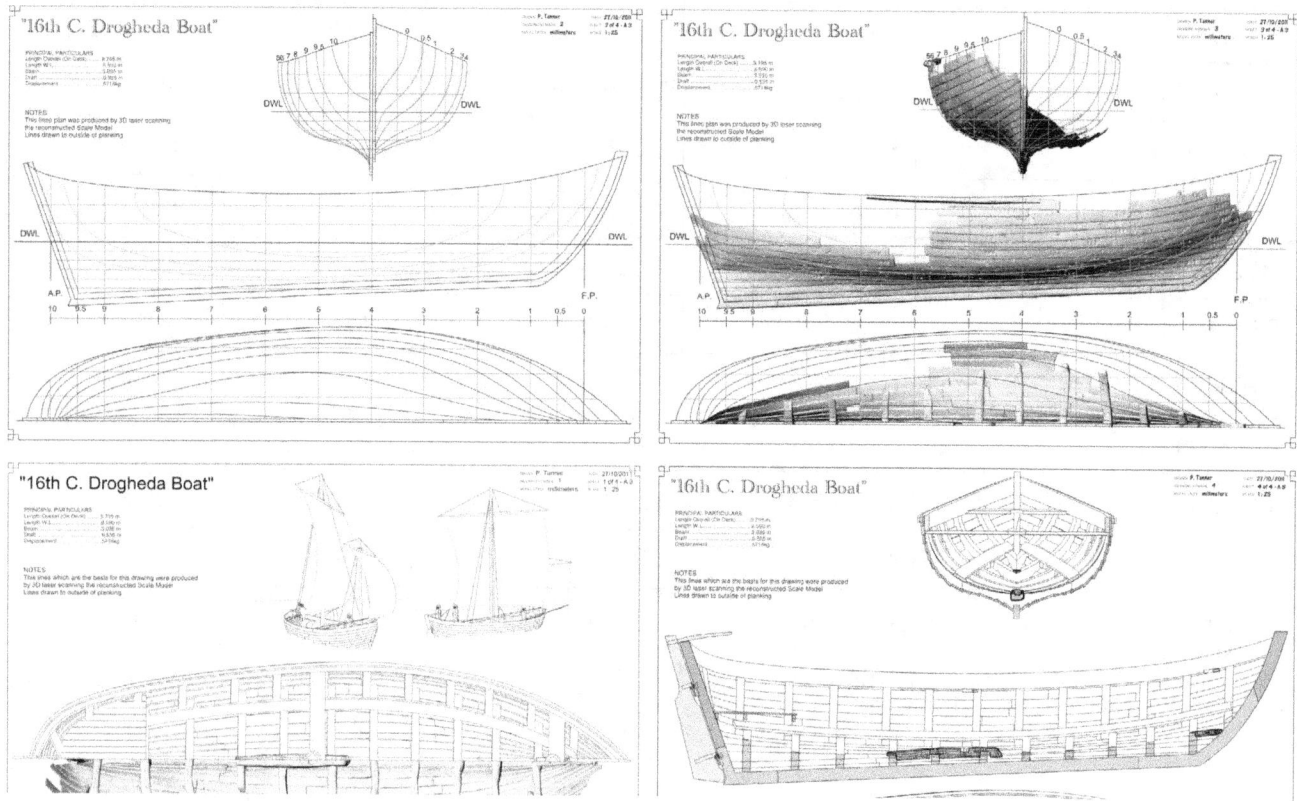

FIGURE 4. FINAL OUTPUT: CLOCKWISE FROM TOP LEFT: LINES PLAN DRAWING, LINES PLAN WITH RECOVERED MATERIAL OVERLAID, CONSTRUCTION DRAWING, GENERAL LAYOUT DRAWING.

waters, small boats were loaded to very little freeboard (McGrail 1978:91). Seagoing data is not readily available, however a medieval Icelandic Law in the Grågås Codex states the minimum freeboard (F) of a cargo ship should be $F=2D/5$ where D=depth of hull amidships (Morken 1980:178). In the case of the Drogheda Boat this would be

$$F = 2 \times 1.66/5 = 0.664 \text{ m}.$$

Static Stability for 75% loading has a freeboard measuring 0.662 m (Table 2).

The use of four "standard freeboards" is suggested (McGrail 1998:199)

1. draft restricted to 300 mm (minimum depth of water)

2. at a standard freeboard of 150 mm (safety consideration)

3. minimum freeboard as a function of transverse stability (upper edge of sides awash at 10° heel)

4. the maximum number of crew there is space for.

The vessel is then examined to determine its floatation condition for four loading states, and further analysed for external influences (Figure 3).

As Built Floatation Condition

This is the empty vessel condition consisting of the constituent parts of hull and rigging only, and excludes any crew, cargo or ballast. This would equate to the draft restricted freeboard, and is an indication of how the vessel would float while sitting empty at a mooring or quayside (Table 1 Column 2).

Lightship Floatation condition

This is empty vessel condition consisting of constituent parts of hull, rigging, 2 crew, and 1 days store each, no cargo or ballast (Table 1 Column 3).

As found Floatation Condition

This is the reconstructed vessel, including hull and rigging together with 12 casks (as recovered) and notionally 2 crew, their stores for 1 day, anchor and warps (Table 1 Column 4).

Max Cargo Floatation Condition

This consists of rebuilt vessel as shown, including hull and rigging together with 42 casks (quantity that could fit within hull volume) and notionally 3 crew, their stores for 2 days, anchor and warps. 42 casks would represent approx 75,600 herring or 8,400 kg weight of herring (of the 15,152 samples of fish remains recovered and tested all were Atlantic Herring) and a total weight of 9,219 kg including casks. In addition this amount of cargo would result in a low freeboard of just 586 mm, while this is still serviceable it would only be so in sheltered waters (Table 1 Column 5).

The As Built condition is of little use in further analysis as the vessel will need inclusion of crew at the very least in order to function, and is only included at this stage to indicate the vessels characteristics while sitting unused. This condition will be excluded from further analysis. The max cargo condition would appear to have insufficient freeboard and is replaced by a 75% loading condition for further analysis.

Lightship Static Stability

The deck edge becomes submerged at 46.2° angle of heel with very little righting moment (823 kgf/m) the boat would be considered very tender or tippy. If heeling due to wind loading is included this condition would probably be considered unsafe in all but the most protected waters (Table 2 column 2).

As Found Static Stability

The deck edge becomes submerged at 38° angle of heel and with a righting moment of 1953 kgf/m the boat would be considered stable (Table 2 column 3).

75% Loading Static Stability

The deck edge becomes submerged at 26° angle of heel and with a righting moment of 2,124 kgf/m the boat would be considered stable, although the low freeboard of 662 mm would probably make the vessel unsuitable for use in open waters with inclement weather (Table 2 column 4).

Lightship Wind Loading Stability

With the boat heeled to 38.8°, and the downflooding angle of 46.2°, this would leave 159 mm of freeboard, (Table 3 column 2) in addition the relatively low righting arm moment of 823 kgf/m means only a slight increase in wind pressure would cause the vessel to be swamped. This indicates the boat, when empty, would be unstable in a light to moderate wind and would almost certainly have carried some form of internal ballast. There was no evidence recovered for internal ballast, save for one piece of limestone measuring circa 320 x 180 x 140 mm,

Vessel Condition	Lightship	As Found
Length Overall	9,795 mm	9,795 mm
Beam Overall	3,095 mm	3,095 mm
Waterline Length	8,372 mm	8,587 mm
Waterline Beam	2,320 mm	2,627 mm
Displacement	3,084 kg	5,718 kg
Draft	684.5 mm	839.5 mm
Freeboard	1,095 mm	922 mm
Waterplane Area Heeled	12.84 m²	16.04 m²
Wetted Surface Area Heeled	19.89 m²	24.68 m²
Sinkage	-152 mm	11 mm
Prismatic Co-Efficient	0.675	0.678
Downflooding angle df	46.2°	38°
Righting moment @ df	823 kgf/m	1953 kgf/m
Sail area	51 m²	51 m²
Wind Speed	15 knots	15 knots
Sail Area Wind Load	2,372.5 N	2,372.5 N
Heel Angle	38.8°	15.8°
Resulting Freeboard	159 mm	497 mm

TABLE 3. HYDROSTATIC AND DYNAMIC STABILITY FOR VARIOUS LOADING STATES IN 15 KNOTS OF WIND.

Length overall LOA	9.795 m
Beam Overall BOA	3.095 m
Waterline length LWL	8.587 m
Waterline Beam BWL	2.627 m
Draft T	0.839 m
Freeboard F	0.922 m
Displacement	5718 kg
Waterplane Area	19.02 m²
Wetted Surface Area	24.68 m²
Prismatic Co-efficient Cp	0.678
Block Coefficient Cb	0.296
Volumetric Coefficient	8.79x10-3
Slenderness Coefficient	3.27
Midship Coefficient Cx	0.436
Downflooding angle	38°
Righting moment at down flooding angle	1,953 kgf/m
Deadweight	2,900 kg
Displacement/Length ratio DLR	251.44
Moment to Trim	71.57 kgf/m
Power required to achieve 3.0 knots	0.2 kW (0.27 hp)
Power required to achieve 3.5 knots	0.3 kW (0.40 hp)
Power required to achieve 4.0 knots	0.5 kW (0.67 hp)
Power required to achieve 4.5 knots	0.8 kW (1.0 hp)
Power required to achieve 5.0 knots	1.1 kW (1.5 hp)
Power required to achieve 5.5 knots	1.8 kW (2.4 hp)
Power required to achieve 6.0 knots	2.5 kW (3.4 hp)
Power required to achieve 6.5 knots	3.5 kW (4.7 hp)
Power required to achieve 7.0 knots	5.3 kW (7.1 hp)

TABLE 4. ANALYSIS RESULTS BASED ON AS FOUND CONDITION

however, it was common practice, especially on the west coast of Ireland, to carry a full cargo without ballast on the outbound or delivery leg of a trip and in the absence of a return load, to replace the cargo weight with locally sourced stone as ballast for the return leg of the trip (Scott 2004:57).

As Found Wind Loading Stability

With an average wind speed of 15 knots the boat could potentially achieve a speed in the region of 5 to 5.5 knots at a heeling angle of up to 16° which would maintain approx 500 mm of freeboard (Table 3 column 3) and a righting moment in the region of 900 kgf/m. A sudden wind gust of 25 knots would heel the boat to 36° while still maintaining 75 mm freeboard and a righting arm moment of approx 1,850 kgf/m. In this configuration, the critical downflooding angle when the gunwale becomes submerged is at 38°.

Assessment of Performance

For the purposes of assessing performance the vessel will be examined in the as-found or general service condition. This represents a vessel with an as built weight of approx 2,900 kg carrying a crew and cargo of approx 2,800 kg, a combined displacement weight of 5,700 kg.

Methods of assessment

Once a reconstruction drawing is available (Figure 4) the performance of the boat it represents may be assessed in several ways using simple coefficients that are based on the boat's overall measurements (Table 4), thus LOA/BOA and BOA/D summarise the overall proportions of the boat and as such give a relative assessment of the boats capabilities. Using hydrostatic curves involves the definition of the waterline(s), underwater shape and calculations of displacements, sectional areas and coefficient based on the underwater geometry, may be used to give forecasts of performance. (McGrail 1998,192).

Speed Potential

Firstly a target speed will need to be set for the vessel. The Irish Sea, in and around

Drogheda experiences a moderate tidal current, with peak spring tidal currents between 2 and 3.5 knots. If the vessel is to work in an area with a tidal rate of two knots, then the vessel will need to achieve a target speed of 4 to 5 knots or more in order to make progress when stemming a foul tide. For a displacement hull like the Drogheda Boat, which is sitting in the water, as it moves forward it generates a bow and stern wave with the boat sitting in the trough between the two waves. As the boat accelerates to higher speeds a greater amount of power is required to overcome this wave resistance, until a stage is reached where the power required to accelerate even more becomes exponential. This point is referred to as the displacement trap. This displacement trap results in a theoretical maximum hull speed, which is calculated as 1.34 times the square root of the waterline length (LWL) in feet. Boats which do achieve speeds where velocity $(V)/(\sqrt{LWL})>1.40$ may appear to be planning. At speeds $(V)/(\sqrt{LWL})>1.70$ dynamic lift begins and boats will be said to be semi planning, and at speeds $(V)/(\sqrt{LWL})>3.20$ boats are truly planning or skimming (Marchaj 1964, fig 158). Displacement boats like the Drogheda Boat can only exceed $(V)/(\sqrt{LWL})=1.40$ in ideal conditions, or with excessive use of mechanical power. From $1.34\sqrt{LWL}$ the Drogheda boat has a theoretical max hull speed of 7.11 knots. A holtrop powering analysis (Holtrop 1984) was carried out using the Orca 3D plug-in for Rhino (Table 4).

Propulsion

A sail area of 550 ft.^{2} (51 m^2) would generate approx 4.9 hp with 10 knots of wind equating to 4.1 knots boat speed approx and 10.9 hp with 15 knots of wind equating to 5.4 knots boat speed.

With an average wind speed of 15 knots the boat could potentially achieve a speed in the region of 5 to 5.5 knots at a heeling angle up to 16°, which would maintain approx 500 mm of freeboard and a righting moment in the region of 900 kgf/m. A sudden wind gust of 25 knots would heel the boat to 36°, while still maintaining a righting arm moment of approximately 1,850 kgf/m. In this configuration, the critical downflooding angle when the gunwale becomes submerged is 38°.

Alternative Methods of Propulsion

The boat would, in all likelihood, have an alternative means of propulsion for use during periods of little or no wind and also for fine control manoeuvring. Figures indicate the maximum output of a man rowing, on a fixed seat, is about 1 hp (750 watts) sustainable for a short time and an average male can deliver approx 0.3 hp (250 watts) for 20 minutes. With a potential rowing speed of between 1.7 and 2.2 knots this would suggest the Drogheda Boat could be propelled by oar for close quarter manoeuvring, entering or leaving a port, or rounding a headland, but would be unlikely to be used as a means of passage-making.

Cargo Capacity and Tonnage

Medieval descriptions of the dimensions of ships may be rare, but references to their tun-nage or burthen are not. However, this does not mean that the use of tunnage figures is straightforward. One immediate problem is that there were many different measures of ship capacity. In England the basis of measurement was the wine tun as wine was an important cargo, and it was enacted by statute that the wine tun should contain 252 gallons. In the Mediterranean the wine barrel was also used as a measure of tunnage, although the actual values accorded to the hotfa, or baril were varied (Zupko 1977,29-30); (Lane 1964,218-9). Zupko equates the tun of 252 gallons to 954 litres, 954 litres equates to 252 U.S. gallons whereas 252 imperial gallons equates to 1145 litres. Bakers old rule (1582) for tonnage states

> *length of keel excluding the false post multiplied by the greatest breadth within the plank and that product multiplied by the depth taken from the breadth to the upper edge of the keel produceth a solid number which divided by 100 gives the content in tons, into which add one third part for tonnage. (Salisbury 1966)*

Using this rule the Drogheda Boat would be

$$25.16 \times 10.15 \times 5.15 = 1315.18 / 100 = 13.15$$
$$\text{plus one third } (4.38) = 17.5 \text{ tons.}$$

The Builders Old Measurement (B.O.M.) was another system introduced in 1834-35, whereby it was not necessary to know the depth of the vessel (a measurement which was difficult to establish while the vessel was afloat) and was calculated as $(L-3/5B) \times B \times 1/2B)/94$. Using this rule the Drogheda Boat would be

$$(32.13 - 3/5(10.15) \times 10.15 \times 1/2(10.15)) / 94 = 14.28 \text{ tons.}$$

A third and more accurate method of assessing cargo capacity is to examine the vessel shape and modelling the casks which were recovered, using these to check what quantity of casks could physically fit within the hull. A typical cask weighing 219.5 kg and a volume of 230 litres was used and 42 of these would fit in the vessel. This would give a total displacement weight including vessel, crew and rigging of 12,418 kg and when you subtract the lightship weight of the vessel which is 2,900 kg gives a gross deadweight of 9,518 kg equal to 9.4 tons. This would probably be an excessive loading as the vessel would have only 568 mm freeboard and 1,170 mm draft.

A more suitable loading might be 75% of max loading which would mean 32 casks giving a total displacement weight including vessel, crew and rigging of 10,223 kg, and when you subtract the lightship weight of the vessel, which is 2,900 kg, gives a gross deadweight of 7,323 kg equal to 7.2 tons. This would result in the vessel having a freeboard of 662 mm and a draft of 1,140 mm.

Conclusion

The result of this methodology is the very accurate (submillimeter) recording of the recovered material, in the form of the initial Faro Arm recording of timbers, and subsequent 3D laser scanning of the physical scale model, combined with an iterative process of testing, in an attempt to produce a more definitive reconstruction. All of the recreated elements for the reconstruction were tested using the Rhinoceros curvature graph analysis, ensuring a fair shape, and any deviation between the recorded and faired shape was closely examined for reasons, such as distortion or damage prior to proceeding.

The resulting reconstruction points towards a vessel with a reasonably narrow entry forward, with a long, fine run aft below the waterline; changing to a fuller shape above, indicating an easily sailed vessel with a good load carrying capacity.

When examined with regard to wind and wave rolling, the reconstructed vessel performs adequately, heeling to 16° in 15 knots of wind, while maintaining 500 mm of freeboard, wind gusting (150% mean wind load) was also examined which would result in 36° heel angle and 75 mm freeboard remaining, with sufficient righting arm moment to recover, and a speed potential in the region of 5 to 5.5 knots.. The vessel would be capable of undertaking coastal voyages within easy reach of a sheltered port or anchorage, but was unlikely to undertake long distance offshore voyages.

References

CHALMERS, MACKENZIE DALZELL EDWIN STEWART, AND EDWARD RICHARD HARDY IVAMY
    1976   *Chalmers' Marine Insurance Act 1906.* Butterworths.

CHRISTENSEN, ARNE EMIL.
    1968   "Sjøvollen Ship." *Viking* 32: 131–53.

CRUMLIN-PEDERSEN, OLE, AND SEÁN MCGRAIL
    2006   Some Principles for the Reconstruction of Ancient Boat Structures. *International Journal of Nautical Archaeology* 35(1):53–57.

HOLTROP, JAN
    1984   A Statistical Re-analysis of Resistance and Propulsion Data. *International Shipbuilding Progress* 31(363):272–276.

JONES, TOBY, AND NIGEL NAYLING
    2011   ShipShape: Creating a 3D Solid Model of the Newport Medieval Ship. *SHA Advisory Council on Underwater Archaeology 2011*:54–60.

KEMP, DIXON
    1897   *Yacht Architecture: a Treatise on the Laws Which Govern the Resistance of Bodies Moving in Water: Propulsion by Steam and Sail; Yacht Designing, and Yacht Building.* Vol. 1. H. Cox.

LANE, F. C.
    1964   Tonnages, Medieval and Modern. *Econ. Hist Review* 17:213–33.

MARCHAJ, C. A.
    1964   *Sailing Theory and Practice.* Adlard Coles.

MCGRAIL, SEÁN
    1978   Logboats of England and Wales. *NMM Archaeological Series*(2).

    1998   *Ancient Boats in North-West Europe: The Archaeology of Water Transport to AD 1500.* Vol. Longman archaeology series. London, Longman.

    2001   *Boats Of The World – From The Stone Age to Medieval Times.* Oxford.

MCKEE, ERIC
    1974   Building and Trials of the Replica of an Ancient Boat: The Gokstad Faering, Part 2: The Sea Trials. NMM Greenwich.

MORETON, WARWICK, STEPHEN FOWLES, AND RICK PEERS
    2000   Note of a Demonstration Laser Scan of a West African Dugout. *MM* 86(4):463–467.

MORKEN, R.
    1980   *Langskip, Knarr Og Kogge.* Bergen.

NAYLING, NIGEL, AND TOBY JONES
   2012   Three-Dimensional Recording and Hull Form Modelling of the Newport (Wales) Medieval Ship. In *Nergis Günsenin (ed) Between Continents : Proceedings of the Twelfth Symposium on Boat and Ship Archaeology*, pp. 319–324.

SALISBURY, WILLIAM
   1966   Early Tonnage Measurements in England: *MM* 52(1):41–51.

SCHWEITZER, HOLGER
   2012   Drogheda Boat: A Story to Tell. In *Nergis Günsenin (ed) Between Continents : Proceedings of the Twelfth Symposium on Boat and Ship Archaeology*, pp. 225–234. Ege Yayinlari.

SCOTT, RICHARD J.
   2004   *The Galway Hookers Sailing Work Boats of Galway Bay*. Fourth. A.K. Ilen, Limerick, Ireland.

ZUPKO, R. E.
   1977   British Weights and Measures. *University of Wisconsin.*

· · · · · · · · · · · · · · · ·

Pat Tanner
Traditional Boats of Ireland Project
32 Rowan Court,
Ballea Woods,
Carrigaline,
Co. Cork,
Ireland
pattanner@eircom.net

Digital Documentation for Many Purposes: The Barcode 6 Boat as a Case Study

Tori Falck
Inger Marie Egenberg
Hilde Vangstad

In 2007 The Norwegian Maritime Museum changed their method of documenting archaeological ship finds to 3D contact digitizing using a FARO-arm and Rhino software. In 2008 thirteen ship finds were uncovered at the so called Barcode site in the old harbor of Oslo. One of these boats, the 'Barcode 6' (AD 1595), has been of particular focus after the excavation. This lapstrake boat is especially suitable for generating a discussion around methodological aspects of digital documentation as it has undergone many stages of documentation and reconstruction after it was recovered in 2008.

Introduction

As with a number of other institutions in Europe, the Norwegian Maritime Museum (NMM) is using FARO-Arm and Rhino 5.0 software when documenting boat-finds digitally in 3D. This technique replaced the former, "pen on transparent foil"-method, and is now more or less considered standard practice in boat recording (Falck 2010, Ravn et al. 2011, Jones and Nayling 2011, Nayling and Jones 2012). The main purpose of the documentation, and the first aim of the NMM, is to provide an accurate record of the boat finds that can be archived for future research. The second aim is to carry out recording to a level that, allows for the ability to create reconstructions of each boat. This process begins with recording the distorted, fragmented wrecks and leads to interpretations and analyses of the original sailing vessels. In Scandinavia, an extensive number of shipwrecks from the medieval period and onwards are known, but the varying level of documentation and publication makes the different material difficult to compare and somewhat inaccessible for research. It is our belief that digitalization both improves the accessibility to these archaeological records, and facilitates comparison.

The main focus of this paper will be to show how digitalization is used throughout our documentation and analyses process at the NMM. After the excavation the first step in the process is the digital 1:1 documentation of the individual boat parts. These drawings are utilized to create scale models and subsequently full-sized reconstructions. The paper will also discuss further uses for the digital output at the NMM. The digitalization of the boat parts has proved to be of great benefit to the teams working with the conservation and exhibition of the original remains. The boat find Barcode 6 is a suitable case study, in that it has been submitted to all of the post-excavation stages mentioned here.

The Barcode Excavation and the Historical Backdrop

The old harbor of Oslo, in the capital of Norway, has undergone extensive archaeological investigations since mid-2000. The excavation of the Barcode site lasted from April 2008 to May 2009, revealing 13 shipwrecks together with large timber constructions that were parts of extensive harbor facilities. In addition approximately 3-4000 artifacts were found (Gundersen 2012, Vangstad 2009, 2012) (Figure 1).

Later, in 2010, 2011, and 2012, the NMM conducted excavations on neighboring areas so that all of these constructions and sites are physically connected in an extensive harbor complex. These sites date from the medieval period to the first part of the 17th century. The dimensions and even the existence of these harbor facilities were unknown before the excavations started. In 1624, the harbor was exposed to a severe fire, probably destroying large parts of the structures above sea level. As a response to this, King Christian IV decided to move the whole town and harbor to the other side of the bay of Bjørvika. The main driving force for doing so was probably to re-establish the town within the secure surrounds of the Castle of *Akershus*, protecting it from the attacks from the Swedish Crown. Written sources indicate that the inhabitants and users of the harbor, in spite of the poor harbor conditions, were reluctant to meet the King's demands. In 1626, the King ordered an armed ship to go to Oslo and burn the old harbor down once more (Probst 1996). It was these structures that were found during the Barcode excavation.

The Barcode 6 (BC-06)

The Barcode 6 boat was originally found as, and assumed to be, two disconnected finds (BC-06 and BC-12). These two parts were excavated months apart, and it was not before the end of the excavation that it became evident that they were fragments of the same vessel. The boat is approximately 7.7 m long, and it consists of 9 strakes held together partly by wooden nails, and partly by clenched iron nails. It is built mainly in oak. The timber is dendrochronologically dated to after AD 1595, and is probably of Southern Norwegian origin. The boat has undergone at least one major rebuild, changing quite radically from having a straight stern post, to having a transom. This evidence makes it the oldest known boat in Norway to have a transom, together with other finds from the same site. It is likely that the rebuild of Barcode 6 was undertaken to increase the cargo capacity of the vessel. The boat will be more thoroughly presented in a forthcoming publication. After the boat arrived at the museum it was documented piece by piece according to the digital standard mentioned in the introduction.

The Building of a 1:5 Scale Model and a Full Scale Reconstruction – a Floating Hypothesis

In the excitement after the excavation the museum decided this was the time to realize an old idea and a dream; to create a proper boat building workshop at the museum. The workshop was intended to pursue a scientific approach to its tasks, and was named the "Boat lab". This fitted well together with the, already up and running, Documentation lab, which opened by spring 2010. The Boat lab's main remit was to build reconstructions of old boats, archaeological or traditional. In addition, it was to test out tools and techniques related to historical boat building. Dr. Terje Planke was the manager of the Boat lab during the whole process of reconstructing the first archaeological boat at the museum. Being an enthusiastic ethnographic researcher of Norwegian traditional boats the project was encouraged by, and undoubtedly enhanced by, his collaboration. The Barcode 6 boat reconstruction was chosen as its first project for several reasons; it was fairly small, fitting exactly in the location of an old *hot dog kiosk* at the museum entrance which had been refurbished for the nobler task of housing the Boat lab. As the Barcode 6 wreck was also close to complete, it was hoped that this would cause fewer interpretive dilemmas than a more incomplete find would have done. The find was also considered to be a suitable size, for a boat to be used as a museum boat, with for instance sailing events connected to museum's activities in education and outreach.

An experienced boat builder of traditional boats, Lars Stålegård, was engaged in the project. He was, in cooperation with the documentation lab and Terje Planke, responsible for the building of a cardboard model in the scale 1:5 (Planke, Falck and Stålegård 2011). The 3D documentation was utilized for the model by printing the strakes in paper and gluing them on to cardboard, with the required thickness. In this way the detailed information from the recording process' layering system was kept with the cardboard planks. What was lost using this method were the many variations in thicknesses and twists

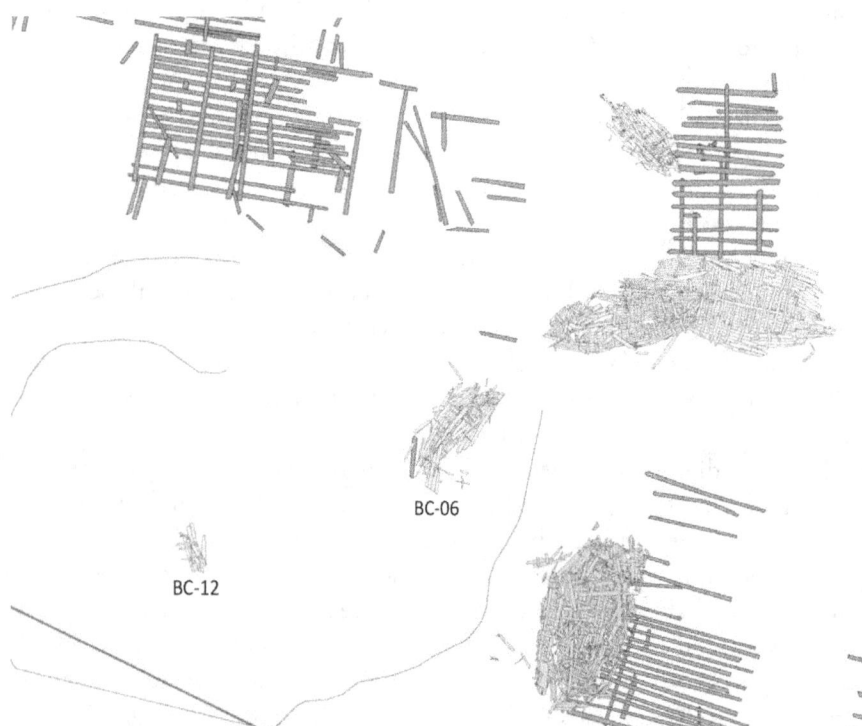

Figure 1. The complex situation on parts of the site, with the timber constructions (harbor facilities) and attached boat finds. The Barcode 6 boat was originally found as two separate finds, the BC-06 and BC-12. Map: NMM.

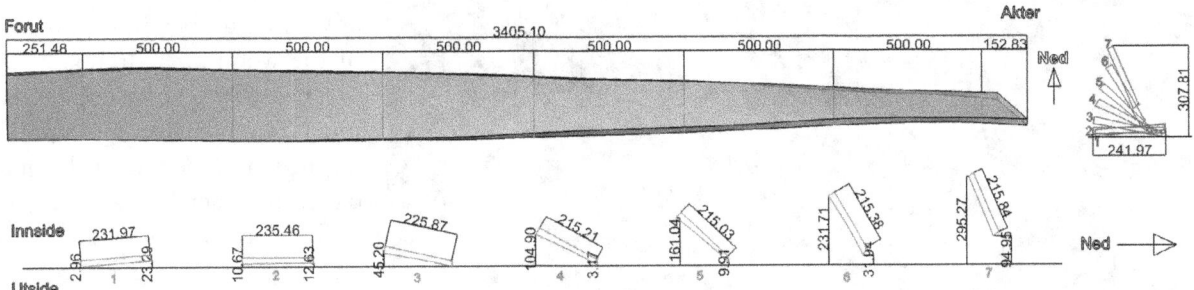

FIGURE 2. THE SOLID MODEL OF PLANK x103, WITH NUMBERED SECTIONS EVERY 0.50 M. ILLUSTRATION: T. FALCK/NMM.

and turns of the planks. Printing 3D drawings in 2D is not without problems, but a procedure was found in the 3D software to straighten out twisted planks to prevent losing surface area in the 2D print outs. The frames, keel, stempost, and sternpost were all printed using a 3D-printer in a polyamide material (rapid prototyping) using the CAD-data. Other projects, like the Newport project, have chosen to print the strakes in 3D also (Jones and Nayling 2011). For another of the Oslo boats, the Vaterland 1, it was decided to print out the garboard planks and second strakes in polyamide, to retain the twisted shapes in the modeling process (Hobberstad 2012). It has been concluded that the methodological decision must be taken for each project based on its needs and desires. There is also an economical question in that the 3D-prints are relatively expensive. In addition to this, each 3D-recording (original Rhino drawing) needs to be re-modeled into *solid models* in order to print them, which is relatively time consuming.

A local company provided the 3D-prints, using a white polyamide material and STL-format. In order to print the parts in 3D, firstly the rhino line-drawings had to be converted to closed solid objects consisting of connected surfaces. The polyamide material is quite strong, but has a slight flexibility making it suitable for the modeling process. The flexibility of the material is even increased if it is heated up carefully (the polyamide is able to take up to 120 degrees Celsius). The Boat lab found using the scale 1:5 for the models provided better control of the details and gave more opportunities to add shape to the hull using the angles of the lands, in particular the lengthwise overlap. On the other hand, these models are large, and this might be a reason for downsizing to a scale of 1:10. As for the choice of using either cardboard or polyamide as a building material, this will have to be a methodological choice taken from one project to another.

The scale model worked as a plan for the actual reconstruction, and was in numerous ways important to how the vessel was interpreted, in particular its outline or shape and rigging. So, in 2011, the Barcode 6 reconstruction was launched, being baptized *Vaaghals*, the *Daredevil* (Figure 4). The name is partly a tribute to the project staff's daring attitude towards the mission in the first place and partly it is named after the oldest known tower in the Castle of *Akershus* in Oslo. On the launching day the boat was rowed to the city bay, Bjørvika, symbolically brought back to where it was actually found. Last summer the boat and its crew participated at the Maritime festival in Brest, France. The process of building the *Vaaghals*, and later projects, can be followed on an online blog.

The conservation of the boat

After some years of experience with the FARO-Arm and the digitalization method the NMM feel quite confident that the results, i.e. the end products, have sufficiently fulfilled the two main goals of the project; to preserve the information for future research and being able to create reconstructions, both as scale models and even as floating hypothesis' as shown in the example of *Vaaghals*, the Barcode 6.

Until 2012, experience of using the digital documentation for the purpose of conservation was scarce. Before the project started, our conservation staff already had knowledge on stabilizing waterlogged timbers for storage and exhibition, but the massive scale of the material from the Barcode project presented them with major challenges. The need for capacity to handle the bulk of timbers resulted in the purchase of a vacuum

Figure 3. The planks as they are about to be freeze dried. The angles from the model in Figure 2 are transferred to boards of plywood, and the oak planks are forced into its right shape and locked in position. Photo: NMM.

freeze dryer, with a diameter of 1.2 m and a length of 6.3 m. The first major challenge was connected to the planned exhibition of the original Barcode 6 wreck in Bjørvika, a project organized in cooperation with the largest Norwegian bank, the DNB, and sponsored by the Savings Banks Foundation (Sparebankstiftelsen DnB NOR). The DNB are building their new national headquarter on the Barcode site, and wanted to use the Barcode 6 as "decoration" or "artistic installation" in their conference area. This meant that the conservators had to plan their first task, not only for storing, but for exhibition.

The conservators chose to stabilize the timbers with a combination of polyethylene glycol impregnation (PEG) and vacuum freeze-drying. PEG is a synthetic wax soluble in water, and the concentration of PEG in the baths was increased from 10% to 40% over a period of two years. Waterlogged wood, mainly oak in the Barcode find, is normally most heavily degraded in the outer layers, resulting in low density of the wood there. The dissolved wax (in this case with a molecular weight of 2000; i.e. PEG2000) penetrates easily into the low density wood, where it prevents the cells from collapsing and the wooden surface layer from cracking or shrinking. It is however not advisable to dry such 40% PEG-impregnated wood atmospherically, since it is a well-documented fact that waterlogged wood can become quite stiff and inflexible after drying, unless fully impregnated (80-90%) (Cronyn 1992: 258ff,

Hoffmann 2009). The brittleness of low percentage impregnated dried wood means that one should avoid any kind of bending and twisting of the wood after drying. Fully impregnated wood on the other hand is much more flexible, but a prolonged impregnation period results in higher costs, considerable weight gain, as well as a dark and waxy appearance. Being able to reconstruct the boat parts, in the shape of how they once had looked, before they were flattened out on the sea bed under tons of clay, demanded a planned strategy. In their original position as boat parts many of the planks were twisted, often in several directions, especially those that meet the stem – and sternpost or transom. In order to be able to create a consistent hull, the retaining of these shapes throughout the whole process of conservation is vital. It must be stressed that the project is yet to be finished, so it is a bit early to conclude that the solutions provided were a success. However, presenting the process so far, will hopefully add some useful ideas to the discussion on how to conserve wood meant for exhibition.

So far, in the process, the closest estimate of the original shape of the planks has been acquired from the 1:5 scale model. In the model, flattened out planks were re-twisted to fit each other as well as the stempost, transom, keel and frames. By measuring the finished model using the FARO-Arm, each part's shape could be re-defined in a digital model of it. Each plank was formed as a closed object of surfaces, a so called solid model mentioned above. Now, the task was to transfer these known angles and shapes to the actual original plank. The idea was to "double freeze" it, so to speak. This meant that at the same time as the planks were freeze dried to prevent the wood from cracking and shrinking, their original shapes were "frozen" as well. It was therefore necessary to find a way to present the digital shapes so that they were easily transferable to the real world and easily read by staff not trained in using 3D software. In addition, the conservators needed to find a preferably non-destructive way to construct molds which would lock the timbers into chosen shapes while freeze drying. Some experience, relevant to the Barcode 6 project, was gained by conservators and other experts associated with the conservation department of the National Museum of Denmark. This is documented in the description on shaping wooden parts of a Danish vessel called the Gislinge boat (Strætkvern et al. 2009). Additionally, another project concerning the Roskilde 6 was used as inspiration; however, it was clear that the method had to be adjusted so that it fitted this specific assignment.

Figure 2 illustrates the solution that was decided on. What the picture shows is the plank as it looked in the scale model and sections through it every 0.50 meters. Several things can be read from this picture, but most importantly is the different measurements from a "floor" the piece is resting on, showing how much the piece needs to be lifted from this floor to create the right bend on the plank lengthways. At the same time the sections show the angles that the timbers need to be bent in the sideways direction. All the lengths and measurements are written on the paper, so that printing in corresponding scale is not necessary.

The shape of the timber in the scale model was, in this manner, transferred to the physical timber (Figure 3). It can be a bit time consuming to make these drawings, but the speed increases with experience. It is hoped that reshaping the planks will make the actual reconstruction of the original boat in the exhibition go smoothly, as they will be already reshaped to fit the larger structure. This will prevent gaps between planks, and also prevent cracks in the planks caused by the need to force the inflexible material into different shapes.

All of these sub-projects have resulted in several representations, or rather interpretations, of the original boat (Figure 4). The interpretations consist of the 1:1 documentation, the scale 1:5 model, the digital version of the scale model, the full scale reconstruction and, in 2015, the original boat as an exhibited and "reshaped" vessel. All of these interpretations were made possible through the digital methods applied. Hopefully the end result is close to the original version once sailing the Oslo fjord.

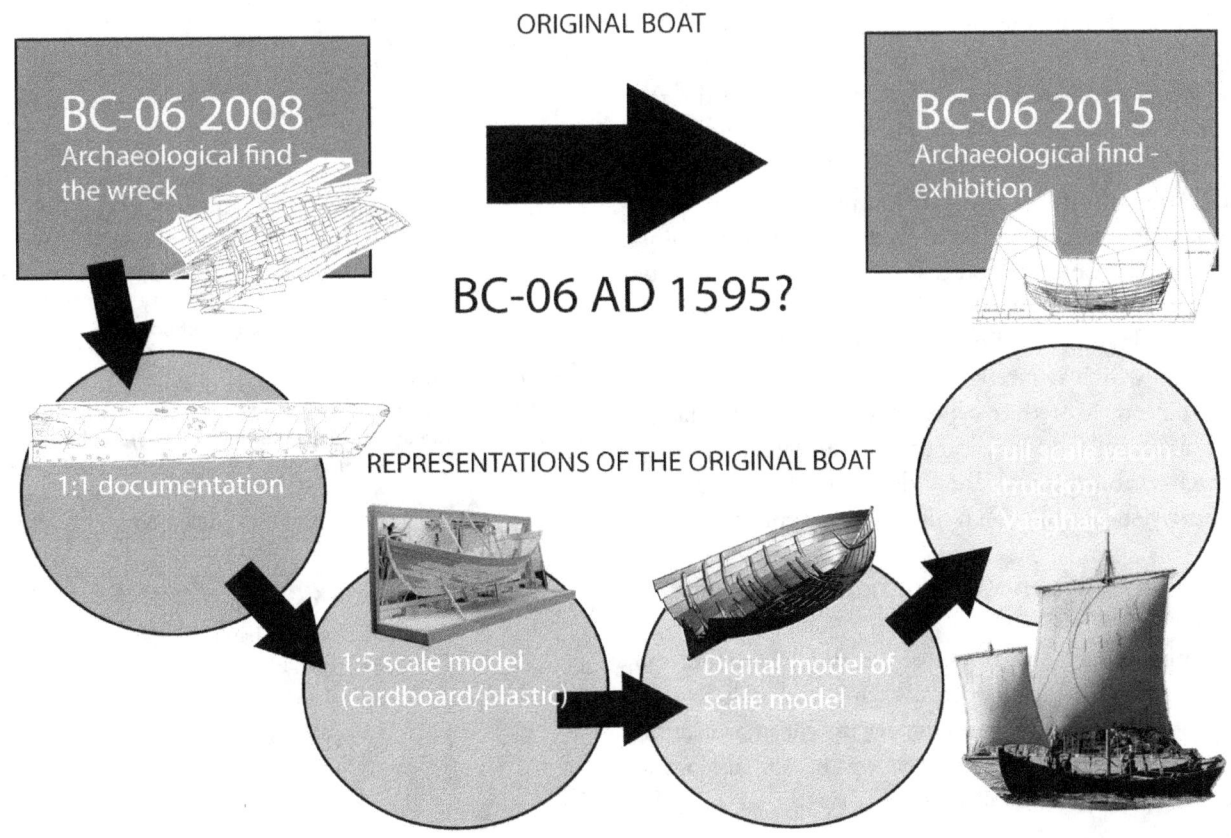

FIGURE 4. THE BARCODE 6 BOAT AND ALL ITS REPRESENTATIONS. THE ARCHAEOLOGICAL FIND, THE 1:1 DIGITAL DOCUMENTATION, THE 1:5 SCALE MODEL IN CARDBOARD AND PLASTIC, THE DIGITAL MODEL, THE FULL SCALE SAILING RECONSTRUCTION. THE LAST VERSION WILL BE THE EXHIBITION PLANNED IN 2015. ILLUSTRATION: T. FALCK/NMM.

New Developments: Photogrammetry

To conclude some of our latest methodological developments will be mentioned briefly. At the moment, new digital methods in the Documentation lab in the NMM are being tested. A photogrammetric solution for parts of our work will be tried out. For this work the software Agisoft Photoscan has been purchased, which allows normal digital cameras to produce images a lot like a "laser scanner". This approach has been chosen instead of a laser scanning for several reasons, price being one and saving time another. Additionally the method promises to provide both the desired accuracy and quality.

The NMM foresees applying this method to fulfil a number of important functions. It can be used for creating the digital models, of the physical scale models. This will mean that it will no longer be necessary to measure the scale model with the FARO-Arm first, which is not an easy task. Instead photos can be taken of the physical model and through them a digital model is generated. This model will have a high level of accuracy and comparable possibilities such as taking measurements of details and the structure as a whole. It will also be possible to photograph the full scale 1:1 reconstruction *Vaaghals*, when it is on land. This again will make it possible to compare the scale model with the full scale model and analyze the discrepancies between them. The digital models of the two versions of the same boat find can be run through the Rhino plug in Orca 3D, to compare their properties and evaluate the two against one another. The method also provides opportunities for on-site documentation, eliminating time consuming hand drawing, without resorting to expensive laser scanning, which is rarely well adapted to the actual on site situation. Moreover it presents a solution for faster, more accurate field documentation underwater, albeit on high-visibility sites. These developments are still in their early stages, but the results so far are promising.

Acknowledgements

Thanks to the invaluable efforts of the documentation staff at the NMM, and special thanks to Sarah Fawsitt for proofreading and commenting on the manuscript. Thanks to FRAUG (Faro and Rhino Archaeological User group) and its inspiring members.

References

CRONYN, J. M.
1992   *The Elements of Archaeological Conservation*. London, Routledge.

GUNDERSEN, J.
2012   Barcode Project, Fifteen Nordic Clinker Built Boats form the 16th and 17th Centuries in the City Centre of Oslo, Norway. In *Between Continents, Proceedings of the Twelfth Symposium on Boat and Ship Archaeology, Istanbul 2009, ISBSA 12*, N. Günsenin, editor, pp. 75-80. Istanbul.

FALCK, T.
2010   Sørenga 7. Å gjenskape en gammel båt i plast og papp eller bytes. Erfaringer midtveisi en prosess. *Nicolay* 110: 20-28.

HOBBERSTAD, L.C.
2012   Lasting og lossing i Oslos middelalderhavn. Båtvraket Vaterland 1. En mulig laste-lossebåt fra 1500-tallets begynnelse. Master's degree, University of Oslo.

HOFFMANN, P.
2009   On the efficiency of stabilisation methods for large waterlogged wooden objects, and on how to choose a method. In *Proceedings of the 10th ICOM Group on Wet Organic Archaeological Materials Conference. Amsterdam 2007*, K. Strætkvern and H. D. J. Huisman, editors, pp. 323-350. Amsterdam, ICOM and RACM.

JONES, T., AND N. NAYLING
2011   ShipShape: Creating a 3D Solid Model of the Newport Medieval Ship. In *Advisory Council on Underwater Archaeology Proceedings 2011*, F. Castro, and L. Thomas, editors. Advisory Council on Underwater Archaeology Publications.

NAYLING, N., AND T. JONES
2012   Three-dimensional recording and hull form modelling of the Newport (Wales) Medieval ship. *In Between Continents, Proceedings of the Twelfth Symposium on Boat and Ship Archaeology, Istanbul 2009, ISBSA 12*, N. Günsenin, editor, pp. 319-324. Istanbul.

PLANKE, T., T. FALCK, AND L. STÅLEGÅRD
2011   Båt i pølsebua, båt i banken og "Barcode" bygges. *Kysten* 3:12-16.

PROBST, N. M.
1996   Christian 4.s flåte. Marinehistorisk selskabs skrift 26, Copenhagen.

Ravn, M., V. Bishoff, A. Englert, and S. Nielsen
:   2011 Recent Advances in Post-excavation Documentation, Reconstruction, and Experimental Maritime Archaeology. In *The Oxford Handbook of Maritime Archaeology*, A. Catsambis, B. Ford, and D. L. Hamilton, editors, pp. 232-249. Oxford University Press. New York.

Strætkvern, K., A. Hjelm-Petersen, J. N. Sørensen, E. Jørgensen, M. Gøthche, and T. Thomassen
:   2009 Successful shaping or destructive devices? Freeze-drying of ship timbers in moulds and frames. In *Proceedings of the 10th ICOM Group on Wet Organic Archaeological Materials Conference. Amsterdam 2007*, K. Strætkvern and H. D. J. Huisman, editors, pp. 439-454. Amsterdam, ICOM and RACM.

Vangstad, H.
:   2009 Ship o' hoi – trygt i havn? Barcodeutgravningen i Bjørvika – en beretning om båtberging i byggegropa med adaptive arkeologiske metoder. *Nicolay* 108: 61-68.

Vangstad, H.
:   2012 Development of an Adaptive Method for the Rescue of 15 Shipwrecks from a Construction Site in Oslo Harbor. Need for speed. In *Between Continents, Proceedings of the Twelfth Symposium on Boat and Ship Archaeology, Istanbul 2009, ISBSA 12*, N. Günsenin, editor, pp. 305-311. Istanbul.

The Boat Lab blog
:   Barcode 6/Vaaghals: http://baatlaben.blogspot.no/ Accessed: March 2013

    The Portørenga boat: http://baatlab.wordpress.com/ Accessed: March 2013

. . . .

Tori Falck
The Norwegian Maritime Museum
Bygdøynesveien 37
N-0286 Oslo
Norway
tori.falck@marmuseum.no

Inger Marie Egenberg
The Norwegian Maritime Museum
Bygdøynesveien 37
N-0286 Oslo
Norway
inger.marie.egenberg@marmuseum.no

Hilde Vangstad
The Norwegian Maritime Museum
Bygdøynesveien 37
N-0286 Oslo
Norway
hilde.vangstad@marmuseum.no

Managing Submerged Prehistoric Landscapes: New Approaches in the Southern North Sea

Edward Salter

Recent developments in the management of submerged prehistoric landscapes in English territorial waters are discussed, with particular reference to a unique piece of work being undertaken in partnership with the marine aggregates industry in the Southern North Sea. The background to this project is introduced, and the most recent developments and findings in the area are discussed. The challenges and opportunities this piece of work presents for the management of submerged prehistory are also considered.

Background

In the North Sea, there is a long history of research and discovery of evidence relating to submerged prehistoric landscapes, those areas of our Continental shelf now submerged, that were once dry land at times of lower sea level. It is 100 years since the geologist Clement Reid published his work on submerged forests, where he postulated that a land bridge once connected Britain to the Continent (Reid 1913). A number of studies in the last 10-15 years demonstrate the recent growing interest in this field of research; Bryony Coles first coined the term 'Doggerland' to refer to the Dogger bank area of the North sea in her seminal work in 1998 (Coles 1998). More recently, a number of studies have sought to improve understanding of the archeological potential, paleo-geomorphology and chronology of the submerged river systems around the UK (Westley et al 2004, Gupta et al 2004, Dix & Sturt 2011). In 2008 a special episode of 'Time Team', a British archeological television programme, on the University of Birmingham's North Sea Prehistory Project entitled 'Britain's Drowned World' helped capture the public imagination (Gaffney 2007). This project is just one example of a long history of collaboration between marine industries and archaeologists in the field of submerged prehistory. In the Netherlands, for example, the fishing industry has, for almost 150 years, been recovering prehistoric finds from the North Sea in the form of faunal remains, and there is a long history of collaboration with paleontologists and archaeologists (Peeters et al 2009).

In English territorial waters, the marine aggregates industry have, for a number of years, been working to ensure that they operate in a sustainable way, with due consideration for the environment. Licensed extraction takes place in a number of regions, or clusters, around the country based on the location of a number of submerged paleo-channels, with reserves of fluvial sand and gravel deposits. The nature of this industry means that they are targeting the very paleo-channel systems that archaeologists are interested in for potential surviving prehistoric cultural materials. However, the two are not incompatible; in fact, much of what we now know about the submerged prehistory of England's territorial waters owes much to finds made by, and work funded via, the Marine Aggregates industry.

Discovery in Licence Area 240

In late 2007 and early 2008 88 Paleolithic flint implements, including 33 hand axes (Figure 1), flakes, cores and a quantity of animal bone were found on the oversize pile of a Dutch wharf by a local archaeologist, Mr. Jan Meulmeester. They had been recovered from an aggregate dredging licence area known as Area 240, located to the east of Great Yarmouth, in a block of aggregate dredging licences off the East Anglian coast. Thanks to a system that tracks the dredger movements, known as Electronic Monitoring System (EMS), the suspected site of the hand axes was quickly protected from further impact in line with an industry specific archaeological protocol (BMAPA and EH 2005). Analysis of the finds was undertaken by a specialist at Leiden University in the Netherlands. It was concluded that the assemblage most likely represented a palimpsest originating from a range of depositional environments, indicating material from both in-situ and secondary contexts (De Loecker 2010). The assemblage included some highly abraded hand axes, but also several examples in a very fresh condition indicating they had been removed from their primary context (Wessex Archaeology 2012).

Further investigations of the site were funded through the Aggregates Levy Sustainability fund, a ring fenced fund for environmental projects taken directly from a tax on aggregate extraction to offset the environmental impacts of the activity. The fund was introduced in

2002, including both a terrestrial and a marine element, and has been of particular use informing decision making and advice by improving our archaeological methods and techniques, enhancing baseline mapping, and providing options for mitigation and management. Unfortunately, funding for the ALSF was withdrawn in the Government spending cuts and the program came to a close in March 2011. The project funded by English Heritage through the Aggregate Levy was undertaken by Wessex Archaeology. They provided a multi phased assessment of the site of the artifacts, and a number of different approaches were adopted, including collection and review of geophysical data, grab sampling, and vibrocore survey and analysis (Wessex Archaeology 2011a). The results were drawn together into a final synthesis report and a picture of the location of the finds and the depositional history of the areas was developed. Over the course of this ALSF project, a number of interesting finds were made, including the discovery of further artifactual material. During the grab sample and beam trawl works for example more worked flint flakes were recovered from transects and grabs taken within the South East corner of the exclusion zone.

The vibrocore and grab samples were subject to a variety of dating techniques and paleo-environmental analysis, including Radiocarbon and Optically Stimulated Luminescence (OSL) dating, and analysis of pollen, foraminifera, ostracods and diatoms. The dating analysis contributed to an interpretation of the chronology and depositional history of the licence area (Wessex Archaeology 2011a). It was postulated that the likely source of the original finds was geological unit 3b, a mixed deposit of sands and gravels. This unit is widespread across the entire Anglian dredging region and thought to have been deposited during the Wolstonian glaciation, dating the finds to between approximately 300 to 130 thousand years before present. This date was consistent with the finds analysis undertaken in the Netherlands (Wessex 2011b), and placed the likely source of the hand axes in the Middle Paleolithic.

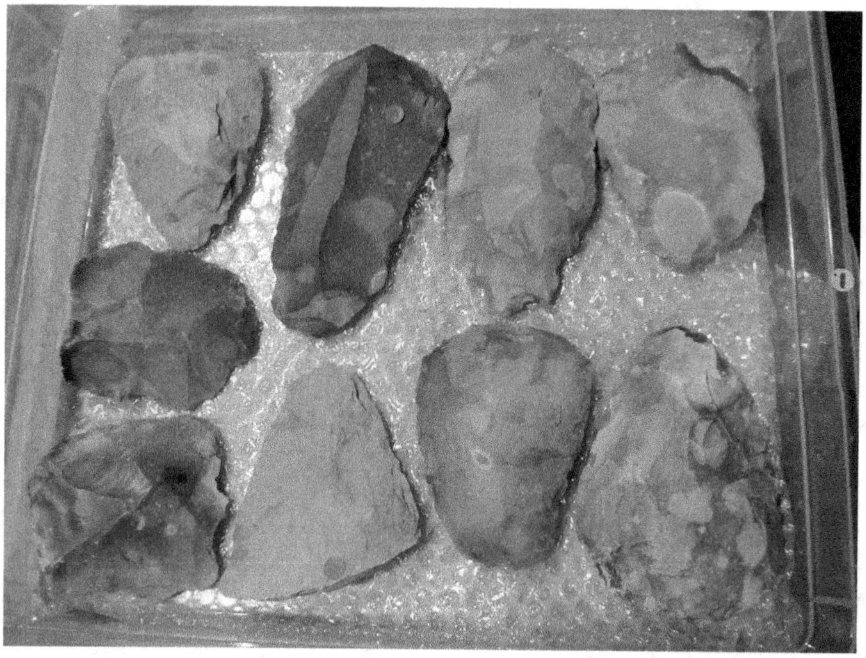

Archaeological Monitoring of Dredging

In August 2011, an opportunity arose to test this working hypothesis. The Licence holders of Area 240 Hanson Aggregates Marine Ltd. (HAML) expressed a desire to English Heritage, the governments' primary advisor for maritime archeology in English waters, to consider the possibility of removal of the exclusion zone to open up the area to future extraction. However, HAML also recognised the significance of the materials recovered from Area 240, and therefore sought discussions with English Heritage to determine the best way forward for the management of the site. Given the apparent national, and potentially international, significance of the artifacts recovered from Area 240, it was decided that further work would be required to determine an appropriate management approach based on an enhanced understanding of their significance and associated seabed context.

To do this a unique approach was developed by Wessex Archaeology and agreed in consultation with English Heritage and HAML. The methodology saw the use of a marine aggregate dredger to take a sample from designated transects both within and outside the exclusion zone in Area 240. HAML collected an 80% cargo from designated lanes within their active dredging zone; this cargo was drained and then field-walked by archaeologists to check for any

FIGURE 1. A COLLECTION OF MIDDLE PALEOLITHIC PREHISTORIC HANDAXES RECOVERED FROM MARINE AGGREGATE LICENCE AREA 240 IN 2007/2008. THE HANDAXES WERE FOUND ON THE OVERSIZE PILE OF A DUTCH WHARF BY A LOCAL ARCHAEOLOGIST, MR JAN MEELMEUSTER WHO PROMPTLY REPORTED THEIR DISCOVERY. IMAGE COPYRIGHT PETER MURPHY.

FIGURE 2. AN ARCHAEOLOGIST FROM WESSEX ARCHAEOLOGY FIELD WALKS A MARINE AGGREGATE CARGO AFTER THE TARGETED EXTRACTION OF MATERIAL IN THE AREA 240 HANDAXE EXCLUSION ZONE. FURTHER ARTIFACTS WERE RECOVERED OVER THE COURSE OF THE SURVEY, WITH EXAMPLES BEING RECOVERED BOTH ON BOARD THE VESSEL AND DURING DISCHARGE OF MATERIAL AT THE FLUSHING WHARF IN THE NETHERLANDS. IMAGE COPYRIGHT WESSEX ARCHAEOLOGY.

archeological materials (Figure 2). Once this was complete the vessel transited to an agreed 500 m transect in the exclusion zone, loaded the final 20% of the cargo, drained and field-walked it once more. In this way the archaeologists could discriminate between materials that had been recovered from both outside and within the exclusion zone, and be confident in the origin of any finds (Wessex Archaeology 2011b). In total, eight transects were run over the course of a two week period (Figure 2). Further wharf inspection was carried out in the Netherlands to ascertain if any further materials were able to be recovered from the load during onshore processing.

The results of this work were very positive. Over 100 pieces were recovered, and of this number 24 were confirmed as definitely artifactual pieces of worked flint. The new assemblage included three hand axes, a number of smaller flint flakes, and a mammoth tooth (Wessex Archaeology 2011b). In addition, an assemblage of wood and a piece of amber were recovered, although these pieces are not now thought to be anthropogenic. The methodology had proved highly successful with finds being recovered both on the vessel and at the wharf. However, to complicate matters somewhat, finds were recovered from both within and outside the exclusion zone. All the evidence was therefore pointing at there being a wider spread of cultural material than originally envisaged. The evidence also supported the hypothesis that that the most likely source of the in situ material was geological unit 3b, with all but one of the finds made onboard being securely located to transects targeting this deposit, and the other find having been recovered from an area where the overlying deposit was

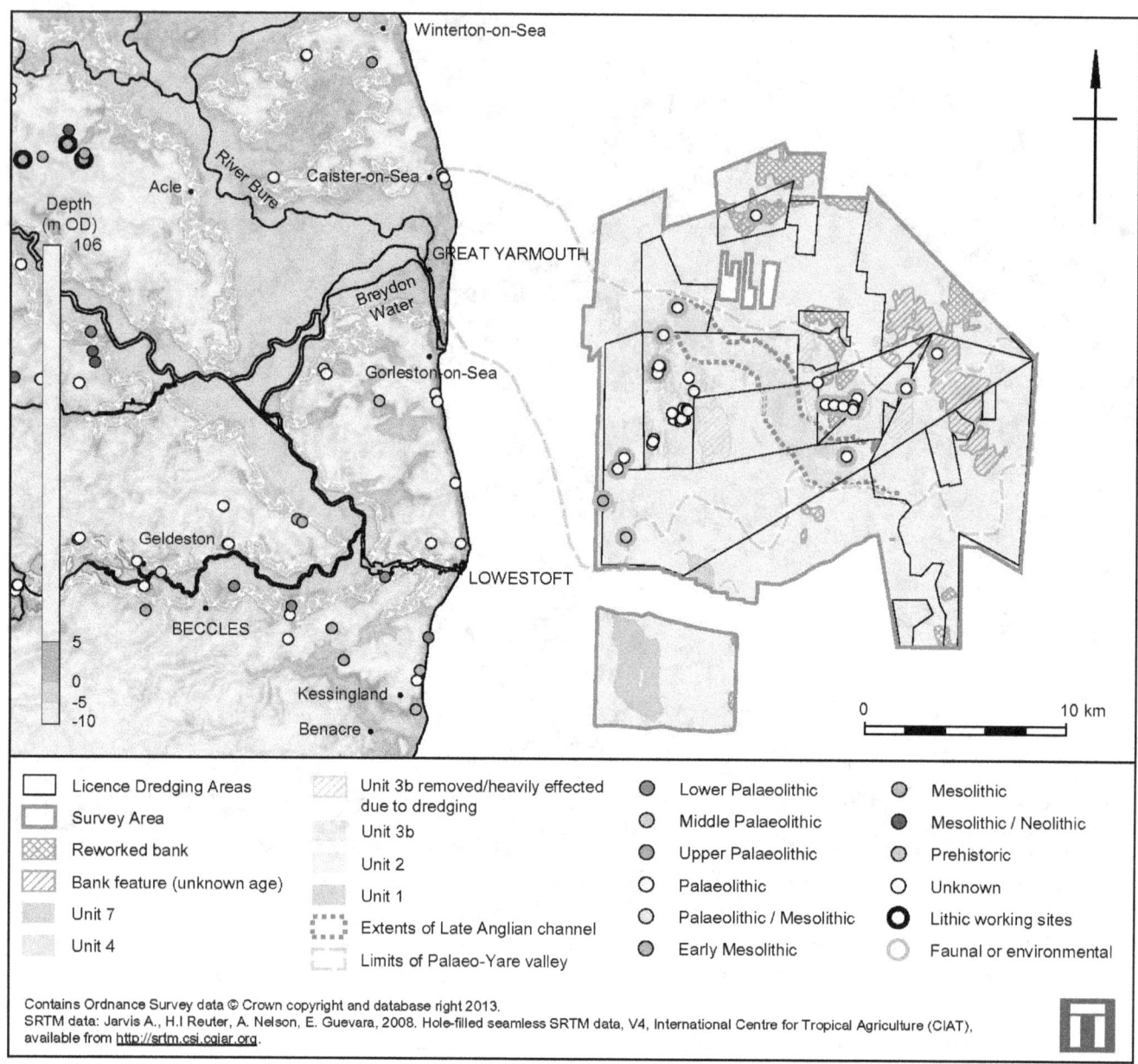

FIGURE 3. INTERPRETATION OF THE SURFICIAL SEDIMENTS ACROSS THE ANGLIAN DREDGING REGION, WHERE LICENCE AREA 240 IS LOCATED, BASED ON AN IN-DEPTH ANALYSIS OF INDUSTRY GEOPHYSICAL AND GEOTECHNICAL DAT. THE UNIT 3B DEPOSIT, THOUGHT TO BE THE SOURCE OF THE HANDAXES, IS DEPICTED IN BLUE. THIS INTERPRETATION WAS MADE POSSIBLE THROUGH FUNDING FROM THE BRITISH MARINE AGGREGATE PRODUCERS ASSOCIATION (BMAPA), THE REPRESENTATIVE TRADE BODY FOR THE BRITISH MARINE AGGREGATE INDUSTRY, AND THE CROWN ESTATE, THE OWNERS OF THE UK TERRITORIAL SEABED. FROM 'THE PALAEO-YARE CATCHMENT ASSESSMENT', COPYRIGHT WESSEX ARCHAEOLOGY.

thought to have been almost completely removed (Euan McNeill, Pers comm.).

The results of this work, while positive, had also left us in somewhat of a quandary. The method had proved productive, but the question of whether there was a wider spread of cultural material associated with unit 3b had arisen. It was, of course, not being suggested that where there was a particular geological deposit in an area there would be cultural material, rather that the deposit had been shown to be archeologically productive, and there was therefore a very real possibility that further sites such as the one in Area 240 might exist across the wider submerged river valley system in which the licence area sits.

Towards a Regional Management Approach

To their great credit, the aggregates industry recognised the significance of these new finds, and the wider potential of the region that this work had demonstrated. To address this, The Crown Estate, owners of the seabed out to 12 nautical miles, and the industry representatives the British Marine Aggregates Producers Association (BMAPA) decided to commission a data audit study to provide an assessment of the wider archeological potential in the region. The 'Palaeo-Yare catchment assessment', so named after the submerged river system that once flowed through the Anglian offshore area, was conducted by Wessex Archaeology, and was based on the premise that geological unit 3b was the likely source of the in situ cultural material found in Area 240. The study covered nine licence areas and four aggregate companies (Wessex Archaeology 2012).

The results of the study included an interpretation of the geology of the entire Anglian dredging region based on an in depth analysis of industry geotechnical and geophysical data. It was found that Unit 3b is a widespread deposit, existing in a number of locations across the dredging region (Figure 3). In some areas, the deposit is located in areas licensed for extraction, in other locations it was found that areas of the deposit exist where they remain untouched by aggregate dredging. The study also determined that there are areas of unit 3b that would be protected from extraction by overlying sandbanks (Wessex Archaeology 2012). The study provided an analysis of historical dredging intensity with the intention of understanding how much of the unit 3b deposit likely remains. A number of the licence areas, including Area 240, have been worked for 30-40 years, and in some cases the unit 3b deposit has been heavily dredged. In other areas it has been lightly dredged, and in other cases it remains as yet untouched (Wessex Archaeology 2012). These findings provide an indication of where future investigations can focus effort to answer key questions about where and how this material survives on the seafloor. Some of the data utilized has limitations, due to factors such as age and data resolution, however, if one accepts the parameters within with this interpretation was produced, it can still become a very powerful tool to guide further investigation through monitoring the archeological potential of an entire marine aggregate dredging region.

Furthermore, recognition must be given to the incredible wealth of industry resources that have been made available to the team at Wessex Archaeology to support this assessment. In total, 1,171 vibrocore logs and approximately 7,000 line km of sub bottom and bathymetry data were assessed as part of the project. In addition, 400 onshore borehole logs were reviewed to provide an assessment of the onshore Yare valley river system (Wessex Archaeology 2012). Very few studies exist where such a vast amount of industry data has been made available solely for archaeological interpretation. This is further proof of the good relations that exist between archaeologists and the aggregate industry in England and highlights just one of the benefits of working with industrial partners to better understand our submerged prehistory.

Based on the results of the study, the aggregates industry are now engaged in further work to assess the wider potential of the Paleo-Yare valley system in partnership with English Heritage and their archeological contractors. This work involves operational sampling and monitoring work over the course of licensed extraction; dredgers periodically target specific areas in their licences, dredge a normal size cargo, and then deliver to an assigned wharf where archaeologists monitor processing to identify any finds. The use of EMS, as described above, tracks the movements of the vessel during operation so that a picture can be developed of the provenance of any finds. Wharf and licence area method statements have been compiled for each company to guide this work. A number of hypotheses have also been developed at the regional catchment scale that will be applied to individual licence areas (Firth 2012). These will help us answer some key questions raised by the research, such as is archaeological material only present in unit 3b, is material only present on the edge of the Paleo-Yare valley system or within the channels themselves, and is material present/or not present in areas that are heavily dredged?

A regional Written Scheme of Investigation (WSI) is also being utilised to ensure that the work continues to meet key objectives for understanding and enhancing the significance of material in the region. The WSI includes the means by which the companies, their consultants, English Heritage, and the government regulators (the Marine Management Organisation) will work together and participate in this process (Firth 2012). It acts as a living document, so that as our understanding and knowledge develops over the course of work, our methodologies and approaches may also develop. All the aggregate companies that operate in the Anglian dredging region have signed up to participate in this work via a licence condition. There are also a number of benefits to

FIGURE 4. THE FIRST TRIAL OF OPERATIONAL MONITORING AT THE HANSON AGGREGATES MARINE LTD OWNED FRINDSBURY WHARF IN NORTH KENT. FURTHER MATERIAL RECOVERED BY TARGETED DREDGING IN LICENCE AREA 240 IS INSPECTED FOR ARTIFACTS AS IT PASSES ARCHAEOLOGISTS ON THE PLANT CONVEYOR. WORKED FLINTS WERE FOUND IN THE TRIAL AND FURTHER WORK ACROSS THE WIDER DREDGING REGION IS BEING UNDERTAKEN TO IMPROVE UNDERSTANDING OF THE ARCHEOLOGICAL POTENTIAL OF THE REGION AND TO IMPROVE MANAGEMENT OF THIS UNIQUE RESOURCE. IMAGE BY THE AUTHOR.

of the wider landscape in which the original material sits, rather than just as a single site in isolation.

A first trial of the wharf monitoring took place in May 2012, at the HAML owned Frindsbury Wharf (Figure 4). Aggregate material was taken from carefully chosen locations within licence area 240, tracked by EMS to show exactly where material was removed, and delivered by vessel to the wharf. This was offloaded in an area that had been cleared to keep the load separate from other materials, then loaded into the plant facility. Fine grained sediments and oversize material greater than 100 mm were removed. Care is taken to ensure that material from previous processing does not remain in the plant to contaminate the load. Archaeologists then had access to material during processing as the grade between 40 mm and 100 mm passed them on a conveyor. They were, in this way, able to spot, inspect, and recover any pieces of interest and then restart the plant. The team also had access to the oversize pile in order to search for and recover finds. Archeological materials, including more worked flints, were found in the trial. While only having access to the over 40 mm grade of material limits our ability to interpret a full assemblage, it improves the chances of finding Middle Paleolithic artifacts, which are generally of a larger size than the more refined later prehistoric technologies. It is also important to note that this method represented the best way for material to be recovered at this particular facility without seriously hampering the companies' ability to process a cargo of sand and gravel, a key consideration of any working methodology. It was a method that was specific to this particular wharf and company; other methodologies are currently being trialled for other facilities.

working on this regional basis, for both the industry and the archaeologists alike. For the industry, they can help answer questions on the regional scale, and not just for their own licence areas as all the results from sampling events will be drawn together into an interpretative report. In addition their working methodologies may be enhanced through sharing of knowledge, experience and understanding. For the archaeologists, the approach ensures that we are able to think about the management

Implications for Future Management

So what are the implications of this work for the future management of our submerged prehistory? If the current work proves successful, then it will be considered to be an option to use this method in the future, as a means of mitigation in other locations where diver-based investigation is not a practical means of assessment. However, it is important to recognize that this is a particular piece of work aimed at an area of already demonstrated significance. Only in areas where similar recovery of material and history of investigation can demonstrate such significance could an approach such as this be considered as an appropriate and proportionate piece of mitigation. Other matters for more immediate consideration are how appropriate is the current exclusion zone; do we now have the evidence to support its continuation, or conversely, its removal or reduction in size? Perhaps this work may highlight other areas that would be more appropriate places to protect? Or conversely, if little is discovered in other areas of the river catchment, and we are confident that this isn't a failing of the sampling and processing methodologies, then the significance of the finds in Area 240 may be further enhanced.

We can also consider whether in situ protection through exclusion zones is, in fact, the most desirable management option for this site. What would the public benefit be of excluding these areas from extraction, but also from future research, due to a lack of permitted access and scarce availability of funds for archaeological research? How stable would these areas be on the seabed if protected in-situ but again with little funds available for their ongoing management? So far the approach has been that for the inconvenience of access, the industry gains a better understanding of the archaeological potential of the dredging region, while we gain greater understanding and knowledge of our submerged prehistory and the survival and location of such sites on the seafloor. This form of 'preservation by record', as opposed to a preservation in situ approach, has worked well in this instance. Naturally should a site of clear significance worthy of in situ protection be discovered, then this would have to be considered where practicable. However, for this site at present, the preservation by record approach outlined above remains the best way of managing the site to understand and enhance its significance.

Answers to a number of the remaining questions this work raises about the location of artifacts, and how our ancestors were using and traversing this landscape in the Middle Paleolithic, will become apparent over the course of the next few years of monitoring work. What is clear today is that working in partnership with marine industries can provide great opportunities to advance understanding of our submerged prehistoric past.

Acknowledgements

I would like to thank Chris Pater and Ian Oxley of English Heritage for their ongoing support and guidance. Special mention must go to Louise Tizzard, Euan McNeill and the team at Wessex Archaeology, Nigel Griffiths of Hanson, and Mark Russell of BMAPA for all their efforts in developing the work described above. Thanks also go to Andrew Bellamy of Tarmac, Will Drake of Volker and Graham Singleton of CEMEX, as well as The Crown Estate and the licensing team at the MMO. Thanks finally to my wife Jessica and son Finley for all their love and support.

References

BMAPA and English Heritage
    2005   *Protocol for reporting finds of archaeological interest.* British Marine Aggregate Producers Association and English Heritage: London.

Coles, Bryony J.
    1998   Doggerland: a Speculative Survey, *Proceedings of the Prehistoric Society* 64:45-81.

Dix, Justin and Fraser Sturt
    2011   *The Relic Palaeo-landscapes of the Thames Estuary.* MEPF Report 09/P126. University of Southampton.

De Loecker, Dimitri
    2010   *Great Yarmouth dredging licence Area 240, Norfolk, United Kingdom. Preliminary report on the lithic artifacts.* Unpublished Report, University of Leiden.

Firth, Antony
    2012   *Provisional Written Scheme of Investigations for the Anglian Region.* Ver.070912. Unpublished document.

Gaffney, Vince, Kenneth Thomson and Simon Fitch
    2007   *Mapping Doggerland: The Mesolithic Landscapes of the Southern North Sea.* Oxford: Archaeopress.

Gupta, Sanjeev, Jenny Collier, Andy Palmer-Felgate, Julie Dickinson, Kerry Bushe and Stuart Humber
    2004   *Submerged Palaeo-Arun River: Reconstruction of Prehistoric Landscapes and Evaluation of Archaeological Resource Potential. Integrated Projects 1 and 2.* Department of Earth Science & Engineering, Imperial College, on behalf of English Heritage. London.

PEETERS, HANS, PETER MURPHY AND NIC FLEMMING (EDS.)
    2009   *North Sea Prehistory Research and Management Framework (NSPRMF) 2009.* Amersfoort: Rijksdienst voor het Cultureel Erfgoed/ English Heritage.

REID, CLEMENT
    1913   *Submerged Forests.* London: Cambridge University Press.

WESSEX ARCHAEOLOGY
    2011a   *Seabed Prehistory: Site Evaluation Techniques (Area 240). Synthesis.* Ref. 70754.03. Salisbury: Wessex Archaeology.

    2011b   *Licence Area 240: Archaeological Monitoring of Dredging.* Ref: 77860.02. Salisbury: Wessex Archaeology.

    2012   *Palaeo-Yare Catchment Assessment. Technical Report.* Ref:83740.02. Salisbury: Wessex Archaeology.

WESTLEY, KIERAN, JUSTIN DIX AND RORY QUINN
    2004   *Re-assessment of the archaeological potential of continental shelves.* English Heritage ALSF project no. 3362. School of Ocean and Earth Science, University of Southampton.

· · · · · · · · · · · · · · · ·

Edward Salter
English Heritage
Eastgate Court
195-205 High Street
Guildford
GU1 3EH
United Kingdom

Developing Foresight, Threat Analysis And Risk Assessment to Further the Management of the Marine Historic Environment Of England

Ian Oxley

Heritage agencies are subject to change due to external and internal impacts. English Heritage, the statutory advisor to the UK Government on the terrestrial and marine historic environment of England, has regularly revised its marine capacity since 2002 when the organisation first assumed marine responsibilities. Recent corporate developments, within the framework of a new National Heritage Protection Plan, have involved the discontinuation of the central Maritime Archaeology Team and the transfer of specialist marine functions such as designation and planning advice to relevant English Heritage Departments where the terrestrial equivalents are delivered. A further innovation is the setting up of a Historic Environment Intelligence Team that includes a marine analyst to carry out foresight and risk assessment functions for the benefit of the sector and English Heritage itself.

Introduction

Many heritage organizations are experiencing budget reductions and staff cuts as a result of the deteriorating economic climate. English Heritage, as the United Kingdom Government's statutory advisor on the historic environment of England, land and sea, is no exception. To mitigate for these pressures, strategies have to be developed to focus available resources and capacity on core activities and responsibilities, while enabling supporting players such as other Government Departments, industry, and the wider sector to play an effective role themselves in the care and protection of the common heritage.

The formal management of the historic environment of any country's marine historic environment is a relatively new development in the curatorial sector. English Heritage, as a national heritage agency, assumed specific responsibilities for the marine historic environment of England in 2002, and even over the short period since its formal involvement, the organisation has taken a series of evolutionary steps to develop its own expert capacity, tools, systems and structures, together with building knowledge and understanding of the surviving heritage.

On a corporate scale, over the last thirteen years a series of reorganisations have changed the shape of the provision of maritime archaeological expertise within English Heritage, against the background of wider social, economic and natural environmental change (Flatman 2009). Such heritage agency development and experience is not normally recorded and published, although country-by-country descriptions of risks and threats to their maritime and underwater heritage are relatively common in conference proceedings (Pater 2009; Henderson 2012).

Therefore it is timely that the organisational challenges in relation to the resilience of structures developed to deliver marine historic environment management are considered. How can strategies be developed that ensure the speedy recovery and timely adaptation of an organisation to impacts beyond its control?

In response to such challenges, and to ensure the continual evolution of its terrestrial and marine historic environment capacity, English Heritage is developing strategies based on understanding, planning, responding and learning. However, re-structuring and budget cuts as a result of the recently deteriorating economic climate have necessitated that new strategies focus resources on core responsibilities.

A National Heritage Protection Plan has been developed by English Heritage to determine priorities based on research and understanding, set up processes, then implement them. Furthermore, it is recognised that an effective intelligence function for any organisation is an essential component of strategic planning, because it underpins workforce planning, anticipates and responds to trends most likely to impact on ability to deliver core corporate objectives.

In this way English Heritage will become more proactive and better able to manage risk and exploit opportunity through the development and implementation of even more robust and resilient policies and strategies. This paper describes the development of, and background to, English Heritage's creation of a Historic Environment Intelligence Team which includes a marine function.

The Marine Historic Environment and Global Change

Natural processes and human activity impact on the heritage. Major events, such as issues for food and farming, weather, terrorism, migration and population change, financial systems stability, humanitarian disaster, energy availability, and climate change, can have catastrophic effects on the historic environment itself but also on the capacity of heritage organisations to function effectively.

The protection of cultural heritage in the face of global change is becoming a major concern for decision-makers, stakeholders and populations. Clearly research is needed to safeguard cultural heritage against impacts. Environmental changes and security risks threaten cultural heritage, potentially exposing it to irreversible damage and losses because of its age and fragility (Flatman 2009; JPI Cultural Heritage 2010).

The marine historic environment is no exception and it does not exist in isolation. It is an integral part of the wider marine environment, surrounded by, and often firmly embedded in, what may be termed the natural marine environment. That wider marine environment is of great economic importance. The United Kingdom marine sector has a total property value of £726m, with £17.7m in revenue coming from marine minerals, £12.7m income from cables and pipelines, and £7.8m from marine renewable energy, and it is estimated that the wider marine-related economy generates around £46bn of the United Kingdom Gross Domestic Product and provides 890,000 jobs (The Crown Estate 2013).

Consequently, Governments and other major organisations are mindful of the benefits of forward corporate business planning which involve foresight and risk assessment methodologies (Bhimji 2009). For example, in the United Kingdom the National Risk Assessment, developed by the Government Office for Science, is designed to increase awareness of the kinds of risk the country faces, and to encourage organizations to think about their own preparedness.

An example of strategic planning in marine sector is the UK Marine Industries Strategic Framework developed to provide an overview of marine industries, their importance to the UK economy and the key issues for the future (Marine Industries Leadership Council 2010).

The Evolution of English Heritage's Marine Historic Environment Capacity

As result of acquiring new marine responsibilities under the National Heritage Act of 2002, English Heritage appointed a Head of Maritime Archaeology to lead a Maritime Archaeology Team which gradually expanded from one additional maritime archaeologist in 2003 to seven staff in 2009.

Successive corporate re-organisations offered the opportunity of enabling a more strategic approach to be taken to addressing marine historic environment and maritime heritage objectives and the sharing of tasks with teams other than that of Maritime Archaeology so that the organisation could continue to:

- gradually build internal capacity to fulfill it's role as national curator/ statutory advisor (Oxley 2007);

- commission key projects from external partners to raise awareness, enable access, develop and promote standards (Tapper and Hooley 2012, Newman 2012);

- promote the debate about frameworks to underpin future research directions (Ransley et al. 2013);

- identify gaps in participation, ownership, and support for the submerged historic environment.

During those developmental years particular specialist roles became necessary such as Protected Wreck licensing management and marine planning advice. These developments together with successive re-structuring phases led to a marine and maritime strategy review in 2009 which proposed that the next evolutionary step was for the specialist functions to be transferred out to those English Heritage Departments where the terrestrial equivalents were accommodated.

Implementation of these proposals led to the discontinuation of the central Maritime Archaeology Team in 2011 and the creation of the marine analyst function in the newly formed English Heritage Historic Environment Intelligence Team. This role is new to marine historic environment management in the United Kingdom and it is an imaginative and forward-looking step for a heritage agency. One aim for the post is to develop structures for acquiring and analysing marine historic environment intelligence through foresight and threat assessment in the context of the National Heritage Protection Plan.

National Heritage Protection Plan

English Heritage has developed an overarching framework to make best use of existing resources so that England's vulnerable historic environment is safeguarded in the most cost-effective way at a time of massive social, environmental, economic, and technological change.

Focussing on those areas and types of heritage that are least understood, most threatened, most significant, and/or most valued by communities, English Heritage's National Heritage Protection Plan, which explicitly includes the marine historic environment, provides the structure to further the protection, management and presentation of England's historic environment (English Heritage 2012a, 2012b).

Key Plan Principles

The Plan represents English Heritage's vision, but the aspiration is for it to be the way that others help achieve the overall aim inspiring them to co-operate and contribute in the delivery of the aim, looking to a shared, sector-wide framework, intended to promote collaborative effort. It focuses on the heritage itself (the assets) and the potential threats to heritage (issues), and it aims to ensure that, while helping to deliver positive and sustainable economic growth, England's heritages: are not needlessly at risk of damage, erosion or loss; are experienced, understood, and enjoyed by communities; and continue to provide memorable places used by people.

The Plan is meant to be a common language for everyone working to protect heritage, responsive, using the term "protection" in a broad sense, and be a long term, iterative and cyclical tool composed of a framework document, an English Heritage Action Plan, and an Activity Programme.

The framework document sets out the need and overarching priorities expressed through eight measures sub-divided into series of activities, which set out shared priorities for cross-sectoral effort in delivering tangible protection results. The framework therefore stands outside and above any specific organisation plan or strategy. The English Heritage Action Plan is a detailed summary of the objectives, methods, outputs and resource which English Heritage itself is committing to the Plan between until March 2015.

Finally the Activity Programme contains eight measures: Foresight; Threat assessment and response; Heritage identification and recognition; Assessment of significance; Protection; Managing change; Managing major historic assets; and, Advice and grant-aid to help owners.

The English Heritage Historic Environment Intelligence Team

The first two Plan measures form the framework for the work of the new Historic Environment Intelligence Team, which provides leadership in forecasting long-raise issues, assessing threat and impacts, and delivering workable and cost-effective responses. The Team contains expertise in development, local government, environmental and climate change, social impacts, professional skills, resource and landscape exploitation, as well as marine issues.

Carrying out the systematic examination of potential threats, opportunities, and likely future developments at the margins of current thinking and planning, a structured methodology is being developed to bring together key people knowledge and ideas that look beyond normal planning horizons in order to inform strategic thinking at a general scale and develop tactical responses to specific issues.

Methodologies and Tools

As discussed above, formal processes of foresight, threat analysis and risk assessment are considered to be fundamental to delivering the National Heritage Protection Plan successfully. In fact sector intelligence and foresight were used to formulate the prioritised Plan itself. There is, therefore, a further requirement to develop different ways of recovering sector intelligence, to identify, as far as possible, knowledge that will be needed in future and to use that knowledge to protect not only the historic environment but the organisation as well.

English Heritage has an existing and ongoing commitment to foresight which is embedded in the structure of the organisation and articulated through the formulation of thematic research and other strategies, and expressed to a greater or lesser extent in day to day operations.

English Heritage will carry out foresight through the strategic analysis of high level threats that have a demonstrable or potential impact on the historic environment. In the context of the Plan this has been combined with intelligence gathering on the state of knowledge pertaining to all aspects of the historic environment in order to provide two key scans: one on understanding and knowledge and one on threat and opportunities.

By analysing the likely severity and immediacy of these threats, and assessing the known or perceived significance of an historic asset EH is developing a strategy for evaluating priorities to ensure that the most urgent needs of the historic environment are met. This strategy crucially includes an evaluation of those themes, areas, and assets about which not enough is known in order to provide effective protection.

Foresight uses intelligence and horizon-scanning from a wide range of sources to identify trends and issues (threats or opportunities) and to assess the implications of change. Foresight also provides a long-term perspective on how external pressures, particularly social, economic, environmental, and political ones are likely to affect the historic environment in order to inform strategic action.

Sector Intelligence, Horizon Scanning, and Scenario Planning

There are many different, and increasingly complex, methodologies for carrying out foresight which depend on maintaining and recovering an adequate level of 'sector intelligence' both through normal day to day operations and by using specific intelligence gathering and review mechanisms (Rhydderch 2009). The simplest foresight mechanism is horizon scanning coupled with basic scenario planning.

Horizon scanning looks for clues and suggestions about future developments at the outer periphery of what is currently known and understood. It identifies emerging trends and issues and gives advance warning of new opportunities and threats by gathering and analysing information from a wide variety of sources such as academic research, formal and informal stakeholder consultation, peer review, and popular or media information.

Scenario planning investigates a range of possible futures to identify the likely scale and significance of potential threats and opportunities. This can include futures which are highly likely and which will have a reasonable or high impact, but can also include the identification of those threats that might have a low probability of occurrence but which would have a very high impact.

Initial Areas of Marine Sector Interest

Preliminary mapping of the marine sector relating to marine historic environment issues indicates a wide range of potential areas for research and scanning. The development of the structures and organisations to deliver the advent of marine planning, marine licensing and Marine Conservation Zones as a result of the passing of the Marine and Coastal Access Act 2009 is causing significant challenges for ensuring that historic interests are adequately taken into account. Secondly an example of a Government initiative where attention to the historic environment could have been better is the first United Kingdom Marine Science Strategy produced in February 2010 (Marine Science Coordinating Committee 2010). It is a fifteen year Strategy developed with significant input from the UK marine science community but without comprehensive attention to marine archaeological heritage.

Other areas of work are expected to include: issues of reporting of the discovery of marine archaeological sites and the declaration of the recovery of finds; mapping of the ownership of marine remains in order to encourage owners to have a role in their management; the disposal of Government marine heritage assets; and, the marine effects of climate change.

Conclusions

English Heritage is continually developing as a heritage agency and recently the direct impact of Government cuts have required an organisation that is smaller, more focussed and more strategic, that is capable of intelligent delivery of essential core functions that are genuinely integrated and relevant to current times. The latest evolutionary step has been to set up the capacity to proactively collect and use historic environment intelligence, explicitly including marine. The objective is to identify marine historic environment knowledge needed in future to ensure that English Heritage continues to work effectively; and deliver the best protection for the marine historic environment; use that knowledge to protect the historic environment and the organisation itself from the impact of new and emerging problems. By developing and using different ways of recovering marine historic environment sector intelligence, English Heritage will not only be able to better protect the common heritage from the impact of new and emerging problems but it will also be able to protect itself.

References

BHIMJI, WAHID
2009   Guidance on the use of strategic futures analysis for policy development in government. Foresight Horizon Scanning Centre, Government Office for Science, London, England. http://www.bis.gov.uk/assets/foresight/docs/horizon-scanning-centre/futuresinpolicyguidance.pdf Accessed 2 Mar. 2013

CULTURAL HERITAGE
 2010 The Joint Programming Initiative on Cultural Heritage and Global Change: a new challenge for Europe Vision Document. Version 17 June 2010. http://www.jpi-culturalheritage.eu/wp-content/uploads/Vision-Document_17-June-20101.pdf Accessed 18 Dec. 2012

ENGLISH HERITAGE
 2010 *Protected Wreck Sites: Moving towards a new way of managing England's historic environment.* English Heritage, London, England. http://www.english-heritage.org.uk/publications/protected-wreck-sites/ Accessed 28 Feb. 2013

 2012a National Heritage Protection Plan; An Introduction. English Heritage, London, England. http://www.english-heritage.org.uk/publications/nhpp-leaflet/nhpp-leaflet.pdf Accessed 18 Dec. 2012

 2012b The National Heritage Protection Plan. Version: 3rd December 2012. English Heritage, London, England. http://www.english-heritage.org.uk/publications/nhpp-plan-framework/nhpp-plan-framework.pdf Accessed 18 Dec. 2012

FLATMAN, JOSEPH
 2009 Conserving Marine Cultural Heritage: Threats, Risks and Future Priorities. *Conservation and Management of Archaeological Sites*, Vol 11 No 1: 5-8

GOVERNMENT OFFICE FOR SCIENCE
 2012 http://www.bis.gov.uk/foresight Accessed 28 Feb. 2013

HENDERSON, JON (EDITOR)
 2012 IKUWA 3 Beyond Boundaries – *Proceedings of The 3rd International Congress on Underwater Archaeology 9th to 12th July 2008, London.* Romisch – Germanische Kommission des Deutschen Archaologischen Instituts and Nautical Archaeology Society, Bonn, Germany

MARINE INDUSTRIES LEADERSHIP COUNCIL
 2010 UK Marine Industries Strategic Framework. Department for Business, Innovation & Skills, London, England

MARINE SCIENCE COORDINATING COMMITTEE
 2010 UK Marine Science Strategy. Department for Environment Food and Rural Affairs, London, England. http://www.defra.gov.uk/mscc/files/uk-marine-science-strategy-.pdf Accessed 18 Dec. 2012

NEWMAN, MARTIN
 2012 A Record of England's Underwater Past that is Fit for the Future. *IKUWA 3 Beyond Boundaries – Proceedings of The 3rd International Congress on Underwater Archaeology 9th to 12th July 2008, London,* Henderson, Jon, editor, pp 113-122. Romisch – Germanische Kommission des Deutschen Archaologischen Instituts and Nautical Archaeology Society, Bonn, Germany

OXLEY, IAN
 2007 Making the submerged historic environment accessible – beyond the National Heritage Act (2002). In *Managing the Marine Cultural Heritage: Defining, Accessing and Managing the Resource.* Satchell, Julie, and Paula Palma, (editors). CBA Research Report 153, Council for British Archaeology, York, England

PATER, CHRIS
 2009 National practice in the English area of the United Kingdom. In Manders, M., Oosting, R and W. Brouwers, eds., 2009, MACHU Managing Cultural Heritage Underwater Final report. MACHU, Rotterdam, The Netherlands: 124-126. http://www.machuproject.eu/documenten/MACHU_report_3.pdf Accessed 26 Feb. 2013

RANSLEY, JESSE, FRASER STURT, JUSTIN DIX, JONATHAN ADAMS, AND LUCY BLUE (EDITORS)
 [2013] *People and the Sea: A Maritime Archaeological Research Agenda for England.* CBA Research Report 171. York: Council for British Archaeology, York, England

RHYDDERCH, ALUN
 2009 Scenario Planning Guidance Note. Foresight Scanning Centre, Government Office for Science, London, England. http://www.bis.gov.uk/assets/foresight/docs/horizon-scanning-centre/foresight_scenario_planning.pdf Accessed 02 Mar. 2013

TAPPER, BRYN, AND DAVE HOOLEY
 2012 England's Historic Seascapes: mapping the character of the marine historic environment. In *IKUWA 3 Beyond Boundaries – Proceedings of The 3rd International Congress on Underwater Archaeology 9th to 12th July 2008, London,* Henderson, Jon, editor, pp 105-111. Romisch – Germanische Kommission des Deutschen Archaologischen Instituts and Nautical Archaeology Society, Bonn, Germany

THE CROWN ESTATE
 2013 http://www.thecrownestate.co.uk/energy-infrastructure/ Accessed 28 Feb. 2013

• • • • • • • • • • • • • • •

Ian Oxley
Historic Environment Intelligence Analyst (Marine)
English Heritage
Fort Cumberland, Fort Cumberland Road
Eastney, Portsmouth
Hants PO4 9LD
United Kingdom

Researching, Protecting and Managing England's Marine Historic Environment

Alison James

English Heritage is the Government's advisor on all aspects of the historic environment in England. One of the statutory functions of English Heritage is to advise on the protection and management of shipwrecks in English territorial waters designated under the Protection of Wrecks Act 1973. Recent marine archaeological discoveries of historic wreck sites that have been designated under the 1973 Act highlight a series of case studies to examine key approaches to site management.

Introduction

Casework surrounding historic shipwrecks falls primarily to the Designation Department of English Heritage, although other departments, including National Planning and Conservation, provide advice and guidance where necessary. It is the role of the Designation Department, through a programme of strategic designation, to identify the important elements of our past and, in doing so, articulate how ship and boat remains contribute so thoroughly to our national story. Most recently, this has been achieved through the online publication of a series of introduction to this type of asset in *Ships & Boats – prehistory to 1840* [1], and *Ships & Boats – 1840 to 1950* [2] and a designation selection guide *Ships & Boats – prehistory to present* [3]. Ships and boats have helped defined our nation; from the migration of prehistoric populations, through the defeat of the Spanish Armada, to the more recent Allied invasion of Normandy.

Ten years ago, the National Heritage Act 2002 transferred general functions for England's maritime archaeology to English Heritage from the Department for Culture, Media and Sport. At the same time, an 'ancient monument' was redefined to include the remains of vessels, aircraft, and movable structures to exist in, on, or under England's territorial seabed. To date (February 2013), 62 shipwrecks in the UK have legal status under the Protection of Wrecks Act 1973 ranging from the remains of Late Bronze Age cargo scatters to early 20th Century submarines. They have highlighted the research potential of shipwreck sites and illuminated diverse topics from early contacts with the Mediterranean through to the detailed understanding of a major Tudor warship. It should be noted that although the Act applies throughout the United Kingdom in waters out to 12 nm, English Heritage, and thus this paper, only deal with the 47 sites in English waters.

Protected Wreck Sites

The Protection of Wrecks Act (PWA) 1973

The Protection of Wrecks Act (PWA) 1973 is an Act to "*secure the protection of wrecks in territorial waters and the sites of such wrecks, from interference by unauthorised persons; and for connected purposes*"[4]. The Act empowers the Secretary of State (for Culture, Media and Sport) to designate a restricted area around a historic wreck on account of the historical, archaeological or artistic importance of the vessel. The Act applies to cargo, which in a number of cases is all that is known to remain.

PWA Licenses

The Act controls any access to and activity on a protected wreck site, which is generally defined by a single position and an area of 200-300m radius around it, although this does vary between sites. Access to sites designated under the Act is restricted and licence based, licensing is undertaken by the Department for Culture, Media and Sport but administered by English Heritage. Four categories of licence can be applied for; Visit, Survey, Surface Recovery and Excavation, applications can be made on the English Heritage website or via the post. The requirements for obtaining a licence become more stringent with each higher category, due to the potential for increased risk to the historic environment. To obtain a Surface Recovery or Excavation licence, a Project Design will need to be produced detailing research objectives and method statements, a suitable repository for artifacts and an appropriate archaeologist will also need to be nominated. Holders of a licence are termed Licensees and approximately 90% of sites have an active Licensee (February 2012).

Licensees and Affiliated Volunteers

The PWA licensing system utilises the volunteer role of Licensee to involve individuals with sites as effective voluntary custodians. Licensees have, in many cases, been involved with the sites over many years; current statistics from a survey undertaken by English Heritage in 2008 show that over 37% of licensees have been involved with the sites for ten years or more [5]. Their support, commitment and enthusiasm for these nationally important sites is crucial for furthering understanding of these sites, enabling stewardship and under-pinning effective management of them into the future. As will be shown later in this paper, licensees play a key role in the management of the sites designated under the Act, a fact recognised by English Heritage through their status as official English Heritage affiliated volunteers.

Managing the Sites

Contract for Archaeological Services in Support of Marine Designation

Since 1986, the Secretary for State has enabled a contract for archaeological services relating to wreck sites of archaeological interest in UK territorial waters [6]. The primary nature of this contract is to allow fieldwork that furthers the understanding and management of sites already designated or being considered for protection. Fieldwork on English sites is directed by English Heritage who plan an annual programme set forward in a series of briefs. The contractor is one of the main sources of information for English Heritage about both designated and non-designated sites.

Heritage at Risk

The Heritage at Risk Programme provides an annual picture of the health of England's heritage including that of protected wreck sites. All wreck sites, whether or not they are protected by the 1973 Act, are vulnerable to both environmental and human impacts. Because they are often in remote locations, their management can also be challenging and changes to their condition are characteristically difficult to anticipate and monitor [7].

In 2007 English Heritage audited all sites in order to gain a baseline survey of their condition and vulnerability, and to assess what needs to be done to ensure that their significance is maintained for both present and future generations. The survey was based upon the methodology developed and set out in *Protected Wreck Sites at Risk: A Risk Management Handbook* [8]. This survey showed that the then 42 of England's protected wreck sites were at high or medium risk from damage, decay or loss, unless action was taken. English Heritage is committed to securing a year-on year reduction in the number of historic sites at risk and to address this the Protected Wreck Sites at Risk Programme was developed as part of our wider Heritage at Risk initiative. The programme sets targets for reducing the types and degree of risk to England's protected wreck sites. At the strategic level, the major sources of risk to the condition of sites have been identified. At the individual site level, practical management needs have been identified and implemented through conservation management plans for high priority sites. In spite of the inherent difficulties in caring for this type of site, careful management must be maintained if we are to pass them on to future generations in as good condition as reasonably possible.

English Heritage is committed to maintaining the Heritage at Risk register and in Autumn 2012 published the most recent register. This shows that there has been a 63% percentage decrease in the number of sites at high risk since the baseline survey took place in 2007. This positive trend has been achieved through ongoing management of the sites, the work that has taken place and encouraging developments such as new Licensees becoming involved.

New Sites and Discoveries

The management approach by English Heritage varies according to the needs of each site that are clearly identified in a site specific Conservation Management Plan. Approaches include mitigation of risk through community involvement, ongoing monitoring work, excavation of high risk sites and public enjoyment on more robust sites. The case studies below highlight a number of recent examples.

Community Engagement on the London

A relatively recent designation is that of the *London* in the Thames Estuary. The *London* was a Second Rate ship built at Chatham in 1656. She formed part of an English Squadron sent to collect Charles II from the Netherlands and restore him to his throne in an effort to end the anarchy which followed the death of Cromwell in 1658. The *London* blew-up on passage from Chatham in March 1665. Further details on the *London* are available on the National Heritage List for England: http://list.english-heritage.org.uk/resultsingle.aspx?uid=1000088.

The site came to the attention of English Heritage during a staged archaeological assessment as part of ongoing mitigation for the London Gateway project. It was immediately apparent that the site was of high significance and it was subsequently designated under the Protection of Wrecks Act in 2008. From the outset management of the site had some unique challenges; it's location in a low visibility, highly tidal environment on the edge of a busy shipping channel meant it was not a easy or attractive site to dive. It was also a high-risk site due to the exposed nature of the site and the abundance of artifacts on the seabed and as a result it was placed onto the Heritage at Risk register. A keen local diver, Steven Ellis, approached English Heritage to apply for a visit license for the site. He undertook most of his diving in the area and was used to the particular challenges of the environment. As a result of his visits he subsequently became enthused with the possibilities of working alongside English Heritage as an Affiliated Volunteer to survey the site. English Heritage have worked with Steven, Wessex Archaeology and Southend Museum to develop a practical community based protocol to enable the recording of the site and in particular the high risk, mobile material. The monitoring and recording is undertaken by the volunteer team led by Steven supported by professional guidance and mentored by a nominated archaeologist and others, Figure 1. The approach has allowed for the maximum amount of information to be gained, indeed the site is now dived on an almost weekly basis, from a site that, for various reasons, could never be fully excavated or stabilised. While the site is still classified as at high risk, the protocol is ensuring that important information is gained that would otherwise be lost.

Ongoing Site Monitoring on the Holland No.5

Designated wreck sites require ongoing monitoring work some of which is achieved by Licensees and their teams as above and some of which is planned by English Heritage and undertaken by the Archaeological Contractor previously discussed. Of the 47 protected wreck sites just three are metal hulled; the submarines *Holland No.5* and HMS/m *A1* and the *Iona II*. As a result, most of the management expertise that has been developed has focused on wooden shipwrecks. In order to readdress this one recent project has sought to develop methodology for testing hull metal thickness to help inform future conservation management of metal wrecks.

FIGURE 1. ARCHAEOLOGISTS FROM ENGLISH HERITAGE AND WESSEX ARCHAEOLOGY WORK ALONGSIDE AFFILIATED VOLUNTEERS TO RECOVER AND RECORD HIGH RISK EXPOSED ARTIFACTS FROM THE LONDON. COPYRIGHT SOUTHEND MUSEUM.

The *Holland No.5* submarine was designated under the Protection of Wrecks Act 1973 in December 2004. Further details on the *Holland No. 5* are available on the National Heritage List for England: http://list.english-heritage.org.uk/resultsingle.aspx?uid=1000081.

The site has formed part of a programme initiated by English Heritage in 2012 to develop specific methodology. Fieldwork on the site has allowed the development of a simple process to collect information about hull thickness using simple hand tools to remove concretion and a Cygnus DIVE gauge to take measurements [9]. Repeatable ultrasonic thickness measurements at key points on the hull of the *Holland No. 5* will help to inform on its future management on the hypothesis that monitoring hull thickness over time can provide information relating to the overall condition, stability, or degradation of the site by essentially measuring the amount of metal that is being lost. To our knowledge, this is the first time it had been utilized for the management of archaeologically significant sites. The 2012 work has formed a baseline survey that can be compared against known makers plans of the site and be used to compare measurements against in future years. This will then allow management responses to be put in place that will allow the *Holland No.5* to be removed from the Heritage at Risk register. It is early days for the work but English Heritage are excited about the management possibilities it presents.

Swash Channel – The Excavation of a High Risk Site

The Swash Channel wreck was discovered in October 2004, during archaeological assessment work undertaken in advance of proposed channel deepening in Poole Harbour, on behalf of Poole Harbour Commissioners. The vessel appeared as a large anomaly during geophysical survey and brief investigation of the site confirmed the significance of the find. All the finds and the visible structure suggested a large seventeenth century armed merchant vessel engaged in trade with the tropics. Further details on the Swash Channel are available on the National Heritage List for England: http://list.english-heritage.org.uk/resultsingle.aspx?uid=1000082.

As a result of its national significance, the wreck was designated under the Protection of Wrecks Act in December 2004. Since the site first came to archaeological attention it continually proved to be unstable and subject to dramatic shifts in exposure levels. It became quickly apparent there were more remains on the site than originally believed; elements of particular interest include spectacular carvings, and the ships rudder, which lies on the site 8.4 m long, topped by a carving of a human head. In 2006 sediment monitoring stakes were positioned on the site by Bournemouth University. By 2008 these stakes revealed up to 300 mm loss in sediment across the site that was resulting in exposed new sections of archaeology.

The exposure and rapid degradation of archaeological material led to the site being classed as high risk on the Heritage at Risk register. While the Swash Channel wreck is similar to the *London* in that it is situated near a shipping lane, it is dramatically different in that it is located in only 6 m of water, with very low tidal action, and in generally excellent visibility. Various trials to stabilise the site including sandbagging and covering areas with geotextile material were trialled but the exposure continued at a fast rate. As a result, in 2010, English Heritage funded Bournemouth University to undertake a major excavation on the site. Work is almost complete and has seen the excavation and recording of major elements including a large section of ships structure and the rudder.

Once the material has been fully recorded and conserved it will be available for public display at Poole Museum. The work has allowed the site to be stabilised and thus removed from the Heritage at Risk register.

Public Enjoyment on the Colossus Dive Trail

It has long been established that the heritage values of wreck sites can also generate social and economic benefits, for example, through being utilised as a learning or recreational resource, or as a generator of tourism [5]. English Heritage's strategy for making the past part of the future includes fostering a dynamic heritage cycle of understanding, valuing, caring, and enjoying the historic environment. Maritime archaeology is often by its very nature inaccessible, lying deep beneath the waves and out of sight of the majority of the population. This means that is it vital to engage audiences with maritime archaeology through specific education and outreach

FIGURE 2. A DIVER USES THE UNDERWATER BOOKLET TO ENJOY A GUIDED DIVE ON THE COLOSSUS. COPYRIGHT CISMAS.

programs, designed to raise the profile of submerged cultural heritage. By making the results of research widely available, it is possible to increase knowledge and understanding, attract new audiences, and prompt new questions, ensuring the historic environment is placed high in the consciousness of future generations. In order to achieve this English Heritage have supported the creation of a number of dive trails on wreck sites designated under the Protection of Wrecks Act. Trails are currently in place on *Hazardous, Coronation* and *Normans Bay* although this paper will only examine the one on HMS *Colossus*.

HMS *Colossus* was a 74-gun third rate ship-of-the-line built at Gravesend, and launched in 1787. Her last naval engagement was at the Battle of Cape St Vincent (1797), during the course of which she was badly damaged. The *Colossus* was stripped of her stores to repair the serving ships, and ordered to return to England, carrying wounded from the battle, along with prize items and part of a collection of Greek antiquities amassed by Sir William Hamilton. The *Colossus* approached the Channel in December 1798, and Captain Murray decided to take anchorage in St Mary's Road in the Isles of Scilly to await favourable winds. On the 10th December the main anchor cable parted in the gale, and the ship dragged her remaining anchors to come aground on Southward Well Rocks. The stern section of the *Colossus* was designated in 2001, and the site includes a large section of ship structure, cannon, and among other items, muskets, mizzen chains and a rudder gudgeon. A carved figure from the portside of the stern of the vessel was also identified, excavated and recovered. Further details on the *Colossus* are available on the National Heritage List for England (NHLE): *http://list.english-heritage.org.uk/resultsingle.aspx?uid=1000078*. There is still large amount to see on the seabed and it was realised that this would make a site that would be of great interest to visiting divers.

The *Colossus* dive trail (Figure 2) was developed by the Cornwall and Isles of Scilly Maritime Archaeology Society (CISMAS) in 2009 using funding from English Heritage [9]. The trail uses numbered buoyed observation stations situated at key points on the site and a waterproof guide book [10] to guide divers between the observation stations, explaining the exposed remains and detailing brief background information on the wreck. The dive trail has been a success in terms of number visiting and the feedback that has been received. Since the dive trail opened in 2009 nearly 1100 divers have visited, used and enjoyed the trail. As a direct result of trails such as this one the number of divers accessing and enjoying England's protected wreck sites has risen year on year.

Conclusions

Protected Wreck Sites are historic shipwreck sites of the highest significance, as shown through their designations. They help define our nation and tell our story yet they are all unique in terms of their locations, problems and challenges. There is no one management approach that is suitable for all the sites and key to their successful management is the ability to develop, adapt and employ approaches that are appropriate for each site to ensure their potential is fulfilled. This paper has examined a series of recent case studies that highlight a number of approaches including community based recording, the development of ongoing recording methodologies, excavation to mitigate risk and opening access through dive trail schemes. It is anticipated that as new sites are identified, researched and protected, and as the management of existing sites progress, that new approaches will need to be developed to ensure that sites are managed appropriately so that their significance is maintained for future generations to enjoy.

Acknowledgements

I would like to thank all licensees, affiliated volunteers, and their team members and nominated archaeologists for the ongoing enthusiasm and commitment that they show to England's protected wreck sites.

References

ENGLISH HERITAGE
   2007   *Protected Wreck Sites at Risk: A risk management handbook*

   2012   *Introduction to Heritage Assets: Ships and Boats Prehistory to 1840*

   2012   *Introduction to Heritage Assets: Ships and Boats 1840 to 1950*

   2012   *Designation Selection Guide: Ships and Boats Prehistory to Present*

   http://www.english-heritage.org.uk/caring/heritage-at-risk/archaeology/protected-wreck-sites-at-risk/

UK GOVERNMENT
   The Protection of Wrecks Act 1973, http://www.legislation.gov.uk/ukpga/1973/33, Accessed 13th November 2012

HAMER, A. AND SATCHELL, J.
    2008   *Engaging Audiences with maritime archaeology: Delivering education, learning and training experiences from the classroom to the field*, Proceedings of the 13th Annual Meeting of the European Association of Archaeologists.

DUNKLEY, M.
    2008   *The Value of Historic Shipwrecks*, Proceedings of the 13th Annual Meeting of the European Association of Archaeologists

WESSEX ARCHAEOLOGY
    2012   *Ultrasonic thickness measurement methodology development and testing:* Holland No.5 *and HMS/m A1'*, Unpublished Report for English Heritage

CAMIDGE, K.
    2009   *HMS* Colossus *Dive Trail Project Report*, Unpublished Report for English Heritage

CISMAS
    2012   *HMS* Colossus *Dive Trail Underwater Guide, www.cismas.org.uk,* Accessed 13th November 2012.

· · · · · · · · · · · · · · · ·

Alison James
English Heritage
Fort Cumberland, Fort Cumberland Road
Eastney, Portsmouth
PO4 9LD
United Kingdom
alison.james@english-heritage.org.uk

Petrolheads: Managing England's Early Submarines

Mark Dunkley
Hanna Steyne

English Heritage, the UK Government's adviser on the historic environment of England, has over a decade of experience in the management of shipwreck sites. This experience is largely based on managing change to the remains of sunken wooden vessels which allowed for the publication of online guidance on pre-Industrial ships and boats in spring 2011.

However, in order to begin to understand the management requirements of metal-hulled ships and boats, English Heritage has commenced a programme of research, investigation, analysis, and non-destructive testing on the remains of two protected early submarines; the Holland 5 and A1.

Utilising an ultrasonic thickness gauge for the first time as an archaeological management tool in British waters, English Heritage plans to better understand the deterioration of metal shipwreck sites so as to manage the recent past for the future.

Introduction

English Heritage has over a decade of experience in the management of historic shipwreck sites. This experience is largely based on managing change to the remains of sunken protected wooden warships (such as HMS *Colossus*, sunk 1798) and armed merchant vessels (such as the seventeenth century Swash Channel Wreck), which allowed for the publication of online guidance on pre-Industrial ships and boats in spring 2012 (English Heritage 2012). However, for UK territorial waters adjacent to England, 96% of known wreck sites post-date 1840 (with the majority post-dating 1914). Such sites hold different values and historical interests to wooden wreck sites (such as power plant development / composite to steel typologies / diversification of craft) and, of course, 'modern' historical watercraft are largely less than 100 years old and lie outwith the 2001 UNESCO Convention on the Protection of the Underwater Cultural Heritage at present.

English Heritage guidance on post-1840 ships and boats therefore followed in early 2013 (English Heritage 2013) and is relevant to classes of metal-hulled vessels related to forthcoming global commemorations; the commencement of the First World War and the 70th Anniversary of D-Day.

However, in order to begin to understand the management requirements of metal-hulled vessels, an initial programme of research, ultrasonic investigation and analysis on the remains of two protected early submarines (the Holland No. 5 and A1) began off England's south coast during the summer of 2012 This work commenced with the necessity of understanding the condition, stability and integrity of steel hulls of historic wreck sites without causing damaging and increased degradation.

Target Sites: Steel-hulled Submarines

The *Holland No. 5*, and the *A1*, are two very early types of petrol-driven submarine in service with the Royal Navy between 1902 and 1911. The *Holland No. 5* sank in 1912 off Beachy Head while the *A1* sank in 1911 in Bracklesham Bay. Following their discovery during two independent expeditions, statutory protection of the two boats followed respectively in 2005 and 1998.

In response to submarines entering service in foreign navies during the late 1890's, the British Admiralty reluctantly decided that they should acquire some submarine boats for the purpose of evaluating their potential as a weapon. Agreement was made with the Holland Torpedo Boat Company that five of their Holland No. X design would be built at Vickers Sons & Maxim Ltd at Barrow-in-Furness. The first submarine was launched in October 1901. *No.5* was launched in May 1902. The boats were built in great secrecy and with direct involvement from the Holland Company. The Admiralty regarded the boats as wholly experimental and extensive trials were carried out. Many developments were made on the boats and several of these ideas were taken back to the USA. Not least of which was the first application of a periscope to a submarine in order to allow surface vision while the boat was submerged, all previous submarines were dependant on porpoising up and down to view through deadlights. The Holland boats served their purpose well and even before the last of the type was launched the improved class that was to supersede them was already being built.

Once their function was fulfilled, the Navy quickly disposed of the Holland's. *No.4* had foundered in 1912, but was raised and expended as a gunnery target, and all the rest were sold to ship breakers. *No.5* foundered on 8th August 1912, while under tow to the breakers yard and lies at a depth of *c*.30m on an even keel. In 2012, 71 visitors were licensed to dive the site. The hull of *No. 1*, the first of the experimental class, was located and salvaged in 1982 and is displayed at the RN Submarine Museum. Due to the nature of their service lives the Holland boats produced a great deal of surviving documentation and photographs; these are now housed in the extensive archive of RN Submarine Museum at Gosport.

Built by Vickers in 1903, the *A1* is the first British designed and built submarine used by the Royal Navy. Although she never saw active service, the *A1* sank twice in her career; the first time (in which all of her crew were killed) was in 1904 after a collision with the SS *Berwick Castle* during exercises. The submarine was recovered soon after and subsequently employed for training and experimental work in anti-submarine warfare. During unmanned trials in 1911, operating under automatic pilot as a submerged target, she was lost off Selsey Bill. The position of *A1*'s sinking was known and the wreck marked but when recovery operations began the next day the submarine had disappeared. Efforts at the time failed to relocate her and were eventually abandoned. It is most likely that the submarine was only partially flooded when she sank, and the remaining buoyancy in the hull allowed the strong tides that run around Selsey to move the wreck some five miles away to where she lies today at a general depth of 9m. She was discovered again by a fisherman in 1989 and sold by the Ministry of Defence in 1994. In 2012, 73 visitors were licensed to dive the site. Further historical and archaeological detail about both submarines is available from the online National Heritage List for England.

The two submarine boats were chosen for study, for they lie relatively close together in the same sea area of the wider English Channel; previous investigations and damage have been restricted owing to their protected status and, more importantly, information on their construction and hull-thickness was readily available from naval historical records.

Non-destructive Testing

Non-destructive Testing (NDT) comprises a wide group of analysis techniques used in science and industry to evaluate the properties of a material, component or system without causing damage.

Ultrasonic thickness gauges are especially useful for non-destructive measurement of thickness testing, particularly where access is restricted to one side of a hull only. These gauges are employed in many industrial applications around the world and were used, for example, in 2003 to measure the hull of the designated dangerous wreck SS *Richard Montgomery* in the Thames Estuary. Here, measurements were taken at 7 m intervals, from positions: 1 m above seabed level, 600-900 mm below deck level, and 300 mm inside the gunwales on the deck (Maritime & Coastguard Agency 2003).

As Ultrasonic thickness gauges listen for echoes, and can measure virtually any material such as plastics, metals, and internally corroded materials, they are ideal archaeological tools. However, fundamental to the success of direct thickness measurement for assessing the current condition of a metal shipwreck is knowing what the original metal thickness was at the time of sinking. This enables the total metal loss to be calculated, and provides a baseline for assessing a sites' stability or deterioration. Both the *Holland No. 5* and *A1* are built out of steel (an alloy of iron and other elements) and a naval publication from 1979 provides the best summary account of the designs of the two classes of submarine. Here, records of the Director of Naval Construction (DNC) show that hull plating on both the *Holland No. 5* and *A1* was 7/16" (11.1 mm) thick.

Previous Work

In 2009/10, during investigations submitted in partial fulfilment of the requirements for the Degree of Master of Science, post-graduate student undertook a licensed *Investigation into Corrosion on the Holland 5 Submarine* (Harwood 2010). Utilising a Cygnus 1 Diver Ultrasonic Thickness Gauge (UTG) was used to collect four measurements from the post side of the submarine and three from the starboard side. The readings appear to have been taken through concretion and were not accurately located to enable repeatability. However, successful readings were taken which ranged from 5.6 mm at the port quarter to 11.7 mm at the starboard beam.

Corresponding measurements were taken on the *Holland No. 1*, which gave differing thicknesses. This can be explained, as concretion has been removed from the *Holland No. 1,* giving access to exposed hull plating.

However, Harwood had proposed an innovative proposal on which to develop repeatable UTG testing of metal-hulled shipwrecks.

UTG Equipment

A Cygnus DIVE underwater UTG was acquired to enable planned research owing to its ease of use and portability (Figure 1). Rated to 300m depth, the Cygnus gauge can be worn on a divers' forearm, enabling a valuable free hand when working underwater. Working on a pulse-echo principle (whereby the probe transmits a short ultrasonic pulse and receives the returning echoes), the probe frequency of 2.25 MHz provides a measurement range of between 3.0 mm and 250 mm. The probe itself was pre-calibrated to match the velocity of sound through mild steel; 5920 m/s.

Importantly, the Cygnus DIVE provides an accuracy of 0.1mm when calibrated and has a data logging capability.

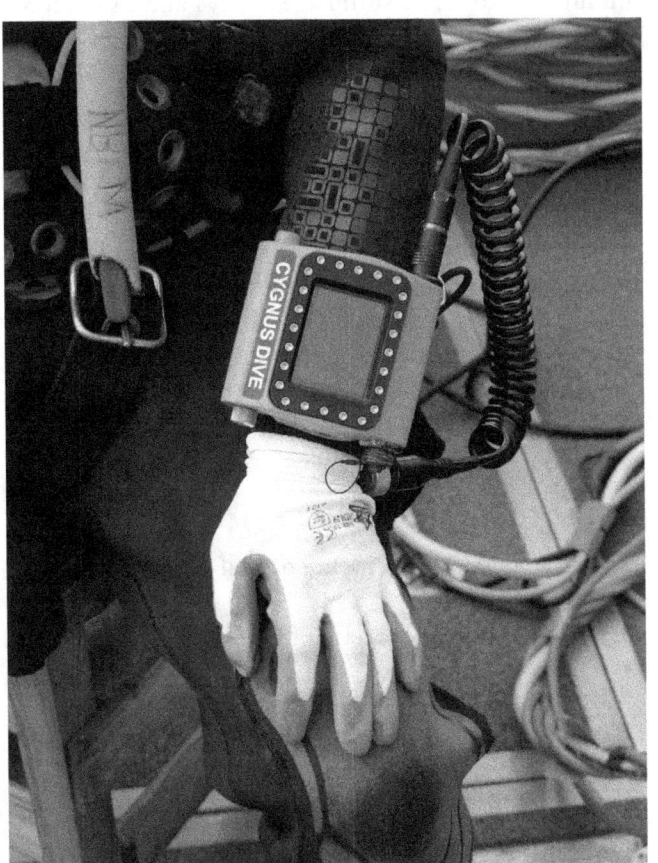

FIGURE 1. THE CYGNUS DIVE UTG SITS COMFORTABLY ON A DIVERS' WRIST (COURTESY M. HAMILTON-SCOTT).

Shipwreck Corrosion

The major factors which affect the corrosion rates of metal shipwrecks in seawater, can be summarised as:

1. The type of metal used for the ship construction (the type of iron or steel);

2. The presence or absence of non-ferrous metal fixings or fixtures, which could inhibit or promote corrosion of the shipwreck;

3. Seawater salinity, where an increased concentration of chloride ions promotes corrosion;

4. Dissolved Oxygen in the water, where an increased concentration of oxygen in the water promotes corrosion;

5. Temperature, where increased temperatures promote chemical reactions, and therefore corrosion;

6. Water movement around the site, where increased water movement affects salinity, dissolved oxygen and water temperature and therefore corrosion;

7. Marine growth, where increased marine growth can create a protective barrier between metal and seawater, thereby inhibiting corrosion.

However, salinity, dissolved oxygen and water temperature were not recorded as fieldwork was, at this time, aimed at developing a methodology for UTG testing.

Underwater Inspection & Methodological Development

Fieldwork was undertaken in May 2012, using surface-supplied diving equipment. The breathing gas was air and atmospheric conditions were fair. Bottom time on the *Holland No. 5* was limited to around 25 minutes and for the *A1* time increased to a maximum of 88 minutes. An acoustic positioning system enabled accurate recording of the location of each measurement.

It was uncertain as to whether the Cygnus DIVE would be able to measure through corrosion product and concretion on the *Holland No.5* and *A1*. To test whether any measurements taken through concretion

FIGURE 2. USING THE CYGNUS DIVE UTG TO MEASURE THE HULL OF THE A1 SUBMARINE (CROWN COPYRIGHT).

or corrosion product were accurate it was planned to remove concretion and take thickness measurements against bare metal, in addition to through concretion.

Furthermore, it was uncertain how the gauge would react to heavily corroded metal, as the operating manual suggested that the uneven surfaces created as a result of corrosion would 'cause the ultrasound echo pulses to scatter and be absorbed. The ultrasound will be reflected from multiple points as there is no one true metal thickness' (Cygnus DIVE Operation Manual). The operating manual suggests the best option is to slowly move the probe around the area of interest to locate areas of least pitting where a reading may be achieved.

The removal of any corrosion product or concretion from the test sites would reintroduce seawater to the metal and potentially increase localised corrosion if left exposed. In order to reduce any potential damage or destabilisation of the metal by such exposure, the removed concretion was replaced with a non-toxic aquatic epoxy putty as soon as thickness tests were completed. Surex Aquastick was selected for use as this product comes in a rod form with the curing agent encapsulated in the base material, which is a contrasting colour. When the two parts are mixed together the epoxy turns from aquamarine to white and can be used in fresh and sea water environments. The working life of Aquastick is 20 minutes at 20°C, its shrinkage is <1% and its compressive strength is 84 N / mm2.

It was also noted that a number of site specific factors were identified which could affect metal thickness readings on the *Holland No. 5* and *A1* at specific measurement locations. These factors can be divided into those which can be identified as directly affecting the thickness of metal being tested (primarily ship construction related), and those which might create differential corrosion rates and therefore variations in metal thickness (primarily environmental). Factors identified as directly affecting metal thickness included:

1. The original 'as built' thickness of the hull plating;

2. The location and nature of hull plating joins;

3. The location of internal frames;

4. The location of external or internal fixtures and fittings, which could affect either the direct thickness of metal in a specific location;

5. Direct damage to the shipwreck hulls, such

as knocks and scrapes caused, for example, by anchor or beam trawling equipment.

The selection of thickness measurement locations, and the design of the methodology was focused to counter any potential variation in metal thickness around the ship, and the possibility for one off, non-representative thickness measurements.

Finally, In order to ensure that measurements were repeatable and indicative of the thickness of the hull in a particular area, four measurements would be taken at two points at each test location, approximately 100-200 mm apart. Two measurements would be taken through the concretion, as it was unclear as to whether the Cygnus DIVE gauge could successfully take measurements through concretion. The concretion would then be removed at these two positions to enable two further measurements on bare metal. It was hoped that this approach would identify any variations in thickness caused by differential corrosion across hull plating, or the accidental location of internal/unseen metal fixtures or fittings such as framing.

Results

Upon inspection underwater, the hulls of both boats were observed to be covered by a layer of concretion (a hard compact mass of corrosion products from iron combined with seawater) colonised by soft marine growth (which for the *Holland No. 5* comprised anemone (*Actinothoe sphyrodeta*) and a variety of seaweeds while seaweeds, anemones and hornwrack (*Flustra foliacea*) were present on the *A1*). For the test areas on each boat, marine growth was cleaned back with a wire brush exposing a 'clean' corrosion surface some 200 mm by 100 mm.

A number of attempts were made to take thickness measurements through the concretion, but the gauge flashed readings between 5.5 mm and 15 mm and no consistent measurements were recorded. A small disc of concretion was therefore removed using a hammer and 20 mm chisel to expose solid metal of the hull. Typically, a circular disc *c.*5 mm thick was removed. The probe of the Cygnus gauge was then held against the exposed steel hull to measure its thickness (and repeated a number of times to confirm the reading) (Figures 2 and 3) and the cavity was made-good with epoxy putty.

Investigation on the *Holland No. 5* was purposely limited to a single reading of 6.5 mm, while readings on the *A1* of 5.6 mm, 5.7 mm and 8.4 mm (against a known 'as built' thickness of 11.1 mm) demonstrate potential variability of hull thickness. These measurements show the need for numerous readings to be taken across a hull to identify erroneous readings and thickness variability in order to locate areas of instability.

Conclusion

From a methodological point of view, the work on the *Holland No.5* and *A1* established that the Cygnus DIVE gauge is capable of taking metal thickness measurements on historic shipwrecks, although see below for further discussion of the actual measurements. Divers found the DIVE gauge easy to deploy and turn on underwater, although some of the divers found that wearing the gauge on the wrist was workable, and others preferred to hold the gauge. The wrist strap was far too big for some of the divers, and a lanyard was used to secure the gauge to

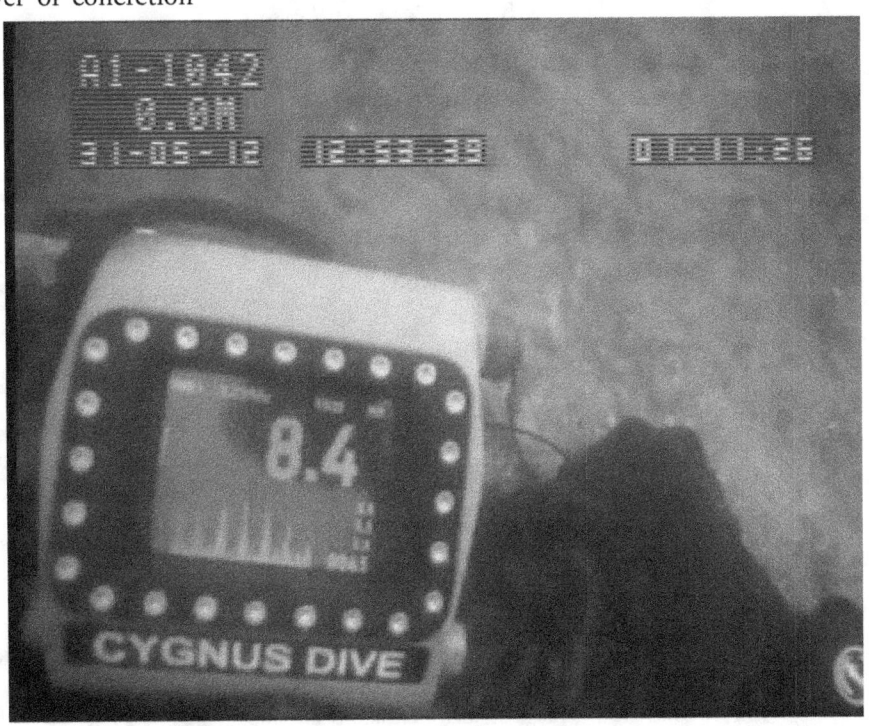

Figure 3. The Cygnus DIVE UTG display, showing (clockwise from top right) thickness reading (8.5 mm), previous logged measurements, echo-verification bars and battery level (Crown Copyright).

the diver instead. The gauge display was easy to read and clearly displayed any verifiable measurements.

Divers found that in some Test Locations the probe needed to be moved around a little to achieve a verifiable measurement, which is likely to be a result of corroded surfaces. As the probe is relatively sensitive to uneven surfaces, it was unpractical for the area of removed concretion to be limited to the *c.* 25 mm of the probe head as originally intended. Instead, larger holes (*c.* 40 mm – 60 mm) were made to find a point at which the probe was able to take a verifiable thickness measurement. One diver noted that an air bubble was present on the probe head, which was preventing measurements being taken. While the probe head membrane is secured with a 'Knurled Ring', it seems that it is relatively easy to catch the edge of the polyurethane membrane, especially when trying to take measurements on rough concretion surfaces, and allow a water/air bubble between the membrane and probe head.

Future visits to the sites of the *Holland No. 5* and *A1* submarines will assess how well the epoxy putty 'repair' is performing and will also commence a programme of temperature recording utilising visiting divers. It is anticipated that salinity and dissolved oxygen measurements will also be recorded in a future research programme in order to fully understand the impacts of corrosion on the two boats.

Utilizing an ultrasonic thickness gauge for the first time as an archaeological management tool in British waters, English Heritage has, with its partners, been able to develop a diver-based methodology to monitor metal hulls of historic wreck sites. This will allow us to implement a programme of active heritage management measures where sites are at risk so as to manage the recent past for the future.

References

DUNKLEY, M.
    2013   Ultrasonic Thickness Testing: New Ways to Manage Marine Heritage, *Nautical Archaeology*, Winter 2013, p.12

ENGLISH HERITAGE
    2012   *Ships and Boats: Prehistory to 1840*. Available: http://www.english-heritage.org.uk/publications/iha-ships-boats/. Last accessed 29 January 2013.

    2013   *Ships and Boats: 1840 to 1950*. Available: http://www.english-heritage.org.uk/publications/iha-ships-boats-1840-1950. Last accessed 29 January 2013.

HAMILTON SCOTT, M.
    2012   Measuring Hull Thickness with an Ultrasonic Unit, *Nautical Archaeology*, Autumn 2012, p.12-13

HARWOOD, D.
    2010   *An Investigation into Corrosion on the Holland 5 Submarine*, thesis is submitted in partial fulfilment of the requirements for the Degree of Master of Science, Cranfield University

MARITIME & COASTGUARD AGENCY, SS RICHARD MONTGOMERY
    2003   *Survey Report 2003*. Available: http://www.dft.gov.uk/mca/mcga07-home/emergencyresponse/mcga-receiverofwreck/mcga-ssrichardmontgomery.htm. Last accessed 29 January 2013.

RUSSELL, M. A., JOHNSON, D. L., WILSON, B. M. & CARR, J. D.
    2006   A minimum-Impact Method for Measuring Corrosion Rate of Steel-Hulled Shipwrecks in Seawater, *The International Journal of Nautical Archaeology*, 35.2: 310-318

STEYNE, H. & MACLEOD, I. D.
    2011   *In-situ* conservation management of historic iron shipwrecks in Port Phillip Bay: a study of *J7* (1924), HMVS *Cerberus* (1926) and the *City of Launceston* (1865), *Bulletin of the Australian Institute for Maritime Archaeology*, 35: 67-80

WESSEX ARCHAEOLOGY
    2012   *Ultrasonic Thickness Measurement Methodology Development and Testing: Holland No. 5 and HMS/m A1*, unpublished report for English Heritage, report ref. 83800.23

• • • • • • • • • • • • • • •

Mark Dunkley
English Heritage
1 Waterhouse Square, 138 - 142 Holborn
London, EC1N 2ST
United Kingdom
mark.dunkley@english-heritage.org.uk

Hanna Steyne
Wessex Archaeology
Portway House
Old Sarum Park, Salisbury
Wilts SP4 6EB
United Kingdom
h.steyne@wessexarch.co.uk

Managing Change on UK Wreck Sites Through Community-Based Recording: The London Recording Project

Graham Scott

In 2012 English Heritage commissioned a National Heritage Protection Plan project led by Wessex Archaeology to support community-based recording of the wreck of the London, a second rate English warship lost in 1665 in the difficult archaeological diving environment of the Thames Estuary. Working as a team with local volunteers and museum professionals, Wessex Archaeology and English Heritage staff designed and trialled a bespoke archaeological recording system. This 'protocol' is intended to be capable of being used as a model for future community-based projects on similar sites.

Introduction

On the 8th March 1665 the Clerk of the Acts of the Navy Board sat down at his desk and began to write. Being the ambitious son of a humble tailor already well on his way to the top of naval administration at the age of 32, vanity may have compelled him to keep a diary. This is what he wrote:

> ...This morning is brought to me to the office the sad news of the London, in which Sir J Lawsons men were all bringing her from Chatham to the Hope, and thence he was to go to sea in her – but a little a-this-side the buoy of the Nower, she suddenly blew up. About 24 and a woman that were in the round house and coach saved; the rest, being 300, drowned – the ship breaking all in pieces – with 80 pieces of brass ordinance. She lies sunk, with her round house above water. Sir J Lawson hath a great loss in this, of so many chosen men, and many relations among them. (Wheatley 2006)

The writer is, of course, the famous Samuel Pepys and his celebrated diary provides the best account of the loss of one of our most important historic shipwrecks, of Charles II's second rate warship *London*.

That ship, depicted in two drawings by the great Dutch maritime artist Van de Velde, is unusual in that it served both monarch and parliament. It was ordered in 1654, by England's post-Civil War republican Commonwealth government. Launched in 1656, at Chatham by its builder Captain John Taylor, it was described as a 'lusty ship'; 123 feet long, with a breadth of 40 feet and a burthen of just over 1000 tons. The *London*, and its sister ship the *Dunbar*, were the first new second rates constructed for the English navy in over 20 years, with three complete decks and, after some argument, no forecastle (Fox 2012: 60-1).

The *London* went on to have an active if unspectacular service history under Parliament, serving as far afield as the Baltic. However, in 1660 the ship went to sea under Vice-Admiral John Lawson as part of the fleet that bore Charles II to his restoration, transporting the king's brother and future king, James Duke of York and his entourage. Thereafter the ship was part of the new Royal Navy, although it spent most of the next few years 'in ordinary', paid off, unarmed and moored in the Medway.

Remobilised by the Earl of Sandwich in 1664, the *London* was prepared for service under Sir John Lawson at the beginning of the Second Dutch War in 1665. Off went Sandwich's men and on came Lawson's newly assembled crew, many of whom we know from Pepys would have been his loyal followers and relatives. Well short of the ship's normal complement of 450, inexperience and ill-discipline may have been responsible for the explosion of what may have been as much as 13 tons of gunpowder.

The wreck of the London, scattered across two sites (Sites 1 & 2) on the edge of the main commercial shipping channel of the Thames off Southend (Figure 1), appears to have faded into obscurity until the late 20th century when bronze guns were recovered from the site by the Port of London Authority during the course of clearance and salvage. These included a demi-culverin captured from the French in 1650-4, a gun now in the collection of the Royal Armouries. However, the site remained largely off the archaeological radar until the beginning of the 21st century, when it was investigated and assessed during the licensing process associated with the construction of the new London Gateway port (Firth et al 2012: 39-44).

Increased visibility may have been partly responsible for a highly controversial commercial salvage operation in 2007. At least two bronze guns from the *London*, a

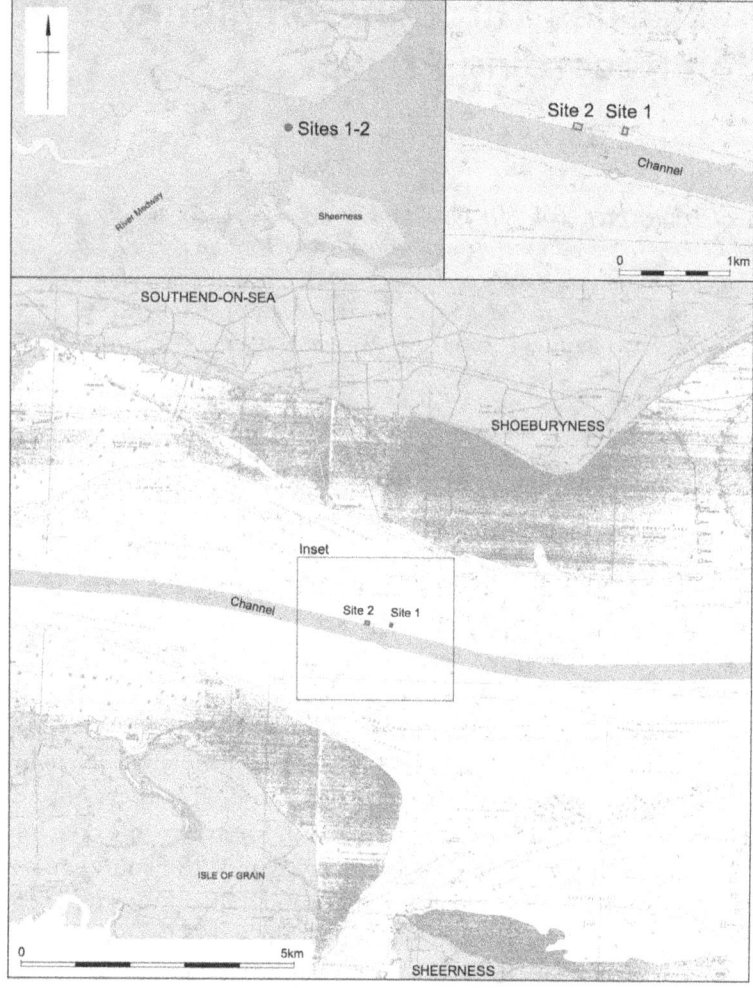

FIGURE 2. GUNS RECOVERED BY THE LONDON SALVORS, INCLUDING THREE DUTCH 24-POUNDERS.

Commonwealth demi-cannon and an unusual English 24-pounder, were recovered and these have been acquired by the Royal Armouries. Three Amsterdam fortress guns (Figure 2), for which a plausible case could otherwise have been made for their being aboard the *London*, were reported by the salvors as having come from another unidentified wreck (Fox 2012: 69-71).

In 2008, the *London* was designated under the Protection of Wrecks Act. Subsequently EH contractors Wessex Archaeology undertook short periods of geophysical and diving survey on both sites in order to provide better baseline archaeological information and to assess their condition.

Geophysical survey involved wide area sidescan survey that identified anomalies for subsequent diver investigation. Parametric sonar was also briefly used. This has demonstrated the probable presence of at least 1m of buried archaeological material on both sites, probably extending well beyond what is exposed on the seabed (Wessex Archaeology 2010a).

Although the London Gateway scheme opted to avoid the sites rather than incur the costs associated with an archaeologically controlled removal, mitigation measures put in place to monitor any changes in the condition of these sites and others during nearby capital dredging works have involved repeated multibeam swath bathymetry surveys.

The geophysical datasets produced during all of this work have become central to the investigation of the sites. In addition to providing base mapping for diver survey, they have provided readily comparable datasets for monitoring changes in the condition of the sites. The results of bathymetric difference analysis difference analysis between 206 and 2010 can be seen in Figure 3. While there is an overall depositional environment in the area, significant localised erosion has been noted, corresponding approximately to upstanding archaeological deposits. No overall dredging impact has been detected and it may be that the changes noted represent the long-term settlement of the site after the late 20th and early 21st century clearance and salvage operations (Wessex Archaeology 2011: 5).

Limited diving work by English Heritage's contractors Wessex Archaeology concentrated on building up a broad understanding of the character of the sites and included sampling of dendrochronological samples and the recovery of vulnerable finds, as well as the ground-truthing of geophysical anomalies. Some discoveries such as an impressive intact shaft and globe bottle of 1650-1665, have provided dating evidence. The recovery of several superbly preserved wooden box parts have demonstrated that an excellent preservation environment exists just below the seabed. Amongst the rich assemblage of organic material scattered across the sites are barrels, piles of rope and shoes.

Survey work was rapid and necessarily fairly coarse. Despite this it has enabled theories to be out forward about what parts of the ship are present, for example a working theory was generated that Site 2 contains part of the hold amidships based upon observation of the ship structure and the presence of barrels, large quantities of rope and probable hearth bricks. Prior to the 1660s the specifications for English warships of this period suggest that the cookroom would have been laid on false beams in the forward hold just before the main hatch (Fox 2012: 61).

One distinctive area of geophysical data within Site 2 proved a conundrum, until diver investigation located cuprous bolts and iron deck beam brackets. Subsequent analysis identified the copper alloy of the fastenings as being Muntz metal, which, in turn, proved that the site contained a second and probably co-incidental wreck of the 19th century (English Heritage 2011).

Growing realisation with regard to the importance and vulnerability of the site and the long term nature of work that would be required to record it led English Heritage to the realisation that the extensive financial commitment required to fully record the site using archaeological contractors was not a realistic option. EH therefore turned to the local community for help.

Seeking out an enthusiastic volunteer they found local Essex diver Steve Ellis. Supported by English Heritage and a range of volunteer specialists, his small local community team quickly become acquainted with the site. Able to dive regularly and throughout the year, they started to make significant discoveries.

If the environment of the Thames Estuary is problematic for diving, it is doubly so for archaeology. The sites are swept by fierce currents, and have visibility that often prevents divers from reading their gauges. Diveable slack water is very short. Like many sites on the east coast of England, the London represents the type of challenge that has often compromised effective archaeological investigation.

While the new team were highly experienced Estuary sports, they were new to archaeology. They therefore faced a steep learning curve if they were to produce the type of archaeological results that they craved, those that were going to produce a lasting public benefit to the local community. A Nautical Archaeology Society course and the help of a number of specialist volunteers from Wessex Archaeology and elsewhere helped but was not the complete solution.

Discussions between English Heritage, Wessex Archaeology and Mr Ellis therefore led in 2012, to a project funded through English Heritage's National Heritage Protection Plan to produce a recording system

FIGURE 2. GUNS RECOVERED BY THE LONDON SALVORS, INCLUDING THREE DUTCH 24-POUNDERS.

or 'Archaeological Protocol' for the London that was suited to the volunteers who would be using it and the difficult environment. A group comprising Wessex Archaeology and including Mr Ellis and his team, maritime and conservation staff from English Heritage and representatives of Southend Museum sat down together in early summer 2012 and devised the protocol (Wessex Archaeology 2013a).

The protocol provides guidelines on how to prioritise the work involved. These decisions are based upon research questions and, because the London is at risk, upon analysis of those areas of the sites thought to be at greatest risk of erosion. The latter in turn relies upon the bathymetric difference analysis and is therefore is a good example of how in the UK data produced during developer-funded marine archaeological work can be fed into the work being carried out by local voluntary groups. In addition to this, the local team's own monitoring work based upon simple diver observations is now producing a picture of a short term cycle of erosion and deposition within the long term pattern revealed by the London Gateway developer's geophysics.

To ensure that the protocol could do what it promised, a short fieldwork trial was undertaken in September 2012 (Wessex Archaeology 2013b). As it provided procedures for identifying when artifacts 'at risk' could be recovered and for their long-term care, the local team had been issued with a Surface Recovery Licence. While Wessex

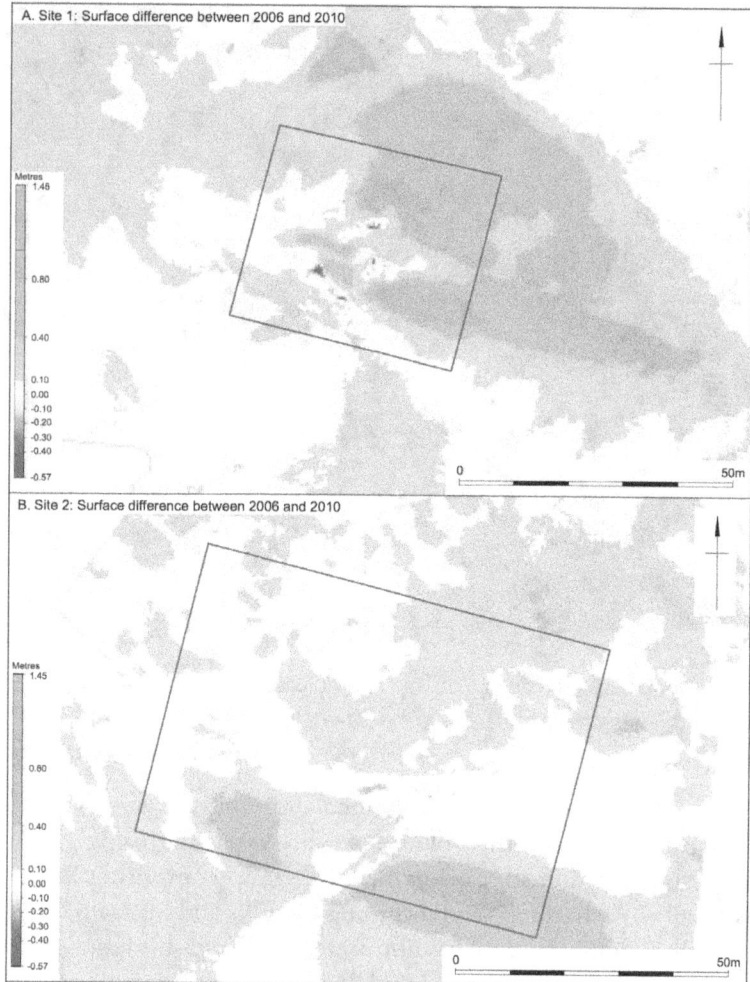

FIGURE 3. DIFFERENCE ANALYSIS OF 2006 AND 2010 BATHYMETRIC DATASETS.

Archaeology concentrated on installing a network of survey control points for them, they were able to carry out and record a number of finds recoveries.

As a result, a number of finds were recovered, recorded and passed to EH via the museum for conservation assessment, including a finger ring with a tobacco tamper and a stoneware jug. More significant discoveries have followed, including a complete leather shoe and human remains. Once conserved, these finds will be accessioned by Southend Museum.

A particular feature of the protocol is a complete suite of recording forms modelled on the type of forms used to record terrestrial archaeological sites. These have been adapted to ensure their suitability for the *London*. Although initially daunting, the local team has since found that they are easy to use and are developing a growing appreciation of the value of systematic recording and archiving.

Another deliberate feature of the protocol is its adaptability. The local team are not experienced archaeologists and the site environment is very difficult. The system for underwater survey that they wanted and which is therefore written into the Protocol is based upon simple trilateration and offset techniques, using a network of control points that are being installed on the sites. At the same time additional data is being collected that will ease any transition to more sophisticated three dimensional recording as the team becomes more experienced and more confident. The team will decide when and how to rewrite the Protocol, depending upon their progress.

The local government environment in the UK is currently one of financial austerity, with severe cuts to local authority museum budgets and many closures or drastic re-organisations. This has exacerbated existing problems concerning archaeological archives. Recent survey has indicated that 27% of museums are now refusing to accept archaeological archives, and 70% lacking a specialist archaeological curator (Edwards 2012). The project is therefore fortunate to have enlisted the active help and support of the forward thinking staff of Southend Borough Council's museum service. They are keen to develop the role of their museum in preserving and presenting the maritime history and archaeology of the Estuary. The recording protocol therefore sets out what needs to be done to ensure that the museum remains a willing partner. By designing the museum's requirements into the recording system and decisions on finds recovery, the community team will hopefully avoid the problems that can beset both volunteer and professional alike when they are seeking to deposit their archives at the completion of an otherwise successful project.

A particular feature of the protocol is the provision of flow charts for deciding what finds should be recovered and what left *in situ* (Figure 4). Apart from a small number of research-related recoveries, it is anticipated that most finds will be left *in situ* unless they are at risk of damage or destruction and adequate conservation and curation can be provided. Not only do the flow charts ensure that these decisions are dealt with consistently but they also enable the Community team to take decisions quickly and without having to refer back to anyone.

The protocol provides advice on how to deal with recovered finds, including temporary storage and recording them both on the seabed and on the surface. At the present time the community team transfers the

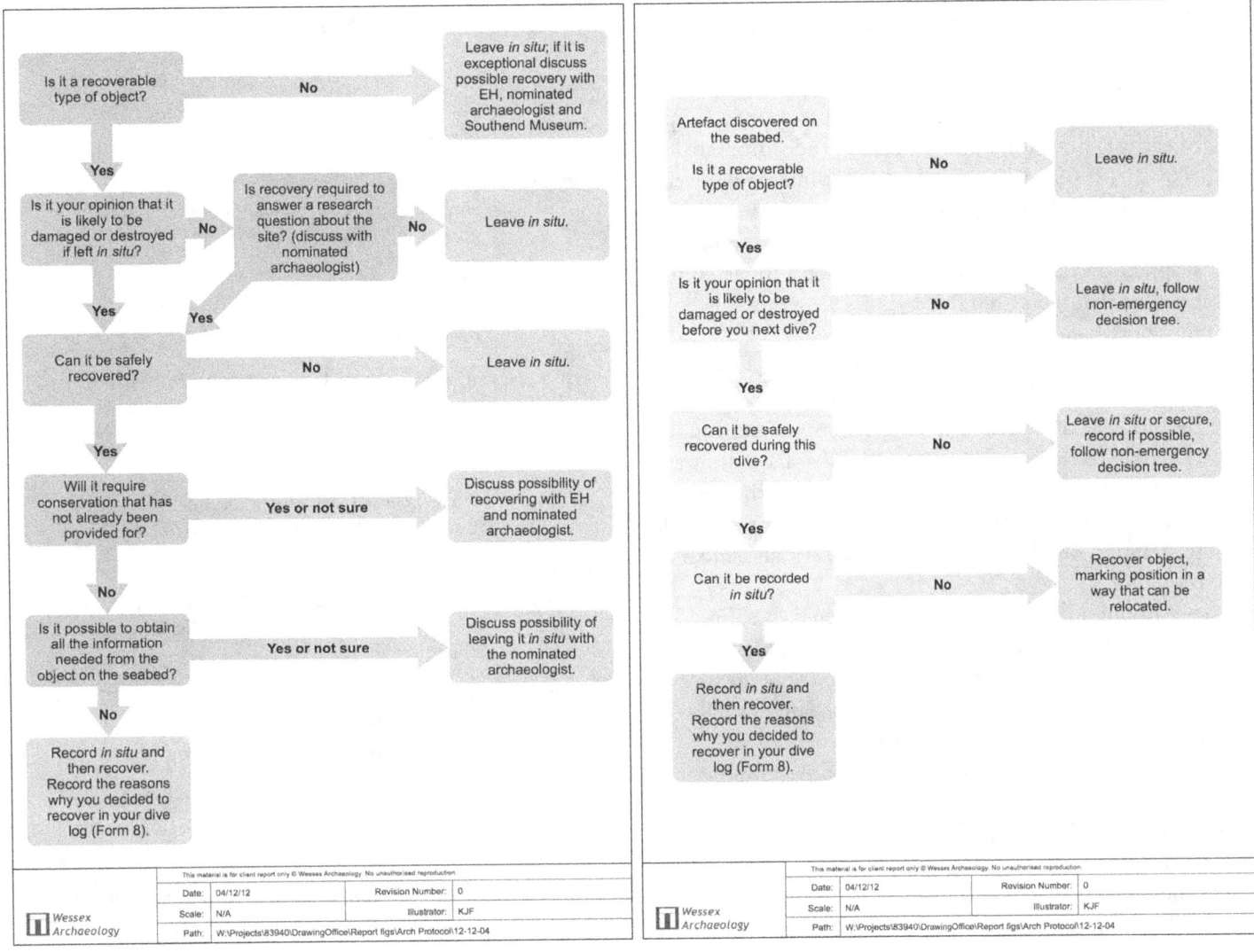

FIGURE 4. RECOVERY DECISION TREE FOR DETERMINING WHETHER FINDS SHOULD BE RECOVERED.

finds to the Museum for temporary storage, from where they go to English Heritage for conservation assessment. The arrangement is working well, although as yet the number of finds is by agreement fairly small.

Human remains are amongst the most interesting finds from this site and have been provided for in the form of an agreement with the local police and coroner, together with willingness on the part of EH to take them for analysis. In particular the recovery of human remains from at least two women of 20-40 years of age, suggests that Pepys was correct that women were onboard (Wessex Archaeology 2010b: 28). Unlike the Georgian navy there is very little evidence that women would have been amongst the crew (Davies 2008: 156). It therefore seems likely that these women were wives, partners, or prostitutes. Their presence would generally have been allowed onboard while the ship was in port at Chatham and mustering at the fleet anchorages of the Nore or the Downs. The human remains within the *London* site therefore present an extremely rare opportunity to study a distinctive section of naval society.

Recording data in an organized and consistent way is a challenge for those new to archaeology and therefore the Protocol includes a series of recording forms. Based upon adaptations of forms tried and tested on other archaeological sites, this aspect of the project seeks to ensure that data recording both during and after a dive is consistently of a high quality.

Another feature of this site is that the work of the community team is being supported by an informal panel of experts set up by the Nominated Archaeologist, including finds specialists and maritime historians. In addition to helping devise a forthcoming research framework which will help direct and prioritise future work and will be incorporated into the Protocol, these specialists provide the community team with advice on their discoveries. This synergy has, for example, allowed stacked iron cannon found in Site 1 to be identified with records of the reballasting of the *London* and has led to the realisation that the site may contain important examples of early 17th century or even earlier Tudor iron artillery (Fox 2012: 68). Interestingly the documents that relate to this ballast indicate that the vessels bringing it down the Thames, possibly from the Tower of London, were stopped by the press gang (CPSD 1664-5). It is quite possible that men from these vessels were pressed aboard the short-handed *London*.

The *London* is very much a community-orientated project and work is on-going to continue to publicise the site and the work of the community team. In addition to two television documentaries that have dealt with the site and forthcoming publication in both academic and popular archaeology press, a program of public talks to a range of different Thames Estuary audiences are on-going.

Although the Protocol was completed in early 2013, continuity will not be lost because English Heritage and Wessex Archaeology specialists will continue to support the work of the community team, the latter as part of a larger advisory group of volunteer specialists.

English Heritage hopes that its initiative in sponsoring the project will also produce benefits that are not limited to one site. It sees the Protocol as potentially offering an adaptable model for helping community-led study of other important but archaeologically challenging sites and for building the type of local partnerships that will be needed for them. While it will not be for everyone, it could prove ideal for new projects on newly discovered or designated wrecks.

Acknowledgements

The author would not have been able to write this paper without the assistance of many volunteers and professionals and thanks are due to all of them. Local volunteer and Site Licensee Steve Ellis, Alison James and Mark Dunkley of English Heritage, Clare Hunt and Ken Crowe of Southend Museum, and Wessex Archaeology Project Manager Nikki Cook deserve special thanks. The Port of London Authority and London Gateway kindly provided data and CPBS provided the diving support vessel used during fieldwork.

References

DAVIES, J.D.
   2008   *Pepys's Navy: Ships Men & Warfare 1649-1689*. Seaforth Publishing.

EDWARDS, R.
   2012   *Archaeological Archives and Museums 2012*. The Society of Museum Archaeologists.

ENGLISH HERITAGE
   2011   *Untitled note on the composition of cuprous fasteners from Site 2*. Unpublished Report.

FIRTH A., N. CALLAN, G. SCOTT, G., T. GANE, S. ARNOTT
   2012a   *London Gateway. Maritime Archaeology in the Thames Estuary*. Wessex Archaeology Report No. 30.

FOX, F.
   2012   *The London of 1656: Her History and Armament*. Transactions of the Naval Dockyard Society: 57-75.

WESSEX ARCHAEOLOGY
   2010a   East of England Designated Wrecks: Marine geophysical Survey and Interpretation, Unpublished Client Report.

   2010b   *HMS London, Southend, Thames Estuary. Designated Assessment: Archaeological Report*, Unpublished Client Report.

   2011   *The London, Southend, Thames Estuary. Designated Site Assessment: Archaeological Report*, Unpublished Client Report.

   2013a   *Managing change on wreck sites through community-based recording: The London recording project. Recording Protocol*. Unpublished Archaeological Protocol Document (WA Document Ref. 83940.05).

   2013b   *Managing change on wreck sites through community-based recording: The London recording project. Technical Report*. Unpublished Client Report (WA Document Ref. 83940.05).

WHEATLEY, H.B. (ED.)
   2006   *The Diary of Samuel Pepys: 1660*. The Echo Library

• • • • • • • • • • • • • • • •

Graham Scott
Senior Archaeologist
Wessex Archaeology
Portway House
Old Sarum Park
Salisbury
SP4 6EB
UK

Underwater Archaeological Parks in Greece: The Cases of Methoni Bay – Sapienza Island and Northern Sporades, from a Culture of Prohibition to a Culture of Engagement

Panagiotis Georgopoulos
Tatiana Fragkopoulou

From a policy of restriction to the permission of recreational diving, the process of valorising, representing and managing underwater archaeological heritage in Greece has been a recent development. When previous legal enforcements required the monitoring and control of underwater archaeological heritage, the discipline suffered from an ineffective means of communication which affected the public image of the underwater archaeologist. This paper examines the role of underwater archaeological parks in representing an extra-national cultural asset, promoting archaeological knowledge and inspiring cultural memory. Focusing on the cases of Methoni Bay-Sapientza Island (SW Peloponnese) and Northern Sporades it argues that the establishment of underwater archaeological parks are a means to ensure preservation and public access as well consolidating underwater archaeology within the contemporary Greek archaeological discipline.

Introduction

With a coastline of 15,000 km, more than 3000 islands and islets and an archaeologically demonstrable maritime tradition since the 11th millennium BC, Greece is an impressively rich country of underwater cultural heritage. Consequently, one would expect to find a well-developed situation regarding its management and promotion in the form of underwater archaeological preserves, shipwreck parks, or maritime heritage trails. Unfortunately, for the time being, there is none of the above. The present paper discusses the possibilities of managing the underwater archaeological sites in Greece and presents two case-studies. Furthermore, it underlines the legal complications that impede the course of underwater archaeological enhancement.

Underwater Archaeological Heritage: Legal Complications.

The minimal progress that has been made so far towards the creation of underwater archaeological parks (UAPs) in Greece could be justified by a series of incomplete and insufficient laws and provisions; along with a certain mindset regarding the submerged archaeological heritage. Consequently, to date these have led to legal and bureaucratic dead-ends.

The complicated geomorphology of the Greek territory comprising in the archipelagic seas of thousands of islands and islets (Dellaporta 2009) as well as the thousands of underwater archaeological sites make their monitoring by the Ephorate of Underwater Antiquities very difficult. The insufficient government support to the Ephorate as well as the consequent lack of personnel, means and instruments (Tragganidas 2007) have made the monitoring of underwater antiquities almost impossible. Looting of underwater sites continued after the foundation of the Ephorate in 1976. By indirectly admitting its inadequacy, the Ephorate of Underwater Antiquities chose the ambivalent policy of imposing an almost complete prohibition of recreational scuba diving for more than two decades; excluding only ten percent of Greek waters (General Port Regulation/1978/258). This measure was revoked in 2005 with the enactment of the new law for recreational diving (Law 3409/ 2005 *Recreational Diving and other Provisions*). This made it possible to dive almost everywhere except on sites that officially declared as archaeological areas. The new legislation brought a new era to recreational scuba-diving in Greece.

It is important to note that 27 years of prevention have damaged the public image of underwater archaeology for divers across the country, with the subject almost a synonym for the abuse of authority or injustice. Fortunately, a series of actions have recently taken place in order to bridge such differences. The Hellenic Society for Law and Archaeology organized a meeting in 2011, presenting to the public the aforementioned legal complications. Moreover, the Hellenic Institute of Marine Archaeology and Research in collaboration with Timeheritage Ltd. (cultural heritage consultants) organized two seminars (June 2007 and June 2009) promoting cultural awareness to divers.

Nevertheless, the Ephorate of Underwater Antiquities is still suspicious and defensive toward recreational divers, who are considered potential looters. The continuation of such an attitude is justified since the change in the law was not followed by any additional government support for the Ephorate of Underwater Antiquities. Moreover, the Ephorate is threatened with complete closure and the absorption of its duties within other administrative branches of the Ministry of Culture. Consequently, the Ephorate's inability to monitor underwater antiquities, which are now more vulnerable due to the liberation of recreational diving in Greece, is still an unpleasant reality.

Within this context, one would understand the mindset of hesitation by the Ephorate of Underwater Antiquities concerning the relaxation of restrictions and the implication for the future formation of UAPs.

Furthermore, the aforementioned law for *Recreational Diving and other Provisions* also provides for the creation of '*Areas of Organized development of diving parks*', stating that the initiative for their creation can be undertaken by private entities, public bodies, or the combination of both. However, this contradicts the provisions of Law 3028/2002 *On the Protection of Antiquities and by and large of Cultural Heritage*, according to which only state facilities have the right to organize activities related to underwater archaeological tourism. Moreover, the Hellenic Council of State has declared that private entities cannot organize visits to underwater archaeological sites. Even if the Ephorate found a way to collaborate with a private entity, according to the law the divers in an UAP should be accompanied by a diver-archaeologist or a diver-custodian. However, there are only about 25 archaeologists, technicians-custodians, and conservators who are able to dive. The diving personnel of the Ephorate, despite all efforts, have not yet been officially recognized as underwater archaeologists by the Greek Ministry of Culture. So should tourist-divers be willing to follow the letter of the the law, there would not be anyone available to accompany them.

Even if all of the above were eventually resolved in some way, there would still be the problem of delimiting the underwater archaeological sites, which could be defined as 'Underwater Museums' and as such could potentially be included in an UAP project. The only requirement, according to the law, is a Common Ministerial Decision which is pending since 2005.

Towards a Public Acknowledgement

While the complexity of laws continues along with ministerial delays and postponements, communities are gradually understanding the necessity of consolidating their underwater archaeological heritage as part of general cultural development. The UAP case in Pylos (W. Peloponnese) reflects such a process where local government, private bodies, and the Ephorate of Underwater Antiquities found a way to cooperate. As a result the first UAP in Greece is about to be created. Similar petitions have been made for the prehistoric submerged settlement of Pavlopetri (SW Laconia, S. Peloponnese) where the University of Nottingham and the local authorities argued that an UAP is imperative for the preservation of the settlement.

Methoni-Sapientza and Nothern Sporades

Methoni Bay – Sapienza Island

Methoni is a coastal town located at the SW promontory of Peloponnese and nearby Sapientza Island is located on the important maritime route that always connected the Italian Peninsula to the Middle East. Due to its protected bay and its strategic location, during the Byzantine period (Middle Ages) and under Venetian rule, Methoni became one of the most important commercial centers in the Eastern Mediterranean.

The Ephorate of Underwater Antiquities has been surveying the area as well promoting its development since 1980. From about twenty shipwrecks and a Middle Helladic submerged settlement which have been identified, extending over an area of 12 hectares, two (i.e. the 'shipwreck of the sarcophagi' and the 'shipwreck of the columns') have been proposed by the Ephorate of Underwater Antiquities to become open to the public.

Both shipwrecks are located at the northern end of Sapientza Island, in an area of significant ecological interest and declared as a protected site within the NATURA 2000 network. The 'Shipwreck of the sarcophagi' dates to the Roman period and carried a number of tombs made of titanium stone. The granite columns of the 'shipwreck of the columns' (Myrilla 2011) lie in pieces (apart from one that is still intact) and most probably belong to the Great Peristyle of Caesarea, which was among other 'treasures' – looted by the Venetians, after the occupation of Jerusalem in 1099. Both shipwrecks, would seem ideal for the creation of an underwater archaeological park, not only because of their location in shallow waters (<8m), but also due to their close proximity and their heavy cargoes, a fact which would make looting a relatively difficult task.

Northern Sporades

The Northern Sporades is an archipelago along the northern-east coast of mainland Greece, in the Aegean Sea. It consists of 24 islands and islets, four of which are permanently inhabited: Alonnissos, Skiathos, Skyros, and Skopelos. It covers a territory of approximately 2260 km² including six smaller islands: Peristera, Kyra – Panagia, Gioura, Psathoura, Piperi and Skantzoura. Moreover, there are 20 uninhabited islets and rocky outcrops. It has been a National Marine Park (National Marine Park of Alonnissos and Northern Sporades) since 1992.

The marine area of the archipelago abounds in shipwrecks and submerged settlements. As such the Northern Sporades island complex would be ideal for the creation of an UAP and the local government and communities have been supportive. Indeed, several efforts (both official and non official) have already been made including the most important *Proposal for an Innovative Development Plan: Northern Sporades Islands* (Magklis 2007). The latter presents a complete plan of cultural, agricultural, natural and archaeological development and management of the Marine Park, with special interest in the underwater archaeological sector. However, along with the bureaucratic complications comes an archaeological concern arising from the extent of the proposed archaeological area and the proposal has not yet been accepted.

Northern Sporades Underwater Cultural Material

The archaeological and historical sites that could be included in the UAP cover a wide chronological range from the prehistoric period to WWII. These include the submerged Neolithic site of Aghios Petros (Efstratiou 1985) dated to the 5th millennium BC. Also the 'Peristera' classical shipwreck (the biggest shipwreck of the period yet known) carrying more than 3000 amphorae that create a 25m long, 10m wide and 3m high mound. The Peristera shipwreck has been partially excavated by the Ephorate of Underwater Antiquities (Hadjidaki 1996). In addition there is the classical shipwreck of 'Phagrou', with a cargo of more than 1500 amphorae.

Concerning the Roman and Byzantine periods, plenty of traces of marine commerce are preserved, such as the enormous 'Vassilikos' Byzantine shipwreck(s?) with a cargo of more than 4000 amphorae (12th century A.D.); the Byzantine shipwreck with the cargo of plates at Aghios Petros bay (Dellaporta 1999; 1020-22); the Byzantine shipwreck off the coast of Peristera (Dellaporta 1999); and the various Roman and Byzantine shipwrecks at Panormos bay (Skopelos island). The submerged remains of a Roman port can also be found at Skopelos Island. Finally, in the Northern Sporades sea there is a number of historical submerged sites such as the sunken Junker, a German bomber monoplane from WWII which crashed and sunk in 1942 and a German Navy's battleship that sunk during 1944.

Structure and Organization of an Underwater Archaeological Park

The establishment of an UAP has a long way to go once it has received the necessary legal approval. One of the main aspects in organizing such an effort has to do with the archaeological procedures that ensure the overall presentation of the site. If the location and delimitation are required for the legal approval, the preservation of the submerged area is crucial for the site's existence itself. Within this context, actions of surveying, excavating and archaeologically studying the proposed site should thoroughly prepare the area for potential public presentation and visits. At this point the issue of safety arises as the basic element of the park.

Risks concerning the site's security as well as the visitor's safety should be resolved long before the inauguration of the park. In general, there are both natural and human causes responsible for putting heritage at risk. Looting has been historically one of the main causes of damaging heritage. As such safeguarding, preservation and conservation activities are crucial and need to take place on a regular basis while on a primary level archaeological care, for instance by retrieving submerged movable findings and keeping heavy archaeological parts on the seabed discourages potentially illegal action.

Underwater Archaeological Parks: a Mediterranean Perspective

There are several cases in the Mediterranean where plans have been formulated for UAPs have been drafted or enacted: Italy, Croatia and Israel already have UAPs while Libya is also due to establish one (Pizzinato et al. 2012). In all cases plans follow the maxim 'research-safety-preservation-interpretation'.

In terms of interpretation it seems important to emphasize the progress that has been made in Ustica and Baia. The marine park at Ustica followed one of the most successful models regarding the representation of the 'exhibiting' space i.e. maps and explanatory signs provide the historical and archaeological concept while proposed paths emphasize the interpretive result (Frost 1990).

In the vast area of the submerged archaeological site of Baia an impressive project has been in development since 2001 (Baia 2012; Stefanile 2012: 57). Following the above model of 'research-safety-preservation-interpretation', the Baia project seems to work in terms of cultural management. Safety issues have been covered with a security network formed by local community, private agencies and authorities. Although, Baia's architectural remains are automatically protected against looting as they are immovable and heavy by nature. What is more, preservation in Baia is perceived as a dynamic and continuous work with regards to more effective site presentation with less emphasis on conservation of the already preserved archaeological remains of the city (Stefanile 2012: 60). Interestingly, especially regarding the legal implications that concern UAPs in Greece, is the role that private entities (dive centers) play in Baia's archaeological area. While guidance is provided through the submerged city where the diver is able to see in-situ archaeological remains as in a museum exhibition, dive centers contribute to Baia's safeguarding (Stefanile 2012: 60).

While Baia's submerged structures are difficult to loot, safeguarding shipwrecks in Greece and elsewhere requires a more subtle procedure because of their nature. Croatia provides an interesting approach in terms of archaeological safety: security cages (Jurisic 2006); however its suitability in the two Greek cases still needs to be examined. Similarly, it is important to note the substantial surface marking of each sea area, the aim of which is to prevent destruction from external human causes (fishery and anchors).

Establishing an Underwater Archaeological Site

In this paper an UAP is conceived as an open (exhibited) concept where interpretive methods aid dynamic integration with the social sphere (Flatman 2003; 151). This means that UAPs project should include a wide range of participants in terms of management and recreation. Furthermore, it is important for each site to comply with the scientific as well as the communicative requirements of an exhibited cultural space. Towards such a 'musealization' of the archaeological area there are parameters that need to be ensured. Accessibility and equipment are essential. In terms of presentation, the site will need to be equipped with explanatory signs as well as marking of proposed paths (Baia 2012). Finally, the creation of an onshore cultural center could possibly provide a repository for mobile artifacts as well as a scientific center for the site. We underline here the importance of a museum closely related to each site.

Issues of Further Development

We have already referred to the term 'multileveled development' following the organization of an underwater archaeological park. In fact despite the obvious differences from an inland archaeological site, an UAP still remains a cultural 'landmark' carrying the multiple benefits of an organized cultural space. To begin with, it is strongly believed that scientific research, documentation and study will gradually change with a permanent cultural context. UAPs could possibly be a medium for an evolution in cultural research in a Greek context. Environmental issues could be incorporated considering the direct connection between environment and archaeological preservation. Finally, it is important to understand the impact that cultural centers can have in terms of social and financial development. In a country where tourism is one of the main sources of income, underwater cultural tourism would undoubtedly boost both the local and national economy.

Conclusions – Proposals

The development and subsequent management of submerged cultural heritage in Greece, sooner or later shall come into existence. UAPs should be seen as a productive opportunity. Whatever their form may be, cultural management should fulfill the requirements for both preservation and public access as declared by the UNESCO Convention on the Protection of the Underwater Cultural Heritage (UNESCO: 2012), while at the same time it should encourage the visitor to value the submerged cultural resource as a tangible element of the past worthy of preservation.

Safety issues have been the main concern of established UAPs in the Mediterranean. In Greece's any proposed UAPs could use a combination of social, archaeological, legislative and authority control to provide an adequate security network. Local communities that understand the benefits of an UAP in their territory could provide immediate supervision of their cultural asset. Moreover a legislative context orientated toward cultural tourism while monitored by local authorities would ensure a better defense against illegal underwater activities.

The improvements can be summarized:

1. The relevant legislation should change to become more eloquent, specific and complete.

2. The Greek government should support the Ephorate of Underwater Antiquities with personnel, means and instruments.

3. Divers and underwater archaeologists have to redefine their relationship, acknowledging that both sides were justified for their past actions while understanding that it is time to move on in a more collaborative way. Initiatives and actions –seminars, symposia or workshops – addressing this goal would play a substantial role.

In terms of cultural heritage:

4. It is imperative to develop an understanding of underwater archaeological heritage as a multi-leveled cultural asset.

5. While the importance of conducting cultural preservation projects appears more urgent, archaeological preservation should not exclude cultural interpretation.

6. Within this context it is crucial for UAP projects to emerge as a tool for heritage preservation but equally to communication cultural heritage in an engaging way.

Acknowledgements

We would like to express our gratitude to the Ephorate's archaeologists –especially to Mr. Elias Spondylis – who despite the aforementioned difficulties gave us the chance to proceed with the underwater archaeological studies. Without their commitment we would not be aware of the existence of such cultural assets neither would we be able to proceed with any theoretical projects.

References

Dellaporta K.
2006 Anafores E.E.A., in *Archaiologikon Deltion (Chronika)*, pp. 1020-22, T.A.P. editions, Athens.

Manglis, A.
2010 I touristiki aksiopoiisi tou enaliou archaeologikou ploutou – diethnis empeiria. Ano Magniton Nisoi, in *Viopoikilotita kai kataditikos tourismos stis hellinices thalasses*, Athens 2010.

Myrilla, D.
2011 Archaia apo saranta kymata, in *Eleytherotypia* newspaper, 24/7/2011, Tegopoulos editions SA, Athens.

Spondylis E.
1994 Anafores E.E.A., in *Archaiologikon Deltion (Chronika)*, pp. 1025-28, T.A.P. Editions, Athens.

Tragganidas, G.
2007 "Vythizetai sta provlimata", in *RIZOSPASTIS* newspaper, 6/5/2007, Sygxroni Epochi editions, Athens.

Hadjidaki, Elpida
1996 'Underwater Excavations of a Late Fifth Century Merchant Ship at Alonnesos, Greece : the 1991-1993 Seasons.' In: *Bulletin de correspondance hellénique*. Volume 120, livraison 2, pp. 561-593, Ecole Francaise d' Athènes, Athens.

Efstratiou, Nicholas
1985 *Agios Petros, a neolithic site in the northern Sporades : Aegean Relationships during the neolithic of the 5th Millennium*, BAR international series: 241, Publisher: B.A.R., Oxford, UK.

Pizzinato C. and Beltrame C.,
2012 A project for the creation of an underwater archaeological park at Apollonia, Libya, in *International Journal of the Society for Underwater Technology*, vol 30, No 4, pp 217–224.

Flatman J.
2003 Cultural Biographies, cognitive landscapes and dirty old bits of boat: 'theory' in maritime archaeology, in *The International Journal of Nautical Archaeology* vol 32, no 2. pp.143-157.

Frost H.
1990 Museum report-tourism aids archaeology: The Ustica experiment. *International Journal of Nautical Archaeology*, vol. 4, no 19 , pp.341-343.

Jurisic M.
2006 La protezione fisica dei siti archeologici sommersi dal fondale merino nell'Adriatico croato in Radic Rossi I. (ed.) *Archeologia subaquea in Croazia., Studi e ricerce*, Marsilio, Venezia, 2006. pp.147-156.

Stefanile M.
2012 Research, protection and musealization in an underwater archaeological park: the case of Baia (Naples – Italy) in *Actas de las IV Jornadas de Jovens em Investigaçao Arqueologica*. Faro 2011. Faro: Promontoria Monografica, pp. 57–63.

Digital Sources

BAIA
2012   The underwater archaeological park of Baiae – from a commercial port to a protected marine area http://www.parcoarcheologicosommersodibaia.it/parco_text.php?id_lingua=en&id=ST. Accessed February 28

HELLENIC SOCIETY FOR LAW AND ARCHAEOLOGY
2011   Underwater Antiquities and the Law < http://www.law-archaeology.gr/Index.asp?C=224 > Accessed March 1

TIME HERITAGE
2007   Three-days' seminar on theoretical aspects of underwater archaeology by members of the Hellenic Institute of Marine Archaeology http://en.timeheritage.gr/Default.aspx?tabid=119&language=el-GR. Accessed March 2

UNITED NATIONS EDUCATIONAL, SCIENTIFC AND CULTURAL ORGANIZATION (UNESCO)
2012   Safeguarding the Under-water Cultural Heritage. www.unesco.org/new/en/culture/themes/underwater-cultural-heritage Accessed February 12

Legal References

LAW 3409
2005   *Recreational Diving and other Provisions.* in Efimeris tis Kyverniseos No. 273, Part I, 4 November 2005.

GENIKOS KANONISMOS LIMENA (GENERAL REGULATION OF PORT)
1978   in Efimeris tis Kyverniseos No. 388, Part B, 27 April 1978.

LAW 3028
2002   *Gia tin prostasia ton archaeotiton ke en geni tis Politistikis Klironomias* (On the Protection of Antiquities and of Cultural Heritage) in Efimeris tis Kyverniseos tis Ellinikis Democratias, No. 153, Part A, 28 June 2002.

....

Panagiotis Georgopoulos
Archaeologist, Museologist MA
Independent Researcher in Cultural Heritage
Exoneon Str. 17 Athens 11851
Greece
pangeo2@hotmail.com

Tatiana Fragkopoulou
http://uniss.academia.edu/tatianafragkopoulou
lo2lecrea@yahoo.gr

www.ingramcontent.com/pod-product-compliance
Lightning Source LLC
Chambersburg PA
CBHW081444070526
44586CB00019B/2224